GREAT POWER DIPLOMACY

Great Power Diplomacy

THE SKILL OF STATECRAFT FROM ATTILA THE HUN TO KISSINGER

A. Wess Mitchell

PRINCETON UNIVERSITY PRESS

PRINCETON & OXFORD

Published by Princeton University Press
41 William Street, Princeton, New Jersey 08540
99 Banbury Road, Oxford OX2 6JX

press.princeton.edu

GPSR Authorized Representative: Easy Access System Europe - Mustamäe tee 50, 10621 Tallinn, Estonia, gpsr.requests@easproject.com

All Rights Reserved

Library of Congress Control Number: 2025937514

ISBN 9780691236872
ISBN (e-book) 9780691236889

British Library Cataloging-in-Publication Data is available

Editorial: Dave McBride, Alena Chekanov
Production Editorial: Elizabeth Byrd
Jacket: Heather Hansen
Production: Erin Suydam
Publicity: James Schneider (US), Kathryn Stevens (UK)
Copyeditor: Michelle Starika

Jacket Credit: William Orpen, *A Peace Conference at the Quai d'Orsay*, oil on canvas, 1919.

10 9 8 7 6 5 4 3 2 1

For my friend and mentor, Larry Hirsch

A soft tongue breaketh the bone.

—PROVERBS 25:15

CONTENTS

THIS IS A BOOK about how great powers use diplomacy to survive and thrive in the daunting arena of competition with other very powerful states.[1] Its unifying theme is the claim that diplomacy finds its highest and most enduring expression not as an agent of abstract peace or as a mere handmaiden to military power, but as an instrument of grand strategy that states use to rearrange power in space and time and avoid tests of strength beyond their ability to bear. Never are the services of the diplomat more urgently needed than when the skills of the general are outmatched by enemies too powerful, numerous, or ferocious to defeat solely by force of arms. It is in these moments of supreme danger that diplomacy finds its essential expression as a tool of strategic statecraft for enduring amid the perils and contradictions of geopolitics. Because of its centrality to the very survival of the state, all of diplomacy's other tasks are of secondary or derivative importance to success in this, its most elemental role.

Diplomacy of this kind is as old as humanity. On countless occasions across the ages, human societies have found themselves confronted, often quite suddenly, with dangerous opponents that could not be defeated by their military means alone. Many succumbed and went the way of Nineveh and Tyre in Kipling's recessional, "valiant dust that builds on dust." But some did not. Many of history's most successful great powers endured because their leaders learned to use what Richelieu called "the art of talking" to flip the gameboard in their favor and overcome seemingly impossible odds.

The results were often nothing short of salvific for the societies involved: great cities spared, old ways of life preserved, and countless everyday people saved from cruel fates. Attila the Hun, Suleiman the Magnificent, Frederick the Great, Napoleon, and Kaiser Wilhelm are just a few of the great captains whose swords were blunted by the quills of diplomats. Had it not been for the efforts of long-forgotten envoys to assemble coalitions of weaker states, the nations of the West might long ago have fallen under the heel of one of the conquerors who comes along every few generations to disturb the peace. Without diplomacy, the world would be a much darker place.

But diplomacy has become something of a lost art in the modern world. Western societies today get security from two sources: the soldier and the lawyer. The soldier protects the nation with an array of technologies so dazzling and terrifying that, it is hoped, no opponent would dare to attack us. The lawyer ensconces the nation in a skein of multilateral rules, presided over by global bodies with portentous names that promise to govern the "global commons" with justice and equity, combat climate change, and, with time, abolish war itself. Standing behind both is the banker, who girds the nation with an arsenal of sanctions that promise to bring even the most powerful opponent to his knees with calibrated precision at the stroke of a keyboard.

In this brave new world, the diplomat has slowly receded into the shadows. To be a diplomat in the era of the *pax Americana* was to operate in a world already made safe by dominant U.S. military power—to dispense "soft power" through public diplomacy, perform nation-building in America's bush wars, and play referee to disputes involving people, places, and problems far from America's shores. Without a great-power rival on the horizon, American diplomacy was able to focus on what was, essentially, a global mopping-up operation of expanding democracy and managing peripheral crises—or, as one recent book on diplomacy put it, "managing other people's problems."[2] In this setting, the role of the Pentagon and Treasury in U.S. foreign policy steadily expanded while that of the State Department shrunk apace.[3]

For the first time in history, diplomacy of the kind that human societies have conducted since the days of the pharaohs seemed to suddenly be obsolete. The soldier and lawyer had everything under control. Strategy in the post–Cold War world became a science of calibrating sanctions until the enemy yells uncle—and if that fails, defeating him with remote-controlled weapons, with televised results. Peace became the science of administration: of getting the right mix of institutions in place, backed by just the right amount of aid, overseen by the proper authorities. None of these tasks had much need for diplomacy in the traditional sense of the term, as the art of negotiating, recruiting allies, and avoiding great-power war.

It's little exaggeration to say that diplomacy is widely thought to be dead.[4] Diplomats have been compared to antique sailing ships, glorified postal carriers, and weary headwaiters in need of a break. Some observers have suggested that embassies should be scrapped and diplomats retrained as social media jockeys; others, that they should cede the field entirely to artificial intelligence, large foundations, or celebrities like Bono and Angelina Jolie. Squeezed by multilateral institutions from one side and a high-tech military from the other, diplomacy apparently has nothing left to offer.

But I beg to differ. The diplomat, this book argues, plays an indispensable role in the life of nations that neither the soldier nor the lawyer can replace. The need for skill in diplomacy has not gone away; it was only rendered temporarily dormant by the greenhouse conditions of the post–Cold War era, when a uniquely powerful country kept the peace. But most of human history didn't look that way, and the future won't either. Already, the sureties of the recent past are vanishing and giving way to a more turbulent, competitive, and withal more perilous era in which continent-sized great powers mightier than anything yet seen under the sun clash over the age-old objects of territory, allies, and prestige that have possessed humankind from its earliest days.[5]

In this dangerous new setting, neither the soldier's substitute to diplomacy, nor that of the jurist, is likely, by themselves, to avail. Not even the most impressive technologies can provide total safety in a world of multiple nuclear-armed powers and uneven economic growth rates. And not even the most idealistic of institutions can exorcise war from the human condition. Whether we like it or not, we will have to survive in a world that looks less like the orderly global village some had hoped for, and more like the red-in-tooth-and-claw savannah that has been the norm throughout history.

In short, we will need to rediscover old-fashioned diplomacy, not as a janitorial service for the military or as a custodian of global norms but as an instrument of grand strategy that states use to magnify their own power and influence, and resist and restrain that of other great powers. Diplomacy of this kind is one of the West's greatest, and most forgotten, inheritances. Through skillful diplomacy, states build the combinations that restrain would-be hegemons and erect temporary bulwarks against the chaos and danger of geopolitics. Historically, it has been the crucial medium by which great powers avoid war and ensure that, if it does come, they will be in a better position than their opponent to win. The leader who knows how to do such things skillfully will have a considerable advantage against the one that does not.

Rediscovering diplomacy's role in this, its classical form, is the purpose of this book. Diplomacy, I argue, has a role to play that is every bit as vital as military force, and a good deal more vital than international law, for ensuring the safety of the nation. Without effective diplomacy, even the grandest armies can be stretched beyond their limits or squandered on unattainable objects, and even the loftiest aspirations founder on the shoals of great-power war. Like everything that comes from the crooked timber of humanity, diplomacy is prone to miscarry; its history is strewn with at least as many knaves and fools as heroes. But when deftly utilized, diplomacy can produce results out of all proportion to the effort and expense it entails, and bring forth deeds every bit as noble and intrepid as warfare, even if they tend to not be remembered as such.

To understand diplomacy's role, we have to look back, beyond the conditions of the past thirty-five years to the many centuries that proceeded them. The post–Cold War generation has not seen great-power diplomacy in conditions of intense rivalry. The Cold War itself is important, and is included in this book. But it is probably a bit overstudied these days because of its near familiarity. Reviewing a longer history allows us to step back and compare different strategies for dealing with multiple great-power rivals. History remains the best resource at our disposal for understanding the dilemmas of our species—the indispensable repository, as Winston Churchill said, wherein "lie all the secrets of statecraft."

To that end, this book offers a meditation on diplomacy through the prism of strategy, from antiquity to the modern era. My aim is to bring diplomacy to life for the reader and convey a sense of the skill, persistence, and—occasionally—adventure that its use has often entailed. Doing that requires us to see the anatomy of diplomacy as it was conceived and conducted by individual leaders in the fog and din of cabinet room and campaign tent in moments that truly mattered: when the lives of great states hung in the balance.

By recalling how diplomacy has been used by past generations, I hope to rediscover some of its attributes as a tool of grand strategy, and separate the timeless from the transient. I also hope to rescue diplomacy from many persistent myths, and recover some small part of the wonder of diplomacy as a field of human endeavor. In doing so, I am not looking for pat lessons for the present. "The value of history," as the English philosopher R. J. Collinwood wrote, "is that it teaches us what man has done and thus what man is."[6] For all that has changed over the millennium and a half covered in this book, human nature assuredly has not. Studying the past gives us an extended opportunity to reflect upon certain ingredients that will be present as long as there are human beings. Only by escaping the myopia and hubris that afflict the human mind when it dwells in the present may we see, however dimly, the outlines of what lies ahead.

I HAVE INCURRED many debts during this book's long gestation. Graham Allison was the first to see merit in the idea of studying diplomacy's role in grand strategy when I proposed it to him as the topic for a paper at Harvard University Belfer Center's Applied History Project many years ago. Andrew May has long encouraged my curiosity about the element of time in strategy, which is an important theme throughout the text. I wish to thank Marin Strmecki at the Smith Richardson Foundation, which provided the grant that made the book possible. Eric Crahan at Princeton University Press had the good sense to nudge me to write the book in a way that would appeal to a broad audience. The Press's Alena Chekanov was a steady resource throughout the drafting process and, along with Bridget Flannery-McCoy, gave me the extra time I needed to complete the manuscript. David McBride helped get the book across the finish line. Angela Piliouras and Michelle Starika were judicious and generous editors.

I am especially grateful to my colleagues at the Marathon Initiative. My mentor Larry Hirsch was a steadfast backer from the outset; without his many years of encouragement and support, an effort of this magnitude would never have been remotely possible. My great friend and partner Elbridge Colby was an inexhaustible source of camaraderie and wisdom on strategy. My dear friend Jakub Grygiel helped refine some of the book's most important ideas and weed out a few bad ones. Chris Vassallo acted as a sounding board and drafted impressive background memoranda on a number of topics covered in the chapters. William Ellison conducted literature reviews, retrieved arcane data, and helped with French translations. Jack Ellis tracked down difficult sources and fielded research requests at all hours of the day and night. Robert Delfeld, Allison Francis, Ilona Teleki, Carsten Schmiedl, Joan Renner, Paul Kentes, and Mohit Chawla provided spirited administrative support.

While working on the manuscript, I benefited from the insights of a number of scholars with specialized knowledge on various themes in the book. Lucien Bély, John Bew, Andrew Ehrhardt, Charles Ingrao, Katja Hoyer, Edward Luttwak, Bronwen McShea, Brendan Simms, Hubert Védrine, and Odd Arne Westad read chapter drafts and offered constructive feedback. Andrew Rhodes furnished the book with one-of-a-kind maps that helped me picture the world from the perspective of historical decision-makers.

My understanding of diplomacy was enriched by my time at the State Department's Bureau of European and Eurasian Affairs. I'm thankful to Rex Tillerson and Mike Pompeo for giving me the opportunity to serve my country as a diplomat, and to those men and women of the foreign and civil service who set an example of professionalism in the modern practice of diplomacy.

Widening the aperture, I have benefited over the years from the support, example, illumination, and friendship of a number of individuals who contributed in one way or another to this book. I would especially like to thank Jamal Al-Mussawi, Gérard Araud, Neal Blue, Tyler Brace, Ulrich Brechbühl, Zbigniew Brzezinski[†], Roger Chickering, Chris Chivvis, Thomas de Maizière, Jackie Deal, Colin Dueck, Eugene Fishel, Rose Gottemoeller, Nick Gvosdev, Emily Haber, Steve Hadley, David Hale, Rebeccah Heinrichs, Roger Hertog, Brad Hirsch, Susan Hirsch, Leonard Hochberg, Brian Hook, Ken Howery, John Hulsman, Dhruva Jaishankar, Reuben Jeffery, Robert Kaplan, Charles Kupchan, Andy Krepinevich, Dan Kurtz-Phelan, Thomas Lehrman, Michael Linse, Evan Loomis, Kent Lucken, Tom Mahnken, Octavian Manea, Jim Mattis, H. R. McMaster, Walter Russell Mead, Andrew Michta, Elisabeth Millard, Jim Mitre, Raja Mohan, Colin Moran, Michael Murphy, Robert C. O'Brien, Asier Parra, Matthew Palmer, Yashar Parsie, Marcin Piatkowski, Matthew Pottinger, Brad Roberts, Andrew Rose, Peter Rough, Eberhard Sandschneider, David Satterfield, Nadia Schadlow, Will Schirano, Griffin Schroeder, Luis Simón, Byron Smith, Will Snellings, Danielle Stoebe, Tomasz Szatkowski, Jan Techau, Ashley Tellis, Maximilian Terhalle, Stefan Theil, Jim Thomas, Michael Thompson, Alex Velez-Green, Chart Westcott, and Justin Winokur.

I thank Rev. Miles Smith and Grace Episcopal Church in Keswick, Virginia, for providing a quiet place to write in the parish library.

Finally, I am grateful to my family for their many years of unflinching support. My parents, Larry and Dessa, and siblings, Wade and Audra, encouraged me in intellectual pursuits from an early age that were, to put it mildly, unusual for a kid growing up in rural Texas. My grandma Elinor Dodd fed my childhood appetite for esoteric knowledge through creative utilization of the local public library. My in-laws Ed and Linda Leon and grandma "Duck" all deserve recognition for their love and support. Most of all, I am thankful to my beloved wife, Elizabeth, who has been a paragon of diplomatic grace, patience, and prudence through what proved to be a very long undertaking. My son, Wesley, offered precocious insights on battles, maps, and human nature. My daughter, Charlotte, helped select the book's illustrations, brought flowers to my study during long drafting sessions, and was a constant reminder of why the pursuit of peace is so precious and important in every era. It was with their futures in mind, and in hopes of a more durable tranquility than now seems likely, that this book was written.

Andrew Rhodes

THE MAPS in this volume emerged from a conversation between a strategic thinker and a mapmaker. Such conversations should happen more often than they do, for the combination can be powerful. It requires a creative dialogue, in which the strategist seeks the aid of a mapmaker to bring an argument into a new and visual frame. The back-and-forth leads to better maps and may even help the strategist see with new eyes and put a fresh perspective on the written argument.

Early in our conversations about the maps for this book (over Zoom because of the COVID-19 pandemic), Wess and I both held up treasured copies of Richard Edes Harrison's classic 1944 book, *Look at the World: The Fortune Atlas of World Strategy*. Harrison was a master of innovative uses of the orthographic projection, which shows the earth as a three-dimensional globe and emphasizes the geographic context of strategic choices on a round earth better than most other projections. Harrison liked to create orthographic maps from a low, oblique angle to give an impression of looking outward from a given point toward the horizon. Doing so allows a reader to view the world through the eyes of people in a specific place. It's especially useful in a book about strategy because it draws attention toward the unquiet frontier, thereby conveying the perspective of leaders eyeing a threat (or threats), as was done by leaders in the historical cases in this book.

I have unabashedly tried to emulate the signature Harrison style in some of the maps that appear in this book. Four (Byzantium, the Republic of Venice, France, and Bismarck's Germany) use the orthographic projection. Two (Interwar Britain and the Cold War–era United States) use the azimuthal equidistant projection, another Harrison favorite, which emphasizes the strategic challenges of the great distances that face global powers in the "air age" because it preserves the property of distance from fixed points.

For some of the maps in this book, the greatest challenge was getting the historical borders right for a particular moment in the never-ending chaos and warfare among great powers that were rising and falling. In other cases the challenge was to go beyond general reference and try to visually capture the geographic perspective of a nation looking warily outward to the threats on its borders, the rising challengers coming nearer or a stable neighbor descending into chaos. Such national outlook is hard to capture with a map on a small page and in black and white. Given the chance, most cartographers would rather create a beautifully colored and professionally printed wall map. But trade-offs are inherent in all media, as in geopolitics, and the constraints sometimes help focus the argument through a ruthless prioritization of what goes on the page.

The maps in this book are simple illustrations; each will undoubtedly have shortcomings, either due to the compromises forced by the medium or due to my own errors. I am grateful to Wess for allowing me to contribute maps and include this cartographic note. I am sure that we both wish for more maps, and better maps, for a book like this. But I will take comfort in the belief that this book will publish more maps, and better maps, than most of its peers.

GREAT POWER DIPLOMACY

CHAPTER ONE

The Lost Art of Diplomacy

*Ambassadors have no battleships at their disposal, or heavy infantry,
or fortresses; their weapons are words and opportunities.*

—DEMOSTHENES

I didn't want to be no Chamberlain umbrella man.

—PRESIDENT LYNDON BAINES JOHNSON

IN THE SUMMER of 432 BC, the leaders of Sparta gathered to consider whether to go to war with their mighty neighbor, Athens. For months, tensions had been building between the two Greek city-states. Months earlier, Sparta's ally Corinth had come to blows with the Athenian navy. Another Spartan ally, Megara, had recently been subjected to an Athenian trade embargo. And a Corinthian colony, Potidaea, now lay under siege by Athenian forces. With each passing month, the Athenians seemed to be tightening the noose around the Peloponnese while Sparta sat idly by, doing nothing. Now Sparta's allies were demanding help: Mobilize and meet the enemy head-on, a group of Corinthian envoys pleaded. Fail to act, they warned, and Sparta might lose not only her allies, but her liberty and honor as well.

Most Spartans wanted to fight. A proud and martial people, they boasted the finest army of the Hellenic world, renowned for its heroic stand against the Persians at Thermopylae fifty years earlier. A group of war hawks, many of them hot-blooded young nobles, longed to test their mettle against the haughty Athenians. They found an able spokesman in the ephor Sthenelaidas, who implored his countrymen to dispense with formalities and take up arms. "Vote . . . for war, as the honor of Sparta demands," he told the assembly, and "with the gods let us advance against the aggressors."[1]

One voice spoke against the clamor for battle. The aging king Archidamus II admonished the assembly to take stock of their situation. The coming war, he said, would be long and terrible. The Athenians had more ships and men than Sparta, and a lot more money. War against such an opponent would be easy to start, but hard to finish. It would grind on for years and require every ounce of national blood and treasure. It would claim the lives of Sparta's sons and daughters, bring ruin to her homeland, and probably result in the devastation of much of the Greek world.

Before rushing to war, Archidamus counseled his countrymen to improve their strategic position. Send emissaries to the Athenians, he advised, to remonstrate for peace in a tone "not too suggestive of war, nor again too suggestive of submission." Use the time gained to rally Sparta's far-flung allies, replenish the treasury, refill the granaries, and restock the armories. If necessary, Archidamus argued, Sparta should even be willing to join forces with the hated Persians to tip the scales in her favor. By making these preparations, he reasoned, Sparta might yet dispose the Athenians to peace, and if that failed, she would be better prepared for war when it eventually came.

At first, Archidamus's address didn't seem to make much of an impression. Egged on by Sthenelaidas, the assembly voted for war. But in the weeks that followed, as the Spartans realized the extent of their unreadiness for battle, the old man's wisdom sunk in.[2] Remembering the king's advice, Sparta sent diplomats far and wide to slow the rush to war and pull the triremes and hoplites of other city-states to her side. When war finally came the following year, Sparta was in a better position to fight than she had been the previous summer. The ensuing conflict was long, and the margins of success were razor-thin. When the final victory came for Sparta more than two decades later, it wasn't because she had a better army than Athens but because she had assembled a bigger and better array of allies— including, crucially, her arch-enemy Persia. Sparta triumphed because her leaders proved adept at exercising the very qualities that Sthenelaidas had scorned as unpatriotic: patience, prudence, flexibility, indirection, and self-control. In short: diplomacy.

⁕

Over the ensuing two and a half millennia, the "Archidamus moment" has played out on innumerable occasions in the cockpits of history's great powers. With clockwork regularity, a city-state, kingdom, empire, nation-state, or superpower has found itself confronted with the impending danger of a big war for which it is underprepared. Just as often, soldiers—men like Sthenelaidas—have promised to save the state and salvage its honor by defeating the enemy in battle. But when the military has proven inadequate to the task, or when the financial resources required for mounting a sustained buildup of armies, fleets, and forts exceeded the state's available means, great powers have invariably turned to diplomacy to build winning coalitions, divide their opponents, and reshuffle the deck in their favor.

This book argues that skill in diplomacy of this kind—strategic, farsighted, and sedulously tactful—is of foundational importance to the survival and prosperity of a successful great power. Its central claim is that diplomacy finds its highest and most enduring expression not as an agent of abstract peace or international order, or as a bag-carrier to an all-powerful military, but as an instrument of grand strategy in its own right, which states use to manage the gaps between finite means and the seemingly infinite ends of a hostile outside environment. Diplomacy is the political medium by which states tap into resources beyond their own to isolate, deflect, or humble menacing opponents. It is the instrument par excellence for manipulating the critical factor of time in competition and achieving what Clausewitz called the "highest and simplest" object of strategy: concentration.[3] The essence of diplomacy in strategy is to rearrange power in space and time so that the state avoids tests of strength beyond its immediate ability to bear. This role is indispensable, timeless, and cannot be performed by any other instrument of state.

By situating diplomacy within the realm of strategy, I challenge two conceptions of diplomacy that have become firmly lodged in the modern mind. One is the notion, borne of America's wars in the 20th Century, that human societies can only find true safety—and honor—in a preponderance of military power, and that diplomacy is a quixotic or pusillanimous enterprise that jeopardizes both. The other is the idea, equally prevalent in recent years, that humanity is progressing inexorably toward a liberal utopia, and that diplomacy's job is to pave the way for that outcome by abolishing war and the nation-state itself from the human experience.

Neither idea is particularly new. They reflect, respectively, the age-old reflex of the soldier, as articulated by Sthenelaidas, and the vision of the lawyer or priest, which is probably just as old. What changed in the modern era is the extent to which both impulses seemed poised to finally realize their full potential. Their ascendancy was occasioned by the existence of a uniquely powerful and dynamic state, in the form of the post–Cold War United States, that seemed to have the potential to remake the world, including its adversaries, in its own image. For the first time in the human story, the competitive principle that had given rise to classical diplomacy, and propelled its development in both form and function, seemed to have been suspended.

But just like past utopias, ours didn't last. Geopolitics, to the extent it ever really went away, returned with all its primal intensity. States remain the building block of international politics, and the very biggest states—the great powers—have the potential to dominate their regions and destroy one another. Survival, not harmony, is as much the central concern of states today as it was in Thucydides's time. Even the United States, the most powerful state in world history to date, must contend with gaps between the means at its disposal and the seemingly infinite ends presented by the threats in its outside environment. The quest to manage those gaps—grand strategy—remains a defining discipline of the successful state. And those states that can mobilize diplomacy as a tool of grand strategy to build and maintain alliances, concentrate military resources, and splinter enemy coalitions are likely to find a decisive advantage over those that cannot.

In this setting, the ancient art of diplomacy deserves a fresh look. What follows is a reflection on diplomacy not as we have come to view it in modern times but as it was understood and practiced by Archidamus, and centuries of Western statesmen (and a few women) who came after him. The book's primary interest is the history itself: the leaders, the choices they faced, and the times in which they lived. The main characters are not just individuals but the great powers they led and diplomacy itself, its logic, uses, and institutions. By taking this deep dive into the past, I hope to rediscover some timeless attributes of diplomacy as an enduring, and remarkably efficacious, human enterprise. That, in turn, will hopefully shed some insights that will prove useful to Western leaders as they face their own "Archidamus moment" in the days ahead.

What Is Diplomacy?

Diplomacy, the British diplomat Sir Ernest Satow wrote in 1917, is "the application of tact and intelligence" to relations between states.[4] But diplomacy far predates the modern state and occurs even when tact and intelligence are in short supply. Stripped to its essence, it is simply communication between sovereign entities for the purpose of reconciling conflicting interests. Diplomacy in this, its most basic form can be found in Homer and the Hebrew Bible. It already existed in a highly sophisticated form by the time of Egypt's Eighteenth Dynasty, some three millennia before the birth of Christ.[5] And we may reasonably assume that the earliest tribes of humans practiced it amid their interminable feuding over horses, hunting grounds, and fertile river valleys.

Like any art, diplomacy is better defined by its outcomes than its processes—and its most important outcome is the constraint of power.[6] Human societies need diplomacy most when they face an enemy that will not submit to their own laws and that cannot be cowed or defeated using the force at their disposal.[7] In a world with infinite resources, or ruled by one all-powerful state, there would be no need for diplomacy, since human interaction would be either intrinsically harmonious or would have the dynamic of master and vassal. Those empires in history that came closest to thoroughly subjugating their surroundings, like the Aztecs, Mongols, or Rome at its peak, left little in the way of a tradition of what could properly be called diplomacy.[8] For them, external relations was an exercise in law and administration rather than negotiation—of judiciously extending their own customs to those neighbors who had the good sense to submit without subjugation by military force.

Diplomacy is endemic, in other words, to competitive settings. It emerges in organized form among the jockeying kingdoms of the ancient Near East and moves to the cramped and striving world of ancient Greece, and thence to inland Europe, whose craggy, crenulated landscape impeded unification under a single ruler. Its modern forms found ignition amid the decay of Rome and the universal Church, first in the wars of the crowded Italian peninsula, then in the struggles of Europe's great dynastic houses north of the Alps, and finally in the global contests of Europe's colonial empires.

Diplomacy's functions developed to give states advantages in competition. Since antiquity, rulers have sent emissaries abroad to gather information, convey messages, and broker deals.[9] Far back also goes the custom of giving envoys safe passage and immunity from the laws of the land to which they are sent. The earliest diplomats were kissing cousins to the spy—like the heralds that Odysseus sent to scout the land of the Lotus-eaters or the Gideonites in the book of Joshua who "did work wilily . . . as if they had been ambassadors" to enmesh the Israelites in a treaty of alliance on false pretenses.[10]

Diplomacy's most important function, and that which ultimately sets it apart from the work of the spy or courier, is negotiation. Negotiation—the promotion of the national interest through compromise—is essential for survival in a competitive landscape where states cannot achieve safety by subduing their neighbors. It is to diplomacy what skill at arms is to war: the central and indispensable competence. Early diplomatic manuals devoted as much attention to the art of negotiating as military manuals do to the art of winning battles. So vital is it to diplomacy's raison d'être that for a long time in the Western world, diplomats were simply called *négotiateurs*.[11]

Negotiation is not deception. A con artist may fool someone once or even twice, but then the game is up. Because states deal with one another repeatedly over long time horizons, the diplomat must operate in some degree of good faith. "Success achieved by force or fraud," the 18th-Century French diplomat François de Callières wrote, "rests on an insecure foundation; conversely, success based on reciprocal advantage gives promise of even further successes to come."[12] Those states in history that have possessed the will and means to impose their will by force have tended to treat diplomacy as *a ruse de guerre*.

Diplomacy's means have evolved to support its functions. These have long been: the ambassador, the embassy, the treaty, and bureaucracy. The resident ambassador appears first among the pocket states of Renaissance Italy as a way of keeping tabs on rivals and seizing opportunities, as one 15th-Century Venetian diplomat put it, to "win or preserve the friendship of princes."[13] The embassy evolved to give the ambassador a permanent perch from which to operate nonstop in peace and in war; "to sleep," as Richelieu said, "like the lion, without closing one's eyes . . . to negotiate ceaselessly, either openly or secretly, and in all places."[14]

What the soldier defends with arms, the diplomat defends with treaties. These exist to lock in advantages gained in negotiations or war. The effects can prove durable; the concepts of sovereignty and territorial integrity that were codified at the Peace of Westphalia in 1648 remain the cornerstone of international relations to this day. But as a rule treaties are seasonal constructs, the validity of which rests, *rebus sic stantibus*, on the conditions that existed when they were signed.[15] Bureaucracy emerges in diplomatic history as a way of equipping the state with the archives and scribes needed to retain knowledge of foreign places and past agreements, and thereby ensure "constant vigilance" in competition with other states.[16]

None of diplomacy's means create power on their own. "Covenants without swords," as Hobbes says, are "but mere words." Their force, as is frequently pointed out, derives from the power of the state that wields them. This takes the form not only of military force but of wealth, which can be proffered or withheld to entice or coerce, and of what today is called "soft power" but is more correctly understood as influence and reputation, which can attract or repel.[17] It is a truism, but nevertheless true, that diplomacy succeeds in proportion to its effective integration with military and economic power.

Yet while diplomats' efficacy is derivative, it should not be concluded from that that they simply transmit power realities the way that metal conducts electricity. Skilled diplomacy can amplify the power of a weak state, while inept diplomacy (what the Greeks called *parapresbeía*) can diminish a state's influence and cause even the mightiest of great powers to under-realize their potential.[18]

The abilities of the individual conducting diplomacy therefore matter greatly—arguably even more than is true of a general. Unlike military commanders, diplomats have no armies at their fingertips; as Demosthenes wrote, "their weapons are words and opportunities." When Callières admonished his prince to select ambassadors with "a spirit fertile in expedients" and "quick penetration to be able to discover the secrets of men's hearts," it was because great matters of state depended on the intellect and character of the person who would bear its image abroad.[19]

Like the soldier, the diplomat's reason for existence is to ensure the survival and welfare of the state. An embassy or treaty is as much a means to this end as is a battleship or cruise missile. For the activities of diplomats to have purpose, they must reflect the policy of the state; to talk about them in isolation is like talking about the movements of the hand without the brain. Diplomacy, in other words, encompasses not just the method by which policy is enacted but also the policy itself.[20]

Strategy's "Younger Brother"

When people hear the word "strategy" they think of generals pouring over maps in wartime. Diplomacy, so the thinking goes, is the stuff that happens when the fighting stops. As the Habsburg émigré Robert Strausz-Hupé wrote during the Cold War, Americans tend to "look upon diplomacy as the antithesis of conflict" in the conviction that "guns will remain silent as long as statesmen confer."[21]

In fact, diplomacy has from the beginning been an integral part of conflict, and therefore of strategy. At its highest level, strategy is "the calculated matching of means to large ends."[22] Danger arises for a state when the gap between the means at its disposal, in the form of military and economic power, and the ends to which it could apply those things, in the form of threats in the outside environment, widen to a point that endangers the state. When this happens, a state faces a difficult choice: accept a higher level of risk than is tolerable, or mount an all-out effort to close the gap using its own resources, which can be hard to sustain for very long.

Diplomacy's role in strategy is to help bridge these gaps. It doesn't do so on its own, since it is not a source of power; rather, it is a political tool that states use to the enhance the means at their disposal externally or reduce the number of threats arrayed against them, or both.

Perhaps the most timeless articulation of diplomacy's role in strategy can be found in Archidamus's address to the Spartan assembly, as related by Thucydides:

> I do bid you not to take up arms at once, but to send and remonstrate with [the Athenians] in a tone not too suggestive of war, nor again too suggestive of submission, and to employ the interval in perfecting our own preparations. The means will be, first, the acquisition of allies, Hellenic or barbarian it matters not, so long as they are an accession to our strength naval or financial—I say Hellenic or barbarian, because the odium of such an accession to all who like us are the objects of the designs of the Athenians is taken away by the law of self-preservation—and secondly, the development of our home resources. If they listen to our embassy, so much the better; but if not, after the lapse of two or three years our position will have become materially strengthened. . . . Perhaps by that time the sight of our preparations, backed by language equally significant, will have disposed them to submission, while their land is still untouched, and while their counsels may be directed to the retention of advantages as yet undestroyed.[23]

At the heart of Archidamus's logic is the idea that states can gain an advantage over adversaries by using diplomacy to impose certain kinds of constraints.

First, diplomacy acts to curb one's own emotions. Don't give in to the passion of the moment and rush into war, Archidamus tells the impetuous young men around him. Take stock, marshal allies, send envoys, appeal to reason. Think before you take the plunge. This is not a counsel of cowardice but of prudence.

Second, leaders use diplomacy to gain control of the clock. Don't engage when the enemy wants it; engage when you are ready. Use the time gained by talking to the enemy to recruit allies and make preparations for battle. War may be averted entirely and, if it cannot be, the state will still be in a substantially better place all-round for waging it than otherwise would have been the case.

Third, and most important, Archidamus says, use diplomacy to constrain the enemy. Gathering states to one's side or even rendering them neutral denies their support to an adversary. This is what Clausewitz meant when he wrote about finding "another way" to increase "the likelihood of success without defeating the enemy's forces"; "to disrupt the opposing alliance, or to paralyze it" and thereby find "a much shorter route to the goal than the destruction of the opposing armies."[24]

By building coalitions, states isolate an opponent and thereby reduce his options for profitable aggression while reducing the range of dangers against which their own resources have to be deployed at a given moment.[25] Doing this repeatedly over long stretches of time allows states to cultivate a balance of power that aggregates other defensive-minded states and stacks the odds against would-be aggressors.

Finally, diplomacy attempts to put limits on war itself. War is expensive—"a matter not so much of arms as of money," as Archimadus says. Even preparing for war places enormous financial strains on the state and its people. By sharing the load with allies, diplomacy alleviates these burdens. Once unleashed, war is a primal force of incalculable ferocity that can quickly get out of control; as Clausewitz wrote, leaders must find ways to keep its exertions commensurate to the object at hand.[26] By giving the policymaker options beyond bloodletting, diplomacy helps maintain political control over the warrior, including by bringing war to an end, if it threatens the destruction of the state.

What all of these functions share is a focus on improving the state's odds of survival at an attainable cost in money and risk. It's not an exercise in sweet reasonableness but the use of forethought and reason to close off an opponent's opportunities for achieving his political ends by military means. Diplomacy may therefore be said to be an inherently conservative and defensive enterprise, both in the sense that it proceeds from a realization of the limits of one's own power and in the sense that it seeks to prevent dangerous accumulations of power by others.

Diplomacy, in other words, arrives at peace not by transcending geopolitics but by excelling in it—through the doorway of high strategy. Strategy, in Strausz-Hupé's memorable formulation, "is diplomacy's elder brother."[27]

"Shit in Silk Stockings"

Diplomacy's role in strategy hasn't won it many admirers across the ages. In the human imagination, the diplomat has always seemed to be a peddler of occult arts. *On n'aime pas ces porteurs de secrets que sont les ambassadeurs,* Jules Cambon said: "We don't like these bearers of secrets known as ambassadors."[28] The Greek poems describe Hermes, god of envoys, as a deity "of many shifts, blandly cunning, a robber, a cattle driver, a bringer of dreams" known for "deeds such as knavish folk pursue in the dark night-time." Sir Henry Wotton memorably described diplomats as "honest men sent abroad to lie for their country." Even Niccolò Machiavelli, who certainly had no qualms about dissimulating for power's sake, deprecated diplomacy as a form of "honorable laziness." And Napoleon put the matter bluntly when he called his chief diplomat, Talleyrand, "shit in silk stockings."

Soldiers in particular have always viewed the diplomat's counsel with suspicion, as summed up in Sthenelaidas's rebuttal to Archidamus: "Let us not be told that it is fitting for us to deliberate under injustice; long deliberation is rather fitting for those who have injustice in contemplation."[29]

The soldier's critique of diplomacy rests on the assumed superiority of *l'arme blanche*. Military force is the most direct and efficient medium by which states pursue their desired ends. Force is agency. Its application, whether in the form of phalanxes or cruise missiles, conveys the precision of a mathematical science. By comparison, diplomacy seems a dilatory and altogether chancier proposition on which to hazard the security of the state.

But Sthenelaidas's declamation wasn't only about efficiency; it was also about honor. War is a primordial act that stirs the passions and excites the imagination. Violence is simply more exhilarating than talking. "There is nothing in [the diplomat's] achievements," the 19th-Century British statesman Lord Salisbury wrote,

> which appeals to the imagination. . . . His victories are made up of a series of microscopic advantages: of a judicious suggestion here, of an opportune civility there; of a wise concession at one moment and a far-sighted persistence at another; of sleepless tact, immovable calmness, and patience that no folly, no provocation, no blunders can shake. But there is nothing exciting in the exercise of excellences such as these. . . . The result is that while the services of a commander are celebrated with almost undiminished enthusiasm from age to age, the services of the diplomatist fade rapidly away from a nation's memory.[30]

Where war leaves behind a roster of great deeds whose luster only grows with the retelling, diplomacy's greatest accomplishments often consist of events that never occur—in crises defused and collisions averted. Where even hopeless wars seem to convey the prospect, however illusory, of glory for those who wage them, diplomacy, with its undercurrents of duplicity and temporization, carries something of the night about it. And where war seems to hold out the promise of satisfyingly definitive solutions, diplomacy involves compromise, which embraces imperfection and entails an acceptance of the limits of power and transience of all human effort.[31]

The jurist's critique of diplomacy is subtler, but probably just as old. Clear back to antiquity, human societies have looked for ways to tame war's chaos without the mess and uncertainty of negotiations, by appealing to the laws of man or the gods. There is an unbroken line that runs from the amphictyonic councils of ancient Greece to the *ius gentim* of Rome and the *res publica Christiana* of St. Augustine to the moral philosophizing of Grotius and Kant to the League of Nations and the United Nations charter and declaration of universal human rights.

Like the soldier, the jurist sees diplomacy as inefficient. Negotiations are opaque and arbitrary; at best, they advance the selfish interests of a handful states and only push conflict off for a bit. But where the soldier offers to deal with danger in kind, the jurist aspires to rise above it by abolishing war itself. Subjected to a higher law, the thinking goes, societies will disarm, get rich, and find harmony. Viewed against these vast potentialities, diplomacy seems not just inadequate but tainted with the same immorality as war, for it impedes the use of reason to remove the *sources* of human strife. As the 19th-Century German liberal philosopher Immanuel Kant wrote, the diplomat's machinations rest on "'dishonorable stratagems' [that are] incompatible with a just world order."[32]

These age-old critiques of diplomacy pale in comparison to the savaging it received in the 20th Century. Western publics blamed diplomats for the loss of life in the two world wars. After the first, U.S. president Woodrow Wilson called for Old World diplomacy to be thrown out entirely and replaced by world government. After the second, American leaders came to associate classical diplomacy with British prime minister Neville Chamberlain's catastrophic attempt to appease Adolf Hitler at Munich.

In the decades since, diplomacy has labored under the long shadows of Wilson and Chamberlain. The resulting mentalities reflect, respectively, the ancient critiques of the lawyer and the soldier. Every U.S. president since Harry Truman has either invoked Munich to justify military intervention or been accused of appeasement by their critics.[33] Even Ronald Reagan, hardly a merchant of "peace at any price," found his photograph juxtaposed with that of Chamberlain in a full-page ad in the *Washington Times* after embarking on nuclear talks with Mikhail Gorbachev. By contrast, Wilson, despite the disastrous failure of his plans, came to symbolize the promise of an egalitarian future that might, with persistence and the right administrative formula, become a reality.

The nail in diplomacy's coffin came after the Cold War. While not scorned in the way they had been after the two world wars, diplomats seemed to lack an obvious role after the collapse of the Soviet Union. There was no grand settlement among the major powers of the sort that had occurred after previous hot wars—no equivalent to the momentous gatherings at Vienna, Versailles or Potsdam. Western diplomats quickly turned their attention to building a capacious new order characterized by multilateral rule-making at the center and nation-building in the periphery.

The main reason diplomacy atrophied after the Cold War was the totality of U.S. supremacy, which far surpassed that of victors in earlier world conflicts. For the first time in history, a global superpower possessed economic and military strength outstripping all of its potential enemies combined. With liberal ideals in the ascendancy, the United States could embrace a foreign-policy program geared not to *shaping* the behavior of rivals but to *transforming* them entirely, into polities resembling itself. The competitive principle that had given rise to classical diplomacy in previous eras was, it seemed, now gone for good. In these remarkable conditions, the substitutes to diplomacy long advocated by the soldier and lawyer appeared to have finally and definitively triumphed, to a degree that removed its purpose altogether.

A (Re)Forgotten Art

Given diplomacy's apparent demise, it is unsurprising to find that it has withered in recent years both as a profession and as a topic of scholarly study. But while the extent of decay is unprecedented, the phenomenon is not. Many times across the ages, human societies enjoyed moments in the sun, when the tools of war or law seemed to be in the ascendancy. Thinking and writing about diplomacy in a serious way, as a tool of strategic statecraft, has frequently been spurred by doubts about the durability of these moments and worries about the inevitable return of the competitive principle.

In modern times, there have been two such "rediscoveries" of diplomacy. The first occurred in Britain after World War I. The prevailing wisdom at that time held that old-school diplomats were incompatible with mass democracy, which demanded a "new diplomacy" whereby elected leaders would conduct negotiations at large summits organized under the auspices of a peace organization, the League of Nations. A few Brits were unconvinced by this fad. In 1917, an Asia hand named Sir Ernest Satow wrote his famous manual on diplomacy as a way of preserving knowledge of diplomacy's historic functions. A few years later, another British diplomat named A. F. Whyte published an English translation of the writings of the 18th-Century French diplomat François de Callières, with an introduction extoling diplomacy as a vital but neglected public service. And on the eve of World War II, Harold Nicolson, a disillusioned Wilsonian, wrote what would become the first in a series of books advocating for a return to the high standards that had characterized Western diplomacy at its zenith.[34]

The second big rediscovery of diplomacy came in the United States during the early Cold War. In the immediate aftermath of World War II, conventional wisdom held that diplomacy was not just outdated but completely dead.[35] Old-fashioned diplomacy seemed counterproductive in the unfolding ideological struggle and pointless in an era of atomic weapons.[36] A handful of Americans, many of them émigrés from Europe, challenged this view. Writers like Hans Morgenthau, Walter Lippmann, and Robert Strausz-Hupé argued that diplomacy was an indispensable component of national power and that a vigorous U.S. diplomacy would be needed to contend with the Soviets.[37]

The most illustrious voice to emerge from this ferment was Henry Kissinger. From the 1950s onward, Kissinger became a prolific advocate for refurbishing diplomacy as an instrument of high policy in the Cold War struggle. A philosopher at heart, Kissinger was beguiled by Kant's notion that humanity is slowly moving toward a global federation that will banish war from the human experience.[38] He developed a lifelong preoccupation with the question of international order, which, invoking Kant, he saw as "the most difficult and the last to be solved by the human race."[39] The job of the diplomat, Kissinger believed, was to solve that problem by devising a series of "intermediary stages," grounded in the balance of power, that would slowly allow humanity to realize Kant's dream.[40]

Both rediscoveries of diplomacy occurred not because of nostalgia but because international exigencies made them necessary. The first was primarily about restoring the professional competence that was lost when politicians took charge of diplomacy; the second was about restoring political control over war that was threatened by the advent of nuclear weapons. Both were rooted in a desire to recover lost constraining functions that are classical diplomacy's stock-in-trade. And both were driven by individuals who looked to history for inspiration and succeeded in producing a rearticulation of diplomacy's core functions suited to the new circumstances of the time.

So far, the post–Cold War world has not produced a similar reappraisal. Peace in our time has seemed more durable and certain than in those earlier eras; confidence in the soldier and jurist runs much deeper. As a result, diplomacy's depreciation since 1991 has been more comprehensive, and the resulting loss more pervasive, than that which occurred after 1919 and 1945.

The effects of this loss can be seen in modern writing on diplomacy. Since the Cold War, the field of diplomatic history has shrunk to a fraction of its former size.[41] A few scholars have kept the torch burning by pointing out diplomacy's indispensable role in international politics.[42] And a handful of practitioners have begun to argue for a renewal of diplomacy to cope with rising world tensions.[43]

For the most part, however, diplomacy has become a province of law. Since the early 1990s, the professional focus has been on multilateral rule-making ("governance diplomacy)" or conflict management ("stabilization diplomacy"). Modern treatises on diplomacy branch in innumerable directions that reflect the interests and desired remit of the international jurist: "refugee diplomacy," humanitarian diplomacy," "digital diplomacy," "climate diplomacy," "health diplomacy," "sports diplomacy," and so on.[44] The emphasis is on navigating international bodies and administering peace as a process *above* the level of the state, not understanding diplomacy's strategic uses *by* the state.

The absence of strategy in works on diplomacy is mirrored by a general neglect of diplomacy in the modern writing about strategy. There are a few important exceptions, mainly in the field of grand strategy, which have done much to illuminate the diplomatic policies of various empires and rulers across the ages.[45] But by and large, post–Cold War strategic studies have shown a heavy bias for the military end of the spectrum. Recent major books on strategy contain entries on counterinsurgency, terrorism, attrition, and deterrence, but very few that deal more than tangentially with diplomacy.[46]

Perhaps the biggest difference about today is that the nature of power itself seems to have changed. When Nicolson or Morgenthau wrote about diplomacy, they could assume as a given that power was understood to be finite, and that the state's ability to impose its will was highly constrained from within and without. It was a short distance from that recognition to the conclusion that the state might need to devise political expedients to bridge gaps in the means at its disposal, at least temporarily, through diplomacy.

By contrast, after the Cold War, the old limits seemed to have vanished. History supposedly ended, at least in ideological terms, and ideals reigned supreme.[47] Power came to be seen as something that could be conjured at will. It took many nebulous and flashy forms: "soft," "smart," "generative," and the like.[48] Untethered from underlying material realities, power became a kind of ideational substance that could be produced without being consumed or depleted. The state itself seemed about to be transcended as geography ceased to matter and sovereignty became a virtual construct.[49] Diplomacy had been "dead" before, but never has the rigor mortis been so advanced.

Argument and Approach

But obituaries of classical diplomacy, this book argues, were premature. Its starting point is that Kant was wrong: Humanity is not progressing toward an apotheosis. War is a permanent condition of human existence. We still inhabit a world of competing states, and their highest goal is survival. Their range of choice remains limited by all kinds of things—geography, finite wealth and weapons, clever enemies. The job of diplomacy is to help the state navigate those realities, while amplifying constraints on opponents. The doorway through which it makes that contribution is strategy: the art of survival.

The aim of the book is to make a fresh articulation of classical diplomacy, both as an art and as a source of stability, for a new and unstable era. In that sense, it can be viewed as a humble attempt to extend the tradition of Callières, Satow, Nicolson, and their successors into the 21st Century. Like them, I look to history to help us understand diplomacy's core role and functions. My approach is to examine how national leaders in past eras used diplomacy to cope with the dangers of great-power competition.

Attempting such an inventory across all of time would fill an entire library and is well beyond the abilities of an author who has a wife, two kids, and a dog that demand his attention. So to reduce the matter to a manageable form, I am narrowing the focus in a handful of ways that allow me to get to the nub of the issue.

First, I'm looking only at the history of diplomacy in the West. This is reasonable, since diplomacy as we know it in its modern form originated in Europe and continues to bear a Western imprint at the global level. The great Eastern empires have fascinating diplomatic traditions, and maybe I will write about those someday. But for the most part those empires did not recognize the concepts of sovereignty for political units of all sizes, or the separation between diplomacy and espionage, that we have come to associate with the Western tradition.

Second, I am interested only in the diplomatic strategies of the great powers. All states practice diplomacy. But only the most powerful ones undertake actions that have the potential to rearrange regions, set the template for global order, and, if things go badly, kill every person on the planet.

Third, I am interested only in what were once called conservative great powers—that is, states that are not attempting to violently overturn the status quo. Genghis Khan, Suleiman the Magnificent, and Adolf Hitler all employed professional diplomats. But the ends to which they used them would more properly be called subterfuge or deception, in that their chief aim was to facilitate conquest. This is not diplomacy but rather the waging of warfare by non-violent means. By definition, classical diplomacy concerns itself with stymying accumulations of power that would allow one great power to dominate the others.[50]

Fourth, I am looking at the actions of individual leaders. History is made up of imperfect people, laboring under the strain of events, who had to live with the consequences of their decisions. Diplomacy in particular is the realm of the mind; as one early 20th-Century historian wrote:

> More than any form of history, perhaps, that of diplomacy brings into prominence in its plenitude the psychological element, the constructive value of human plan and purpose. It reveals the mind of an individual, or the sagacity of a group of statesmen, grasping the conditions of a situation in which vast combinations of force may be thwarted by other combinations, and the interests of a nation, or of civilization itself, secured by a sound public policy.[51]

To understand history at this level, we have to see the world as decision-makers at the time saw it. We have to know the leaders themselves: what they feared, who they loved, what they had for breakfast. Doing that requires us to look past the patina of bronze busts to underlying follies and peccadillos. There is a tendency in diplomatic history to lionize a rotating cast of virtuosos who seem to walk in the clouds and commune directly with the gods. This book casts a broader net. Richelieu, Metternich, and Bismarck all make appearances in the following chapters. They are considered the "greats" for a reason. But diplomacy has never only been the exclusive province of geniuses. It is also the story of eunuchs, courtesans, alcoholics, and moms who were just trying to help their kids stay out of trouble. Seeing this full panoply of actors makes diplomacy at once more accessible and, when it succeeds, more remarkable.

Finally, I am interested in moments that truly mattered: when the stakes were high and strategy had life-or-death consequences. All too often, historians study how diplomats built order *after* wars ended. Those are important episodes, and a few of them appear in the book. But they aren't really the best situations to see diplomacy's role in strategy for the obvious reason that by the time great powers reach the peace table, the military has already had its say on the battlefield. The opposite problem applies when studying diplomacy *during* wartime. Once the fighting starts, the options shrink, reaction cycles takes over, and strategy becomes a quest for physically overpowering an opponent by main force.

Instead, this book's main interest lies in the period leading up to a potential war, when savvy strategists can see a major conflict looming on the horizon, but before the straitjacket of "crisis management" has taken over. It is during these instants—let's call them the "Archidamus moment"—when the dangers of scarcity are most keenly felt, and when diplomacy offers the greatest promise for shifting the odds in one's favor.

Historically, the times that have brought these realities most starkly into focus are wars against more than one great power simultaneously.[52] Two-front war is a uniquely dangerous threat in the life of even very powerful states, because it is then that the gaps between means and ends are widest. Sitting "between the devil and the deep blue sea" forces states to clarify what they care about and fear the most—and what they are willing to give up. The moments when such wars are foreseeable but leaders have not yet been overtaken by events provide the purest laboratory we are likely to find for assessing diplomacy's place in strategy.

With these factors in mind, I chose to look at episodes of great danger drawn from the lives of seven great powers that span roughly a millennium and a half, from the arrival of Attila the Hun on the Danube in the mid-5th Century AD to the end of Richard Nixon's first term in November 1972. Across these episodes, I trace four threads that jointly comprise the book's argument.

First, I contend that the need for diplomacy in strategy arises in inverse proportion to the amount or efficacy of military strength that a great power has on hand to address the threats it faces. The realization of this deficit is far from automatic; to the contrary, great powers almost always reach instinctively for the military option when they are threatened. It is only when that option proves inadequate to the task, or the costs involved with ramping up militarily would saddle the state with an intolerable financial burden, that leaders turn, often reluctantly, to diplomacy as an expedient for securing the state. Diplomacy's role in strategy is to construct political expedients that help states bridge these dangerous gaps between the means at their disposal and the threats arrayed against them.

Second, in managing these gaps, I argue that diplomacy gives the state an advantage in influencing the factor of time in strategic competition.[53] By limiting the uses to which force is likely to be applied at any given moment, diplomacy helps the state conserve, redirect, and concentrate its power. The essence of diplomacy in strategy is to rearrange power in space and time in order to achieve its utmost political aims while avoiding tests of strength beyond the state's ability to bear. This role is indispensable, timeless, and cannot be performed by any other instrument of state.

Third, I argue that diplomacy's use in strategy comes with costs and trade-offs, management of which are themselves part of the measure of its success. Sometimes these costs are tangible and strategic; sometimes they are moral and reputational. Dealing with them requires leaders to make gut-wrenching choices involving long-cherished goals or aspirations. No analysis of diplomacy's role in strategy can be complete without examining these trade-offs and asking, "Was it worth it?"

Finally and relatedly, I argue that effective diplomacy relates power back to a national mission that is greater than the state itself and transcends profane power politics. Great states, like individuals, "cannot live by bread alone"; they seek survival for reasons that are not purely material but cultural, spiritual, and particular to their histories. Alone among the instruments of state power, diplomacy provides a medium for connecting the exercise of power to a higher sense of purpose in the world. It seeks to transmit not just the "how" but the "why" of power.

Plan of the Book

The chapters are arranged chronologically.

Chapter 2 begins with the frantic efforts of the young Byzantine emperor Theodosius the Younger and his wily court chamberlain Chrysaphius to deal with the unstoppable hordes of Attila without taking their eye off of powerful Sassanid neighbors to the east.

Chapter 3 moves to Renaissance Italy, where we find the aging Venetian doge Francesco Foscari attempting to settle accounts with mainland rival Milan so that he can turn his attention to the threat from the Ottoman warlord Mehmed II, who has just sacked the great Christian citadel of Constantinople.

Chapter 4 has two parts. The first chronicles the Valois queen-regent Marie of Savoy's efforts to entice the Ottoman sultan Suleiman the Magnificent into an alliance against the emperor Charles V. The second examines Cardinal Richelieu's quest to court the heretic Protestant princes of

Germany and free the kingdom of Louis XIII from the encircling grasp of the Habsburg Empire.

Chapter 5 moves to Habsburg Austria, where the empress Maria Theresa and her eccentric minister Count Kaunitz manuever to form an alliance with archrival France to save their empire from the cunning soldier-king Frederick the Great. The second half of the chapter looks at how the statesman Klemens von Metternich built an elaborate system of diplomacy that extended Austria's lifespan as a great power and created one of the longest periods of great-power peace in history.

Chapter 6 shifts the focus north to Germany, where we find the bilious chancellor Otto von Bismarck spinning elaborate webs to keep his empire out of a two-front war with France and Russia.

Chapter 7 looks at how British leaders on the eve of two world wars attempted to use diplomacy to secure the British Empire from multidirectional attacks, with very different results.

Chapter 8 brings us to the Cold War, where we find Richard Nixon and Henry Kissinger sending secret messages to Mao Zedong and Zhou Enlai in a bold gambit to discomfit Leonid Brezhnev and extricate America from the war in Vietnam.

Each chapter follows a similar mold. I start by examining the geography of the great power in question and explaining the dilemmas that confronted it at a moment of particular danger. Next, I describe the constraints facing the group of leaders in question and catalogue the military and financial resources at their disposal. I outline their strategic options and describe the often very intense debates that raged at the time. I devote particular attention to understanding the mindset of the leaders themselves—how they thought about their options, and why they chose a particular path. I then show the results of their decisions and ask what could have been done differently. At the end of each chapter, I offer some thoughts on what the great power in question contributed to the development of diplomacy as a profession and as an instrument of grand strategy.

A central claim of the book is that the pressure of competition spurs developments in diplomacy's forms and uses. To drive this home, I track a handful of themes from one chapter to the next. One is *fluctuations in military technology*, whose periodic spikes in lethality, from the compound reflex bow to the atom bomb, have served to both help and hinder the task of diplomats. Another is the *changing use of money in diplomacy*, from the era of gold ducats to the end of Bretton Woods, as a way of gaining advantage in great-power competition. A third is *bureaucracy*, which emerges in the storyline with the Byzantines creating a "bureau of barbarians" to get a handle on the wild assortment of tribes around their borders, and ends with Henry Kissinger's efforts to sideline the bureaucrats at the U.S. State Department.

The diversity of experiences across the chapters is itself part of the point of the book. Whatever a 15th-Century Venetian doge and a 20th-Century U.S. president may not have had in common, they shared an imperative to protect their homelands against omnidirectional enemies that possessed powerful weapons and were motivated by antagonistic worldviews. It is in tracing this recurrent theme of the need to match finite means to seemingly infinite ends across a shifting mosaic of situations that we are able to see what has changed over time in diplomacy's institutions and conventions, and what has remained the same in its underlying logic in strategy.

In writing this book, I didn't go in search of any "lessons" for the present.[54] There can be no doubt that great-power competition is upon us in the early 21st Century, and that the conditions percolating in the world today resemble the dangerously competitive dynamics that were the norm in earlier ages. At the end of the book, I identify some recuring traits of great powers that employed strategic diplomacy successfully that are likely to remain valid in the future. But there are no clear and easy instructions that Theodosius the Younger or Metternich can give us for how to deal with Xi Jinping or Vladimir Putin.

History's primary usefulness lies not in pat lessons but in what it tells us, mirrorlike, about the human condition. In a modern era that has lost the shared reference points that bound together past generations, history has become one of the few things at our disposal for creating a shared sense of identity and purpose.[55] At a time when reality itself seems startlingly malleable, history is a reminder of certain constraints that do not change: geography, human nature, and the logic of strategy being chief among those. History is a good solvent to hubris, and to the conceit that we moderns know everything and can solve everything. If this book does nothing but remind us of our mortal frames—and perhaps challenge Lord Salisbury's claim that there is nothing in the achievements of the diplomat capable of sparking the human imagination—then it will have achieved its aim.

The Eunuch and the Barbarian

Behold, the wolves, not of Arabia, but of the North, were let loose upon us last year from the far-off rocks of Caucasus, and in a little while overran great provinces.

—ST. JEROME

[The Romans became] the slaves of the barbarians and were subjected into slavery by the confession of written documents.

—NESTORIUS

IN THE SPRING of 450 AD, or 5958 on the Eastern calendar, a small party of Byzantine diplomats crossed the Danube into the territory of the Huns. Traveling south to meet them from his stronghold on the Pannonian Plain was Attila, the fierce and wily leader of a loose confederation of nomadic tribes, dominated by the Huns, that for the past several decades had waged intermittent warfare against the northern territories of the Eastern Roman Empire.[1] Leading the Byzantine delegation was a certain Anatolius, a trusted servant of the emperor Theodosius II and veteran of the empire's Persian wars, who had negotiated an earlier truce with the Huns. Anatolius's instructions from the emperor were simple: "Abate Attila's anger and persuade him to preserve the peace according to their agreements."[2]

A lot was riding on the success of Anatolius's mission. Just a few months earlier, a previous Byzantine embassy to the Huns had ended in disaster when Attila discovered that the interpreter accompanying the envoys was involved in a plot to assassinate him. In the wake of that failed mission, there was every reason to believe that the Huns were preparing a fresh assault on Theodosius's empire.

As Anatolius traveled north, he would have witnessed firsthand the devastation that such an invasion could produce, as he passed through a moonscape of wrecked towns and farmlands that had once been thriving provinces of the empire. Priscus of Panium, a junior official who had accompanied the previous mission to Attila, gives us some sense of the scenes that greeted them: cities reduced to rubble, villages emptied of inhabitants, crucified Christians dotting the roadside, piles of bones littering the open fields. These scars of war would have served as vivid illustrations to the Byzantine diplomats of what would happen if they failed in their task.

In seeking to "abate Attila's anger," Anatolius was continuing a policy of patient, if often deceptive, diplomacy toward the Huns that had been established years earlier by Theodosius and his chamberlain, the powerful eunuch Chrysaphius. The policy was far from popular back in Constantinople. An influential faction at court that included the empire's top generals, churchmen, and members of the imperial family chafed at what they saw as craven attempts to appease the "wolves of the North."

And yet as a result of Anatolius's mission, Priscus tells us, the fearsome Attila was "won over by the abundance of gifts and, softened by their gentle words, he swore to keep the peace . . . to withdraw from Roman territory . . . and to stop badgering the emperor."[3] When, just a few months later, the Huns hit the warpath again, they chose Rome, not Byzantium, as their target. For all its apparent fecklessness, Chrysaphius's cunning diplomacy helped to save his empire and lay the foundation for a highly strategic, distinctively Byzantine, and remarkably successful style of diplomacy that would continue in various forms until the empire's final days, a thousand years later.[4]

The Hunnic Menace

The nomadic adversaries with whom Anatolius and his companions had to negotiate were relative newcomers to the geopolitics of the late Roman Empire.[5] Less than a century had passed since the Huns had irrupted, suddenly and violently, from their misty homeland somewhere in the Eurasian steppe.[6] In 376, Byzantine commanders on the Danube had first begun to send worried reports back to Constantinople about a mysterious new group of horsemen who were bulldozing other tribes, pell-mell, into Roman territory. When in the winter of 395 the Danube froze over, the Huns crossed the river in force, easily overwhelming local defenses and spreading panic in the surrounding provinces.

The speed and savagery of Hun attacks left a deep impression on the Romans.[7] A sense of the fear that these fast-moving armies of mounted archers created in towns and monasteries across the empire can be gleaned from the accounts of contemporary chroniclers. The Roman historian Ammianus Marcellinus described them almost like travelers from another dimension, "a race of men which had never been seen before . . . which had arisen from some secret corner of the earth . . . destroying everything that came in its way." St. Jerome saw in the Huns the Four Horsemen of the Apocalypse, while Jordanes, repeating the fireside tales of the Goths, suggested that they were the unholy offspring of witches and demons. For the pious Byzantines, the Huns were as much a spiritual as a physical menace—a scourge sent by God to chastise one or another of the various heresies then sweeping the Eastern Empire.

By the late 300s, the Huns were firmly ensconced in the grasslands of the Alföld, north of the Danube, in modern-day Hungary. From this sanctuary their horsemen could sally at will into the Byzantine Empire's Balkan provinces. After years of intermittent raiding, they invaded in force in 408, 422, and 434. Moving swiftly, the Huns would surprise sleepy garrisons and take even very large towns by storm, leading entire swaths of the countryside away into slavery. As time passed, they grew bolder. In 441 a big force of Huns made it as far south as Thrace and, wheeling eastward through the snowbound passes of the Caucasus, sacked the empire's richest territories. Two years later they struck again, below the Danube, laying waste to the strategic cities of Naissus (modern-day Niš), Serdica (Sofia), and Philippopolis (Plovdiv).

These early incursions were but a foretaste of the destruction that Attila meted out in 447. Crossing the frontier en masse and bypassing recently repaired fortifications, the Huns zipped down the full length of the Balkans, taking more than a hundred towns before lapping up against the walls of Constantinople. A large Byzantine army, commanded by the empire's best generals, marched out to meet them, only to be crushed at Chersonesus, on the European side of the Hellespont.[8] In the wake of this battle, the entirety of imperial territory between the Danube and the Bosporus—a total of some seven provinces—fell under Hunnic control. Whatever status Attila may have held before this war, as the captain of a mélange of marauding tribes, he was now, as a leading authority on the Huns tells us, "the ruler of a great power."[9]

The Byzantine Predicament

On their own, the Huns were difficult enough. But trouble rarely came in less than threes or fours for the Eastern Roman state. From the time of its emergence as an independent power in 395, Byzantium was beset by danger on all sides.

At the empire's center sat the capital, Constantinople, a magnificent metropolis of 200,000 inhabitants that was already well on its way to becoming the glistening seat of Eastern Christendom. The city itself was eminently defensible, lying at the apex of the triangular peninsula formed by the confluence of three bodies of water near the junction of the Mediterranean and Black seas. Successive emperors had strengthened its defenses by constructing lines of walls along the city's landward approaches, including most recently a formidable double row of battlements some three and a half miles in length, completed by Theodosius II in 439.

From their perch on the Bosporus, Theodosius and his advisors looked out on a vast estate of dizzying complexity whose frontiers stretched from the Adriatic to the Euphrates and from the Danube to the Nile.[10]

In every direction, trouble beckoned.

To the north and west of Constantinople lay the Balkan peninsula, whose central spine of mountains afforded little protection from the nomadic tribes, often numbering in the hundreds of thousands, that were now appearing at regular intervals from across the highway of grass that ran from Thrace, through the coastal lowlands of the Wallachian Plain, all the way to Mongolia. By the time of the Huns' arrival, the empire's northern frontier was already home to Goths, Alans, Avars, Sueves, and other groups of Germanic, Slavic, or unknown origin in varying stages of decampment as the Völkerwanderung reached its high tide.

To the south and west of Constantinople lay the Mediterranean Sea and, beyond it, the North African provinces of Libya and Egypt, which constituted a major revenue base and the primary source of grain for most of the empire. These territories were objects of frequent raids by Arabs, Ethiopians, and various desert tribes and, by the 5th Century, seaborne assaults by groups of Vandals, Alans, and Goths, a combined force of which, under their enterprising leader Gaiseric, had already taken Carthage in 439 and, a year later, attacked Sicily.

To the east and south of Constantinople lay the fertile coastal fringe of Asia Minor, the arid Anatolian massif, and, beyond that, the long eastern frontier with Persia, which ran from the mountains of Armenia down the length of the Levant to the eastern shore of the Red Sea. This had long been the empire's most strategically important frontier, partly owing to the tax receipts yielded by Egypt and the empire's two Syrian provinces, and partly owing to the fact that it was the only frontier that neighbored another great power—Persia.

Rivalry with Persia, first under the Seleucid dynasty, then the Parthians, and now the Sassanids, was a leitmotif of Roman foreign policy back to the days of the late Republic. Alone among the empire's enemies, Persia possessed the military sophistication, resources, and universalist aspirations to seriously contest Roman primacy on an ongoing basis. Over the centuries, many Roman legions, and three different emperors, had marched into the Syrian deserts, never to return.

Dealing with the Persians required diligence—and resources. Since the time of the Flavian emperors, Rome had maintained a chain of fortresses, linked by well-maintained roads, down the full length of the thousand-mile frontier from modern-day Georgia to the Sinai. By the late 4th Century, fully two-thirds of the Byzantine military establishment was concentrated on this front, including 150,000 *limitanei* (garrison troops) divided into fifteen independent commands and backed by 20,000 *comitatenses* (mobile troops).[11] Military parity between Byzantium and Persia produced long periods of stalemate in which diplomats swapped border strips and brokered formal treaties (the first of their kind) of varying duration. These seasons of peace were often uneasy; episodic border crises necessitated not only a watchful eye, especially during dynastic transitions, but also the standing presence of large Byzantine garrisons even in times of peace.

By comparison with the empire's eastern frontier, its Mediterranean and Balkan theaters tended to receive less attention. In early Byzantine history, large swaths of both regions were jointly managed with the Western Roman Empire. Prior to the Huns' arrival, the Balkans had usually been the lowest priority for Byzantine military resources.[12] The need for greater focus on this frontier had, however, been growing for some time, as the military prowess of the tribes emerging from the steppe became apparent. To counter these threats, the Byzantines relied on the Danubian *limes*—a miniature version of their eastern defenses, consisting of interconnected forts, palisades, and naval flotillas along the southern banks of the Lower Danube.

The components of the Byzantine security system tended to work in tandem: eastern forts sheltered the empire's rich eastern provinces, which provided the revenue for its field armies. The northern *limes* freed up manpower for the east or for occasional expeditions to relieve maritime pressure on the Mediterranean grain supply. Together, these components enabled a concentration of force in the east while leaving room to manage smaller threats in the other theaters. With this system Byzantium had the flexibility to handle one major war and a second smaller, regional war at the same time.

This finely tuned system collapsed entirely under the weight of the Hunnic invasions. The system's logic had hinged on maintaining a light

FIGURE 2.1. The Byzantine Empire in the reign of Theodosius II
(Credit: Andrew Rhodes)

military presence on every frontier except in the east. With the arrival of the Huns in force along its northern territories, the empire faced the danger of a two-front war beyond its ability to manage. Responding to that new threat would require a permanent military presence in the north that would mean drawing down forces in the east, thus exposing the empire to the danger of a Persian attack; attempting to secure both fronts by military means would require an expansion of the empire's field armies to proportions that would have strained the finances of the empire's largely agrarian economy. What had started as raids by a mysterious tribe of "mounted wolves" had become a strategic problem of the first magnitude for the Eastern Roman Empire.

Eunuch Diplomacy

The ruler on whose shoulders it fell to manage this dangerous predicament was Theodosius the Younger, grandson of Theodosius I and the third of his dynasty to hold the Eastern scepter.[13] Theodosius's entire reign—the longest of any Byzantine emperor—fell within the confines of the Hunnic menace. Born in the purple in 401, not long after the Huns had first crossed the Danube, he had ascended to the throne in 408 and died after falling from his horse while hunting in the summer of 450, the year of Anatolius's final mission to Attila.

What little we know about Theodosius does not bespeak the qualities of a great statesman. One chronicler describes him as "by nature handsome, white-skinned, well-built, with a good nose, a good chest, black eyebrows, straight hair, a thick beard . . . magnanimous, charming and eloquent."[14] John of Antioch wrote that he enjoyed "liberal books," was "unwarlike," and was "under the control of his eunuchs in everything."[15] What is certain is that, like his father, Theodosius was surrounded from a young age by powerful officials who tended to dominate policymaking.

Decision-making in the Byzantine Empire of Theodosius's time centered on a small group of palace bureaucrats and counselors. At the top stood the imperial council, or *consistorium*, composed of both civilian and military officials, many of whom were also members of the Senate.[16] Within this body, the chief official was the *magister officorum*, who oversaw the imperial bureaucracy, followed by the *praetorian prefects* of the east and Illyricum, the *quaestor* (legal advisory), and the city prefect of Constantinople. Counterbalancing, and often overshadowing this body, was a second group composed of the emperor's household staff, the so-called *cubiculum* or "bedroom" advisors, many of whom were eunuchs.

It is among the latter group that we find the most influential figure of Theodosius's late reign, the court chamberlain and eunuch Chrysaphius, who appears to have held a predominant role in the empire's foreign policy from 443 onward.[17] Eunuchs frequently ascended to positions of influence in the Byzantine court, partly on account of the fact that they were barred from the throne and thus posed no threat to the emperor and partly because their inability to have children meant they could not build up multigenerational centers of influence that would challenge the power of the aristocracy.[18]

In Chrysaphius's case, there appears to have been an added X factor, some combination of charisma, intelligence, and other qualities that captivated Theodosius to an unusual degree. The chronicler John Malalas tells us that Theodosius was "passionately in love" with Chrysaphius, "since he was extremely handsome," that the emperor "gave him . . . whatever he asked for," and that he granted Chrysaphius "control over all affairs."[19] Using this influence, the eunuch gained a decisive upper hand against his rivals at court, who included the emperor's sister, Pulcheria, and wife, Eudocia.

Well before Chrysaphius's rise to prominence, Theodosius had gotten a taste of the problems that barbarian invasions could create for imperial strategy. When the Huns attacked in 422, the Byzantine army was preoccupied with the Persians hundreds of miles away in the east. When they attacked in 434, the army was helping the Western Empire deal with the Vandals in North Africa. Most spectacularly, the Hun invasion of 441 had come at a moment when the bulk of the Byzantine army, some fifty thousand men on eleven hundred ships, was dealing with Gaiseric's threat to the Mediterranean grain supply *and* scrambling to react to a Persian move against Armenia.[20]

As these events showed, the Huns were well aware of the empire's multifront dilemma and adept at exploiting it to their advantage.[21] So impeccable was their sense of timing that one cannot help but wonder if the Byzantine prelates weren't right to ascribe supernatural qualities to them.

Through these experiences, Theodosius developed a preference for dealing with the Huns through diplomacy rather than force, whenever possible. Before the arrival of the Huns, Theodosius's father, Arcadius, had pursued a similar policy toward the Visigoths, buying off their leader Alaric through subsidies and grants of territory in the borderlands between the Eastern and Western Empires.[22] Building on this tradition, Theodosius's childhood guardian, the prefect Anthemius, had used gold to thwart an invasion by the Hun leader Uldin in 408.

Theodosius regularized and expanded upon these practices. After the 422 invasion, diplomats of the adolescent emperor had brokered a treaty under which the empire would pay 350 pounds of gold a year in tribute to Attila's uncle Rua not to attack the empire. In 435 Theodosius's diplomats had brought to conclusion the subsequent war by negotiating the so-called Peace of Margus with Attila and his brother Bleda, who were then co-rulers, and consenting to an annual tribute of 700 pounds of gold plus tariff-free access to Byzantine markets.[23] And in 443 a delegation led by Anatolius negotiated a third peace, this time probably requiring 1,400 pounds of gold per year to keep the peace.[24]

By the time of Anatolius's mission in 450, therefore, Theodosius's government had been conducting systematic diplomacy with the Huns for several decades. Journeys of envoys to Attila's capital were a frequent occurrence. Frequent, too, was the arrival of Hunnic emissaries to Constantinople, usually to extort more gold or demand exchanges of hostages.

In these protracted dealings with the Huns, the emperor and his advisors could draw upon a large and mature state apparatus with well-developed institutions and traditions of diplomacy.[25] One historian estimates that by the reign of Diocletian, more than a century before Theodosius, the professional bureaucracy of the Eastern Empire numbered around fifteen thousand, and that its administration was already more advanced than that of the Western Empire.[26]

By the time of Theodosius's reign there probably already existed the famous Bureau of Barbarians, or Skrinion Barbaron, which combined the roles of foreign ministry, diplomatic archives, and intelligence apparatus.[27] The bureau prepared detailed studies of the habits and languages of foreign lands, provided professional interpreters for diplomatic missions, kept track of the texts of treaties, received and handled foreign envoys, and maintained elaborate systems of protocol for ranking the bewildering assortment of nations and tribes around the empire's borders.

The existence of the Skrinion Barbaron is a testament to the importance that the Byzantines attached to informed reflection on foreign affairs. The Byzantines are a rare example in history of a great power whose public servants wrote down their thoughts about war and statecraft. In later centuries the empire would generate a substantial strategic literature, far exceeding that of ancient Rome in its breadth and sophistication, that included the famous *Strategikon*, a treatise on warfare credited to the emperor Maurice, the *Tactica* of Leo VI, the *Praecepta Militaria* of the emperor Nicephorus Phocas, and Constantine VII Porphyrogenitus's *De Administrando Imperio*, a substantial portion of which dealt with the subject of diplomacy with tribes on the northern frontier.[28]

While all of this lay in the future in Theodosius's time, he and his advisors would have had access to a large body of didactic Latin and Greek literature on history and war, including Polybius's analyses on the roots of Rome's success in its struggle with Carthage, Arrian of Nicomedia's history of the campaigns of Alexander, and Aelianus Tacitus's treatise on Greek tactics, to name a few.

Whatever the extent of Chrysaphius's reading or the reasons for his sway over the emperor, it is clear that he was in undisputed control of Byzantine grand strategy at the time of Attila's latest, and most ambitious, invasion. And it was with him that authorship of the diplomatic strategy pursued toward Attila, of which Anatolius's latest mission was the latest iteration, probably rests.

To restore peace on the northern frontier, in 448 Chrysaphius had bought off Attila on a scale that surpassed the tribute promised under previous treaties, promising more than a ton of gold annually along with three tons in arrears.[29] This was more than three times the amount promised annually under the Treaty of Margus in 435, and nearly seven times the amount that the Byzantines had promised to the Hun leader Rua in 431. In addition, the Byzantines consented to Attila's demand that Roman

FIGURE 2.2. Playboy emperor: Theodosius II (Credit: Peter Horree / Alamy)

territory between the imperial capital and the northern frontier, a space of three hundred miles or five days' travel on foot, be evacuated.[30] In practical terms, this meant not only that the Byzantine population could not continue with farming and settlement but that, unlike after previous invasions, the government could not rebuild the region's defenses—in other words, the de facto demilitarization of provinces that had been Roman for nearly half a millennium.

Of all the treaties the Byzantines had agreed with the Huns since their sudden emergence in the late 4th Century, the peace of 448 was by far the most expensive, the most humiliating for the empire, and the most damaging to Theodosius's reputation.

The Military Itch

It is unsurprising to find that Chrysaphius's policy toward the Huns met with stiff resistance from key elements of the Byzantine elite.[31] Equally unsurprising is the fact that the fiercest opposition came from the empire's top generals. By this stage in its history, the Eastern Empire's military leadership was of largely Germanic extraction, descendants of the Goths and Visigoths who had settled inside the empire over the past few generations and who, on account of their martial qualities, had quickly come to dominate its upper echelons. In the reign of Theodosius's father, Arcadius, the power of these barbarian generals had been so great that they were often able to effectively sideline the emperor and his civilian counselors. By Theodosius's time, this influence had abated somewhat, as the newcomers' assimilation increased. But it was still very great.

The most influential of the generals was Aspar, scion of a family of Gothic soldiers, of Arian faith, who had seen service against Persia and the Vandals alongside his father, Ardabur, and would rise to the rank of *magister militum*, or master of soldiers. Another very powerful non-Germanic general was Zeno, an Isaurian leader who had risen to prominence by organizing the defense of Constantinople when Attila's armies reached the city's outskirts in 447.

The generals weren't Chrysaphius's only opponents. The emperor's elder sister, Pulcheria, who held considerable influence early in his reign, was a special target of the eunuch's machinations and a prominent ally of Aspar. Many church leaders, too, tended to align with the war hawks at court, perhaps partly because of the spiritual dimensions that they attributed to the struggle with the Huns but mainly because of Chrysaphius's stance in theological debates.

While their motives differed, all of these factions shared a disgust for Chrysaphius's diplomacy as a form of feckless surrender to the barbarians. This is the line of criticism that jumps out at us from the pages of the chroniclers. Priscus, who was politically aligned with the hawks at court and would later hold a position in the administration of Aspar's protégé Marcian, describes Chrysaphius as "hated" and his negotiations as "craven," while John of Antioch criticized the eunuch for winning peace "by money not arms."[32] Nestorius writes that Chrysaphius's diplomacy subjected the Byzantines to "slavery by the confession of written documents."[33] Later historians like Gibbon followed this line, accusing Theodosius and his chief minister of pusillanimity on a scale that stained the empire's honor and endangered its existence.[34]

Chrysaphius's critics, in his own time and later, saw his diplomacy as a form of surrender, echoing in sentiment the Roman senator Lampadius's denunciation of Rome's payments to Alaric a few years earlier, *"Non es ista pax, sed pactio servitutis"*—This isn't peace, it's servitude.[35] Underlying this criticism is the unspoken assumption that the emperor had a viable option other than diplomacy, in the form of force—that the Byzantines could, by mustering sufficient courage and willpower, have mounted a military answer to the Huns that would have cauterized the threat at its source and removed the need to negotiate with them.

But that is not the case. Attila's armies were larger, faster, and more lethal than the forces of earlier enemies that had emerged from the Eurasian interior. Owen Lattimore has documented the decisive military edge that the compound reflex bow and mastery of the horse gave to nomads over settled societies.[36] More recently, Edward Luttwak has calculated that Attila's mounted archers enjoyed a stunning 2-to-1 speed advantage over Byzantine cavalry and were capable not only of deep strikes into Roman territory but of defeating in detail any force they met along the way.[37] Critically, unlike earlier steppe tribes encountered by the Romans, the Huns possessed the technology for conducting successful sieges against walled cities. Together, these traits meant that, in contrast to the empire's previous opponents, Byzantine armies had no hope of either setting the pace of operations against, or establishing escalation dominance over, Hun armies—facts that gave Attila not only a tactical and strategic advantage over Byzantine forces, but a psychological one as well.

By the late 440s, the Huns' military superiority over the Romans had been repeatedly and painfully demonstrated. In campaign after campaign, the Huns had not only been able to overpower the empire's frontier defenses but had, on almost every occasion, made short work of even very large, first-rate formations that marched out to meet them in open battle. In the 447 war, this had happened twice: first just within the frontier, near Marcianopolis, where the Huns destroyed an army under Arnegisclus, the master of soldiers in Thrace; and a second time, more spectacularly, at the Chersonesus, where in a running series of battles Attila annihilated the flower of the Byzantine field army under Aspar.

These encounters showed that Theodosius did not have a viable military option for securing his northern frontier. Against every other adversary around their borders, be it Vandals, Arabs, or Persians, the Byzantines could reliably expect to hold their own, if not triumph outright, in most military encounters. But not against the Huns. On the basis of capabilities alone, this was an enemy unlike the Eastern Empire or indeed Roman civilization had ever faced.

Crucially, the 447 war raised troubling questions about how Attila intended to wield this enormous destructive power. Earlier nomadic tribes encountered by the Romans were interested mainly in plundering raids or in settling down, usually with some degree of brokered subservience, beneath the imperial aegis. At first this had seemed to be true of the Huns as well. But Attila appeared to have bigger ambitions. His grasp for power could be seen in the skill with which, after murdering his brother Bleda to seize sole leadership, he had charmed and coerced a score of other tribes—Alans, Gepids, Heruli, Greuthungi, Ostrogoths, Rugi, Sciri, Suebi—into a powerful confederacy more formidable than anything ever commanded by previous Hun leaders.[38] Politically significant was the fact that many tribes under Attila's thrall were formal supplicants to the emperor. The sheer geographic extent of the territory over which this collection of tribes ranged, from Crimea to the river Elbe, suggested an expansive potential indeed.

But the Romans didn't have to guess at Attila's intentions. Under the terms of the 448 peace, he had demonstrated his capacity to think in terms of territory rather than merely plunder, when he stipulated the creation of a vast buffer zone that would put the imperial capital at his mercy in the next war. The Hun leader had repeatedly threatened to sack Constantinople and was known to be sizing up the Western Empire as well. As a delegation of Roman diplomats explained to Priscus during his time in the Hun camp, Attila also planned to subjugate the Persian Empire as soon as circumstances allowed. The latter prospect was in some ways more alarming than an attack on the Byzantine capital, with its virtually impregnable defenses. The Persians, who had often been bested by the Romans, would probably prove easy prey for Attila, potentially putting much greater resources at his disposal to use against the Romans. "If he should bring the Parthians, Medes, and Persians under his sway," Priscus records, "[Attila] would no longer tolerate the Romans' depriving him of power . . . [but] openly consider them his servants."[39]

Given these calculations, Theodosius and his advisors could reasonably assume—indeed, it would have been irresponsible for them not to do so—that, as one of Priscus's Roman interlocutors had told him in Attila's camp, the Hun "was aiming at more than his present achievements." Like the leaders of many a great power before and since, they faced a novel opponent that they could not defeat and could not hide from.

Buying Time

Such was the dismal state of affairs in which the Eastern Empire found itself at the end of the war of 447. As we have seen, the answer of Chrysaphius had been to negotiate a new peace, underwritten by much larger subsidies than had ever been undertaken. That this amounted to bribery cannot be denied. But it would be a mistake to see in these methods an exercise in either naivety or rank appeasement.[40] Chrysaphius may have been a eunuch, and a scheming one at that, and Theodosius may have enjoyed hunting boars more than governing, but that doesn't mean, as their critics have alleged, that either was a fool or a coward. The emperor and his chamberlain pursued negotiations with the Huns not because they believed that talking to them, or for that matter paying them, would avoid the danger in itself. Rather, they were employing diplomacy as a tool of strategy to rearrange the limited military power at their disposal against the main threat.

Viewed through the lens of strategy, a different picture comes into view of Chrysaphius's diplomacy than the caricature presented by his opponents. Its unifying thread, or logic, was the manipulation of the element of time to gain advantage over a militarily stronger opponent without losing sight of other, still very dangerous opponents on other frontiers. Priscus, certainly no fan of Chrysaphius, points to this logic when he writes, the year before Anatolius's mission:

> Not only were they avoiding starting a war against [Attila], but they also feared the Parthians who were in a state of preparation, the Vandals who were drawing up in formation by the sea, the Isaurians who were again practicing banditry, the Saracens who were overrunning the eastern end of their dominion, and the Ethiopian races who were

unifying. Humbled, therefore, *the Romans were blandishing Attila while gathering their forces and appointing generals to try to marshal their troops.*[41]

Stalling for time was not a new concept for Byzantine diplomacy. Since the arrival of the Huns, successive Roman governments had used lulls in fighting to repair the palisades along the Danube. Prefiguring Chrysaphius's methods, Eutropius, the eunuch chamberlain to Theodosius's father, had paid court and coin to Alaric while quietly reinforcing Roman forces in the Balkans.[42] During the ceasefires of the early 440s, Theodosius had used a truce to keep the Huns at bay while he recalled the expeditionary force from Sicily and extended the battlements along Constantinople's western approaches. Critically, when these periods of recuperation had been completed, the Byzantines usually stopped sending payments to the Huns. This is precisely what Chrysaphius appears to have done as early as 444.[43]

The fact that the Byzantines typically stopped payment once they had amassed a position of military strength shows that they were using diplomacy not for *war avoidance*, which was anyhow impossible with an adversary whose society and economy depended on raiding. Instead, they were using diplomacy to prepare for war when it inevitably resumed. To appreciate the sophistication of these techniques, one has to understand the other ways that Byzantine leaders were using the breathing space created by their payments to the Huns to improve the empire's overall position.

One of these was the resolution of conflicts on other frontiers. The most dramatic example can be seen in the Byzantines' handling, during the period of the Hunnic threat, of the relationship with Persia. With astonishing regularity, every time the Huns attacked in force, we find the Byzantines quickly getting their affairs in order with the Persians. In 408, the year that Theodosius became emperor and Uldin invaded, the two empires concluded what was intended to be a hundred-year peace. Again in 422, when Rua attacked, the Byzantines and Persians came to terms in similar fashion. And in 442, when Attila and Bleda attacked, yet another agreement was reached under which the two empires would cease hostilities and new fortress construction.[44]

The Byzantines conducted diplomacy toward the Persians differently than they did toward the Huns. In Persia, the Byzantines recognized a great-power rival that was a civilizational as well as a military peer. By the 5th Century, the two empires had lived alongside one another in one incarnation or another for more than half a millennium, and were well acquainted with one another's institutions and manners. Through these interactions they had developed a shared culture of diplomacy with jointly accepted conventions and protocols.[45] In 384 Theodosius's grandfather had concluded a comprehensive peace treaty with the shah Shapur III, centered on the partition of Armenia, that laid the foundation for almost a century of peace between the two empires. The importance of this treaty can be seen in the speedy resolution that it enabled to the two Persian crises of Theodosius II's reign, in 421 and 441, both of which were settled by developing addendums to the treaty of 384, and the second of which was negotiated by Anatolius.[46]

The ability to peacefully cohabit with the Persians through diplomacy, despite the long and bitter rivalry between the two empires, brought significant strategic benefits for the Byzantines. Most obviously, it alleviated the severity of their multifront dilemma, aiding their efforts to buy time and allowing them, with reasonable confidence, to redeploy forces against the Huns without undue risk vis-à-vis Persia. More than that, the empire's Persian diplomacy opened the way for the two powers to actually cooperate against the Huns, a tribal offshoot of which, the so-called White Huns, threatened Persia as well. Thus we see the two empires coordinating their moves in the Caucasus when circumstances required it, with the Persians, for a price, keeping watch over the mountain passes to avoid a surprise Hun attack on Byzantium's eastern provinces. At the time of the 447 war, the 442 annex to the 384 treaty with Persia had operated reliably for five years and would ultimately go on to last sixty more, securing what was perhaps the longest period of peace in the history of the two empires.

Taming the Huns

However impressive Byzantine diplomacy may have been at alleviating the pressures bearing down on the empire's various frontiers, this was not its most important, or impressive, feat. In their dealings with the barbarians, the Eastern emperors aimed at something altogether more ambitious: the pacification of their adversary, not through one-off acts of tribute but through exposure to, and assimilation into, Byzantine culture and economy.

As with other aspects of Byzantine diplomacy, this was hardly new. For centuries, the Roman Empire had expanded not only by conquest but by attracting outsiders to the civilizational benefits of life in the Orbis Romanus. For the ancient Romans, this enterprise had usually been aided by a preponderant, and offensive, military apparatus that was capable of violently subduing those who did not accept the toga. For the Byzantines, subjugation was rarely an option: the enemies around the empire were too numerous and powerful to dominate militarily for more than short periods. As one historian of the Byzantine Empire has argued, theirs was a "defensive imperialism," rooted not in territorial acquisition but in self-preservation.[47] Diplomacy occupied a prominent role in this conception of empire, precisely because of the relative unavailability of military strength. To a much greater extent than their Roman predecessors, the Byzantines needed to domesticate rather than dominate their opponents.

One means by which they sought to do so was through the spread of the Christian faith. The Byzantines saw their empire as no mere state in the modern sense of that term but rather as an instrument of divine purpose on earth, imbued with a calling to spread Christianity in adjacent territories. Byzantine rulers conceived of the empire in apostolic terms, as a *sanctum imperium*, whose foreign policy was infused by a sanctifying imperial mission grounded in Christian universalism.[48] Proselytization of neighboring peoples was valuable not only because it offered salvation for pagan souls, but because it brought otherwise alien peoples within the civilizational ambit of Constantinople. Already by Theodosius's time, Christian missionaries had built lasting foundations for the spread of the faith in Armenia and modern-day Georgia and Ethiopia.[49]

As pagans went, the Huns were not an easy lot to convert. Theodoret of Cyrus tells us that John Chrysostom, patriarch of Constantinople in the reign of Theodosius II's father, sent missionaries to the Huns and that they met with some success. Niceta, a bishop in Dacia, is also supposed to have lived and preached among them.[50] But to a greater extent than earlier nomadic arrivals, who had often sought out and embraced Christianity as a gateway to a better life inside the empire, the Huns were reluctant to abandon their pagan beliefs, which appear to have consisted of a form of shamanism rooted, as one would expect from a group of Stone Age horsemen, in haruspicy (the reading of entrails) and osteomancy (the reading of bones).[51]

The Byzantines had to be pragmatic in their use of Christianity as a tool of diplomacy. Some groups were simply more susceptible to the genial influences of the Gospel than others. In the case of the Huns, the reason may have been a warlike propensity and nomadic lifestyle; in the case of the Persians and later Arabs, it was the countervailing influences of a rival religion and civilization. Unlike the later Ottoman or Spanish empires at their zeniths, the Eastern Romans lacked the martial strength to pursue a religiously tinged military imperialism. They had to be flexible in how they pursued their empire's sanctifying mission. They would come to identify prudence (*synesis*) as the chief trait of a successful diplomat—a mindset that can be seen in the use of foreign custom and even dress on diplomatic missions and willingness to accept non-Christian oaths at treaty signings.[52]

Another instrument in the Byzantines' diplomatic repertoire was Roman law, which they used to enmesh wild neighbors in a shared order and worldview. This occurred partly through voluntary emulation, the so-called *imitatio imperii*, whereby weaker nations would emulate Byzantine social, political, and economic behavior. Successive tribes were drawn to the stability and prosperity plainly visible beyond the *limes*, and they voluntarily sought to obtain these benefits by migrating into the empire en masse. It was this magnetic effect that had enabled earlier emperors on occasion to entice and pacify the more settled and agrarian tribes, and the means by which so many Germans had already by Theodosius's reign become integrated members of Roman power structures. Even in the cases of groups like the Huns, the influence of Roman laws and customs was so strong that their leaders often invoked them when formulating their arguments and demands against the empire.[53]

The process of *imitatio imperii* did not only occur by osmosis; Byzantine diplomats took an active hand in promoting it. The fact that most of the nomadic groups they encountered possessed at best rudimentary legal systems, and in many cases lacked written languages, put the Byzantines in a position to inculcate hybrid legal codes on the Roman model.[54] They did so, in the first instance, through treaties, which, as instruments for stipulating mutual obligations, served as inseminators of Roman laws and customs. And as time went on, they did it in more overt ways, through hands-on transmission and training. It's possible that this is what Theodosius had in mind when he deposited a certain *quaestor*, Epigenes, who Priscus describes as having a "superlative reputation for wisdom" and who, perhaps not coincidentally, had been a member of the recent commission to create the empire's new legal code, the Theodosian Code, to live among the Huns.[55]

Whether by imitation or treaties or advisors, the crucial thing that Byzantine law could convey or withhold was *legitimacy*.[56] The Byzantines were well aware of the advantages that this legitimizing power presented, and they wielded it expertly. The job of the empire's diplomats was to cultivate it and extract every ounce of leverage from it that they could. One way they did so was by instilling a sense of awe about the Greek-Roman civilization undergirding the empire. Perhaps their greatest asset in this quest was the imperial capital of Constantinople. The city's impregnable walls, broad pavilions, ornate palaces, churches, hippodrome, and baths made a profound impression on steppe visitors.[57] Foreign visitors received a carefully choreographed reception designed to emphasize the power, wealth, and majesty of Byzantine civilization. The impact that such a reception could have on a pastoral people like the Huns is amply demonstrated by the reaction that Priscus records from Attila's emissary Edekon on his visit in 449:

> Edekon expressed astonishment at the lavishness of the imperial buildings. As the barbarian conversed with Chrysaphius, Vigilas said in translation that Edekon commended the palace and congratulated Chrysaphius on its wealth. Chrysaphius said that he too would possess wealth, including gold-roofed houses, if he were to put aside Scythian interests and prefer Roman.[58]

Here we have the empire's most powerful minister, conversing with an emissary of a hostile power in his native tongue through the medium of an interpreter presumably trained at the Skrinion Barbaron, about the wealth of Constantinople—and channeling admiration for the capital's beauty into a motivation for a peaceful settlement. The Byzantines would later expand and refine these methods and use them to good effect against groups as diverse as Bulgars, Arabs, and Mongols.

Undergirding Byzantine diplomatic influence was a system of court ceremony and protocol. From the 3rd Century onward, the Eastern Romans employed an elaborate diplomatic hierarchy, modeled on family relationships, with the emperor at the top as "spiritual father," the Persian shah as a "brother," and weaker states echeloned below as elder, younger, or, as circumstances warranted, prodigal "sons."[59] Within this scheme, the tribes and states around the empire were accorded honors in accordance with where they stood in relation to the Byzantine *oikouménē*, or civilized world, the center of which was the person of the emperor.[60] At its zenith, this system of diplomatic patronage would act as a powerful amplifier of Byzantine influence in the regions around the empire, as potentates from as far away as Lazica and Crimea came to Constantinople to be baptized and endowed with the impedimenta of kingship by the emperor.[61]

The use of titles was an important component in this system. Leaders of nomadic societies were particularly susceptible to the elevation in status that came with receiving a title from the emperor, usually accompanied by elaborate gifts, a regular stipend, and other emoluments. This practice was well-established by the time of Theodosius II's reign. The elevation of the Goth leader Gainas to the position of *magister militum* by the emperor's grandfather Theodosius I was one recent precedent; that of the Visigoth leader Alaric to the position of *magister militum per Illyricum* by the eunuch Eutropius, under Theodosius's father, Arcadius, was another.[62] As both of these examples showed, conveying imperial titles could be a double-edged sword; closely managed, barbarian leaders could be an effective antidote to an emperor's domestic rivals or other marauding tribes, but they could also become centers of power in their own right that destabilized the empire.

Attila, too, was given the title of *magister militum* in the Western Empire, and he likely would have received a similar one in the east had he lived longer. Such ceremony and titles proved to be powerful devices for Byzantine diplomats interacting with barbarian tribes, whose leaders craved not only the wealth but also the honor and legitimacy they conveyed. A tribal chieftain who began life as a cowherd and clawed his way to the top of the tribal pyramid through cunning and violence might be able to boast of a thousand horses and a hundred wives. But only Christ's vice regent, in the form of the Byzantine emperor, could make a cowherd a proper king.

The Gold Weapon

The gold payments that Chrysaphius made to Attila have to be viewed in the context of this wider strategy of enmeshing, pacifying, and assimilating the Huns.[63] As with law-giving and ceremonial titles, the Byzantines' use of tribute was grounded in a close reading of the characteristics of their adversary. By this stage in their history, the Byzantines had become well-acquainted with the military attributes of the various steppe peoples emerging from Eurasia as well as their tribal structures, politics, and economies. Gathering intelligence about these groups' weaknesses and internal rivalries was, after all, an important job of Byzantine diplomats. Through that intelligence, the Byzantines learned how to use gold strategically to create dependencies that could be used to the empire's advantage as time went on. Viewed in this light, the payments (almost all of which came back to Byzantium with the merchants who peddled their wares among the Huns) were not an indication of subservience on the empire's part, as critics alleged, but rather a central component of a patronage system that would render the Huns an economic and political client to the empire.[64]

The Byzantines used gold to exploit as a vulnerability what might seem to be one of the Huns' greatest advantages: their strong leaders. To hold together the various factions and clans that made up the Hunnic confederation, a leader like Attila needed not only a propensity for calculated violence but also a competence for generating predictable flows of largesse to his followers, in the form of plunder.[65] If he failed to supply that, he was susceptible to being murdered and replaced by a leader who could procure loot more effectively. The value of Byzantine gold was heightened by the fact that the Huns had no other ready source of it; theirs was an agrarian, barter-based economy that ran on horse and cow herds. By contrast, the Byzantine economy was built on large towns that generated a regular supply of gold and a treasury that, in Theodosius's reign, tended to run a healthy surplus.

By giving gold to Attila, the Byzantines were therefore supplying something that the Huns lacked but they had in abundance, the provision of which met a basic need of the Hun economy and fulfilled an essential prerequisite of Attila's kingship. This created leverage for the empire. The convoys carrying tribute northward were a visible testament to the Huns' dependency on the Byzantine emperor to "feed" their thirst for gold and to allow Attila to continue renting the loyalty of the various lesser chieftains under him. True, Attila could threaten war if the payments stopped. But a sudden halt to the flow of gold would also endanger Attila's position and sow instability within the Hunnic ranks. The Byzantines understood this and stopped payments in the lead-up to the outbreak of the 447 war. Under a weaker Hun leader, this probably would have sparked a leadership struggle.

The Byzantines didn't have to take the risk of stopping payments to use their gold as a weapon; they could simply disperse it in ways that opened up cleavages within Attila's power base. Those cleavages were abundant: in addition to his own notoriously quarrelsome Huns, Attila had to hold together numerous other tribes. In later years, Byzantine diplomacy would become adept at exploiting these fault lines to splinter hostile barbarian groups and pit them against one another.

Already by Theodosius's time, the potential value of such a strategy was well understood. When the emperor was just seven years old, in the first year of his reign, his guardian prefect Athemius had effectively thwarted Uldin's invasion by bribing lesser Hun chieftains to defect.[66] Priscus tells us that Theodosius had something similar in mind when he sent payments to the leaders of the various clans of the Akateri, one of the tribes of the Hunnic confederation, "hoping that they would all put aside their alliance with Attila and welcome peace with the Romans."[67] The scheme only collapsed when, in a rare instance of failure by Byzantine diplomatic intelligence, the official distributing the gold managed to overlook and insult a tribal leader, who exposed the scheme to Attila.

Even when gold failed to divide enemies at the tribal level, it held out the prospect of doing so at the leadership level, in the clique surrounding the top chieftain. This is clearly what Chrysaphius had in mind when, the year before Anatolius's mission, he had attempted to bribe Attila's emissary Edekon into assassinating and replacing Attila.[68] This was not unprecedented; in 412 a group of Byzantine emissaries had traveled to the camp of an earlier Hun leader called Donatus, killed him, and won the friendship of his successor with elaborate gifts.

That Chrysaphius had even been able to contemplate such a plot against Attila during the mission of 449 demonstrates the opportunities presented by the combination of ready gold and close study of the empire's opponents. The failure of the mission was more a reflection of Attila's traits as an unusually effective leader than of failure of imagination or planning on the part of the Byzantines. Under a different chief, the plot could very well have succeeded, as it had against Donatus. And while there is no evidence that the Byzantines played any role in Attila's mysterious death—which occurred on his wedding night a few years later, apparently as a result of a nosebleed after a night of heavy drinking—it certainly would have been consistent with their means and methods to have made the attempt.

Giving the Eunuch His Due

In short, there was much more to Chrysaphius's policy toward the Huns than the base appeasement alleged by his critics. His moves were part of a hard-nosed strategy aimed at using the nonmilitary means (religion, law, customs, gold) at the empire's disposal to keep a threat at bay that could not be handled on the basis of military force. The role of diplomacy was to manipulate the element of time, first in a narrow sense of enabling the Byzantines to husband strength and prepare for the next inevitable blow, and also in a wider sense, by positioning the empire to wait out events.

At the root of Chrysaphius's methods was the recognition that time changes things: Tribes ebb and flow, and eventually move on to new lands. Leaders come and go. Even the mighty Attila eventually dies. Chrysaphius used diplomacy to ensure that the passage of time left the empire stronger and its enemy weaker.

This was the strategic background to Anatolius's journey in early 450. We don't know a lot about the details of that mission, beyond what Priscus tells us: that Attila demanded Chrysaphius's head following the failed assassination, that he asked for Anatolius by name as a skilled negotiator with whom he had worked in the past, that the latter traveled north with at least fifty pounds of gold to ransom Byzantine hostages, that he was instructed to convince Attila to keep the terms of the peace agreed after the 448 war, and that he was empowered to negotiate in Theodosius's name. Priscus tells us that Anatolius not only achieved his instructions but also convinced Attila to drop the most onerous provisions from the recent truce and allow Byzantine subjects to return home in the empire's war-torn northern provinces. These were no mean accomplishments, especially considering that the Byzantines were in arrears in tribute and had just botched an attempt on Attila's life.

Priscus tells us that Anatolius achieved these results by an "abundance of gifts" and "gentle words." But of course the diplomat was able to draw on much more than his skills of rhetoric and the bags of gold he had carried from Constantinople. Underlying his diplomacy was the knowledge that the Hun leader, for all his ferocity, needed Roman gold to satiate his followers' appetite for plunder, that he craved Roman titles and legitimacy, and that the empire had used the interval since the last war to strengthen its defenses, reaffirm its friendship with Persia, and shift forces to the northern frontier from the east—in short, that time was on Byzantium's side.

The outcome of Anatolius's mission was an event that did not occur: another Hun invasion of Thrace. When, in 451, Attila finally did return to the warpath, it was toward the Western Empire and not the Byzantine lands that he and his forces turned their attention. Within a few years, the only references to the Huns in Byzantine sources would be in their new capacity as auxiliary cavalry in the service of the Eastern emperor. That these fearsome foes would become a footnote to Byzantine history and not a punctuation mark, as to some extent they were for the Roman state, is at least in part a result of Chrysaphius's careful and persistent—if also sometimes deceptive—diplomacy, however much it might have been deprecated by the emperor's sister and the Gothic generals in Constantinople.

Chrysaphius's methods weren't without costs. They carried a price in Byzantine prestige, in the opportunity costs of foregoing objectives on other frontiers, and, most obviously, in gold. Yet Byzantine payments to the Huns, while not insignificant, were but a small fraction of what the empire spent on walls and soldiers.[69] The cost of the eunuch's payments to Attila has to be compared against the outlays that would have been needed to obtain security against the Huns by force. Opting for an offensive response to Attila would have required enormous sums and inevitably entailed long periods of lost revenue from territories seized by the Huns as well as the indirect costs in agriculture and lost revenue of soldiers being absent at harvest. Even then, it would probably would have failed. Viewed in this light, the subsidies were a cost-effective means of security that was much less expensive than the alternative.[70]

The cost to the empire's prestige, at least in the eyes of many of its own elite, and to Chrysaphius personally, were altogether different matters. In his dealings with the Huns, Chrysaphius's rivals saw a political weapon with which to defame and eventually unseat him. The diplomatic missions to Attila were easily depicted as an act of cowardice that brought dishonor to the empire.

Chrysaphius could withstand this criticism as long as his protector Theodosius, whom he loved, lived. But when the emperor died in a hunting accident in the summer of 450 and his sister Pulcheria took power, the tides suddenly turned against him. One of Pulcheria's first acts was to have Chrysaphius executed. Pulcheria, like her ally Aspar, whose lieutenant Marcian she promptly married and made emperor, had plenty of other reason to want to see Chrysaphius dead, including, no doubt, the confiscation of his wealth. But his policy of "appeasing" the Huns provided the main pretext. For not the last time in history, the architect of a successful policy of diplomacy succeeded abroad but failed at home.

Theodosius's successor, the emperor Marcian, abruptly discontinued tribute to Attila and embarked on exactly the offensive military policy that his predecessor had long avoided. The Hun response was swift; in the fall of 451, Attila launched another raid into Illyricum.[71] Marcian responded with a military offensive deep into Hun territory, which succeeded only because Attila was by then gone, with most of his forces, on his invasion of the Western Empire. When Attila returned, he began to prepare his forces for a large-scale invasion of Byzantium, against which the Eastern Empire's defenses would almost certainly have proven just as inadequate as they had in 441, 442, and 447. "Within a few months of [Marcian's] accession," Thompson concludes, "he had brought the Eastern Romans to the edge of the abyss, and all but lost what Theodosius had won by eleven years of patient, exacting and costly effort."[72] Only Attila's sudden death prevented what would likely have been a catastrophe for the Byzantines at a crucial moment in the early development of the eastern state.

The Byzantine Legacy: Diplomacy First

Tellingly, in the decades following Theodosius's reign, it was the diplomacy-centric approach practiced by Chrysaphius, rather than the more forceful, and supposedly more honorable, methods of Aspar and

Marcian, that would become the default template for Byzantine strategy. In the late 450s the emperor Leo I used a similar combination of subsidies, titles, and emoluments not unlike those that Chrysaphius had used with Attila to deal effectively with the Ostrogoths. In the 470s Zeno the Younger repeated the formula to keep the same tribes from coalescing into a militarily irresistible force. In the early 500s the emperor Anastasius used similar techniques on the empire's southern frontier, to keep peace with the Arabs so that he could fend off renewed threats from Persia. And in 532 the emperor Justinian signed a new treaty with Persia, lubricated with an eye-popping 11,000 pounds of gold, before launching his reconquest of North Africa and Italy.

The relative stability that the Eastern Empire experienced in this period, juxtaposed against the deathbed convulsions of its Western twin, are in part due to diplomacy. While the East's stabler finances and the sheltered geography of its capital helped, these would not have sufficed to keep it afloat in an era of incessant invasions and Persian pressure without an effective foreign policy. If the Eastern Empire had faced full-scale invasion from a large warlike group like the Huns and from the Persians at the same time, just to name the most obvious catastrophic scenario of this period, it might have endured a similar fate to that of the Western Empire. That this didn't happen has to be attributed, in large measure, to the persistent, strategic use of diplomacy.

Much would change in Byzantine diplomacy over the empire's long history. But a handful of central traits or themes can be identified that were already in evidence in Theodosius's time and would evolve into quintessentially Byzantine contributions to the history of diplomacy.

THE INTEGRATION OF STRATEGY AND DIPLOMACY

While the Byzantines drew upon Roman customs and practices in their approach to diplomacy, they differed from classical Rome at its zenith in the extent of their need for nonmilitary tools to cope with the demands of their surrounding environment. If there was one constant across the long centuries of Byzantium's existence, it was the breathtaking disparity between the military resources at the empire's disposal and the multitude of dangers of its surrounding environment. At no point from the emergence of the barbarian menace to the rise of Islam were the empire's armed forces sufficient to the task of securing its long borders.

It was this wide gulf between available means and necessary ends that drove the development of diplomacy as a tool of first, rather than last, resort in Byzantine statecraft.[73] Underlying Chrysaphius's quarrels with the generals was the gnawing, unavoidable fact that the empire's army wasn't up to the task of securing it. Whatever the eunuch's vices as an intriguer, he would never have triumphed over the generals if his preferred policies had not aligned better than theirs with immutable facts of power and geography. For the Byzantines, the strategic use of diplomacy was necessary to compensate for the inadequacy of military power that, even when it could be utilized to the full, usually did not avail for very long, or sometimes at all. Diplomacy emerges as an expedient for bridging the gap, however imperfectly, between perennially inadequate military means and ever-proliferating, far-flung, and insuperable ends.

Diplomacy did not fill this gap for the Byzantines on its own but by acting as a delivery mechanism for nonmilitary forms of power in the empire's arsenal. These included, in the most direct form, gold, but also Byzantine religion, culture, and law, and the prestige and glory of Eastern Roman civilization, all of which to varying degrees carried benefits to alien peoples and leveled the playing field to the empire's advantage against even militarily superior adversaries. Deploying these assets required a clear conception of how individual threats related to the "big picture" of the empire's available resources and the competing demands on those resources in various theaters—in other words, strategy. For the Byzantines, perhaps to a greater extent than any other great power in history, diplomacy truly was, and had to be, "strategy's younger brother."

THE INTEGRATION OF DIPLOMACY
AND INTELLIGENCE

Knowledge of the "big picture," however, was not sufficient; the Byzantines needed accurate local knowledge of the habits and resources of their adversaries. Diplomacy is situational and specific; a method that works well in dealings with the Persians might not work with the Huns, and vice versa. To deploy their impressive panoply of nonmilitary tools effectively, the Byzantines needed to know what made their enemies "tick"—how their economies functioned, what they lacked, how they chose their leaders, what fissures lay beneath the surface of their leadership councils, and how they thought about the world and made decisions.

Byzantine diplomats needed this information not in an encyclopedic sense, or because they believed peace would emerge on the basis of a deeper understanding of their neighbors, but in order to be able to predict, manipulate, and gain leverage over their adversaries. Knowledge of the Huns' gold thirst, tribal factions, and kingship structures allowed the Byzantines to devise tailored diplomatic techniques that reduced the risk of war while opening up possibilities to undermine their enemies' offensive power and foster long-term dependencies on the empire. Knowledge of the Persians' more formal institutional power structures, territorial appetites, and fear of the White Huns allowed the Byzantines to tailor different techniques, anchored in a great-power parity, that also reduced the risk of war without undermining the empire's long-term security on the eastern frontier.

In both cases, effective diplomacy for the Byzantines depended on detailed knowledge of their neighbors' history, culture, language, and leadership personalities and the integration of that knowledge into diplomatic tools and methods *ab ovo*. Their diplomacy was not one-size-fits-all; it had to be painstakingly developed through close study and contact over a period of many years.

THE DEVELOPMENT OF DIPLOMATIC INSTITUTIONS

It is no coincidence that the empire in history that probably did the most to advance the strategic use of diplomacy also pioneered the development of advanced diplomatic institutions. Byzantine rulers treated skillful diplomacy as a form of precious strategic knowledge, retention of which conveyed important advantages in geopolitical competition. The knowledge in question was simply too valuable to be left to the abilities of individual diplomats, however talented. The empire's survival demanded that it be cultivated on a systematic rather than ad hoc basis, disseminated within the empire's elite, and preserved from one generation to the next in permanent, institutional form.

The most obvious manifestation of this institutional impulse was the Skrinion Barbaron. Giving diplomacy institutional expression within the Byzantine system of government, with its own bureaucracy and resources, deepened the skill, preparation, and professionalism of imperial diplomats and therefore increased their odds of success. When Theodosius needed to dispatch a mission to Attila, he wasn't gambling the empire's future on a group of favorites or amateurs; he could rely on a well-resourced cadre of officials to prepare the mission, staff it with interpreters and gifts, and back-brief it with the most up-to-date intelligence as well as archived copies of past treaties with the Huns, detailed knowledge of which constituted an advantage in negotiations. In addition, the existence of a standing diplomatic bureaucracy helped to increase the clout of civilian officials like

Chrysaphius in strategic debates by at least partially offsetting the weight that the generals enjoyed of having a large organization at their back.

Valuable, too, was the content of the strategic knowledge that institutions preserved and passed down. This included, in the first instance, the accumulated wisdom of many generations of Byzantine diplomats, amassed through years of hands-on experience, about what kinds of diplomatic methods worked or didn't with specific groups around the empire's borders. The detailed instructions left by the 10th-Century emperor Constantine VII Porphyrogenitus to his son Romanos in *De Administrando Imperio*, to cite the most famous example, about how to preserve the imperial inheritance weren't the result of one man's private stock of wisdom but rather the distilled essence of the wisdom of many generations of rulers, eunuchs, spies, and emissaries, the preservation of which had been made possible by a standing bureaucracy dedicated expressly to that task.

In addition to this institutional memory bank, there was the body of ceremonial rules and protocols that the empire's diplomats employed in the field, to which its institutions acted as custodian. Retention of these practices put the empire in the advantageous position of being the rule-maker of how interactions between states should occur. The ultimate testament to the empire's success in this regard can be seen in the fact that, even when Attila complained about breaches of etiquette or protocol, he was using standards that had been set by, and transmitted to his people by, Constantinople.

DIPLOMACY AS AN AGENT OF ORDER

Under the ancient Roman Empire, order had primarily been an expression of military might and the ability that it gave for subjugating one's neighbors, with diplomacy playing an important but ultimately supporting role. Under the Byzantines, the relationship was reversed, and diplomacy came into its own as an agent of order, with the military performing the supporting role. For Rome at its height, the decisive medium was power; for Constantinople, it was legitimacy. Because they could not depend on large offensive armies to secure their borders, the Byzantines had to look to other means to entice, attract, and assimilate. This was the aim to which their rulers aspired over the long term even as they temporized, bribed, divided, and played for time over the short term. The immediate aim was imperial survival and security; the outworking was order around the empire's near frontiers.

Domestication was the path that Theodosius had in mind for the Huns, thinking no doubt of the precedent of the earlier barbarians who had been gradually absorbed into the empire's ways. The very German generals who argued with Chrysaphius over the direction of policy—and whose fathers or grandfathers had, just a few years earlier, fought against the empire they now served—were themselves a manifestation of the success that it could achieve in this regard. While we will never know if these methods would have succeeded in the long run against the Huns, who disappeared from history as mysteriously as they had appeared, we can see the order-inducing effects of Byzantine diplomacy in countless other groups in the decades that followed. In the empire's prime, between the reigns of Justinian I and Constantine VII Porphyrogenitus, these methods allowed it to develop an extensive system of tributary states, the so-called foederate principalities or *limitrophes*, lining its borders from the Caucasian kingdom of Lazica in the north to Abyssinia in the south, and encompassing tributaries as disparate as Visigoths, Bulgars, Ghassanids, and Arabs.[74]

The development and maintenance of this broader footprint of territories beyond the empire's formal frontiers, whose rulers held titles from the emperor, emulated Byzantine dress and custom, drew upon Byzantine codes of law, and were integrated to varying degrees within the empire's system of commerce, is perhaps the highest accomplishment of Byzantine diplomacy. In addition to providing a buffer zone that enhanced its security in a narrow sense, these various polities acted as a significant force multiplier that extended Byzantine power out of all proportion to the empire's actual strength.

Byzantium fills an important chapter in the history of diplomacy between antiquity and the early modern era. In its elaborate protocols, systems of patronage and tribute, and talent for artifice, it shows the influences of diplomatic practices from the ancient Near East and classical Greece; in its use of law as a tool of assimilation and facility for driving wedges among opponents, it shows the legacy of Rome; in its pursuit of a higher conception of order rooted in Christian universalism, it prefigures Medieval Europe; and in its centralized bureaucracy and professional diplomatic corps it anticipates the advent of modern diplomacy in Renaissance Italy.

Byzantium also fills an important chapter in the history of strategy because, perhaps more than any other empire or great power in history, it shows what could be accomplished through the intelligent use of nonmilitary means to outwit or outlast martially superior opponents. The Byzantines practiced diplomacy with an aim that would have been equally recognizable to Sun Tzu and Clausewitz, of "improving the odds of success without defeating the enemy's forces." They elevated diplomacy to the highest plateaus of statecraft, wrote about and reflected on its uses, and developed the institutions, mindset, and techniques to realize its full potential. Their application of diplomacy was conservative and defensive, employed to fend off stronger foes and achieve an affordable safety. The ultimate testament to how well they mastered the art of diplomacy is the empire's peculiar longevity in an unusually rough neighborhood. In this, the Byzantine experience anticipated that of other geographically exposed, militarily-weak empires, such as the Song Dynasty and Habsburg Monarchy, where necessity prompted the cultivation of strategic diplomacy to a high art form. But the most direct and immediate inheritor of the Byzantine tradition of diplomacy would be its one-time possession and protégé, the Republic of Venice, where our attention now turns.

CHAPTER THREE

Ducats for the Sultan

Now Mohammad reigns over us. Now the Turk hangs over our very heads. The Black Sea is closed to us, the Don has become inaccessible. Now the Vlachs must obey the Turk. Next his sword will reach the Hungarians, and then the Germans.

—POPE PIUS II

The first duty of an ambassador is exactly the same as that of any other servant of a government, that is, to do, say, advise and think whatever may best serve the preservation and aggrandizement of his own state.

—ERMOLAO BARBARO

ON JULY 17, 1453, the Venetian Senate sent an urgent message to its emissary Bartolomeo Marcello, who at that moment was afloat somewhere in the Eastern Mediterranean on his way to the besieged city of Constantinople.[1] Just two months earlier, Marcello had set sail from Venice aboard the flagship of Giacomo Loredan, captain-general of the Venetian fleet, with instructions to mediate a truce between the Ottoman sultan Mehmed II and the Byzantine emperor Constantine XI Palaiologos, who for weeks had been gamely holding out in Constantinople with a remnant of defenders against an Ottoman force of 160,000. Before Marcello could reach the city, however, Mehmed II's army had succeeded in their siege, breaching the famous walls that Theodosius II had built to resist the Huns and bringing the thousand-year reign of the Byzantine emperors to an end.[2]

The fall of Constantinople put the Republic of Venice in a precarious position, to put it mildly. More than any other European state, Venice had contributed to the great city's defense, sending several warships, stores of weapons, and the largest detachment of foreign volunteers. More than five hundred Venetians perished on the ramparts when Constantinople fell, including sons of the republic's greatest noble families—Barbaros, Mocenigos, Grittis, and Loredans.[3] Girolamo Minotto, the Venetian *bailo*, a kind of combined resident envoy and commercial agent, had personally overseen the defense of a critical section of the walls and had been beheaded, along with his son, when the Turks entered the city. In short, as Marcello sat bobbing on Loredan's ship in the Bosphorus awaiting a pledge of safe conduct, he would have had every reason to fear that Mehmed would view the Venetians as belligerents and simply switch his sights to the scattered outposts of the nearby Aegean that made up the ragged tail end of the Venetian Stato da Mar, or overseas empire.

As Marcello, the Senate, and the sultan all knew, Venice was in no shape to fight a war, should it come to that. On the day Constantinople fell, the republic's attention was fully absorbed with events eight hundred miles away on the Italian mainland, or *terraferma*, where for three decades it had been engaged in a running conflict with its main rival, Milan. In addition to pulling the republic's limited military resources in the opposite direction from the Turkish threat, the wars in Italy had sapped its morale and depleted its finances. That summer Venice ran short of grain and gold, while a significant portion of its merchant fleet and upwards of half a million ducats in inventory now lay in Ottoman hands.[4] Within a few weeks, one of Venice's largest banks would fold, triggering a string of defaults and, just before year's end, the collapse of the Monte Vecchio, the public fund the republic was using to finance the war.

It was in this atmosphere of mounting crisis that the Venetian Senate composed its new instructions to Marcello. On July 12 it wrote, telling the envoy to raise from five hundred ducats to twelve hundred the "gift" he had been authorized to give the sultan. Five days later the Senate wrote again, in more detailed form: let the sultan know of Venice's "firm intention" to respect the peace that it made with his father, Murad II, a few years earlier; demand the return of her cargo ships; and "if peace is confirmed," ask for the return of Venetian vessels to Constantinople, helpfully suggesting the previous treaty with Byzantium as a template, copy in hand. Almost as an afterthought, the Senate instructed Marcello to request the return of such Venetian citizens as had not yet been decapitated.

In parallel, the Senate also sent instructions to the captain-general Loredan, whose ship Marcello was on: while negotiations are underway, move with haste to strengthen the defenses of the Venetian colonies that lay within Mehmed's striking distance in anticipation of "more disastrous consequences" yet to come. While hoping for the best from Marcello's mission of peace, Venice's leaders were preparing for the storm that loomed ahead, once Mehmed had finished absorbing his latest conquest.

The Ottoman Peril

The Venetians were right to be worried. From the time of their arrival from Central Asia as vassals of the Seljuk Turks two centuries earlier, the Ottomans had spread like wildfire across Anatolia and the Balkans.[5] By the beginning of the 15th Century, the Turks were the undisputed masters of a large swath of formerly Christian territories that stretched from the outskirts of Constantinople north to the Danube, south to the Mediterranean, and east to the Black Sea. By the time Mehmed II took Constantinople in 1453, the Byzantine state was already a spent force, its capital a shrinking Christian island in a rising Ottoman sea.

No one felt the irruption of Ottoman power more acutely than the Republic of Venice. From its origins in the 8th Century as a prosperous outpost of the Byzantine Empire, Venice had expanded to become the naval and economic powerhouse of the Eastern Mediterranean.[6] A cluster of islands off of Italy's northeast coast, Venice's geography gave her a fair degree of safety from outside danger. In hard times, the Venetians could sit tight in their silty lagoons and wait for the trouble to blow over. In good times, they made a fortune as middleman in the booming trade between Europe and the Orient.

Venice's favorable geography encouraged the development of republican institutions.[7] Power resided with a tightknit circle of patrician families—no more than 160 in the city's heyday—whose members served in a pyramid of interlocking councils that prevented the accumulation of power by any one individual.[8] At the top stood the doge, a kinglike figure, elected for life, whose prerogatives were circumscribed by a constitutional contract—the so-called *promiso ducalis*. Beneath the doge sat the Council of Ten, also known as the Signoria, which effectively acted as the executive branch, and beneath that the Council of Forty, which functioned as a kind of high court, a Senate, and a Great Council, which acted as a legislature. While not a democracy in the modern sense, Venice's republican institutions were a source of both civic pride and stability in an era dominated by despotism.*

---

* Power in Venice was restricted to the elite families, which made it more of an oligarchy than a republic, strictly speaking. Glorification of the Venetian regime dates to the 15th Century and is a reflection of intra-Italian jealousies; Florence and Milan were never as dictatorial, nor Venice as democratic, as her champions made out.

Venice's unusual combination of good geography and steady government propelled her to early economic success. From their perch on the Adriatic, the Venetians became the commercial intermediary between the thriving textile towns of Medieval Europe and the spice and luxury markets of the Levant. From Asia came spices and silk; from the Black Sea came slaves and wheat. In the opposite direction, Venetian ships ferried Flemish cloth, English wool, and German metals.[9]

To carry and protect this commerce, Venice had amassed Europe's largest merchant fleet and a powerful, modern navy. To succor her fleets, she had gradually acquired a string of ports, islands, and headlands stretching along the sea road from the Gulf of Venice down the length of the Dalmatian coastline to the Peloponnese, across to the Aegean and up to the mouth of the Dardanelles and the approaches to Constantinople.

It was this sprawling oceanic estate, the Stato da Mar, as the Venetians called it, that, with Constantinople's fall, now stood at the mouth of the Ottoman furnace. Venice had faced threats before. Most seriously, and persistently, there had been the feud with archrival Genoa, a kind of doppelgänger on the opposite side of the Italian boot, which in a series of four wars from the mid-13th Century to the late 14th had contested Venice's bid for overseas markets and naval supremacy. The last of these wars had been especially intense, with Genoese forces managing to threaten Venice itself. Only with great exertion had the Venetians prevailed, ejecting their great rival from the Adriatic and forming a monopoly over eastern trade routes.

The struggles with Genoa, however, would not have prepared Venice for the danger she now faced from the East. Unlike the republic's small, maritime Italian opponents, the Turks were primarily a land power. The Ottoman elite were the products of an Anatolian warrior culture accustomed to subjugating large expanses of prairie, forest, and mountains.[10] They fought not for market access and ports like the Genoese but for physical space to hold, fortify, and tax.

Most alarmingly for the Venetians, the Ottomans were bent on converting their resources into sea power.[11] It was not hard for the Venetians to foresee a day when the Turks would carry their vast army across the narrow seas separating Anatolia from the Stato da Mar and gobble up their tiny outposts one at a time. It had been with this grim prospect in mind that the Senate had instructed Loredan to urgently look to the republic's defenses in the region.

But the safety of Venice's maritime possessions was not the only thing preoccupying the thoughts of Bartolomeo Marcello as he awaited permission to meet with Mehmed. There was also the urgent question of

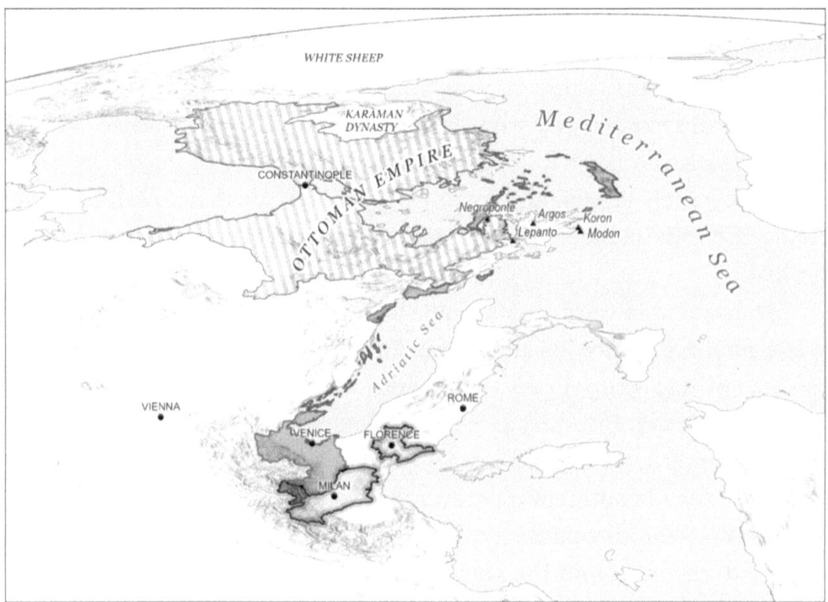

FIGURE 3.1. The Republic of Venice in the time of Francesco Foscari
(Credit: Andrew Rhodes)

Venice's trading rights. For generations under the Byzantine emperors, the Venetians had been able to operate in eastern lands on highly favorable terms, keeping a *bailo* in Constantinople who set duties more or less as he pleased.[12] Even as the Byzantine Empire's outlying territories had slipped away, the empire's capital had continued to secure Venetian access to the Eastern trade routes upon which the republic depended for its lifeblood.

The instant that Constantinople fell, all of this—and with it, Venice's entire economic and strategic position—was suddenly in doubt. As the Senate knew, and as its instructions to Marcello made clear, the Most Serene Republic of Venice—known colloquially as La Serenissima—*had* to find a speedy and favorable understanding with the victorious young sultan. In the Turks, the Venetians faced the worst combination of an enemy that is by all appearances undefeatable but whose good graces are desperately needed to sustain one's own wealth, and the power to resist that comes from it.

The Venetian Predicament

If Mehmed II had been the extent of Venice's problems, it would have been bad enough. But the situation in Europe also demanded attention. For thirty years, Venice had been enmeshed in a draining conflict on the

Italian mainland. The roots of these conflicts were complex, but the proximate cause was territorial expansion by the Duchy of Milan under the ambitious Visconti family. In 1425 Venice had entered the fray as an ally of Florence, a smaller city whose independence Milan threatened. What followed was a protracted struggle in which armies of *condotierri*, or mercenaries, marched back and forth across Italy's northern plains, towns changed hands, belligerents switched sides, and truces were signed and broken.

Involvement in wars of this kind—lengthy, expensive, and indecisive—was something Venice usually avoided. For most of its history, the republic's leaders had scrupulously eschewed entanglement in the boggy affairs of the *terraferma*. By doing so, they had kept a free hand to manage their overseas empire and steered clear of the kind of generational enmities so characteristic of continental politics that could jeopardize their status as an East-West middleman.[13]

The decision to join the wars against Milan came under the tenure of Francesco Foscari, Venice's longest-serving doge.[14] Eighty years old at the time of Marcello's mission in 1453, Foscari had come of age in Venice's wars against Genoa and was determined to make the most of the favorable setting that emerged following the defeat of this great rival. His instincts ran counter to those of his immediate predecessor, Tommaso Mocenigo, who had been hesitant to get drawn too deeply into *terraferma* disputes.[15]

Once committed to the mainland struggle, Foscari strained every nerve to defeat Milan. Unable to field large armies, Venice bought, or rather rented, armies of *condotierri* with murky loyalties and a perverse incentive in drawing out the conflict to increase their wages. By late in the war, Venice was spending half a million ducats a year on the war effort.[16] To sustain these exertions, Foscari stripped the navy and overseas fortresses to the bone and, in one remarkable incident, had Venetian galleys hauled overland and deployed on Italian lakes.

Venice's involvement in the mainland wars gave her a weak hand for dealing with the growing danger in the East.[17]Thirty years of neglecting the Stato da Mar meant smaller fleets and dilapidated fortresses in the Aegean. Preoccupation with the *terraferma* diverted private investment from commerce and disrupted trade routes. The traditional Venetian method for paying for war via forced loans collapsed, as the burden of protracted conflict necessitated continual postponements of interest payments. As Frederic Lane notes, the price of Venetian bonds plummeted by eighty percent in the fifty years between 1423 and 1474, forcing Venice's leaders to turn to levies and higher taxes to fund the military.[18]

Foscari could reasonably expect that all of this effort would eventually be worth it, once the revenues generated by Venice's acquisitions on the *terraferma* started to come online. But that assumed Venice would be able to *keep* what it had gained in Italy—and that was far from certain. The entry of France into the struggle on Milan's side meant that the tide of the war was sure to turn against Venice, jeopardizing her gains in Italy at exactly the moment when the Ottoman threat was mounting in the East. Should Mehmed decide to press his advantage after the fall of Constantinople, there wasn't much Venice could do to stop him. The republic was tired and lacking in strength on both its eastern and its western frontiers. What Venice needed was time to replenish her strength.

The New Diplomacy

In surveying this desperate state of affairs, Foscari and the Senate could not rely on either the naval power or the financial heft that had worked so decisively to Venice's advantage in the past. But there was another asset at their disposal for which the Serene Republic was already famous by this point in its history: skilled diplomacy.[19]

Diplomacy had long been a necessity for Venice. The prompt was partly commercial. Like other Italian city-states of the time, Venetian banks maintained representatives in other countries to protect their interests. As Venice's trade networks grew, it increasingly made use of consuls to look after its economic interests.[20] Along with the republic's sailors and merchants, her consuls provided a deep pool of foreign expertise and fed a steady supply of information back to the capital about goings-on in the varied and far-flung lands through which Venetian trade passed.

Like the Byzantines, the Venetians sought out strategic information through diplomatic channels. A law of 1268 specified that ambassadors must report back within fifteen days of returning from a foreign trip on anything that could bring "profit and honor" to the republic.[21] From this requirement sprang Venice's famous *relazioni*—special diplomatic reports that were delivered to the Senate by returning ambassadors.[22] While other Italian city-states also had documents of the same name, Venice's *relazioni* were of an altogether unique character, equal parts dispatch and intelligence brief. A Venetian *relazione* provided a full accounting of a foreign power's political, geographical, and historical topography, on the logic, as one Venetian ambassador put it, that nothing "is of greater benefit to a well-ordered republic than a detailed understanding of the government, power and disposition of all the great lords and princes of the world."[23]

The primary spur for diplomacy's elevated development in Venice was, however, geopolitical in nature. The historian Garrett Mattingly has shown that the development of modern diplomacy went hand-in-hand with the emergence of a self-contained system of Italian states competing for security and influence during this period.[24] The evolution of this system had its origins in the Medieval struggle between the papacy and German emperors for primacy in Italy, and then between the papacy and individual Italian city-states. These contests gradually uprooted feudal structures and paved the way for the appearance of sovereign, secular states unbound by ecclesiastical or imperial loyalties.[25] The resulting competition was predatory in the extreme, with city-states rubbing up against one another in a never-ending game of survival.

As one would expect in such a setting, Italy's small states developed specialized behaviors to improve their odds of endurance. They sought bigger territories to tax and created centralized bureaucracies to mobilize resources for war. Up to this point, the norm had been to dispatch ambassadors for a specific mission and then bring them home. But as competition intensified, rulers found advantage in deploying diplomats for longer stretches. By the 1370s, Mantua and Milan were exchanging resident ambassadors. By the 1420s, Milan kept an accredited envoy at the court of the future Holy Roman Emperor, Sigismund. And by the outbreak of the Lombard wars, it's likely that Venice had an ambassador regularly stationed at the Visconti court.[26]

All of this was but a prelude, however, to the changes in diplomacy that would occur as a result of the Lombard wars. As Venice discovered in the protracted fighting with Milan, warfare in the age of the Renaissance was an inconclusive affair. The marching and counter-marching of *condotierri* did little to decide matters. However sturdy its finances or skilled its prince, a city-state could stay at war for years without reaching a meaningful outcome. Diplomacy offered a way out of this trap, giving rulers a means of imposing political control and circumventing inconclusive events on the battlefield.[27]

From the Lombard wars there emerged a new kind of diplomat—one who was permanently ensconced in the capital of a foreign land with a standing brief to advance his country's interests. The change was not only in the mechanics of how diplomats were deployed, and for how long, but in how people thought about their role in relation to the business of state. Where Byzantine and Medieval European diplomacy both had, to varying degrees, been grounded in the idea of Christian universalism, the new Italian diplomacy was unabashedly secular in its aims. Its job—and that of the individual ambassador—was not, as had long been conceived, to find peace for the common good of Christendom, but rather to meet the needs of a specific state.[28]

The popular view of the diplomacy of this period is bound up in the legacy of Niccolò Machiavelli, who, writing a few decades later in Florence, would outline a starkly amoral vision for politics and statecraft rooted in a tragic view of human nature. Harold Nicolson later described it as a ruthless, no-holes-barred scramble for *combinazioni* in which diplomats did whatever it took to gain even a slender advantage over their adversaries: "a game of hazard for high immediate stakes . . . conducted in an atmosphere of excitement, and with that combination of cunning, recklessness and ruthlessness which they lauded as '*Virtù.*'"[29]

The Machiavellian depiction is, however, not indicative of diplomacy as it was practiced at the time. The prevailing attitude is better captured in the work of the late 15th-Century Venetian diplomat Ermalao Barbaro, who wrote that while the ambassador is indeed called upon to "do, say, advise and think whatever may best serve the preservation and aggrandizement of his own state," he must remember that the ultimate aim is "to win or preserve the friendship of princes."[30] The highest service an ambassador can render to the state, in other words, is to gain and keep the confidence of the leaders of other states. Whatever temporary advantages may arise from subterfuge are likely to come at the expense of this deeper, far more valuable long-term advantage. Precisely because they were now charged with embodying the state and ensuring its survival and success, diplomats could not afford to engage in tactics that undermined the reputation on which their missions ultimately depended. That reputation, and that of the state, depended on keeping channels open, avoiding indiscretion, and, above all, on active listening.

Foscari's Two Treaties

The need for effective diplomacy would have been especially evident to the octogenarian Foscari as the Lombard wars wound down and the full extent of Venice's predicament came to be felt. Venice could not hope to put off the Turks using force in the Aegean, nor could she do much better in her exhausted condition in Italy. Viewed in strategic terms, the gap between the republic's external needs and internal resources was wide indeed.

The response of Venice's leaders was to undertake major diplomatic initiatives on both of the republic's enflamed frontiers simultaneously. The most urgent of these was Bartolomeo Marcello's mission to Mehmed II. As we have seen, Marcello's instructions from the Senate were to convince the sultan, by hook or by crook, to extend the status quo of Venice's privileged commercial access to eastern lands. Underlying the mission was a wager: that Mehmed II would, rather like a python after a large meal, need to pause and digest his most recent victim. This was an intelligent deduction based on past Ottoman behavior: "one assumes," the Senate wrote, that Mehmed "will do what his father did after capturing Thessalonica: he will seek to live in peace with the Serenissima."[31]

After several months of negotiation, Marcello succeeded in his task, almost to the letter. In the Treaty of Constantinople, signed on April 18, 1454, the sultan allowed Venice to retain its special trade status in the East, recover its ships at Constantinople, continue operating its warehouses there, and retain a *bailo* with far-reaching powers.[32] The only concession that Mehmed insisted on was that Venetian merchants would now have to pay a 2 percent duty on all goods that passed through Ottoman territories. When one considers how lopsided the republic's previous arrangement with the Byzantines really had been, how unfavorable the military balance with the Ottomans now stood, and how roughly the Turks now dealt with other Italian states who were also begging for favorable terms at the time, Marcello's treaty is an impressive accomplishment, "almost taking on the appearance," as one historian put it, "of a diplomatic victory for the Venetians."[33]

Why did the Turks consent to such a treaty? As we've seen, after Constantinople's fall, Mehmed II possessed a military machine that could, without undue exertion, probably have just continued rolling into the Aegean and taken whichever of Venice's territories he wanted. The bribe Marcello paid to the Sultan wasn't very much by the standards of the day.[34] And the Venetian navy was in too shabby a state to offer much of a deterrent at that moment.[35]

Marcello's real leverage was economic. Put simply, Mehmed grasped the extent to which his empire, and he personally, would benefit from the continuation of Venice's well-oiled commercial networks. Venetian trade in both directions was a boon for the Ottoman Empire. Of course, someone else could do the same, but not immediately; only the Venetians had the accumulated financing and transport infrastructure to make it all run. Removing the Venetians from the equation would not only be catastrophic for the Venetians, it would also be very painful for the Ottomans. By allowing the status quo to continue unaltered, Mehmed gave himself time to consume his latest gains while reserving the potential to supplant the

FIGURE 3.2. Aging lion: Francesco Foscari, Doge of Venice
(Credit: CPA Media Pte Ltd / Alamy)

Venetians in their intermediary role when he was better positioned to do so. It was Venice's correct appraisal of this underlying Turkish self-interest that propelled Marcello's efforts to success.

But Marcello's mission wasn't Venice's greatest diplomatic success at this time. That occurred hundreds of miles away in Italy, where emissaries had been working for months, in parallel with the negotiations in Constantinople, to bring the Lombard wars to an end.

The main protagonist of this effort was not a professional diplomat but a man of the cloth, Simone da Camerino, the Augustinian prior of Padua. His efforts had begun months earlier, separately from the official (and ultimately unsuccessful) negotiations being chaired by the pope in Rome, in what would today be called "track 2" talks with two other Franciscan friars, Giovanni Rocco Porzi da Pavia and Agostino Cazzuli da Crema.[36]

Simone and his counterparts came to terms just a few days before Marcello completed his negotiations with the Turks. The Peace of Lodi, signed on April 1, 1454, was a diplomatic masterstroke for Venice.[37] Milan gave up many of its conquests and agreed to new boundaries that significantly expanded Venetian holdings on the mainland. From Venice's perspective, the treaty both provided a reasonable prospect of defensibility in the next war and, critically, increased the revenue base that the Serenissima would need to regain strength for the coming collision with the Ottomans.

The Peace of Lodi provided a foundation for preventing a recurrence of fighting on the *terraferma*. Through long and tedious negotiations after the treaty was ratified, Simone worked to remove the lingering sources of animosity that were sure to fester and poison intra-Italian relations in the years ahead. This included, remarkably and at Foscari's direction, amnesty for any citizens of Venice's newly acquired territories who had sided with Milan in the recent wars.[38]

Through these efforts, the Venetians were able to build support among the other Italian states for a second and more general agreement, which was signed in August. Under its terms, the peninsula's largest powers agreed to a twenty-five-year truce during which they pledged to respect the newly agreed borders, set limits on the size of their armies, eschew bilateral alliances, and come to one another's aid if attacked.

The resulting arrangement, known as the Italian League, was a remarkable innovation for its time—an early attempt at mitigating, if not eliminating entirely, the foreseeable sources of conflict among a group of rivalrous states through a calculated harmonization of interests. The league system was beneficial for all of Italy, which was badly in need of a respite after thirty years of continual warfare. But it was especially advantageous for Venice, which had done more than any other power to bring it to fruition and which, with Constantinople's fall, was now fully exposed to the storm that was bearing down on all of Christendom from the East.

The Long, Cold Peace

By the fall of 1454, therefore, Venice's strategic situation looked very different than it had just a few months earlier. The back-to-back treaties of Constantinople and Lodi provided the breathing space that Venice desperately needed to recuperate and reorient her attention and resources to the main threat in the East. Both treaties had been necessary to achieve this outcome: the first because it kept the Venetians out of a war with the Turks that they almost certainly would have lost; the latter because it extracted them from a war with Italians that they could not win.

The benefits of the two treaties were quickly felt. Under the provisions of Lodi, the Italian states agreed to cap the size of their armies. As a maritime state, Venice gained disproportionately from this arrangement, which allowed her to shift defense resources from land to naval power without triggering a countervailing buildup by her rivals.[39] Before the ink on either treaty was dry, the republic accelerated shipbuilding to expand the size of the fleet. In the years that followed, she undertook a systematic, multi-year effort to repair and replenish neglected Aegean fortresses.

In tandem, the resumption of East-West commerce allowed Venice to repair her damaged economy. Here too, the effects of the two treaties were complementary: the favorable trade terms granted by the sultan allowed Venetian merchants to resume their customary routes, while the end of hostilities on the *terraferma* brought stability to the republic's finances.[40]

Yet even as their fortunes improved, the Venetians kept a wary eye on the Eastern Mediterranean. They didn't have to wait long to see Mehmed II's intentions. Barely a year after signing the treaty with Marcello, the sultan resumed his march into the Christian world. In 1455 he began gobbling up non-Venetian islands in the Aegean. In 1456 he attacked Hungary, in 1458 he took Athens, in 1459 he defeated Serbia, in 1460 he cleared most of the Peloponnese, in 1461 he took control of the northern and southern shores of the Black Sea, in 1462 he re-subjugated Wallachia and seized the island of Lesbos, and in 1463 he took Bosnia.[41]

Mehmed was careful to avoid attacking Venetian possessions outright. But his path of conquest fell uncomfortably close to Venetian outposts. With each swing of the Ottoman scythe, the Stato da Mar became a little more vulnerable. And with each swing, La Serenissima grew more worried, as reports poured in detailing Ottoman atrocities. In 1458, Mehmed seized Athens and led a cavalry detachment to the Venetian outpost of Negroponte, casually riding into the city and ogling its defenses.[42] Three years later, while completing the conquest of Morea, he ordered the execution of a Venetian delegation that attempted to greet him as he passed by the Venetian fortresses at Modon and Coron.

Even as Mehmed grew more aggressive, Venice clung unswervingly to its policy of diplomatic engagement. The Senate instructed the *bailo* to do everything in his power to avoid provoking the sultan's wrath. In 1460, just as Mehmed's forces were taking possession of the Peloponnese, the Venetians renewed the terms of the Treaty of Constantinople and "made themselves appear as hospitable as they could."[43] Come what may, the Senate was determined to preserve the lucrative trade with the sultan's domains.

Yet it would be wrong to conclude from this that Venetian diplomacy in this period was passive. In fact, behind the façade of trade treaties, Venetian diplomats were waging a quiet but determined effort across the Mediterranean and Anatolia to undermine Mehmed's power, gain influence over his decisions, and build alliances for the coming conflict.

In this Renaissance cold war, the republic enjoyed some advantages that helped to offset the vastly greater military strength of its adversary. One was intelligence. Through centuries of commerce, the Venetians had accumulated extensive information networks throughout the territories occupied by the Ottomans. Venetian sailors and merchants took careful observations and were debriefed after their voyages, while Venetian diplomats and informants provided a steady stream of dispatches detailing everything from Ottoman ship construction and troop movements to harem gossip and the mood of the sultan. This intelligence helped the Venetians maintain an up-to-date, accurate picture of Ottoman intentions and capabilities, and an early warning system on their adversary's likely next moves.

Another Venetian advantage was money. By the second half of the 15th Century, Venice was at its apogee as the financial powerhouse of the Mediterranean. The Venetian ducat served as an international currency, in much the way that Britain's pound sterling would do in a later era.[44] Ducats were especially sought after in the East, where the Ottomans were not yet able to produce coinage of the same quality, and where the Senate imposed strict rules about their distribution. Realizing this power, Venetian diplomats engaged in wholesale bribery inside the Ottoman court. Spending from accounts earmarked for the purpose, Venetian envoys spread gold liberally among the viziers, slaves, and concubines of the Ottoman court to ensure that at least some of the advice that reached the sultan's ears comported with Venetian interests.[45]

The Venetians also used ducats to try to have Mehmed replaced by a more agreeable ruler. While Venetian diplomacy in the West in this period was jettisoning chicanery and subterfuge, such methods seem to have still been acceptable in dealings with the Ottomans.[46] Using techniques that would have been recognizable to the Byzantine eunuch Chrysaphius, the Venetians repeatedly tried to have the sultan assassinated. One historian has counted no fewer than fourteen such attempts in the twenty-three years between 1456 and 1479. The frequency of these attempts, averaging more than one per year, is an indication of the cold-blooded determination that permeated Venice's view of the situation in the East even as its diplomats focused on maintaining stable relations. The variety of the plots, involving a cast of characters that included "a Dalmatian seaman, a Florentine nobleman, an Albanian barber, a Pole from Kraków," and even Mehmed's personal physician, shows just how far Venice's ducats could reach. While all appear to have been orchestrated directly by the Council of Ten, it's incomprehensible that the *bailo* and senior Venetian diplomats were unaware of them.[47]

Ducats also helped in recruiting and motivating regional allies. Early in the Ottoman ascendancy, the Venetians had realized the potential value of inflaming antagonisms in their adversary's rear, among the various Turkic-Mongol factions that spanned Anatolia, Persia, and Central Asia at the time. A demonstration of the destructive power that such groups could wield can be seen in the early years of the century, when the Turcoman conqueror Timur (or Tamerlane) had abruptly invaded Anatolia, shattered a large Ottoman army outside Ankara, and captured the sultan Bayezid I. So devastating was Timur's defeat of the Ottomans that one historian has argued it delayed the conquest of Constantinople by half a century.[48]

Learning from this episode, Venetian diplomats assiduously cultivated the descendants of Timur and other nearby groups, using methods not unlike those that Theodosius II and his successors had employed to divide steppe adversaries in a past age. As early as the siege of Thessalonica in 1429, we find the Venetians sending envoys to seek common cause with Timur's son, Shahrukh, against Murad II. Another frequent object of Venetian courtship was the Karaman dynasty, an offshoot of the Oghuz Turks who ruled a powerful beylik in southeastern Anatolia. And most importantly, by midcentury, the Venetians had begun to look at options for an alliance with Uzun Hasan, the leader of a Persianized Turkoman confederation known as the White Sheep that controlled a wide swath of territories across Armenia, eastern Anatolia, and western Iran.[49]

Closer to home, the Venetians cultivated Christian communities in the Balkans, many of which had until recently been their adversaries. The most notable of these was the kingdom of Hungary, which in an earlier era had often sided with Genoa in its wars against the Venetians and just half a century earlier had fought a war against Venice for control of the Dalmatian coastline. Another was the backwoods principality of Albania, whose eccentric ruler, Skanderbeg, was a former janissary and Ottoman governor turned "Champion of Christ" who had only a decade earlier been locked in a bitter war with Venice in the Albanian mountains.[50]

Whatever gripes Venice and these neighbors had formerly had with one another, they paled in comparison to the shared necessity of defending against the Ottoman juggernaut. Even as they played for time in their trade negotiations with the sultan, Venice's diplomats encouraged these states to resist his Balkan inroads not only with words but also with money and weapons.

Venice's Missing Western Alliances

It was one thing to form alliances with Albanian march lords and Turkoman chieftains, but what Venice needed was the active military and political support of western Europe. The natural starting point for such a coalition should have been the states of Italy. In addition to their geographic, linguistic, and cultural proximity, the Italian states had, as we have seen, recently constructed a diplomatic system that sought to avoid war with one another and had at least in theory committed them to a certain degree of mutual support.

But Venice never found a way to convert the Italian league into an anti-Ottoman alliance. Beneath the league's elaborate façade lay the same animosities that had always divided the peninsula's city-states. Far from being a means for transcending their rivalry, the diplomatic innovations introduced by Lodi were used as a means for waging that competition more effectively. The Italians deployed standing diplomats to keep tabs on, and gain advantage over, one another. "Most of them believed," as Mattingly puts it, "that if the lamb had to lie down with the lion, or even if one wolf lay down with another, a wise animal kept one eye open."[51]

These jealousies carried over into Eastern policy. Venice's privileged position in carrying Ottoman commerce did not go unnoticed by neighboring city-states. Even as they parlayed about maintaining the equilibrium on the *terraferma*, Venice's Italian rivals inveighed against her at Mehmed's court, provoking the Ottomans to seize her colonies and even helping gather intelligence about the topography and defenses of the Venetian lagoon for planning a future attack.[52]

Venice's reputation wasn't much better in mainland Europe. In her successive rounds of *terraferma* expansion, Venice had collided with the interests of other large players. In the years after Lodi, Venetian interests came more and more into conflict with the so-called Regnum Italicum, or Italian holdings of the German emperors.[53] In opposing Milan, they also found themselves increasingly at odds with France, whose king had allied with the Sforzas in the recent war and would eventually formulate a dynastic claim to the city. All of this placed hard limits on how far Venetian diplomacy could go in building a common Christian front against the Turks.

The ideal vehicle for doing so would have been to organize a crusade. Already by the mid-15th Century, several such endeavors had been attempted against the Ottomans, most of which had ended disastrously. In 1459, just as Venetian territories were beginning to feel the pressure of nearby Ottoman conquests, Pope Pius II convened a council of Christian rulers in Mantua to plan a joint expedition. But instead of encouraging this effort, the Venetians worked to engineer its failure.[54]

The root of Venice's hesitation was not a lack of piety but rather a sober recognition of the limits and dangers of crusades for providing safety for the republic. Given their exposed location, the Venetians could not take the chance of joining undertakings that were likely to prove militarily ineffectual while provoking Turkish retaliation, which was bound to fall disproportionately on Venice. Paraphrasing the historian Kenneth Meyer Setton, Venice needed either all of Europe at her back or to punctiliously maintain the status quo of Venice's uncomfortable but lucrative relationship with the sultan.[55] The worst of all worlds would be to organize a crusade and see it fail while having to bear the brunt of the consequences. The result would be not only war with the sultan but also the likely loss of Venice's overseas empire and trading privileges in the east, which constituted the main bases of her economic and military strength.

Lonely Lion

When Venice's long-expected war with the Ottomans finally came, the republic faced it alone, without the backing of a major Western power. The signs had been growing that Mehmed was preparing to attack; in 1460 he abruptly increased the tariff on Venetian trade to 5 percent and stepped up harassment of Venetian ships and colonies.[56] In the summer of 1462 the Ottomans launched an unsuccessful surprise attack on the Venetian fortress of Lepanto, and the following spring, they succeeded in taking the Venetian outpost of Argos on the Aegean, after which the Senate voted in favor of a declaration of war.

In the ensuing conflict, Venice finally attempted in earnest to organize a crusade, an enterprise that Pius II eagerly embraced but was resisted by the other Italian states and ultimately collapsed when the pope died. Nevertheless, many of the advantages cultivated by Venetian diplomacy over the preceding decade came into play in the republic's favor. The Senate approved a formal alliance with the Hungarian leader Matthew Corvinus, sent military aid to the Albanians under Skanderbeg, and dispatched emissaries to the Karaman dynasty and Usun Hasan's White Sheep. Outreach to Hasan led to an exchange of ambassadors and, ultimately, an alliance aimed at launching a simultaneous attack on the Ottomans from east and west.[57]

All of these efforts, however, proved insufficient to defeat Mehmed's vastly greater military machine, which included not only substantially larger land forces than the republic and her allies could field but, as the war went on, naval forces equal in size to the Venetian navy. After a decade and a half of war, the Venetians accepted defeat. In the ensuing Treaty of Constantinople, they lost many of their most valuable possessions in the Aegean and were forced to pay an annual fee of ten thousand ducats to continue trading in the sultan's territories.[58] Unlike the treaty made by Marcello in 1454, the 1479 treaty represented an unmistakable downshift in Venice's status in both economic and military-political terms, from leading power of the Eastern Mediterranean to a second-tier player. While the republic remained immensely rich and would continue to be capable of deploying fleets and shaping events for some time to come, the 1463–1479 war unquestionably marked the beginning of the end of Venice as a great power.

Given the scale of Venice's defeat in this, perhaps its most important war, it is tempting to conclude that her diplomacy from the time of Constantinople's fall was a failure. In what proved to be the defining moment in Venice's life as a great state, her diplomats proved incapable of delivering the one thing that their republic needed most: an effective great-power ally. If diplomacy's highest end in strategy is to mobilize factors from abroad that help bridge the gap between domestic means and external ends, then diplomacy was a particular necessity for the Venetians, given their material deficiencies against, and high degree of geographic exposure to, the Ottoman threat. Venice needed diplomacy in the fullest strategic sense, as a means of compensating for military weakness against what turned out to be an insuperable foe. And yet when the chips were down, she was virtually alone and certainly outgunned.

A full accounting of Venice's diplomacy in this period, however, would take a broader view. The service that diplomats like Marcello and Simone rendered was to provide the republic with that most precious of commodities in the dangerous years immediately following the loss of Constantinople: time. About a decade passed from the start of Bartolomeo Marcello's negotiations with Mehmed II until the Senate declared war on Mehmed in 1463. In that time, Venice enjoyed peace with the advancing Turks on favorable terms that enabled her to continue the lucrative trade in the Levant and Black Sea, fill her depleted coffers and ensure that, when war finally did break out, she was fully recovered and ready for hardship.

The Peace of Lodi had a similar if more durable effect. Altogether, its provisions would remain in place with occasional interruptions for four decades and only collapse after Italy was invaded by a foreign power, France, in 1494. During that time, Venice was largely able to forget about the *terraferma* in military terms and give her undivided attention to the Peloponnese without wondering if doing so would create an opening for the Milanese to move against her.

This was far from a self-perpetuating state of affairs; maintaining it required diligent, round-the-clock diplomacy, with professional ambassadors permanently deployed like forward sentinels to preserve the peace and defend the republic's interests. It also required patient diplomacy in adjudicating a lenient peace among the elite and populaces of the territories won by Venice during the Lombard wars. The measure of Venice's success in both regards can be seen in the fact that when the Ottoman war of 1463 broke out, Venice's Italian rivals did not use it as an opportunity to attack the republic from behind and that her newly acquired territories contributed to the war effort without rising in revolt—in other words, that Venice didn't face a two-front war, as might very well have otherwise been the case.

Taken together, the 1454 treaties of Constantinople and Lodi gave Venice the ability to concentrate military power in space and time where it was needed most, against the main threat. From around thirty ships at the time of Constantinople's fall, the Venetian navy grew to more than forty ships in 1462 and seventy ships in 1466.[59] Venetian fortresses that had been neglected and stripped of garrisons in 1453 were by 1463 strengthened and reinforced. If Venice couldn't have a Europe-wide coalition, or even an Italian one, actively helping her, at least she would have every ounce of her own strength on hand to grapple with the main danger.

While aiding in her own concentration for war, Venice's diplomacy worked to degrade the Ottomans' ability to concentrate by confronting Mehmed with his own multifront dilemma. Every Janissary deployed to fight Matthew Corvinus's Hungarians or Scanderbeg's Albanians was a Janissary unavailable to attack Venice. In all of these cases, diplomacy delivered allies that possessed what Venice needed most: ground troops. In the Serene Republic's darkest hour, her Ottoman enemy's greatest strength, land power, was tied up in the Balkans and Anatolia and unable to imperil her existence. So successful was Venice in activating a serious threat to the Ottoman flank from Uzun Hasan's White Sheep that this alliance very nearly succeeded in winning the war and truncating Mehmed's reign; that it failed to do so was due not to deficiencies in Venetian diplomatic finesse but military foresight and initiative.[60]

Venice's diplomatic successes, however, could only do so much to mitigate her material deficiencies; for all its cunning, the republic remained a small cluster of islands off the Po Delta, backed by a handful of holdings on the Italian mainland, pitted against an Ottoman land and sea empire that stretched from the Danube to the Euphrates. To have adequately compensated for this deficiency would have required nothing short of uniting Renaissance Christendom, with all of its divisions and squabbles, for a protracted, multi-year struggle against the Turks. This feat proved too much for Venice, not so much because her diplomats lacked the requisite skills to organize a coalition but because of the impossibility, in peacetime, of participating in such coalitions without jeopardizing the very bases of strength from which her ability to resist the Turk derived.

Herein lay the true tragedy of Venice's predicament and the burden of her diplomacy. In order to deal with the Ottoman threat, Venice needed to summon powers greater than her own, but in order to summon those powers, she would have to sacrifice the commercial relationship with the Ottomans on which her great-power status depended. In moving toward one she forfeited the other. The highest conceivable object of Venetian diplomacy was never remotely attainable, for even to pursue it would have imperiled the great-power status upon which both the republic's safety against the Turks and its position of influence in the West ultimately rested. What was left was the less glorious but tried-and-tested path of playing for time and getting rich for as long as possible, in the calculated hope that the resources thus amassed would be sufficient to weather the storm when it eventually came.

This path was safer for Venice in the short term but also generated distrust and estranged potential allies. The effect was felt in the inability to recruit friends, but also carried over into Venice's future dealings with Christian powers. The full costs eventually came due when, thirty years after the conclusion of their war against the Turks, the Venetians found virtually all of Europe arrayed against her in a coalition—the so-called League of Cambrai—that included not just the usual Italian rivals but continental giants France, Spain, and the German Empire. This isolation was the bitter fruit of Venice's years of noncommittal diplomacy and attempts at maintaining a middle position between Christendom and the Turks. The fact that Venice's options in these years were so constrained didn't make the eventual consequences any less painful.

The Venetian Legacy: Diplomacy and State Power

The decades between the fall of Constantinople and the conclusion of Venice's second treaty with Mehmed II in 1479 were pivotal ones for the republic's life as a great power. In retrospect, it is obvious that a small maritime city-state with limited resources would eventually be eclipsed by the large, centralized empires coalescing on either side of it: to the east, the Ottomans, and to the west, Valois France and Habsburg Spain. The fact that Venice endured as long as it did as a great power is due in no small part to the exertions of Venetian diplomacy.[61]

It is in this same period that we see diplomacy begin to take on something like a modern form, as an enterprise by the state for the state, carried out by accredited professionals on a standing basis. That these methods would emerge in the highly pressurized and self-contained setting of Renaissance Italy underscores the role that competitive forces play in driving the development of both the state and diplomacy as its instrument. That the methods in question would be practiced to high effect by a militarily constrained state beset by an acute form of the two-front problem underscores diplomacy's central role in strategy, as an expedient for managing gaps between ends and means.

From Venice's experiences, and those of northern Italy in general in this period, a handful of themes stand out as especially important in the development of diplomacy.

DIPLOMACY AS AN INSTRUMENT OF STATE POWER

It is in the Italian Renaissance that diplomacy begins to come into its own as an implement of the secular state in its fullest expression, stripped of ecclesiastical or dynastic motivations and constraints. At a time when the larger powers of Europe were still congealing as states and encumbered by both large distances and the last vestiges of feudalism, the jostling city-states of the Italian peninsula were pioneering methods of strategic statecraft without much regard for the influence of popes or emperors. The frenzied struggles for supremacy among Venice, Milan, and their neighbors are a kind of microcosm of balance-of-power politics in Europe of a later era.[62] Competition in the absence of a mitigating higher authority exerted discipline in all realms of state behavior, prompting the Italians to centralize and professionalize the way that they organized resources and exerted themselves in both peace and war.

Venice was well-placed to lead in the transition to the new diplomacy because of its mature political institutions, a culture that prized skill in negotiation for commerce, and diplomatic practices that had already been well-honed through long exposure to international trade. The *terraferma* struggles catapulted the strategic and political application of these practices, demonstrating diplomacy's low cost and high value as a way for the state to circumvent and control military dynamics that, once set in motion, were hard to steer to desired effect. Much as the state needed a standing army to guard its territory in war, it needed the capacity for purposeful political communication and influence abroad to bring wars to an end and advance its interests in peacetime. With reliable methods of this kind in hand, the state could monitor and affect the moves of rivals; without it, the state was blind abroad and susceptible to being outmaneuvered, surprised, and defeated. The advent of permanent resident ambassadors, deployed round-the-clock on both allied and enemy soil, was the ultimate expression of this necessity.

The exaltation of the secular state can be seen not only in the kinds of diplomatic instruments that Venice developed but also in the content and substance of its diplomacy. Prioritization of state interests over other considerations is plainly visible in Venice's interactions with Ottomans and Christians alike. In an era when appeals to Christian solidarity were commonplace, the Venetians had no qualms about maintaining their understandings with the Muslim Turks, shunning even the appearance of participation in crusades and prioritizing their republic's wealth, safety, and freedom of maneuver over the common good of Christendom.

PROFESSIONALIZATION OF DIPLOMACY

The advent of regularized diplomacy went hand-in-hand with the emergence of a system of states on the Italian mainland held together in some semblance of equilibrium. The result of the Lombard wars was an Italian peninsula in which no one state, or pair of states, was strong enough to dominate the whole. Professional diplomacy comes into play as a way of managing the stability of this ecosystem. It was not a one-off act, like forming an alliance or negotiating a boundary dispute, but rather a continual process that demanded unsleeping attention to power relationships. It required a cadre of trained professionals with specialized knowledge, backed by permanent institutions, with an emphasis on defusing crises as they emerged and preventing them from becoming confrontations.

The other Italian states also developed professionalized diplomacy in this era. What sets Venice apart was the scale on which she implemented these new techniques, across a space that included most of the

Mediterranean Basin, and the fact that, to a greater extent than any other power of the time, she mastered diplomatic techniques that were sized to very different customs, geographies, and political dynamics of two separate worlds (East and West).

THE INTEGRATION OF DIPLOMACY AND COMMERCE

While they lacked the military resources of a traditional great power, the Venetians possessed economic power in abundance and utilized it as a source of advantage in their diplomacy. From the standpoint of Mehmed II after the fall of Constantinople, it made more sense to continue benefiting from the positive side-effects of Venetian commerce in his own lands than to go to war with them, at least immediately. Venetian diplomats were conscious of this dynamic and cultivated it by drawing the Ottomans into treaties that provided mutual benefits over long time horizons. Where the Byzantines had used money to bribe or pay tribute and temporarily gain reprieve from war, the Venetians used it to entice the Turks into partnering with Venice rather than her commercial rival, Genoa.

Commerce also facilitated Venetian diplomacy in another way: by providing networks that could be utilized for intelligence and alliance-building. The trade routes that Venetian merchants plied throughout the Levant, Anatolia, and the Black Sea generated relationships with various groups who benefited from Venetian trade as much as the Ottomans. These, too, represented mutual dependencies that Venetian diplomats could leverage for organizing anti-Ottoman coalitions and bringing pressure to bear on the sultan. A ruler like Uzun Hasan was motivated to ally with Venice as much by the prospect of supplanting the Ottomans' lucrative position in East-West trade as by mutual hatred of Mehmed II and by the arms provided by Venice.

THE LIMITS OF DIPLOMACY

Whatever its accomplishments, Venetian diplomacy ultimately demonstrated beyond any doubt the limits of what can be achieved in international politics without the backing of adequate military power. The Venetians were, of course, capable of generating significant amounts of force, including the largest fleets in the Mediterranean at the time and, when assisted by mercenaries and allies, substantial land forces. But it was significantly less than what their main enemy could generate (including at sea) and well short of what was needed for protecting both

Venetian holdings on the Italian peninsula and the far-flung possessions of the Stato da Mar.

Venetian diplomats could only do so much to compensate for military weakness using commercial heft. The strength of diplomacy backed by wealth lies in its ability to attract; the strength of diplomacy backed by force lies in its ability to compel. The latter stems not from the promise of gain but from a capacity to generate fear. And one doesn't get the impression that Venice's main rival in Anatolia feared her very much. By the time Bartolomeo Marcello met Mehmed II, his state was in an increasingly asymmetric position vis-à-vis the Ottoman court. Mehmed went along with the diplomatic arrangements that Venice proposed only long enough to get into a position to do away with Venice's commercial middleman role. Venice's western interlocutors, too, felt little motivation to back her when she was in danger; the smaller ones were jealous of her wealth and hoped to see her humbled while the bigger ones would have preferred to consume her outright.

In its dealings with both East and West, Venice was, by the middle decades of the 15th Century, playing with a weak hand. That the republic endured as long as she did was a feat of ingenuity and endurance. The underlying power disparities only grew more lopsided as time passed. Venetian diplomacy did much to manage these yawning gaps between the military means at her disposal and the looming outside threats. But the gap ultimately proved too wide.

⚜

There is something undeniably beguiling about the Republic of Venice—perhaps not as grand as the "habit of heroism" that Ruskin claimed to see as the central thread of her story, but certainly a delicate hardihood that seems at times to transcend, and defy, geopolitical reality. Venice's rise to wealth and power was unlikely; the extent and longevity of the greatness she attained unlikelier still. Like the Byzantines, the Venetians probably should have succumbed to the pressures of geopolitics sooner than they did. Like the Byzantines, the Venetians were drawn to diplomacy because their geography indicated both its necessity and possibility. Like the Byzantines, they excelled in diplomacy not just in a narrow positional or tactical sense but by creating systems of political influence that increased their security without saddling them with the full costs of empire. But to an even greater extent than the Byzantines, who, though encircled, could draw upon the resources of a large hinterland, the Venetians lacked the strategic depth to sustain their position by military means against a large, determined opponent.

In the history of diplomacy, Venice forms a bridge between the Middle Ages and the era of large European nation-states. In their integration of diplomacy with strategy and intelligence, the Venetians show the influences of the Byzantines; in their secular conception of the state and use of permanent resident ambassadors to manage a system of competing rivals, they look ahead to post-Westphalian Europe. In the Italian League's efforts to hold together a territorial balance of power we see a precursor, in parvo, of the Concert of Europe following the Vienna Congress. The diplomatic methods pioneered by the Venetians and their Italian neighbors would ultimately spread to become the template in Europe and across the world, down to the present day. They would find their highest expression not in the cramped confines of Renaissance Italy but in the large, centralizing administrative states—the true great powers—then congealing north of the Alps. And among the princes of Europe, none would embrace the strategic potential of the new diplomacy more determinedly, or wield it more expertly, than the Valois kings of France, where our attention now turns.

CHAPTER FOUR

Black Queen, Red Cardinal

Every Christian Prince ought to lay it down as a principal maxim of his government, not to have recourse to arms for the maintenance of his right, until he has once tried what he can do by force of reason and persuasion.

—FRANÇOIS DE CALLIÈRES

States receive so much benefit from uninterrupted foreign negotiations, if they are conducted with prudence, that it is unbelievable unless known from experience.

—CARDINAL RICHELIEU

SEVEN DECADES AFTER Marcello Bartolomeo's mission to Mehmed II, another European diplomat made his way to the Ottoman court. The envoy's mission was secret and urgent; to avoid detection, he and his entourage traveled overland, snaking their way to Constantinople through the perilous mountain passes of the Balkans.

It was near one such pass in modern-day Bosnia, just a few days shy of their destination, that the traveler and his companions were ambushed by retainers of the local pasha, and their throats were slit. While ransacking the baggage train, the assassins found two remarkable objects. The first was a ruby of unusual size and exquisite color, intended as a gift for the sultan, Suleiman I. The second, equally extraordinary, was a letter from the queen regent of France, Louise of Savoy, inquiring if Suleiman would be willing to rescue her son, King Francis I, from an Italian prison cell, where he sat in ignoble captivity to the Habsburg emperor Charles V.[1]

It wasn't every day that a French monarch whose titles included "Most Christian King" begged the help of the world's most powerful infidel. At the time of his coronation in 1515, Francis I, first of the House of Valois's

Angoulême line, had seemed destined to become a second Charlemagne.[2] Tall, broad-shouldered, and sporting, *le roi chevalier* possessed "so great a majesty," one contemporary wrote, "that the realm of France should ever seem unto him a small matter."[3] Even the young king's vices ("hunting or whoring," as a Venetian diplomat described them) suggested a rude athleticism that boded well for France on the battlefield.

At first, Francis had lived up to the expectations. At Marignano on the banks of the Lambro just after his coronation, he smashed an army of Swiss mercenaries and reclaimed the duchy of Milan from the Habsburgs. The victory stunned Europe; afterwards, Francis had a medal struck comparing himself to Augustus and thrilled the pope by declaring his intention to lead a crusade to the gates of Constantinople.

But it wasn't to be. On the Lombard plain outside the Italian city of Pavia in 1525, Francis's army suffered one of the worst defeats in French military history. By day's end, the flower of the French nobility was dead or captured. In the chaos of battle, Francis was knocked from his horse and taken prisoner. Afterwards, from a cell in nearby Pizzighettone fortress, the king wrote to his mother, "all that is left to me is my honor and my life . . ."[4]

It was in the aftermath of the catastrophe at Pavia that the king's mother had dispatched her ill-fated envoy to the sultan. Diplomacy of this kind was not the traditional strong suit of Valois kings. For generations, French monarchs had made their names mainly through conquest.[5] Diplomacy on the Venetian mold was known vicariously, from Italian exiles, but not much imitated. The kingdom that could boast the first regular army since the Caesars lacked a professional diplomatic corps.[6] Diplomacy for House Valois was about creating pretexts and itineraries for war. Strategy was about bloodlines and spurs.

The defeat at Pavia, however, jolted France into the business of diplomacy on a much more systematic basis. In its wake, Louise of Savoy dispatched emissaries in every direction—to the English, the Italians, even to the Ottomans, all with the same burning task: to free the king and undermine the power of the Habsburgs. Unfazed by the loss of her first envoy to the sultan, Louise sent a second one before year's end, this time headed by a Croat, Jean Frangipani, who carried the queen's letter in the sole of his shoe. While the contents of Louise's message are lost, Suleiman's reply survives. "Being defeated and captured is not an astonishing situation for kings," the sultan wrote. "Keep your heart contented and do not grieve. . . . Our horses are always saddled and our swords are always belted."[7]

Louise's outreach to Suleiman scandalized Christendom. But with time her diplomacy would enable France to recover its king, rebuild its military, and turn the tables on the Habsburg Empire. In the years that followed, the shock of Pavia spurred the French to embrace the kind of professional diplomacy pioneered by the Venetians in the previous century. While the queen regent's moves may have been acts of improvisation, they suggested a blueprint for a continent-wide grand strategy rooted in the use of alliances and state interests that would culminate, a century later, in France's rise to European preeminence and the creation of the modern states system under one of diplomacy's greatest practitioners, Armand-Jean du Plessis, Cardinal de Richelieu.

The Habsburg Vise

The situation confronting Francis I from his prison cell in Madrid's Alcázar fortress in the months after Pavia was grim. The striking power of his army had been shattered. France lacked allies. The kingdom was bankrupt, its granaries depleted by a series of bad harvests. To pay for Francis's wars, French nobles had been reduced to melting down gold plate.[8] The king's most powerful domestic enemy, the renegade Duke Charles III de Bourbon, was in open rebellion and had taken the field against him at Pavia. It seemed to many onlookers that France's star was fading, and that the battle was the harbinger of the realm's coming collapse—"the beginning," as the Italian writer Guicciardini wrote, "of worse ruin."[9]

In every direction, France faced danger. To the northwest, England's Tudor king Henry VIII plotted to retake the French territories that England had lost in the Hundred Years' War. To the north, east, and south, France was hemmed in by the empire of the Habsburg dynast Emperor Charles V, whose family's territories encompassed most of Central Europe, much of Italy, and the Iberian peninsula.

France had never encountered a threat like Charles V. Five years younger than Francis, he was colder than the French king in temperament, but his plodding nature masked an iron determination to expand his inheritance by all means necessary.[10] In one person, at least on paper, the slack-jawed emperor commanded the major bulk of the European continent. In 1516 he had ascended to the throne of Spain; three years later, he was elected emperor of the Holy Roman Empire.[11] Charles's aunt, Margaret of Austria, ruled as his proxy in the Netherlands; his brother Ferdinand ruled in Austria.

The threat that the Habsburg conglomerate posed to Francis I's kingdom is plainly visible on a map; as Cardinal Wolsey wrote, France was "envyronned on three parts, and scituated, as it wer, in the mydde of

FIGURE 4.1. France in the time of Francis I (Credit: Andrew Rhodes)

th'emperors countries."[12] Charles claimed many of the same territories as Francis, including the Duchy of Milan, which had been an imperial fief since the 14th Century, and the Duchy of Burgundy, which Charles claimed through his paternal great-grandfather and namesake, Charles the Bold.* To these European holdings, from the 1520s, would be added substantial Habsburg possessions in the New World, which would come to provide a steady stream of gold and silver to bankroll the dynasty's European wars.[13]

In retrospect, it is clear that Charles V's diverse holdings presented gigantic difficulties of imperial management. But to many observers at the time, the Habsburg juggernaut seemed well on its way to achieving European hegemony. "A generation earlier," as Geoffrey Parker writes, "five major powers—England, France, Spain, Burgundy and the Empire— had competed for the upper hand: now the same ruler controlled the last three."[14] Of the rulers of the remaining two powers, one controlled half an island and the other was sitting in a Habsburg prison. With the odds stacked so heavily in the Habsburgs' favor, the moment seemed ripe, after Pavia, for carving up Francis's territories. "Now is the time for the Emperor

---

*The Duchy of Burgundy—in this book, referred to simply as "Burgundy"—was annexed by France in 1477; it is not to be confused with the County of Burgundy, or "Franche Comté," bordering it to the east, which was ruled from the Habsburg Netherlands.

and myself to devise means of getting full satisfaction from France," as Henry VIII wrote. "Not an hour is to be lost."[15]

A Natural Great Power

Against this menagerie of dangers, Francis's realm enjoyed some important geographic advantages. Compared to Charles's patchwork empire, France was already by this point in history a large, contiguous country bounded by obstacles on almost every side.[16] To the French kingdom's west and northwest lay the Atlantic and English Channel, to the south loomed the Pyrenees, to the southeast the Mediterranean; and to the east, the Alps. Only in the northeast did it lack for natural defenses.

France's big, arable heartland could support a large population. By 1500 the French king ruled over a country whose population of fifteen million was double that of Spain and quadruple that of England.[17] In Francis I's time, France was experiencing a boom of sorts as it bounced back from the Hundred Years' War. Demographic growth drove an expansion in towns, industry, and credit. In the north, French textiles competed with Flemish cloths; in the south, the acquisition in 1481 of Provence allowed French merchants to vie with Venice for markets in the Levant.[18] Revenue from trade filled the royal coffers, as did the largess of large fiefs that fell, one by one, to the monarchy. As Machiavelli observed at the time, "The Crown and the King of France are at this time more flourishing, rich, and powerful than they have ever been."[19]

French geography encouraged political centralization. As the early 20th-Century British geographer James Fairgrieve noted, there is an unusual concentration of deep, navigable rivers in France's northern basin: the Seine, Oise, Marne, Yonne, and Loire all converge on the area around Paris, while the Rhône-Saône valley connects the whole to the southern half of the country.[20] These rivers facilitated the development of a strong political center in much the same way that the Tiber had done for the Romans, but on a grander scale and without the presence of extensive interior mountain ranges to impede the consolidation of royal authority.

In Francis's time, that process was far from complete; indeed, France was in many ways still a medieval realm. Monarchic authority was constrained by the particular privileges of towns and provinces, by the persistence of large ducal fiefs and foreign enclaves, and by the absence of a shared language and code of law.[21] But already by Francis's reign, those restraints were weakening. A major driver was warfare. Armies were becoming larger and more professional, courtesy of new military technologies that necessitated specialized training.[22] The need to build and maintain larger armies spurred kings to assert greater central control over the resources of their realms, which meant reining in the feudal lords with whom they had long shared power.

France had a head start in that process. While absolutism still lay in the future, it could already be said in Francis I's time that the king shared little power with any other person or entity.[23] The Estates-General, a representative body dating from the Middle Ages, lacked the power of the purse enjoyed by the English Parliament or Spanish *cortes*; under the so-called *taille*, a French king could extract taxes directly to finance war and maintain a standing army.[24] The Parlement of Paris, a judicature combining the roles of high court and upper chamber, derived its powers from the king, as did the seven smaller provincial parlements.[25]

The growing concentration of authority in the person of the king shaped the way that the French thought about political power. In place of the old feudal notion of monarchs as "first among equals," the king in France was evolving into a sovereignty-in-being, accountable only to God.[26] The ascending mentality is exemplified in the writings of French jurists like Charles de Grassaille, who described the French king as infused with the qualities of a deity. In a similar vein, Claude de Seyssel, a former advisor to Louis XII, wrote a treatise early in Francis's reign that promoted the idea of a system of government centered on a strong and wise king.[27] And Guillaume Budé argued a few years later in *De l'institution du prince* that French kings were bound neither by duty to the populace nor by obligations to the nobility, but only to the dictates of divine and natural law.

These writers departed from the Medieval view that monarchs should apply their power to the promotion of Christian virtue. Instead, French humanists saw the king's chief duty as being the protection of his earthly realm.[28] They were following in the footsteps of the Italians, whose strivings in the previous century had prompted a more secular conception of the state and its interests. Except in France, the king's authority would eventually become near-total. Francis anticipated this evolution when he told a delegation from the Paris Parlement, "There will be only one King in France. . . . I will take good care that there is no Senate in France as there is in Venice."[29]

The Mother of Invention

Francis wouldn't have felt very omnipotent as he sat in his prison cell in the aftermath of Pavia. The thankless task of cleaning up after his Italian *mésaventure* fell to his mother, the queen regent, Louise of Savoy.[30] That was a tall order. In exchange for Francis's release, Charles V demanded that France cede a chunk of her best territories; grant Francis's French rival, the Duc de Bourbon, a kind of state-in-miniature inside France; and give England's Henry VIII the territories he demanded in the north.[31] With French forces in disarray, Louise didn't appear to hold a strong hand; her task was to secure her son's release without giving away the store—or as one contemporary observer put it, "mak[ing] best use of what was left."[32]

Fortunately for France, Louise was a leader of unusual intelligence and perspicacity. Widely considered the most beautiful woman in France, she was also pious, known for her mystical visions and for dressing in the black habit of a nun when she went into public.[33] She was well-acquainted with the realities of power through years of efforts to protect her son in the court of Louis XII. Guicciardini wrote that she was "ambitious and very tenacious of government," while a Venetian diplomat observed, "she is very adroit, and once she has taken something into her head she will have it by any means whether with tears or laughter."[34] In the words of one modern biographer, Louise "was realist, skeptical, hardheaded"—"stronger than Henry, with his increasing addiction to [vanity, sex and sport], or than Charles with his egotism and narrow asceticism."[35] As events would show, she was probably also superior to her son as a grand strategist, diplomat, and administrator.

In April 1525, Louise dispatched François de Tournon, the archbishop of Embrun, as an emissary to Charles V. In her written instructions, she told Tournon to "achieve peace and friendship with the emperor . . . and the freedom and deliverance of the king."[36] Her tactical approach was straightforward: appeal to the emperor's sense of duty (and pride) as a ruler aspiring to represent all of Christendom while taking a pragmatic stance on the particulars. Politely brushing aside Charles's initial demands as excessive ("big and high"), Louise expressed a willingness to quickly come to terms as long as it did not involve "giving away French territory."

Louise's opening move hints at what would become a French redline in subsequent dealings with the Habsburgs. Charles V clearly had a lot of leverage, but Louise knew that giving him the thing he wanted most, even if it resulted in the king's release, would only make France worse-off in the next phase of the struggle. That thing was Burgundy. Charles coveted that territory as an heirloom from his great-grandfather's dream of building a great Burgundian state. But for France, Burgundy's importance wasn't just symbolic or dynastic, it was consequentially strategic. Burgundy reached deep into the French heartland and sat adjacent to the one frontier least defined by natural obstacles. Losing it would be giving the German emperor a bridgehead inside France.[37] Come what may, Louise was determined that her son would return home to a kingdom intact. She told her diplomats to be flexible on everything else—Italy, Flanders, cash payments. But not Burgundy.

In parallel with Tournon's mission, Louise sent a royal commission into Burgundy to quietly strengthen its defenses. She took up a conciliatory stance toward its residents to tamp down any grievances and forestall the emergence of fifth columns.[38] And shrewdly, she sent emissaries to Charles V's aunt, Margaret, governor of the Habsburg Netherlands, to renew an earlier agreement prohibiting the transit of military forces through nearby territories in the event of war. These moves make it clear that Louise had no intention of giving up Burgundy, irrespective of what she would have to promise the emperor to get her son out of jail.

Louise was right to take precautions. Charles was very determined to get Burgundy; at one point during the negotiations he even added the stipulation that Francis build four convents to pray around the clock for the soul of one of his ancestors, Duke John of Burgundy, who had been killed by the French.[39] In the end, Francis relented and agreed to give up the coveted territory, on the condition that he be permitted to return home and convince his subjects to support the transfer.[40] Under the Treaty of Madrid, signed in January 1526, Burgundy was relinquished, along with Flanders and Artois; Francis dropped his claims in Italy; and, in a final humiliation, he agreed to deliver his two sons into Habsburg custody as collateral.

All of this must have seemed like a triumph to Charles V as he left, after signing the treaty, for his honeymoon with the Infanta Isabella of Portugal in the Alhambra, where the future Philip II would shortly be conceived.[41] But his satisfaction was premature. Hours earlier, Francis had signed a secret document, prepared by Tournon, stating that the whole thing was a charade and not worth the paper on which it was printed.[42] Louise agreed; on the day Francis returned from captivity, one scholar writes, "he rode straight to Louise, who greeted him with the maternal advice not to observe promises made under duress."[43]

Lighting Fires

If the machinations leading up to the Treaty of Madrid had been the entirety of Louise's diplomacy, she would be little more than an interesting footnote in French history. But negotiations with Charles V were only one small part of her diplomatic strategy. In the months after Pavia, she

FIGURE 4.2. Unsung strategist: Louise of Savoy, Queen Regent of France
(Credit: Penta Springs Limited / Alamy)

also sent envoys and agents further afield, with instructions to salve differences with other powers big and small, and to look for alliances where they could be found. Her immediate motivation was to increase France's leverage vis-à-vis Charles by creating problems in his rear areas. But in looking for that leverage, she was also strengthening France's overall position for the coming phase of competition with the Habsburgs.

The factor that worked most in Louise's favor was fear. In the aftermath of Pavia, Habsburg power was greater than ever, and that worried the empire's other neighbors. If the emperor could defeat and capture the French king, who could he not defeat? Even France's traditional enemies— including the fickle Henry VIII—stood to lose if her power were permanently abased on the scale that Charles envisioned. In that fear lay an opportunity for Louise to stoke opposition to the Habsburgs, rooted not in sympathy for Francis's plight but in their own self-preservation.

The idea of building alliances in this fashion wasn't new. French kings had long sought to stir up opposition to Habsburg and English rulers. Since the Middle Ages, France's Capetian kings had abetted the Scots in an effort to draw the attention of their Plantagenet rivals northward in times of war. Francis's predecessors had sent envoys to the Poles, Hungarians, and Turks. And a few years after his coronation, Francis had courted the friendship of Henry VIII, in their extravagantly expensive but fruitless meeting at the Field of the Cloth of Gold. What changed in Louise's regency was both the urgency of alliances, as a way of coping with the exigencies created by Francis's captivity without a viable military option for securing the kingdom, and the scale and sophistication of the designs she pursued.

The hinge of Louise's strategy was England. As long as the island kingdom was aligned with Charles, France would face a threat of two-front war; dislodge that alliance, and France would be able to concentrate resources on the Habsburg threat. Louise's efforts to entice Henry VIII to switch sides had begun before Pavia, when she sent two envoys, Gian Giacomo Passano and Jean Brinon, to reconnoiter the English court. Baiting the hook wasn't easy; as she had done with Charles, Louise refused to cede any French territory to Henry. In her written instructions, she suggested a different lubricant: cash.[44] Brinon bought off the English at the princely sum of two million écus, to be paid out over a twenty-year period.[45] In the Treaty of the More, signed in August 1525, Henry ceased his raids on the French coast and promised to pressure Charles to release Francis. In one stroke, Louise had alleviated France's two-front problem.

The queen regent also proved adept at causing headaches for the Habsburgs on the continent. She sent agents to the German princes siding with Martin Luther in his escalating dispute with the emperor. She was especially active in Italy, where fear of Habsburg hegemony ran high after Pavia. While Louise's envoys were at work in London, she sent a representative, Luc de Champaigne, to Venice and Rome to propose a defensive coalition for ejecting the Habsburgs from the peninsula. In doing so, she adroitly repositioned France's role from that of a potential conqueror to the protector of the liberties of Italy's small states against Habsburg domination.

She promised the Italians money, to the tune of forty thousand écus per month.[46] And she hinted at eventual French military support, but wouldn't commit much for fear of derailing the talks to free Francis.

It was against this backdrop of high-tempo diplomacy that Louise dispatched her boldest diplomatic initiative, to the court of Suleiman the Magnificent. It's likely that Louise had been giving thought to this option for a while; years earlier, she sent a friar named Jean Thenaud on a scouting expedition with a French trade delegation to the Levant.[47] In courting the Turks, Louise must have known that she risked exciting the ire of Christendom. Yet the idea found support in emergent French political thought. In his 1515 treatise, Seyssel invoked Scripture to justify alliances with heretics: "Any good prince is allowed . . . to stir up and maintain dissensions among those whose agreement he knows would wrongfully harm him and his subjects."[48]

Louise was aware of the effect that Turkish predations had in diverting Habsburg resources and wasn't shy about reminding Charles V of his vulnerability; as one of her envoys reported from Madrid, he had warned the emperor that "peace is necessary in this time more than ever, because he sees before his eyes that the countries of Hungary and Poland are being invaded and molested by the infidels."[49] And while we don't know the exact instructions Louise gave to either Frangipani or his unlucky predecessor, both of which operated under strict scrutiny, it is likely that at a minimum they were told to assess the Ottomans' receptivity to an alliance against Charles.

The King's Rebound

As Francis returned to France from Habsburg captivity in March 1526, the prospects facing his kingdom were, thanks to Louise's diplomacy, less dire than they had been in the immediate aftermath of the Battle of Pavia. In the space of a year, Louise's maneuvers had altered the strategic equation to France's advantage, splintering the Anglo-Imperial alliance, fanning flames of opposition to Habsburg rule in Italy, and opening the door to a Franco-Ottoman alliance that created the potential for coordination between the powers on Charles's flanks.

To have a strategic framework was one thing. But to get out from under the commitments he had made in the Treaty of Madrid, Francis needed to seize the moral high ground. This was no small task, given that breaking a treaty would call into question Francis's honor as a prince and reliability as a partner to allies. His solution was an early example of what we would call public diplomacy. He published a "royal apologia" justifying noncompliance with the treaty on the grounds that under natural law, a ruler could not give away any part of his demesne without obtaining the permission of his people.[50]

Francis's resolve to hold onto Burgundy advertised his determination to continue the contest with Charles. In this endeavor, the position of England remained key. Any sudden renewal of the Anglo-Imperial friendship would force France back into a defensive posture and make retaining Burgundy, much less resuming the bid for Italy, difficult. Francis therefore continued Louise's English diplomacy. He lavished attention on Henry VIII and expanded on her earlier treaty to form a formal military alliance, signed at Westminster in spring 1527.[51]

In Italy, too, Francis continued Louise's policy. Within weeks of returning to France he was in talks with Venetian envoys about forming a pan-Italian alliance, which eventually bore fruit in the form of the League of Cognac, a defensive pact between France, Venice, Florence, Milan, Rome, and, later, England. Francis maintained his mother's practice of disavowing French territorial ambitions there; his aim, as Guicciardini put it, was "not to recover the state of Milan for himself, or otherwise to increase his power," but to "obtain . . . [for] Italy her liberty."[52]

Francis was especially active in Germany, where he sought to drive wedges between the Habsburg emperor and his German vassals. Francis's opportunity came in early 1531, when Charles V's brother, the Archduke Ferdinand, became king of the Romans—the elective title by which an emperor's heir was named prior to his coronation by the pope.[53] The move excited German fears of Habsburg domination and aroused Protestant insecurities by tilting the balance in imperial politics in favor of the Catholics. The resulting turmoil presented an opening for French intrigue inside Charles's empire. Taking a page from the Italian playbook, Francis dispatched an envoy, Gervais Wain, to mediate an alliance between the Catholic Bavarian dukes and the Protestant princes of the Schmalkaldic League aimed at protecting German "liberties."[54]

Francis also intensified Louise's diplomacy in the East. In the spring of 1527 he dispatched Antonio Rincón on a series of missions to the far side of the Habsburg Empire. Rincón's first visit was to the Voivode of Transylvania, followed by a trip to King Sigismund of Poland, and then to Constantinople.[55] In 1528 Suleiman granted a *hatti-sherif* opening the Egyptian market to French merchants. Francis followed up this success a few years later by sending a delegation led by Jean de la Forêt, who brokered an agreement known as the *Capitulations* giving France what would today be called most-favored-nation trade status, legal and religious protections for its citizens, and the right to maintain a resident ambassador in Istanbul.[56] In all likelihood, the agreement was accompanied by a secret military annex of some kind outlining plans for a coordinated attack on Italy.

The breadth and audacity of this Franco-Ottoman alliance shocked Europe. The "blasphemous union of the lily and the crescent," as it came to be known, was widely denounced as an act of feckless opportunism that endangered Christianity itself put the destiny of Francis's soul in doubt.[57] The Italian satirist Pietro Aretino summed up the mood when he wrote to Francis: "You have thrust the sword of the Ottoman into the heart of Christendom!"[58]

The Ladies' Peace

Whatever effect they had on Francis's conscience, the alliances with Ottomans and Lutherans drained and distracted the Habsburgs. Louise's diplomacy enabled her son, within a few years of returning from captivity, to turn the tables on the Habsburgs and undo the damage from the disaster at Pavia. When his contest with Charles resumed, the emperor found himself confronted with much less favorable odds than before: England, unavailable and aligned with France; most of Italy unified against him; the Ottomans more alive to his western predicament and on the march in the east.

The sea change was palpable, and personal. When Charles received a pro-French demarche from the ambassadors of the League of Cognac, he flew into a rage and challenged Francis to a duel.[59] With much of Europe effectively aligned behind France and Suleiman's army invading Hungary, Charles now faced the prospect of a two-front war, as Francis had two years before. These pressures forced Charles onto the defensive and diverted him from his preferred priority of dealing with the Lutherans, whose help he now needed against the Turks. All of this diminished the imperial aura that had surrounded Charles, forcing him to delay plans for a triumphant coronation in Rome.[60]

In the ensuing war of the League of Cognac, Charles was able to fend off Francis's moves in Italy, but at the expense of much of what he thought he gained after Pavia. When peace came, it was through the efforts of Louise of Savoy and Charles's aunt, Margaret. Under the 1529 Treaty of Cambrai, or the "Ladies' Peace" as it came to be called, Charles gave up his claim to Burgundy and agreed to release Francis's sons in exchange for a large ransom, while Francis foreswore Milan, Flanders, and Artois.[61] The treaty put a punctuation mark on Francis's quest to take Milan. But it freed him from the worst provisions of the Treaty of Madrid and removed the threat to Burgundy.

The Ladies' Peace lasted six years, making it the longest truce brokered by treaty in the Habsburg-Valois contest.[62] But it proved only a respite in Francis's feud with Charles, which would persist for the better part of the next two decades. Within a few years Francis was back at war, his advantages gone and his enemies combining against him. Eventually the French homeland was invaded and the king's fortunes were saved only by the military incompetence of his opponents.

By the end of his reign, Francis had frittered away on the battlefield most of what his mother had achieved at the negotiating table. Shortly before he died on the last day of March in 1547, probably from syphilis, he is rumored to have been troubled by dark visions and to have repented of the blasphemy of his alliance with the Turks.[63] His main foreign-policy accomplishment was the retention of Burgundy. But mainly, he is known today for the splendid châteaux that were commissioned during his reign in the Loire Valley, whose mantles and barrel-vaulted ceilings bear his symbol, a fire-breathing salamander.

Evaluating Louise and Francis

The significance of Francis's reign in the history of diplomacy lies less in what he accomplished than in the potentialities that his mother's methods suggested for using systematic diplomacy to gain advantage in competitive politics. The shattering of French offensive power at Pavia forced France to more seriously contemplate means other than force for its security.[64] Before Pavia, the illusion still existed of Francis as a great warlord who might fulfill his dream of conquest in Italy. After Pavia, France was forced to accelerate the development of diplomacy as a tool of strategy in order to escape the noose of Habsburg encirclement, as embodied by the provisions of the Treaty of Madrid.

The period after the Ladies' Peace saw the adoption in earnest of Italian methods of diplomacy in France. Many of the representatives sent abroad after Pavia stayed on to become France's first permanent ambassadors in those countries. On the day of Francis's coronation, France had two resident ambassadors abroad; on the day he died, there were ten. After the Ladies' Peace, the king designated one of his councils for the formulation of foreign policy and increased from two to four the number of regionally divided *secrétaires d'état* responsible for relations with bordering states.[65] It is in this period too that we begin to see a larger cadre of seasoned negotiators emerge in the service of the French king, supported by a scattering of clerks and notetakers.

It is also during Francis's reign that we see the contours start to emerge of a conceptual framework for a French grand strategy centered on diplomacy. Louise's initiatives may have been pursued extemporaneously, but they suggested an overarching logic: To free itself from multifront danger, France had to foist the problem back onto the Habsburgs. That meant lighting fires on the flanks and rear of Habsburg power, in order to draw the emperor's energies away from France. That, in turn, required a willingness to work with infidels and heretics against a fellow Catholic monarch.

Finally, it is in Francis's reign that we see the stirrings of a French school of diplomacy geared to the conscious cultivation of a European states system. Garrett Mattingly is undoubtedly right when he writes of the transition from dynastic principle to national interests that "nobody noticed at the time."[66] But in retrospect, we can see that Francis's frenzied jockeying with Henry and Charles anticipated the development of a European order grounded in the balance of power.

⟨⸙⸙⸙⸙Ⓦ⸙⸙⸙⸙⟩

Within a generation of Francis I's death, France was plunged into the Wars of Religion, a prolonged nightmare in which upwards of an eighth of the population died at the hands of their countrymen. Civil strife sapped the country's strength and pulled its attention inward.[67] It is in the closing phases of this national trauma that the curtain rises again, in dramatic fashion, on French diplomacy. In August 1624, almost exactly a century after Francis's defeat at Pavia, Louis XIII appointed as his principal minister Armand-Jean du Plessis, Cardinal (and from 1629, Duc de) Richelieu.[68]

The moment is a seminal one in the history of diplomacy, analogous, by some accounts, to the appearance of light in the Book of Genesis. Hilaire Belloc described Richelieu as the creator of modern Europe. Henry Kissinger began his account of Western diplomacy with Richelieu and proclaimed him the "father of the modern state system." One recent biographer has compared his impact on the world of statecraft to Galileo's impact on the world of science.[69]

At the time he became Louis XIII's chief minister, Richelieu was not yet forty and had served the Bourbon court intermittently for almost a decade. He had been catapulted to prominence as a young bishop from Luçon after his sermons caught the attention of Marie de' Medici, France's queen regent since the assassination of her husband and Louis's father, Henry IV, in 1610.[70] Initially an advisor to de' Medici, Richelieu narrowly avoided imprisonment when Louis came of age and asserted his kingship. In a preview of his diplomatic virtuosity, Richelieu mediated a reconciliation between mother and son before ingratiating himself with the new king, forming a co-dependent bond with Louis that would make Richelieu France's most powerful man until his death in 1642.

The struggle between Marie and Louis illustrates how unstable France had become since Francis I's reign. As Richelieu later wrote, "The royal dignity was so far removed from what it should have been . . . that it was almost impossible to recognize it."[71] France was a divided country, split between a Catholic majority and a Protestant minority known as Huguenots, who controlled a large swath of the kingdom.[72] France's influence was at a nadir, while foreign courts held sway in its internal affairs. Much as it had been after Pavia, France after the Wars of Religion was at a low ebb.

The "Murderous Encirclement"

When Richelieu joined the Council of State in April 1624, the international situation resembled, in broad form, the scene that had confronted Francis I a century earlier. The encircling Habsburg Empire remained France's main opponent. But some important things had changed. Shortly before his death, Charles V had divided his empire between his son and brother, thus bifurcating the Habsburg conglomerate into Spanish and Austrian lines. The two branches were usually aligned, but not always. The attention of the Austrian Habsburgs was pulled more and more toward Central Europe and the Danube Basin, while the Spanish Habsburgs were drawn west, toward the Atlantic.

Of the two, Spain was the greater threat. The influence of the Spanish Court had penetrated deeply into French internal affairs during the religious wars, during which Spain had deployed troops on French soil and attempted to overthrow Louis XIII's father, Henry IV. By the end of the 16th Century, Charles V's heirs seemed well on their way to realizing the Habsburg dream of universal empire; as the Calabrian refugee Tommaso Campanella wrote in 1600, "The King of Spain might grow more Powerful yet, and might attain to the Dominion of the Whole World."[73] Even if it couldn't achieve that lofty goal, there was a very real danger that Spain would come to exert a controlling influence over the Austrian branch—and with it, the affairs of Germany.[74]

Another change was the intensification of religious conflict as a leitmotif of European politics. In Francis I's time, the sting of Luther's challenge to the Roman Church was still fresh, and the full geopolitical ramifications of the Protestant-Catholic schism remained unclear. By Richelieu's time, the tension had boiled over into open conflict; in 1618, Protestant nobles rose in revolt to prevent the arch-Catholic Ferdinand II's election to the throne of Bohemia. What started as a localized crisis had quickly morphed into a wider Central European struggle.[75] By the time Richelieu took the helm in France, the fighting had drawn in Austria, Spain, and most of Germany.

It would have been natural for France to ally with the Habsburgs in this conflict. The Bourbons were a Catholic dynasty, linked to the Habsburgs by marriage. While Richelieu's predecessor had already begun to break from de' Medici's pro-Spanish line, the momentum at court remained with the so-called *dévots*, who favored an alliance with their Catholic co-religionists.

If France had stuck to the Catholic camp, there wouldn't have been much need for the diplomacy for which Richelieu would become famous. All that France would have had to do was toss an army or two across the Rhine to help the Habsburg forces campaigning there. That would have aligned France with what seemed likely to be the winning side in the conflict, at a moment when the Habsburgs were scoring victory after victory.

Those very Habsburg victories, however, posed a danger for France. Much as a Habsburg triumph might advance the confessional cause of the Church of Rome, it would leave the Catholic French monarchy more susceptible to Habsburg co-optation once the dust had settled. Avoiding such an outcome was Richelieu's chief foreign policy goal—or, as he described it, "to save the world from the tyranny of Spain and to free his country from her murderous encirclement."[76]

La Guerre Couverte

France was in no position to challenge Spain at the start of Richelieu's tenure. What military resources France could deploy at that moment were needed internally against the Huguenots and, in any event, would have been inadequate to the task of fighting the combined might of Spain and Austria.

Rather than confront Spain directly, Richelieu's strategy was to use alliances to sap its strength while husbanding France's energies for the eventual confrontation. Richelieu called this *la guerre couverte,*—"masked war," as Burckhardt translates it. "France's only thought," Richelieu wrote to the king, "must be to strengthen herself and to open doors so that she may enter the states of all her neighbors to protect them from Spain's oppression when the opportunities to do so arise . . ."[77] Such a strategy required France to remain officially at peace with Spain for the time being.

That was easier said than done, given the number of friction points between the two powers. One involved a running dispute over a valley in present-day Italy known as the Valtelline, which formed part of the critical corridor—the so-called Spanish Road—connecting Habsburg possessions in Italy and Flanders.[78] In 1620 Spain had seized and fortified the valley. When Spanish promises to demilitarize it went unfulfilled, Richelieu sent in French forces.[79] The 1626 Treaty of Monçon, which committed Spain to raze its forts and restore equal access to the valley, didn't go as far as France's allies had hoped. But it achieved Richelieu's goal of preventing Habsburg acquisition of a strategic artery without risking major war before France was ready.

Richelieu's strategy was threatened again the following year, when Vincent II, duke of Mantua and Montferrat, died without issue, and a French noble, Charles de Gonzague-Nevers, stood to inherit his duchy. Mantua was a fief of the Holy Roman Emperor and occupied a strategic location astride the route from Austria to the Spanish Road; Gonzague-Nevers's succession would, de facto, place the territory within the French sphere of influence. The situation exploded when Gonzague-Nevers took possession without the emperor Ferdinand II's blessing, triggering a Spanish military intervention. Seeing an opportunity to weaken Habsburg influence in Italy, Richelieu approved a French military response. The ensuing campaign cost the Habsburgs much more than it did the French, drawing Spanish troops away from Flanders, diverting Austrian troops from Germany, and exposing daylight between the strategic objectives of the dynasty's two branches.[80] Under the 1631 Treaty of Cherasco, Gonzague-Nevers was confirmed as Vincent's heir, and Richelieu gained control of important fortresses in the Piedmont—an unambiguous French victory.

What's notable about both crises is how Richelieu responded to the situations at hand without losing sight of his overarching strategy. He used military force, but kept it limited, and used diplomacy to consolidate positive outcomes on the battlefield. His strategy didn't only require avoiding a wider war; it also required avoiding a disadvantageous peace. During this period, Richelieu resisted Habsburg attempts to broker a general peace that would have limited his ability to wage proxy war. He kept France out of open conflict with Spain, but kept France's hands free to build alliances against the Habsburgs in Italy and Germany.

Capuchin Diplomacy

Richelieu scrupulously avoided Francis I's mistake of being sucked too deeply into Italian affairs. For Richelieu, the main theater of competition was Germany. If the Habsburgs could consolidate their power there, they would command a large and centralized power base from which to isolate France. But if the Habsburgs could be stopped in Germany, they would remain, from France's perspective, a largely peripheral empire confined to Spain and Austria.[81]

The principles guiding Richelieu's German diplomacy were spelled out early on, in a 1616 memorandum that he helped compose to Henri de Schomberg, the French envoy in Germany. Schomberg was to recruit allies by stressing the natural alignment of interests between Germany's small states and France—a power that pursued "no designs, but the good of the Empire" and sought only to defeat attempts by "the King of Spain, to set the crowns of Hungary, Bohemia, the King of the Romans, and the Empire, upon the Head of a Child of Spain."[82]

After becoming principal minister, Richelieu pursued a fairly consistent policy aimed at keeping Germany's Protestants in the fight against the Habsburgs and driving a wedge between Germany's Catholic Electors and the Habsburgs.[83] Foremost among the latter was Maximilian I of Bavaria, leader of a powerful coalition called the Catholic League, whose members were nominally aligned with the emperor but feared the growth of Habsburg power. One of Richelieu's first acts after becoming minister was to send an envoy to sound out Maximilian for an alliance. This was followed by a long effort to woo the Bavarian Elector and his Catholic confederates away from the Imperial cause, which eventually bore fruit in a secret treaty, signed in May 1631 at Fontainebleau, committing France and Bavaria to an eight-year defensive alliance.

Much of Richelieu's German diplomacy was conducted by a mysterious network of individuals, many of them fellow churchmen, who comprised Richelieu's inner circle, led by the famous Father Joseph, a Capuchin friar often called the "Gray Eminence," who had been Richelieu's confidant since early in his career.[84] Under Father Joseph's direction, Richelieu's friars and agents traversed Germany, gathering information, distributing money, sewing dissension, and formulating treaties in the courts of states large and small—sometimes, apparently, without the knowledge of France's formal ambassadors and bureaucrats.

While Father Joseph's network was active in Germany, Richelieu looked for ways to sustain resistance to the Habsburgs from other corners. A natural focal point was the Low Countries, where since the reign of Philip II the newly established Dutch Republic had been in revolt against the Spanish Crown. The Dutch wars absorbed Spanish resources that otherwise would have been deployed in Germany. Under the Treaty of Compiègne, signed in June 1624, France committed to subsidizing the Dutch in exchange for trading privileges and help building up the French navy.[85]

Another focal point was Denmark, whose Protestant king, Christian IV, was threatened by the proximity of Habsburg forces to the Baltic coast. It will be remembered that Francis I had sent France's first resident ambassador to Denmark and Sweden, in a bid to erect a northern counterpoise to Charles V. That diplomatic presence now paid off; the French ambassador, Courmenin Deshayes, used liberal promises of French financial aid to stiffen Christian's resolve and bring Denmark into the war.[86] While Christian's forces later suffered catastrophic defeat, the Danish intervention fulfilled its purposes in French strategy, of buying time for Richelieu to focus on the Huguenots and activate opposition to the Habsburgs in other parts of Europe.[87]

None of Richelieu's gambits, however, would prove as decisive as his cultivation of the king of Sweden, Gustavus Adolphus.[88] In early 1629 Richelieu sent the Baron de Charnacé, a relative by marriage, to entice Gustavus into entering the war in Germany against the Habsburgs.[89] To do that, Charnacé first had to broker an end to the fighting between Gustavus and the Swedish king's cousin, Sigismund III Vasa, king of the Polish-Lithuanian Commonwealth. These efforts succeeded in the fall of 1629 with the French-brokered peace of Altmark.[90]

Richelieu's envoy now set about negotiating a Franco-Swedish alliance. After protracted haggling over price, these labors culminated in the Treaty of Bärwalde, signed on January 23, 1631. The treaty committed France to an annual subsidy of one million livres, in exchange for which Sweden pledged to "bring to and maintain in Germany 30,000 foot and 6,000 heavy-armed cavalry" for a period of three years and to "observe friendship and neutrality" toward France's Catholic allies, Bavaria and the Catholic League.[91]

Sweden's entry into the war quickly turned the tide in the Protestants' favor, delivering a string of victories that shattered the myth of Habsburg invincibility. For a time, it looked as though Gustavus—the "Goth," as Richelieu called him—might conquer all of Germany and make himself emperor. It was undoubtedly with relief that Richelieu learned of the Swedish king's death in battle at Lützen in November 1632. With Protestant prospects flagging and France still unready for war, Richelieu once again used diplomacy to plug the gap; at Heilbronn the following spring, at France's instigation, Sweden and the German Protestants forged a new coalition to continue the war.

Richelieu's Diplomatic Revolution

The length and complexity of European conflicts during Richelieu's tenure underscores a salient feature of 17th-Century military power: it wasn't very decisive. Once set in motion, wars produced unpredictable consequences, lasting longer than expected and unleashing hordes of marauding soldiers that roamed the countryside like hungry insects.[92] As Richelieu observed, "The . . . astonishing thing about this war is the size of the armies and the huge sums that have been spent to wage it."[93]

The historian Michael Roberts famously argued that these changes in warfare prompted the development of the modern state, as larger standing armies required larger central administrative complexes to fund and wield. One aspect of this change was what Roberts calls a "revolution in strategy," as "simultaneous operations on two or more fronts" became the norm.[94] The development of improved diplomacy was a natural outworking of that revolution. As wars increased in cost, duration, and territorial scope, diplomacy grew more valuable as an instrument for placing limits on all three. As states kept ever-larger and more expensive standing armies, they needed specially trained diplomats, controlled from the center, to set limits to the length and ferocity of war, and thereby reduce the burdens and risks bearing down on the state.

Richelieu played a critical role in this diplomatic revolution. He rose to prominence in an era when European monarchs had begun to employ principal ministers to manage the increasingly complex business of their realms.[95] These powerful figures were second in power only to the king and wielded near-total authority over both foreign and domestic affairs.

The need to manage such a large portfolio drove innovations to French diplomatic bureaucracy. At the start of Richelieu's tenure, French decision-making structures weren't very different from what they had been in Francis I's time.[96] A small circle of retainers met in the format of the state council, or *conseil d'en haut,* to advise the king on matters of war and peace. To administer policy, there were four secretaries of state, each of whom oversaw a cluster of provinces within France in addition to a group of countries abutting those provinces.[97]

Like other leaders across the ages, Richelieu's instinct was to bypass formal channels and conduct diplomacy through reliable confidants, like Father Joseph. But there were limits to what he could achieve by such methods. To handle the scale of state business, France needed a more efficient bureaucracy.[98] To streamline decision-making, Richelieu shrunk the state council and delegated less important business to specialized sub-councils. He designated a single official with responsibility for the administration, if not yet formulation, of all foreign policy, thus laying the foundation for what would become the ministry of foreign affairs.[99] This wasn't much to behold at first—a handful of weary clerks tucked into a back office. But the very creation of such an entity gave institutional expression to diplomacy as a standing preoccupation of the state, distinct from war, with its own budget, staff, and voice in high policy.

These refinements to France's diplomatic machinery were necessitated by the competitive circumstances of the time. In an era of continual warfare, the country gained value from competent individuals tending to its interests round-the-clock in foreign capitals, tightly tethered to a professional secretariat back home. "It is absolutely necessary to the well-being of the state," Richelieu wrote, "to negotiate ceaselessly, either openly or secretly, and in all places, even in those from which no present fruits are reaped and still more in those for which no future prospects as yet seem likely."[100] "Even if it does no other good on some occasions than gain time, which often is the sole outcome," he wrote, "its employment would be commendable and useful to states, since it frequently takes only an instant to divert a storm."

Continuous diplomacy demanded a higher tempo of political intercourse with friend and foe alike and a conscious elevation by the diplomat of the image and representation of the state on the foreign stage. It also required greater political control over diplomats, to ensure that their words and actions were in lockstep with the state's policy.[101] And it required a strong administrative and cerebral center, embodied by the king's top minister, always alert, always active, and always pursuing the good of the state, "primal and eternal," as his highest end, above all other considerations.

Richelieu's adaptations to bureaucracy would become part of the warp and woof of French, and ultimately European, diplomatic practice. These would find their apogee in the reign of Louis XIV, who came to power

FIGURE 4.3. Early Cold Warrior: Cardinal Richelieu
(Credit: The Print Collector / Alamy)

shortly after Richelieu's death. Writing in 1715, the French diplomat François de Callières admonished the warlike Louis to remember what Richelieu's methods had accomplished for the French state. "A small number of ministers, well-chosen and disposed in the several States of Europe," he wrote, "are capable of rendering to the Prince, or State which employs them very great services; who with a small expense do frequently as much service as standing armies would be able to do because they know how to employ the forces of the country where they reside, in favor of the interests of the Prince whom they serve."[102]

Richelieu's End Game

Richelieu's diplomatic maneuverings during the decade following his appointment as principal minister succeeded in his objective of humbling the House of Austria. In his *Political Testament*, Richelieu summed up for the king what diplomacy had gained for France during this period:

> If it is a result of your singular prudence in keeping all the forces of your enemies at bay for ten whole years with those of your allies by the use of your purse instead of your sword and in going to war only when your allies could no longer subsist alone were not enough, your courage and your wisdom all together are ample proof that by keeping your kingdom at peace, you have been just like those administrators who have known just when to save and just when to spend in order to protect themselves from a greater loss.[103]

A more lucid articulation of diplomacy's strategic potential in any era would be hard to find. Using diplomacy, Richelieu had bought time to recuperate from the wars of religion, deal effectively with the threats from within France, and set the state on surer foundations for war with Spain. When that war finally came, France's adversary was weaker than it otherwise would have been, its energies having been depleted through a decade of war with powers other than France. After its official entry into the Thirty Years' War in 1635, France could count on allies to continue harassing and draining its adversary from the rear, thus reducing the direct burdens of the conflict on itself.

Richelieu's diplomacy hadn't been without costs. Most obviously, there were the subsidies that the cardinal used to keep his scraggly band of allies in the field for so long. There were also the unintended consequences of his machinations, the most obvious example of which was the catastrophic collision between two of his own allies, Sweden and Bavaria. Finally and most seriously, there is the question of whether Richelieu's "continuous diplomacy," by propping up war-weary participants that might have otherwise dropped out earlier, caused the war to run longer than it otherwise would have, thereby prolonging a European nightmare that eventually claimed the lives of as much as half the population in some parts of Germany.[104]

Yet the costs and risks of Richelieu's prewar diplomacy have to be weighed against the alternatives. His subsidies to allies—more than a million livres a year for Sweden and eventually double that for Holland, to name two prominent examples—allowed France to keep a relatively small military establishment in the tens of thousands of troops at an annual expenditure of around twenty million livres. Once France entered the war, those numbers mushroomed, to more than a hundred thousand men at a cost of two to three times the previous budget, with predictable strains on French society.[105] Subsidizing allies had allowed France's leaders to delay those costs and focus on regaining economic and social strength at a moment when both were desperately needed after years of domestic turmoil.

Setting aside the cost savings, Richelieu's policy of *guerre couverte* was arguably the only viable path for France at the time. The alternatives of assisting the Habsburgs in the subjugation of Central Europe in the name of Counter-Reformation, or staying entirely neutral, were unrealistic; either course would have likely led to a postwar environment in which France found itself a virtual island surrounded, if not by outright Habsburg control of, then increased influence in, historically independent territories. The danger was not so much, as Henry Kissinger put it, that France would become "Finlandized," but that it would have eventually faced a war on much less favorable terms, its natural allies having been neutralized or subsumed into a victorious Habsburg colossus.[106] The main accomplishment of Richelieu's diplomacy is that that didn't happen.[107]

Longer term, Richelieu's diplomacy helped to shape a European order favorable to French interests. Richelieu's vision was for a Europe of sovereign states, Catholic and Protestant, whose rights would be enshrined in law and held together by an equilibrium underwritten by its largest powers. France would "hold the scales" in this arrangement, protecting Europe's smaller powers and preserving the common good of Christendom (*"le repos de la chrétienté"*).[108] After Richelieu's death, this concept would guide French diplomacy at the Congress of Westphalia. While the idea was never realized, the concluding treaties of Osnabrück and Münster reaffirmed the right of German states to determine their own religion and conclude international treaties, and acknowledged the French and Swedish crowns as guarantors of the German constitution.[109]

The Peace of Westphalia has been heralded as a milestone in the history of diplomacy that laid the foundation for a system of sovereign nation-states existing under some semblance of international law. What's important for our purposes is that it represented an unmistakable victory for Richelieu's grand strategy, and for French national interests broadly. France had long sought such a state of affairs in Germany, in order to form a breakwater to Habsburg expansion. Westphalia made this objective a reality, enshrined it in precepts of legitimacy and ancient right, and positioned France to be Europe's leading power going forward.

The French Legacy: Great-Power Diplomacy

Richelieu is justly regarded as a foundational figure in the history of diplomacy. Yet it does not detract from his accomplishments to observe that he owes an underacknowledged debt of gratitude to earlier French rulers and, in particular, to Louise of Savoy. In his use of alliances to resist the Spanish Crown, and his construction of combinations on grounds of necessity rather than faith, Richelieu was replicating on a larger and more systematic scale Louise's methods against Charles V. If, as one recent biographer claims, Richelieu is the Galileo of statecraft, in that he conceived a European states system with France at its center, then perhaps it's not a stretch to say that Louise is its Copernicus, in that she conceived a winning grand strategy with diplomacy at its center.[110]

The organizing problem facing France in both eras was multifront pressure from the Habsburg Empire. The search for ways to cope with this challenge fueled the adoption and refinement of Italian diplomatic techniques to fit France's unique geographic circumstances. What made this evolution necessary was a combination of vulnerability and the inability to achieve security by primarily military means. France after Pavia was in a state of shock, with its army destroyed and its king imprisoned. France after the religious wars was regaining its unity, power, and prestige after prolonged sectarian violence.

Recovering from these episodes spurred the development of diplomacy as an instrument of strategy, in much the same way that Byzantium's predicament after the appearance of the Huns, and Venice's predicament after the fall of Constantinople to the Turks, had done in those cases. As had been true for those powers, the process in France was initially reactive and became more systematic over time, as expedients devised in extremis crystalized into standing habits that were expanded and systematized. And as had been the case in Venice and Byzantium, France made a number of distinctive contributions to diplomatic thought and practice.

DIPLOMACY AT SCALE

In diplomacy, size matters. The techniques that France adopted in the period covered in this chapter were not, in and of themselves, all that novel: as we have seen, many were already in widespread use in Italy a full century before Francis I's reign. What made France different was its size and power. The Republic of Venice might maintain resident ambassadors all over Europe, but it remained, at the end of the day, an island republic off the coast of Italy. The kingdom of France was something altogether grander. In French kings we see executive authority in a highly distilled form, wielded over the resources of Europe's largest and most populous state, playing at a level of continental scale and purpose.

France's heft as a big power enhanced the prestige and persuasion of its diplomacy. French diplomats could credibly threaten and promise quite a lot; to deploy them across the length and breadth of Europe was to embed springs and levers with which to move and shake the whole gameboard. That power was conveyed in the first instance in financial terms; even in dire circumstances, French diplomats could usually mobilize large cash payments to allies, as Louise of Savoy did after Pavia and Richelieu did on a far more spectacular scale in Germany, the Low Countries, and Scandinavia in the years leading up to France's formal entry in the Thirty Years' War.

But what ultimately gave French diplomacy its compelling energy was the country's capacity for large-scale military action. The fact that France could generate big armies and wage war beyond its home area meant that the words of its envoys could not be lightly disregarded. To be effective, that military power had to be demonstrated from time to time. The Italian states were wary of agreeing to an alliance with Louise as long as she withheld military commitments. The Danes and Germans in Richelieu's time continually sought more concrete manifestations of French military action than Richelieu was willing to give. Therein lay the dilemma for French diplomacy: the greatest service it could render was to build foreign alliances that allowed France to avoid direct confrontations with its rivals, but to endure, those alliances eventually required France to act militarily beyond its borders. This dilemma never went away entirely, resurfacing in dramatic fashion in the 20th Century, in France's relations with the countries of Eastern Europe between the world wars.

POWER AND MISSION

France's experience shows the benefits that a great power reaps from endowing diplomacy with a higher mission. Precisely because France was so powerful, it needed to relate the exercise of its power to a principle of legitimacy. Without doubt, both Francis I and Louis XIII were motivated by a desire to advance the interests of their kingdom. But both found utility in justifying their actions in ethical and legal terms.

The best illustration is France's embrace of an emphasis on defending small-state "liberties" as a rationale for anti-Habsburg policies in Italy and Germany. It made good strategic sense for a power in France's position that lacked the strength to organize these middle spaces in its own image to keep them divided as a defensive barrier to Habsburg power. By appealing to custom and law as the basis for this policy, rather than the power principle, French kings elevated self-interest to a national mission. In doing so, they offered an alternative vision of order to that of their Habsburg rivals that was attainable and compelling to other states. It was a natural progression from seeking pluralism in Europe's middle zones to promoting equilibrium at the European level, as embodied in Richelieu's concept of a general peace grounded in sovereignty and law.[111]

France's diplomatic power in this period sprang primarily from the promise of self-restraint, as the powerful but benign force protecting the weak. The minute it switched to a policy of active conquest it would be seen not as a protector but as an opportunistic predator. This is precisely what happened later, when Louis XIII's son, Louis XIV, the "Sun King," discarded the defensive strategies of Richelieu and Mazarin and sought security through conquest, triggering counterbalancing by Europe's other powers using many of Richelieu's own methods.

DIPLOMACY AS STRATEGIC ART

The intensity and duration of France's competition with the Habsburgs, involving political maneuvering across Europe over more than two centuries, encouraged the development of diplomacy as an instrument of strategic excellence in the French state. The multifront pressures bearing down on France in these contests could not be borne by military means without incurring ruinous expenses. Diplomacy offered an alternative for securing the state without the full brunt of war's costs and risks. The quest to realize that potential spurred reflection on diplomacy's highest use within the framework of strategy.

Strategic art is reflected in the concepts of French diplomatic policy. Nothing illustrates this point better than the skill with which France cultivated *alliances de revers* with players on the far side of the Habsburg dominions. Louise of Savoy's outreach to Suleiman and Richelieu's courtship of Gustavus Adolphus followed the same logic of pushing the two-front burden onto their adversary—or, as Richelieu put it, keeping enemies "so busy everywhere that they could not win anywhere."[112] Such methods would become part of the fabric of French diplomacy, culminating in France's construction of a bulwark of Eastern states against Nazi Germany, the so-called Little Entente, in the years leading up to World War II.

Strategic art is reflected, too, in French diplomatic methods. France's coalitions didn't build themselves. French diplomats had to work for years studying weedy local dynamics, reconciling local interests with those of France, and managing the knock-on effects of their combinations. Some of the greatest feats of French diplomacy involved mediating disputes between two third parties in which France's only stake was the redirecting of one or both of the parties toward a shared enemy. Even when these efforts failed, they demonstrated the employment of diplomacy at a very high level of abstraction and sophistication.

Finally, strategic art is reflected in the people and institutions of French diplomacy. The treatises of Seyssel and Callières bespeak a culture of reflection on the high ends of state policy. The development of diplomacy as a prestigious state career encouraged professionalism and reflection on the art of negotiation.[113] The institutionalization of Richelieu's methods would form the basis for a culture of diplomatic virtuosity that enabled France to weather the wars of Louis XIV with its accumulated diplomatic tools and instincts intact. The resulting repository of diplomatic skill, preserved from one generation to the next, represented a national strategic advantage every bit as important as the cultivation of military arts.

⟨⟩

France occupies a distinguished place in the history of diplomacy. It is the first modern great power in the full sense of that term—a large state with a centralized administrative apparatus and ability to decisively shape events well beyond its borders. Like Byzantium, France was a land power that was forced to excel in diplomacy as a result of the competitive environment around it. Like Venice, France was an early disciple of the state as an all-important object to which all other considerations were subordinate.

But unlike its predecessors, France possessed the prerequisites for a broad and durable national greatness. French kings ruled over a land that was more productive, compact, and defensible than the sprawling and vulnerable estates of the Byzantine emperors, and could summon offensive military power beyond the wildest dreams of a Venetian doge. Such a kingdom could aspire to more than a stingy baseline safety; it had the makings of Europe's grandest state. Even in France's bleakest moments—after Pavia, and indeed even after the wreckage of the religious wars—that allure of greatness hovered in the near distance.

Warmer-blooded French leaders than Richelieu would in later generations return to the path of conquest that had beguiled Francis and his ancestors. Within a generation of the cardinal's death, his master's son, Louis XIV, the "Sun King," would resume the quest for military glory, followed, in later years, by Napoleon Bonaparte. These spasms of conquest elicited from Europe's other powers the same coalitional responses that Louise of Savoy and Richelieu had used to curb the power of the Habsburgs. The gods of geopolitics being both fickle and ironic, the mantle of resisting France fell to none other than the Habsburg dynasty, to whom our attention now turns.

The Spider's Web

To resist two enemies at the same time . . . is an impossible task.

—WENZEL ANTON VON KAUNITZ-RITTBERG

I have a feeling that I am in the middle of a web which I am spinning in the style of my friends the spiders. . . . A net of this kind is good to behold, woven with artistry, and strong enough to withstand a light attack, even if it cannot survive a mighty gust of wind.

—KLEMENS VON METTERNICH

ON A LATE summer's day in 1755, the Austrian minister in Paris, Count Georg Adam von Starhemberg, paid an unscheduled visit to the residence of Madame de Pompadour, the longtime mistress of Louis XV. Earlier that day, Starhemberg had received an urgent message from Vienna, instructing him to deliver a secret letter to Louis from the empress Maria Theresa. Starhemberg could make his approach, his instructions said, either through the king's cousin, the prestigious Prince de Conti, or through Pompadour, a beautiful woman of high influence but low birth whose affair with Louis had scandalized Europe.[1]

Starhemberg chose Pompadour. The letter that he handed to her explained that he carried a message concerning "matters of the greatest importance," and that he needed someone he could trust—someone of extraordinary discretion—to make sure it reached the king.

Approaching Pompadour wasn't strictly proper; protocol dictated that official communications go through the foreign ministry. It also risked the good name of the Habsburg empress, a pious ruler who would have blanched at the idea of passing notes to a fellow Catholic monarch in the boudoir of an adulteress. But Starhemberg's gambit was worth the risk. For contained in the letter to Louis was a proposal for the houses of Habsburg and Bourbon to lay aside their differences and form an alliance against Prussia.

The idea was audacious. For three hundred years, Austria and France had been locked in a bitter contest for European supremacy. The rivalry was intense—and personal; only a few years earlier, this same Louis had joined the Prussian king Frederick II ("the Great") in an attempt to carve up Maria Theresa's empire and elect a non-Habsburg candidate as Holy Roman Emperor. Austria had survived, but only after a bruising war that lasted eight years and came at the cost of her richest territory, Silesia.

The initiative to woo Louis away from Frederick was the brainchild of Austria's eccentric top diplomat, Count (later Prince) Wenzel Anton von Kaunitz-Rittberg. For years, Kaunitz had waged a determined campaign to align Austria with France before the next inevitable clash with Frederick broke out. His scheme wasn't without danger. At the time Starhemberg approached Pompadour, France remained an ally of Prussia, and Austria an ally of England. This pattern of alliances had held for decades; to scramble it was to risk throwing all of Europe into disarray.

Yet, for Austria, the alternative was even more dangerous. For in Frederick, the Habsburg monarchy faced an opponent of seemingly supernatural animus—and talent. In the period since the previous war, the Prussian king had rebuilt his army, and he was known to be preparing to take another bite out of the Monarchy's territories. It was only a matter of time before he struck again. The last war had shown the catastrophic consequences of being caught without effective allies against such an opponent. Austria was not going to recover Silesia and find lasting safety against Prussia on the basis of her military strength alone. She needed new friends, even if they were old enemies, and even if she had to go through unsavory channels to reach them.

The "Monster"

The source of Kaunitz's angst was a Prussian soldier-king whom Carl von Clausewitz called "a general above all others, ever ready for battle." Not yet thirty when he came to the throne in 1740, Frederick II was a misanthropic genius who despised the Habsburgs, hated women, and already had a fair claim to being the greatest conqueror since Alexander the Great.[2]

At the moment of Frederick's accession, the kingdom of Brandenburg-Prussia wasn't much to behold—"a kind of hermaphrodite, rather more an electorate than a kingdom," as Frederick himself said.[3] Yet the new king had inherited from his father Frederick William I two strategic assets that compensated for Prussia's weaknesses: a healthy budget surplus and a large, splendid army.

Frederick didn't have to wait long to put these assets to use. Just five months after his coronation, the Habsburg emperor Charles VI died unexpectedly, without a male heir. This presented a serious problem, for under Salic Law, the ancient code governing royal successions, Charles' daughter Maria Theresa was barred from following him to the throne. Foreseeing such an eventuality, Charles had years earlier promulgated an edict known as the Pragmatic Sanction, which stipulated that his hereditary possessions would pass *in toto* to his daughter.[4] In the years leading up to his death, Charles's top diplomat, Johann Christoph von Bartenstein, had waged a seemingly successful campaign across the courts of Europe to solicit support for this document as a kind of insurance policy for Maria Theresa's ascension to the throne.

All of that came to naught the moment Charles died. With French encouragement, the Elector of Bavaria, Charles Albert, contested the succession, laying claim to both the imperial title and a swath of the Habsburgs' German possessions. The resulting crisis presented an irresistible opportunity for Frederick. In December 1740, in an early display of the restless energy that would define his reign, he crossed the frontier at the head of 27,000 soldiers, ejected the small Austrian garrison, and seized the Habsburg province of Silesia.

Silesia was no mere border strip: at the time Frederick invaded, it was Austria's most valuable territory, with a population of a million people (equivalent to half of Prussia) and a booming textile industry that generated a fourth of the Habsburg monarchy's annual tax receipts, making it, as Bartenstein said, "the true jewel of the House of Austria."[5]

Frederick's assault came at a delicate moment for Austria. When her father died, Maria Theresa was twenty-three years old and pregnant. The realm she inherited was in a shabby state, with a depleted treasury and an army that was reeling from a humiliating defeat at the hands of the Turks. The young archduchess was inexperienced in matters of state and attended by advisors who were decrepit and defeatist. As Maria Theresa later wrote, she found herself "without money, without credit, without army, . . . without counsel."[6]

The ensuing struggle lasted eight years and brought Austria to the brink of extinction as a great power. Austria was attacked from every quarter, as predators of all sizes joined in the feeding frenzy. It was a defining moment for Maria Theresa, who summoned unexpected qualities as a wartime leader and strategist and fought Frederick to a standstill.[7] Austria survived, but its armies were unable to recover Silesia.

The succession war showed that Frederick was a different kind of opponent than anything the Habsburgs had faced in their long history. The Prussian army was better drilled, equipped, and disciplined than the Austrian army—and better handled.[8] Moving swiftly through Austria's porous northern frontier, Frederick's armies had been able to penetrate the Habsburg heartland with little warning and place themselves within striking distance of Vienna. Once there, they could live off the land for extended periods of time, forcing Austria to keep large forces in the field to defend the capital while depriving it of revenue and manpower from the monarchy's richest provinces.

What made Frederick most dangerous of all to Austria, however, was the man himself. Beneath his rationalist façade, the Prussian king was motivated by a deeply-felt resentment toward the Habsburg dynasty that bordered on obsession. The devout Maria Theresa perceived in him a spiritual darkness; he was a "monster" determined to terrorize her realm and carry it into the "abyss."[9] Beyond simply rounding off the kingdom of Prussia, Frederick wanted to permanently truncate Austria and relegate it to the status of a minor kingdom—and he almost succeeded.[10]

Europe's Storm Center

Dealing with an opponent of Frederick's caliber would have been difficult for even the most powerful of empires. But the Habsburg monarchy was not a "normal" great power in the mold of France or Prussia. It was a wild assortment of territories, inhabited by more than a dozen ethnicities, that had been cobbled together in preceding centuries through conquest and marriage, all of which was bound together only by fealty to the Habsburg family.[11] Austria's makeup complicated its leaders' ability to create a powerful central government capable of mobilizing resources for war.[12]

As had been the case for France, Austria's formation as a state was aided by geography. The empire found a spacious heartland along the Danube River that was fenced on almost every side by mountains.[13] These characteristics made the Habsburg monarchy a natural defensive space, the contours of which are visible on a topographical map as the hermit-crab-shaped recess between the Alps and the Eurasian steppe.

In every direction, the Austrians faced enemies.[14] For centuries, the greatest threat came from the Ottoman Empire. By the early 18th Century, Turkish power had begun to attenuate. But the two empires continued

FIGURE 5.1. The Habsburg Monarchy after the Austrian Succession War
(Credit: Andrew Rhodes)

to rub up against one another uncomfortably on a long frontier from the Adriatic to the Carpathians.

The threat that attracted by far the most Habsburg attention before Frederick's appearance was France. The Habsburgs and Bourbons competed for influence across the middle mass of the European continent, from Italy to modern-day Belgium. As the Austrian succession conflict had demonstrated, France was also capable of mounting a full-scale invasion of the Habsburg heartland, especially when aided by a Germanic ally.

Austria's frontier with Russia was comparatively quiet. The existence between the two empires of the Polish-Lithuanian Commonwealth, a feeble giant incapable of offensive military action, had long enabled Habsburg rulers to forgo standing defenses in this theater. Yet as Poland's decay accelerated and Ottoman power weakened, points of conflict were bound to multiply, even as Austria needed Russia as an ally more and more against Prussia.

The nightmare scenario for Austria was that wars would erupt in two or more of these theaters simultaneously. This had already happened on more than one occasion. In the 1680s, Louis XIV encouraged an attack on Austria by the Ottomans and their Hungarian allies that culminated with an unsuccessful siege of Vienna.[15] Twenty years later, Austria found herself assailed by an even bigger enemy coalition, with concurrent fighting in Italy, Germany, and Hungary.

These earlier emergencies paled, however, to the trauma that Frederick meted out in the War of Austrian Succession. Prussian armies invaded from the north while Spanish and French forces attacked Habsburg possessions in Italy and French and Bavarian armies entered Austria from the west, eventually taking Prague and making it to the outskirts of Vienna. Austria had survived only by waging grueling attritional campaigns that inflicted almost as much damage on her own provinces as they did on the enemy.

Kaunitz's Gambit

The Austrian succession crisis showed beyond any doubt that Austria's established foreign policy was not up to the task of providing security against an opponent of Frederick's lethality. In its aftermath, in the spring of 1749 Maria Theresa convened the Privy Conference, Austria's top decision-making council, for a series of meetings to reassess the foundations of Habsburg grand strategy.[16] The empress instructed her councilors to take two weeks and formulate their thoughts, in memo form, on the future of the empire's foreign policy. After submission to the empress, the position papers would be debated in council and a summary of conclusions drawn up for consideration as a basis for future policy.

In the ensuing debates, one voice stood out from the rest. Wenzel Anton von Kaunitz-Rittberg had just turned thirty-eight when he joined the Privy Conference in 1749 and was by far its youngest member.[17] The Kaunitzes were an old family with deep roots in the Bohemian nobility. Wenzel's grandfather had served under the Habsburg emperor Leopold I. As a young man, he already had given a solid account of his abilities, serving as a diplomat in Turin and the Austrian Netherlands, and most recently as head of the Austrian negotiating team in the talks that concluded the succession war. Kaunitz's ascent in the years that followed was swift: in 1750 he became Austrian representative in France; in 1753 he was named state chancellor and foreign minister, a post he would occupy for nearly four decades, until 1792.

Kaunitz was an unusual man. Contemporaries describe an eccentric genius with behavior that today would be called obsessive-compulsive.[18] Stories abound of his odd behavior: how he maintained a diet of chicken and fruit and had a habit of brushing his teeth in public; his outlandish wardrobe and famed collection of erotica; how he forbade use of the word "death" in his presence and once held a meeting with the pope while wearing a kimono.[19] These quirks were apparent to Maria Theresa, but they were outweighed by Kaunitz's extraordinary intellect, by which he came to exercise a talismanic hold over his queen, "like that of a demonic seducer."[20]

The memorandum that Kaunitz presented to the Privy Conference in the spring of 1749 suggested nothing less than a comprehensive overhaul of Habsburg foreign policy.[21] After reviewing the postwar situation and analyzing the interests of the major powers in turn, Kaunitz concluded that Frederick would be Austria's "greatest, most dangerous, most intransigent enemy" for the foreseeable future, and that urgent preparations had to be made against his machinations. The only remedy to such a threat, he wrote, was "setting on [Frederick] as many enemies as possible"—even if doing so required Austria to seek détente with her archenemy, France.[22]

Kaunitz's idea was revolutionary.[23] Rivalry with the Bourbons was part of the fixed furniture of Habsburg statecraft; everyone in the room had lost relatives in the French wars and had spent their careers designing policies aimed at gaining advantage against the French *Erbfeind*. To make common cause with this enemy meant, inevitably, endangering Austria's old alliances with England and Holland. Instead of these distant sea powers, Kaunitz argued, Austria needed the help of nearby land powers—big players, with real military heft, like France and Russia—if it was going to have any chance of defeating Frederick.[24]

Kaunitz's proposal landed like a bombshell. On hearing it, Maria Theresa's husband, the emperor Francis Stephen, exploded in a rage, pounding his fist on the table and shouting, "Such an unnatural alliance is impracticable and shall never take place"![25] Another Privy Conference member, the aging Count Friedrich von Harrach, argued that France remained Austria's most dangerous opponent, and that Austria's interests would continue to be best served by making common cause with England.

Outnumbered as he may have been in these debates, Kaunitz appears to have won over the one person whose opinion mattered most: Maria Theresa. A few months later, the empress named Kaunitz ambassador to France, with instructions to see if he could persuade the French to go along with his scheme. That proved to be a tall order. At Versailles, old grievances were as entrenched as they were in Vienna. Louis XV's attention was firmly focused on overseas competition with England, and it wasn't immediately clear how Austria could help him with that problem. After three years of apparently fruitless effort, Maria Theresa recalled Kaunitz to Vienna to serve as state chancellor. While he did not return

FIGURE 5.2. Tenacious opponent: The Empress Maria Theresa
(Credit: incamerastock / Alamy)

with a treaty, he had used his time in Paris wisely by building alliances within Louis' court—including with Madame de Pompadour.

Kaunitz's Diplomatic Revolution

In his new role as state chancellor, Kaunitz, pursued the strengthening of the state with single-minded determination, prioritizing raison d'état over dynastic or other considerations. Only by rigorously pursuing Austria's "real state interests," Kaunitz believed, would his empress be able to set her monarchy on a secure foundation and avoid a repeat of the catastrophe that had almost destroyed it in the recent war.[26]

Like Cardinal Richelieu, Kaunitz sought to refine the bureaucratic instruments at his disposal for advancing these goals. When he became state chancellor, Austria's foreign-policymaking bodies were in a state of transition prompted by Austria's recent wars.[27] The key deliberative body was the Privy Conference, which formed the rough equivalent of a National Security Council. Beneath it stood the Austrian Court Chancellery, whose head, the Austrian chancellor, was the de facto foreign minister. The appointment in 1726 of the brilliant but idiosyncratic Bartenstein to the new post of state secretary had brought seriousness of purpose and a larger staff. From here, a chancellery of state emerged, first as the foreign affairs department of the Austrian Court Chancellery and, from 1742, as a stand-alone entity. But even as these institutions matured on paper, Bartenstein's failure to delegate or create basic record-keeping systems made them a tangled mass of inefficiency.

Kaunitz did a lot to iron out this mess. As a precondition of becoming state chancellor, he insisted that Maria Theresa dismiss the aging Bartenstein, who lingered as the deus ex machina, and streamline the bureaucracy. In place of Bartenstein's slapdash methods, Kaunitz installed modern administration on the French model.[28] He expanded the number of senior officials to four (a deputy minister and three department heads), instituted regular reporting, standardized routine functions, and stamped out corruption and petty intrigues, including the habit of foreign diplomats making direct approaches to the empress's advisors.[29]

These changes produced an efficient diplomatic machinery over which Kaunitz exercised as much control as Frederick did over his well-drilled regiments. Over time, Kaunitz succeeded in making the Chancellery, not the Privy Conference, the real locus of policy. By tightening the bureaucracy and aligning it with his and the empress's will, he ensured that "the Habsburg Monarchy always spoke with one clear and consistent voice, and [that] all officials were animated by the same spirit" of raison d'état.[30]

The Renversement des Alliances

From the time of his appointment as state chancellor in May 1753, Kaunitz labored to prepare Austria for the coming clash with Prussia. "Since your Majesty is surrounded by numerous enemies, which only serve to increase the danger from Frederick," Kaunitz wrote to Maria Theresa in a memorandum in June 27, 1755, "the weakening of this king must remain the main object at all times, and be pursued in such a way that, above all, strengthens the security of the House of Austria and exposes it to as little danger as possible." He then outlined three options:

1. Double down on Austria's traditional alliance against the House of Bourbon by strengthening ties with the maritime powers, England and Holland.
2. Split from the maritime powers and build a coalition composed of France and other Catholic countries aimed at the reduction of Prussian power.
3. Separate France and Prussia without fully allying with France, and while trying to preserve the alliance with the maritime powers.[31]

The first option made no sense at a moment when Frederick was preparing around-the-clock for war. The third option was what Austria had been pursuing, fruitlessly, since 1749. Austria's only viable way forward, Kaunitz argued, was option two.

Kaunitz's opportunity came later that summer as a result of events five thousand miles away, in the Ohio River Valley. The defeat of British General Edward Braddock by a French and Indian force in July 1755 sent shock waves through European politics.[32] England and France scrambled to invoke their alliances in preparation for a global confrontation. Austria could no longer sit on the fence; she had to choose.

At an emergency session of the Privy Conference in August, Kaunitz made a spirited case for jettisoning England and wooing France into the Habsburg fold. To sweeten the deal, he proposed offering Louis XV a slice of the Austrian Netherlands (modern-day Belgium), in exchange for territories in Italy.[33] This is the plan that Starhemberg communicated, at Kaunitz's request, by way of Madame de Pompadour to the French king.

The gambit worked. Within days, Louis XV had designated an emissary, Abbé de Bernis, to negotiate with Starhemberg, secretly and in contravention of the French foreign ministry.[34] The talks were initially difficult but got an unexpected boost when, in the first weeks of 1756, word arrived that Prussia had reached an agreement with England in which Frederick guaranteed Hanover in exchange for England eschewing aid for any Austrian effort to retake Silesia.[35]

Stung by Prussia's defection, France quickly came to terms. Under the Treaty of Versailles, signed in early May 1756, Louis XV pledged to come to Austria's aid with 24,000 troops if she were attacked by a third party. A year later, France promised even more: 105,000 troops to fight Frederick in Germany plus 30,000 for Austria itself, along with twelve million livres in aid (the equivalent of 15 percent of France's total peacetime expenditures) to replace Austria's lost English subsidies.

It would be hard to find a more lopsidedly advantageous arrangement in diplomatic history. In exchange for a future promise to cede the Austrian Netherlands, which Kaunitz didn't want anyway, he got immediate and tangible French help for regaining Silesia, as well as French recognition of Italy as a Habsburg sphere of influence. A France that faced no real threat from Prussia agreed to send thousands of troops to the Rhine that she desperately needed in Canada.[36]

Kaunitz's efforts were not confined to France. In parallel with Starhemberg's mission, Austrian diplomats crisscrossed the Holy Roman Empire, much as Richelieu's envoys had done in the previous century, in hopes of provoking a collective German response to Frederick. Also like Richelieu, Kaunitz worked to recruit Sweden and Poland and create a northern front against Frederick, offering both a slice of Prussian territories if they joined the Austrian cause.

Not surprisingly, Kaunitz devoted particular attention to Europe's largest land power, Russia. Late in the succession war, Maria Theresa had formed a defensive alliance with Tsarina Elisabeth of Russia aimed at thwarting Prussian moves into Poland. Kaunitz expanded this into an offensive arrangement, with the explicit goal of "mak[ing] war against the King of Prussia" and placing Frederick "in a position whereby he could no longer disturb the peace."[37] Under the new terms, Russia committed to sending 80,000 troops to help Austria and agreed to a secret provision to repatriate Silesia and partition Prussia.

Kaunitz was careful not to neglect Austria's southern neighbor. In a war with Prussia, Vienna needed relations with the Ottoman Empire to remain quiet. In scenes reminiscent of a Cold War spy novel, Austrian agents worked the back channels of the sultan's court, bribing concubines and pashas in a successful bid to keep the Turks from entering the war on Prussia's side.[38]

In all of these efforts, Kaunitz remained laser-focused on his central goal, of convincing as many countries as possible to join Austria's side, or at least remain neutral, so that she would not face a war on many fronts as she had done last time around—and foisting the problem of encirclement back onto Frederick. While his goal remained fixed, he tailored his diplomatic techniques to the countries he courted, based on a careful reading of their own interests. Where fear was a common glue, he invoked it; where it was not, he used promises of territory or simply cash.

The results were astonishing. In the space of a couple of years, Kaunitz was able to rearrange the European gameboard decisively to Austria's advantage. His *renversement des alliances*, as it came to be known, effectively placed the bulk of the continent's fighting power behind the Habsburg monarchy, including the armies of many states that had fought against Austria in the previous war. Prussia now found herself geopolitically isolated, backed only by England, whose navy could do little to shape events in Central Europe. "Posterity will hardly believe," Maria Theresa later wrote, that "I succeeded not only in pacifying the previous sworn enemy of my Archducal House, but . . . in steering everything towards a single final objective on which the welfare, repose and indeed the very survival of my Archducal House principally depends."[39]

Frederick Slips the Net

As a result of Kaunitz's maneuverings, Austria was in a much better position to defend herself when Frederick's second invasion came than she had been the first time around. Whereas Habsburg forces had in the previous war fought virtually unaided on land, they now enjoyed active help from the armies of France, Russia, and a host of smaller German states, a total of around half a million men, which was more than double Frederick's available manpower.[40]

Even with all that, Austria proved unable to bring Frederick to heel. Over a grueling seven-year struggle, the Habsburg-led coalition inflicted crushing defeats on the Prussian king, forcing him to slowly recoil into the Prussian interior.[41] But each time, cautious Austrian commanders frittered away their victories and allowed Frederick to bounce back. In the sixth year of the war, just as the "monster" seemed to be ready to collapse, fickle fate played her hand when Tsarina Elisabeth died and was succeeded by her erratic son, Peter III. Russia abruptly switched sides, allowing Frederick to focus his full attention on Austria and force Maria Theresa to the negotiating table.

The concluding Treaty of Hubertusburg wasn't a complete loss for Austria, for she was able to preserve the independence of ally Saxony and secure Prussian support for Maria Theresa's son in the next imperial election. But the Habsburg monarchy failed to achieve its main wartime objective of recovering Silesia.

Kaunitz can hardly be faulted for any of this; indeed, it was by his diplomacy that Austria came as close as she did to winning the war. Frederick's reprieve was called the "Miracle of the House of Brandenburg" for a reason: He had escaped the destiny prepared for him by Kaunitz. He was saved by his military genius—and by Europe's largest land power changing sides at the last minute. Even then, Kaunitz's diplomacy had succeeded in transforming the House of Habsburg's prospects from where they had stood at the end of the succession struggle a few years earlier. Frederick had been prevented from taking Bohemia, and Austria was confirmed in her status as a top-tier power.

Still, the war revealed in a vivid way the limitations of power balancing as a means of alleviating the Habsburg monarchy's strategic predicament. The aim of Kaunitz's diplomacy had never been just to regain Silesia. It had been to restore an element of balance to the European order that had been lost when Frederick launched his first invasion. Kaunitz's vision was "a post-war environment without the evil of 'remaining armed beyond our means and burdening loyal subjects with still more taxes rather than granting relief from their burdens.'"[42]

The outcome of the war showed just how elusive that goal would be. To maintain the balance of power, Europe's vulnerable central empire would have to work tirelessly to keep the springs and coils operating to her advantage. Even then, she would have to remain on a war footing to guard against renewed Prussian attacks, even as she kept a wary eye on her other neighbors.

If You Can't Beat Them . . .

Austria's dilemmas were most acute in the East. For more than a century, the Habsburgs had worked to prop up the Polish-Lithuanian Commonwealth as a buffer between their empire and its two eastern neighbors, Prussia and Russia. By maintaining a weak but independent Poland, Austria had been able to keep these rivals at arm's length without the expense of fortifying its eastern frontiers.[43]

In the decade following the Seven Years' War, this policy became difficult to maintain, as domestic turmoil in Poland invited interventions from Prussia and Russia.[44] Austria was confronted with an unenviable choice: she could stand on the sidelines while her two rivals increased their territories, or join in the vivisection of what had long been her most valuable buffer.[45]

Opting for the lesser of two evils, in 1772 Austria took part in the first partition of Poland, by which each of the three eastern powers was apportioned a chunk of commonwealth territory. In addition to acquiring a swath of southern Poland, Kaunitz managed to pry from the Ottoman sultan a portion of the Bukovina in return for limiting Russia's advance, thereby acquiring for the monarchy a small land bridge between Transylvania and the monarchy's newly acquired Polish province of Galicia.

Tactically, Kaunitz's handling of the negotiations was a success; at the stroke of a quill, he had avoided war and added 31,600 square miles and 2.65 million inhabitants to the Habsburg monarchy.[46] But the partition came with long-term costs for Austria. In addition to eroding Austria's eastern glacis, it brought in new territories that would have to be administered. The partition made Austria more dependent on its alliance with Russia, both to counterbalance an enlarged Prussia and to avoid having to fortify Austria's newly elongated eastern frontier.

"Do unto Others . . ."

Austria's travails in the East underscored what she had learned in the wars with Frederick: that the balance of power was a shaky foundation for Austrian security.[47] Passivity was impossible—one was either ordering food or on the menu. To avoid being the latter, one had to actively participate in exchanges of territory as the system's chief currency. And as Europe's sprawling middle power, Austria could never win in these games. If she wanted to avoid becoming a target, she had to participate in predatory geopolitics, which in practice tended to undercut the very stability on which the Habsburg monarchy depended for its long-term survival.

Late in his career, Kaunitz wrote about these dynamics in a memorandum entitled "Reflections on the Concept of the Balance of Power in Europe":

> Any rational, fair and thinking being would agree that in order for a human society to be established and maintained, its first rule must be that no individual can ever attempt to take another's property. Thus follows: no state can infringe on any property gained legitimately, nor afford, without obvious injustice, to demand this of any other states, under any pretext, however special the circumstances. . . . What we refer to as the "balance" has always been found again, and will continue to be constantly found. It will be found in the protection that each individual state has to maintain for itself a large enough number of allies in Europe, to use in its own interest, in the face of an unfair aggressor. Therefore, it is very desirable that we let go once and for all of the concept of a so-called balance being a monster, and that we tell ourselves . . . "Do unto others as you would have done unto you (*Quod tibi non vis fieri alteri ne feceris*)."[48]

Kaunitz's rationalization of the balance of power was at once a defense and rebuttal of the concept. The state chancellor embraced balancing as part of a "political algebra," whereby attempts at hegemony were automatically punished; yet, in the same breath he appeals to human ethics, in the form of the Golden Rule, as that lends legitimacy to its workings.[49]

The fact that Kaunitz, the most talented practitioner of raison d'état of his time, would look for ways to relate its workings to a higher law underscores not only Austria's peace-loving qualities but also the extent of its predicament as a great power. One would not have found Frederick the Great or, in an earlier era, Louis XIV, extolling law as a mechanism to check an "unfair aggressor," or invoking Scripture as a basis of statecraft. Their recourse was to superior force. Austria didn't have that luxury; her best hope was to engineer a stable balance of power—and tether it to a wider conception of order that made disturbances of the peace a European, rather than merely Austria, concern.

A New Menace

Prince Kaunitz did not live to see his ideas come to fruition. He did, however, live to see the emergence of a new menace that would bring about the collapse of the European states system over which he had presided so skillfully. The outbreak of the French Revolution in the spring of 1789 introduced an entropic force into Western politics that was the antithesis of the principles of enlightened equilibrium that had been the hallmark of Kaunitz's statecraft.

The ensuing struggle lasted twenty years and brought Austria to the brink of ruin as a great power. In that time, Austria found herself at war with France on no fewer than six occasions and lost in all but the last two. From the start, it was clear that the new France was a different kind of enemy than anything Austria had previously faced. Militarily, it was capable of generating armies that combined the scale of the Ottoman hordes that the Habsburgs had encountered in prior centuries with the tactical sophistication and battlefield superiority of Frederick II. Politically, it embodied a system of government that was antithetical to the monarchical principle on which the legitimacy of the House of Habsburg, and Europe's other ruling dynasties, had been founded.

In responding to the new French threat, Austria employed the same methods that she had used against Frederick II. Kaunitz's successors made common cause with Austria's erstwhile enemy Prussia, muted disagreements with Russia, and kept things quiet on the Ottoman frontier.

FIGURE 5.3. The Austrian Empire after the Congress of Vienna
(Credit: Andrew Rhodes)

Reactivating the old alliance with England, Austria became the continental linchpin in a series of coalitions that were grander in scale than anything since the wars of Louis XIV. In war after war, Austria's diplomacy worked to ensure that the Habsburgs were on the side with the largest armies, deepest pockets, and best odds of success.

And yet, time and again, the Habsburgs were defeated. In 1797 they lost the Austrian Netherlands and Lombardy. In 1806 Napoleon unceremoniously dismantled the Holy Roman Empire and replaced it with a new French-controlled confederation. In 1807 Austria's supreme nightmare transpired when Napoleon and the Russian tsar Alexander I met at Tilsit and effectively divided Europe between them. In 1809 Austria lashed out in a brief, lonely war that ended with her comprehensive defeat. In the peace that followed, the Habsburg monarchy was shorn of some thirty-two thousand square miles of territory and became a tributary state of the French Empire. In an act of desperation, to bind his empire more closely to the one force capable of enacting its extinction, the Austrian emperor gave his eldest daughter, Marie Louise—Marie Antoinette's great-niece—in propitiatory marriage to the Corsican ogre.

When Napoleon was finally defeated in 1814, Austria was among the foremost victors. But it had come at a terrible cost. Over two decades of fighting, Austria suffered more combat fatalities than any other allied combatant.[50] She had lost a third of her territory and population as spoils of war, and taken on millions in war loans, mainly from Great Britain. Like the rest of Europe, Austria longed for peace. But to an even greater extent than her neighbors, she needed peace to repair the foundations on which her status as a great power rested.

An Austrian Peace

It was fitting, after all that Austria had sacrificed to defeat Napoleon, that the negotiations to shape the postwar order should occur in the Habsburg capital of Vienna.[51] The Congress of Vienna would prove to be one of the most consequential events in the history of diplomacy—the only time when the entirety of the European ruling class would gather in one place to determine their collective future.[52] Neither the deliberations at Westphalia in 1648 nor the peace conferences at Paris in 1919 and Yalta in 1945 equal the proceedings at Vienna in splendor, ambition, or duration of effect.[53]

The architect of this remarkable gathering was Austria's dazzling foreign minister, Klemens Wenzel Count (later Prince) von Metternich.[54] At the time of the Vienna Congress, Metternich was forty-one and at the peak of his career. A Rhinelander by birth, he and his family had witnessed the chaos of the French Revolution firsthand when they were ejected by invading French forces from their ancestral estates near Trier. He entered the Austrian diplomatic service in 1801 as minister to the Saxon court and rose to the rank of foreign minister after Austria's disastrous 1809 campaign. He would retain this post (in tandem, from 1821, with the position of state chancellor) until the revolutions of 1848, making him, alongside Kaunitz, one of Austria's longest-serving statesmen.

Few individuals in the history of diplomacy have been more gifted in its arts. A scion of the old German Reich reared in the waning days of the Enlightenment, Metternich embodied, in his tastes and worldview, the grand nobility of the ancien régime at its pre-Revolution zenith. Handsome and vain, he navigated the intricacies of salon diplomacy, as Treitschke wrote, "as happily as a fish in [a] glittering whirlpool." Yet for all of his supposed cynicism, Metternich was a sentimentalist at heart who wept at performances of Rossini, wrote sappy epistles to his mistresses, and left crumbs on the floor for the mice inhabiting his office at the Ballhausplatz.[55] His numerous love affairs were legendary even by the standards of his day and included Napoleon's sister Caroline and the influential Wilhelmine de Sagan, whom he momentarily shared as a lover with the Tsar of Russia.[56]

FIGURE 5.4. Salon warrior: Klemens von Metternich
(Credit: Heritage Image Partnership Ltd / Alamy)

Like his idol Kaunitz, whose granddaughter he married, Metternich was a connoisseur of power. This he gained, as Kaunitz and Richelieu had done, through assiduous cultivation of the person at the top—that being, in Metternich's case, the cautious and plodding Austrian emperor Francis I. "The emperor always does what I want him to do," Metternich once said, "but I never want him to do anything else but what he has to do."[57] Over a career spanning nearly four decades, his name would become synonymous with a system of diplomacy that laid the foundation for the longest period of systemic peace in Western history.

Metternich's Vision

Metternich would later write that his aim at the Vienna Congress was to foster a "long general peace" to give the Habsburg monarchy time to recover from "the after-pains of a two-and-twenty years' war."[58] The words evoke Kaunitz's quest for a peace that would allow Austria to avoid "remaining armed beyond our means" after the Seven Years' War.

The year before the Congress, Metternich outlined a set of principles to guide Austrian diplomacy in a postwar settlement, the first two of which were placing "the geographic and political relations of the powers on a just and therefore durable basis" and "establish[ing] a new state of affairs that conforms to all interests."[59] The bulk of his time at the Congress was spent on engineering that outcome by reapportioning Europe's territories and populations in a way that would deprive any one state of a preponderance of power with which to threaten its neighbors.

Yet Metternich's approach to peace can't simply be understood as a mechanistic reinstatement of the balance of power. It would be insufficient, he later wrote, to broker a "second edition of the former peace in rather a different form."[60] What he envisioned, rather, was nothing less than a renunciation of the methods by which the major powers had sought security in the past—"the rejection," as he put it, "of the system of conquest, and the establishment of the system of restitution and equivalents in the forming of kingdoms and states." He wanted this "rejection" to occur not just once, but repeatedly over time, by grounding the repaired territorial equilibrium in international law to be supervised through routine consultation among the great powers.

Metternich set down his views on power and law in a passage of his memoirs that bears quoting at length:

That which characterizes the modern world . . . is the tendency of nations to draw near to each other, and in some fashion to enter into a social league . . . [recalling] the precept of the Book of books, "Do unto others as ye would they should do unto you." . . . In the ancient world, policy . . . exercised the most absolute selfishness, without any other curb than that of prudence. . . . Modern history, on the other hand, exhibits the principle of the solidarity of nations and of the balance of power, and furnishes the spectacle of the combined endeavors of several states against the temporary predominance of any one to impede the extension of this principle, and to constrain it to return to the common law. The establishment of international relations upon the basis of reciprocity, under the guarantee of respect for acquired rights, and the conscientious observance of plighted faith, constitutes, at the present day, the essence of politics, of which diplomacy is only the daily application.[61]

Metternich's musings recall Kaunitz's 1789 memorandum in seeking some way to mitigate the effects of naked power balancing. Like Kaunitz, Metternich wanted to escape the old cycle of warfare to which Austria had been subjected over the preceding century.

The only way to do so, Metternich believed, was to place certain constraints, or "curbs," on the behavior of states. The balance of power was one such curb, insofar as it represented a kind of automatic check on attempts at hegemony. But to create a lasting peace, Metternich believed, two additional constraints were needed: adherence to treaty rights, and some mechanism for achieving close and regular coordination among the great powers.

In both respects, Metternich was going well beyond Kaunitz's conception of diplomacy. He was positing a political order in which peace would be preserved not on a reactive basis, through the cobbling-together of coalitions once a war had already broken out, but proactively, on the basis of binding obligations supervised by the great powers. In this design we see an evolution beyond the notion of the balance of power as it was understood in the 18th Century toward an essentially federative arrangement rooted in collective security.[62]

Metternich believed that Austria was ideally positioned to act as the mainspring for such an arrangement. Austria's special status arose from the antiquity of her ruling dynasty, her long role as defender of the constitution of the Holy Roman Empire, and her legacy as an exemplar of treaty rights.

Austria's vulnerability only enhanced her credibility; since she stood to suffer disproportionately from crises, she had the greatest stake in preserving stability.[63] Uniquely among Europe's big powers, she could not enhance her security through conquest, even if she wanted to.[64] These built-in limitations lent moral credibility to Austrian diplomacy, and by extension lent authority to Metternich as the pivotal figure of the Vienna Congress.

Metternich's "Central Dike"

It would be a mistake to conclude from all of this, however, that Metternich's diplomacy rested entirely on a cosmopolitan agenda. The writings of Henry Kissinger have cemented a popular image of him as a European statesman for whom the establishment of peace in Europe was the paramount goal. Metternich actively cultivated this image. "For a long time now, Europe has had for me the value of a mother country," he once commented to the Duke of Wellington. His greatest labors, he attested late in life, had been inspired by "[no] purpose other than to give solidarity to the leading European powers in maintaining the common peace."[65]

But it's important to remember that Metternich was, first and foremost, an Austrian diplomat charged with ensuring the security of the Habsburg monarchy.[66] His approach to the Vienna settlement has to be understood in that light, as fostering outcomes that would be most likely to spare Austria the full defensive burdens of her exposed central position going forward. Doing so required not just peace in a generic sense but a specific set of territorial and political configurations that would enhance Austria's status as the linchpin in the system.

The idea that animated Metternich's strategy was an interdependent middle zone—a "central dike," as Metternich's aide Friedrich von Gentz called it—strong enough to resist encroachments from the flanking powers.[67] At its heart would be a strengthened Habsburg monarchy, its resource base expanded through the restoration of its lost territories. Around this core would be a belt of smaller states connected to Austria by political and economic ties, to share the burdens of defending her central position. In Germany, Metternich presided over the creation of a new Austrian-led entity, the German Confederation, which had a mutual defense clause not unlike NATO's Article 5. Together with Austria's Italian territories, Metternich hoped over time to form these states into a kind of proto–federation linked to Austria by common infrastructure and commercial policies. As Gentz put it, the resulting cluster was Austria's best hope of forming a "true rampart of the common security of Europe; [while] the colossi that occupy the two extremities, breaking against this central dike for as long as it lasts, must for a long time to come seek their advantage and their glory in preserving an order of things they cannot hope to destroy."[68]

The pieces of Metternich's diplomatic vision reinforced one another in ways that enhanced Austrian national security. Habsburg leadership in Central Europe increased Austria's weight vis-à-vis the other great powers, while her coordination with the latter allowed her to devote limited military resources to policing crises in the middle zone. Both roles implied a utility for Austria that made her, in a sense, irreplaceable: To Austria's buffer states, she was just strong enough to provide protection against the flanking powers but not strong enough to become threatening herself; to the other great powers, she was strong enough to prevent an outbreak of revolution inside her empire and buffer regions but not strong enough to pose a direct military threat to her rivals.

The Vienna System

The Final Act of the Vienna Congress, signed on June 9, 1815, was a landmark of European diplomacy. It combined under one cover a Treaty on the General Peace, corresponding to the Congress's main decisions, alongside nine agreements dealing with smaller matters. Taken as a whole, it amounted to a comprehensive alteration of the territorial and legal underpinnings of politics in the Western world. While it would later become fashionable to talk of the task of the Vienna Congress as restoration, it is perhaps more accurate to describe it as renovation—the grafting of new materials, in the form of redrawn boundaries and institutions, onto the old foundation of monarchical principle to render the structure as a whole sturdier.[69]

Even after all this effort, it's conceivable that Europe might have lapsed, after a short interlude, to the old familiar cycle of crisis and conflict. But the abrupt return of Napoleon from his exile on the Mediterranean island of Elba in the spring of 1815and subsequent, final defeat at the Battle of Waterloo, provided a sobering reminder of the suddenness with which war could return and the value to be obtained from prolonging the spirit as well as the letter of the Vienna Final Act. These events spurred the development of two parallel diplomatic arrangements that would be twin pillars of Austrian security in the ensuing years.

One was the Quadruple Alliance—a standing peacetime arrangement that Metternich helped to engineer in the aftermath of Waterloo, whereby Austria, Russia, Prussia, and Britain pledged to contain French aggression and suppress revolutionary outbursts on the continent. Under Article VI of the treaty, the major powers agreed to meet at routine intervals in the style of the Vienna Congress, not only to ensure France's compliance with the terms of peace but also to coordinate on wider matters of "common interest and benefit" as events required.[70]

The other security arrangement was the Holy Alliance—a secret treaty whereby Austria, Prussia, and Russia agreed to uphold the monarchical principle against revolutionary impulses.[71] The original idea, as conceived by Tsar Alexander, had been to form a fraternal association of Christian princes committed to guaranteeing one another's territories and granting liberal constitutions to their subjects. While privately contemptuous of the mystical underpinnings of this construction—"a loud sounding nothing," he called it—Metternich saw the Holy Alliance as a way to co-opt Alexander's enthusiasms and keep Russia constructively engaged in Europe. He essentially hijacked the tsar's idea by expunging the provisions for advancing liberalism and converting it into an autocratic club committed to perpetuating the domestic stability of the three eastern empires.

From an Austrian strategic perspective, these alliances, for as long as they could be maintained, helped to alleviate the two-front danger posed by France and Russia. The Quadruple Alliance enlisted Britain, Prussia, and Russia into containing France, while the Holy Alliance, for all its hollow pretense, provided a practical means for Austria to restrain Russia from pursuing a scale of ambition, particularly in the East, that could have thrust the continent back into conflict.

As important as the alliances themselves, from Metternich's perspective, was the principle that they embodied of routine consultation among Europe's great powers. In the years following the Vienna Congress, Metternich presided over a series of congresses aimed at averting major crises: at Aix-la-Chapelle in 1818, to navigate the thorny question of France's entry into the Quadruple (now Quintuple) Alliance; at Troppau in 1820 and at Laibach the following year, to coordinate responses to uprisings in Naples, Piedmont, and Moldavia and avert a Russo-Turkish confrontation in Greece. In each of these congresses, Metternich used the principles and methods devised at Vienna to avoid a major breach among the big powers and maintain stability on the continent.

It's worth noting that Metternich resisted occasional calls at the time to give the Congress system an institutional expression by endowing it with a secretariat of the kind that we associate with collective security in the modern era. Doing so, he believed, would have fueled the growth of a permanent bureaucracy with its own separate agenda. By keeping congresses regular but problem-driven, Metternich believed that the great powers could maintain focus where it belonged, on heading off big storms before they could form.[72]

The Russian Backstop

It didn't take long for those storms to appear. The Vienna system masked diverging interests that could not be reconciled indefinitely. As Metternich had anticipated, Britain was drawn more and more to its traditional foreign policy of avoiding peacetime alliances on the European continent. France, too, while too tired to mount a renewed bid for European primacy, was drawn inexorably back to its historic policy of contesting Habsburg influence in Italy and Germany. Both chafed at the autocratic principles of the Holy Alliance, whose members claimed a right of intervention in the affairs of sovereign states in order to stamp out liberal opposition.

Cracks had already begun to appear early at Troppau; by the time the powers met in Verona in 1822 to discuss the prospect of joint intervention in Spain, the breach was virtually irreparable. The death of British foreign secretary Viscount Castlereagh, with whom Metternich had formed a close partnership at the Vienna Congress, in 1822, and replacement by his domestic opponent George Canning—followed within months by the appointment of Réné de Chateaubriand, who saw France's participation in the Vienna system as a national humiliation, as French foreign minister— marked the end of the Quintuple Alliance and the era of close cooperation among the five great powers.[73]

The alliance with Russia presented its own challenge for Austria. For all his protestations of monarchical solidarity, Alexander was perfectly willing to sow the seeds of liberal agitation in the Austrian sphere of influence. More seriously, the accelerating decay of the Ottoman Empire created constant temptations for Russia to expand its influence in the Balkans, under the guise of protecting Orthodox Christians. Initially Metternich was able to use his sway over the tsar to thwart these impulses. But by the mid-1820s the game was up, as new uprisings in Greece presented an irresistible opportunity for Russia to exploit Turkish decay. A gathering of the major powers in St. Petersburg in 1825 failed to defuse the crisis, after which Russia and Britain imposed a bilateral solution without the consent of the other powers, thereby signifying the effective end of the congress system.

As these gaps widened, Metternich faced a choice, of either trying to hold together the entire edifice, and potentially alienating Russia, or aligning with Russia and alienating France and Britain. He chose the second option. At Troppau and Laibach, he sided with the tsar in sanctioning intervention against liberal movements. In the years that followed, he stuck with that choice, eventually devising a set of agreements in 1833, known collectively as the Treaty of Münchengrätz, whereby Austria and Russia committed to preserving the status quo in Turkey and Poland and pledging mutual support in the event of internal rebellion.[74]

For Austria, alliance with Russia was the only conceivable option, in the absence of the Quintuple Alliance, by which to secure the Central Europe dike. That depended, above all, on Prussia's coordination with, and subordination to, Austria in German affairs. Allowing a split to emerge between

Austria and Russia would have created the possibility for Prussia to challenge Austrian leadership in Germany, potentially with Russian or French backing.

By staying diplomatically aligned with Russia and Prussia, Metternich enabled the Austrian army to concentrate its scarce resources against the main threat facing Austria, which was France.[75] Metternich's new German Confederation provided a powerful makeweight to these arrangements, effectively allowing Austria to call upon the combined military resources of her Germanic neighbors in the event of a crisis and equipping her with a military deterrent of last resort against both France and Russia.

Only when viewed through the lens of Austrian strategic requirements, rather than European peace in the abstract, does Metternich's logic make sense. Tellingly, he saw the retention of Russia after the loss of England and France as one of his greatest achievements, calling it "a blessing which cannot be sufficiently valued. . . . Who would have believed that Austria could march in a moral union with Russia and Prussia, with Germany and all the Italian princes?"[76]

A Rock of Order

It's not hard to see why many historians view Metternich's system as more smoke than substance—an elegant façade masking a wide disconnect between Austria's responsibilities as a great power and the real power capabilities at her disposal.[77] At base, his methods were those of an unusually cunning diplomat at the helm of a militarily weak state. Metternich himself acknowledged as much when he described the Vienna system as a spider's web, "good to behold, woven with artistry, and strong enough to withstand a light attack, even if it cannot survive a mighty gust of wind."[78]

And yet, the undeniable fact is that Metternich's web, for all of its apparent frailty, *did* withstand the gusts of wind that could have shattered the peace well into the 19th Century.[79] There were plenty of flashpoints in the decades after the Vienna Congress that could have led to a European war but did not, including the eastern crisis of 1821–1823, the Belgian crisis of 1830–1832, and innumerable near-collisions between France and Austria in Italy.[80] Even the settling of the Greek crisis of 1825–1826, while occurring technically outside the boundaries of the congress format, invoked its spirit in reaching an understanding without war.

It is when the management of these crises is viewed in the context of Austrian security requirements that Metternich's accomplishments come into sharpest focus. A full accounting of his success would include not only the European-level storms it helped to defuse but also the smaller regional squalls that it enabled Austria to manage throughout the first half of the 19th Century. These included uprisings in Italy in the 1820s (Naples and Piedmont) and 1840s (Parma and Modena); frontier conflicts in the Balkans in 1819, 1831, 1834, and 1845–1846; and internal unrest in 1844 (Bohemia) and 1846 (Croatia and Poland).[81] In all of these cases Austria enjoyed the diplomatic backing of most of Europe's great powers and, in many of them, the active military assistance of Russia or Prussia or both.

Perhaps the ultimate validation of Metternich's diplomacy came, ironically, in 1848–1849, when Austria faced the full-scale revolution that he had long feared. At its peak, the violence reached Vienna, endangering the Habsburg family and forcing Metternich to flee to England. At this moment of supreme emergency, Austria was able to call on Russia's help in suppressing uprisings inside the monarchy's own borders, and on Prussia's help restoring order in Germany. Had Metternich not engineered a common front with Austria's eastern rivals over the preceding years, the Habsburg army would have faced these internal challenges alone, while carrying the burdens of pacifying Germany, manning the Italian frontier, and guarding its eastern flank. In the event, Metternich's diplomacy helped ensure not only that Austria's geopolitical rivalries were pacified but that the rivals themselves were active participants in her salvation.

It was not until the Crimea crisis of 1854–1856 that the great powers went to war with one another for the first time since the wars with Napoleon. It's noteworthy that this breakdown occurred after Metternich's successors departed from the cornerstone principles of his diplomacy by aligning against Russia. Even then, the resulting conflict did not become a general conflagration involving all of the major powers. Only in 1859, nearly a half-century after the Congress of Vienna and after the impetuous young emperor Franz Joseph had discarded Metternich's conservative methods in favor of a new grand strategy centered on offensive military power, did Austria find herself at war with a major rival, France. Aspects of Metternich's system would continue to guide European diplomacy through the end of the 19th Century and only fully dissolve in the cataclysm of 1914–1918.

Compared to either the century that came before the Vienna system or the one that followed, Metternich is surely justified in the claim, made near the end of his life, that he was a "rock of order" that spared Austria—and by extension Europe—a recurrence of the madness that had nearly consumed them in the years leading up to 1815.

The Austrian Legacy: Confederal Diplomacy

It seems inevitable that a great power of Austria's many vulnerabilities would eventually succumb to the pressures of geopolitics. The Habsburg monarchy's geography exposed her to a parade of dangers, while her makeup placed limits on her ability to deal effectively with those dangers. More than Europe's other great powers, Austria's "responsibilities far exceeded" her resources; she could neither dominate nor hide from her surroundings.[82]

That Austria endured for so long was the result of effective diplomacy. Austria's wars habituated her leaders to conceptualizing diplomacy as a component of strategy and to practicing it at a high level of proficiency. Both Kaunitz and Metternich studied the history of Austria's attempts to deal with its predicament; both closely analyzed Austria's interests alongside those of other powers to inform their policy options; and both developed "big picture" frameworks for thinking about how to manipulate European outcomes to Austria's advantage. From their diplomatic résumés, some common themes emerge.

CO-OPTIVE STATECRAFT

The notion of a self-correcting balance of power held special appeal for Europe's quintessential central power, yet the pursuit of that ideal proved ephemeral, as the end of each conflict gave way, after a short interlude of peace, to some new season of conquest that was certain to draw it into the fray. These realities drove Austrian statesmen to look for ways to mitigate the destructive aspects of the balance of power through appeals to a higher set of principles.[83] The instinct is on display in Bartenstein's search for a pan-European legal sanction for Maria Theresa's succession and Kaunitz's search for a "just" equilibrium after the wars with Frederick the Great. Metternich's concept was a logical culmination of this quest, albeit on a much more ambitious scale.

This was not a naïve attempt to transcend the realities of geopolitics. At base it represented an effort to rope other powers into sharing the burdens of maintaining Austria's exposed position. Emphasis on law played to Austria's special mission as a composite great power built on the principles of legitimacy and treaty rights. The appeal was ultimately not to law per se but rather the other great powers' self-interest in preventing the appearance of a vacuum at the middle of the European gameboard. The essence of Habsburg diplomacy was to convert Austria weaknesses—its exposure to geopolitical storms and susceptibility to revolutionary movements—into assets by advertising the benefits that other powers derived from voluntarily helping it resist these dangers, on the logic that Austria's preservation was a necessity for the stability of Europe.

CONFEDERAL DIPLOMACY

Austrian conceptions of the balance of power were a natural outgrowth of the fissiparous nature of power in the territories of the Habsburg monarchy and Holy Roman Empire. To a greater extent than other European rulers, Habsburg monarchs found their writ circumscribed by the peculiarities of their realm, which militated against effective centralization.[84] Habsburg leaders had to rely more on persuasion and toleration than on threats and subordination.

These realities gave Habsburg diplomacy a confederal quality, in the sense that Austria sought to position herself as a leader of pluralistic groupings that she would not have been able to dominate by force alone. The normal logic of empires is that power increases in proportion to the ability to exert direct control over territory and resources. In Austria's case, it was often the opposite. The Habsburg monarchy's moral authority among the great powers increased in proportion to her eschewal of the "law of conquest." Her influence in Central Europe increased in proportion to her willingness to work with the grain of her smaller neighbors' desire to be independent. And, as Metternich correctly saw, her susceptibility to internal revolution decreased in proportion to the willingness of her leaders to decentralize and respect particularist rights.

In all of these cases, Austria pursued federative solutions not because she was an inherently benevolent power but because doing so was the most effective way to advance the security of the Habsburg state.

BUFFER STATES

The idea of using diplomacy to maintain intermediary zones in the spaces between one's own territory and one's rivals is as old as diplomacy itself. As we saw in an earlier chapter, the Byzantines managed extensive buffers in the turbulent areas around their frontiers, and France under Richelieu propped up the small states of Germany as a way of checking the growth of Spanish power in Central Europe. But it may be fairly said that the Austrians brought the management of buffer zones to its highest art and made it the sine qua non of their diplomacy.

Austria's geographic centrality and relative weakness meant that to survive as a great power, she had to be capable of preventing the spaces around her from falling under the control of a hostile power. The effort to preserve the existence of weaker players like Saxony, the Polish-Lithuanian Commonwealth, the Danubian Principalities, and the Ottoman Empire runs like a golden thread through Habsburg diplomacy.[85] Both Kaunitz and Metternich would have preferred to preserve Poland; both were willing to fight wars to keep it and other Austrian buffers from falling into their neighbors' hands intact.

The strategic benefit of buffer states for Austria was that they interposed space around what was a relatively fragile core. They played a role in Austria's strategy that was roughly equivalent to the role that the English Channel played for Britain or the endless steppe played for Russia: they bought her time when threatened and, in peacetime, reduced the necessity of maintaining large-scale defenses on every side. The job of Habsburg diplomacy was to compete for positive influence in these spaces—to resist the spread of rival or revolutionary tendrils there, to tilt them toward Austria, and, in any event, to keep them alive as independent actors to the extent possible. Habsburg diplomacy performed these tasks admirably for more than two centuries; the eventual loss of these intermediary spaces marked the beginning of the end of Austria as a great power.

TIME-BASED DIPLOMACY

Austrian diplomacy excelled in managing the element of time in strategic competition. As we have seen, the Byzantines, Venetians, and French were all cognizant of diplomacy's value in this respect. But in Austria's case, the need to do so was a central requirement created by the harsh necessities of geography. The existence of big-power threats in every direction from the Habsburg home area put a premium on being able to concentrate scarce military resources against the primary threat du jour without compromising Austrian security on other frontiers.

The requirement to shift focus to each new danger as it emerged, rather than any overarching conception of order, tended to dictate the main task of Habsburg diplomacy at a given moment. The urgent need to concentrate effort against Frederick II demanded that Kaunitz make common cause with Austria's traditional enemy, Bourbon France, while the need to concentrate against Revolutionary France demanded that Kaunitz's successors make common cause with Prussia to concentrate against France.

The identity of the main threat was usually obvious, though it's worth noting that both Kaunitz and Metternich devoted considerable attention in their memoranda to analyzing likely permutations in the future threat environment.

Through these experiences, Austria's diplomats developed a talent for ameliorating old rivalries and sustaining effective coalitions. Yet Habsburg contests against Prussia and France also showed the inevitable strains generated by such an approach, as Austria became the garrison and pivot for each new coalition to thwart a disturber of the peace. The genius of Metternich's system of European diplomacy can only be fully grasped in this light, as an attempt to break out of the cycle and give Austria breathing space to recuperate from two decades of war. His goal remained that of earlier Austrian diplomats, of gaining control of the factor of time before the next war began. But his aspiration was to do so over a much longer horizon, by way of a regularized system that tried to keep Austria ahead of storms before they could break out. The mainspring was a rational quest, not for peace in a generic sense, though that was certainly welcome, but to spare Austria the costs and risks of maintaining her precarious position for as long as possible.

✦

Austria occupies a sui generis place in the history of diplomacy. It is in the Austrian empire of the Habsburgs that the techniques of the "new diplomacy" that had emerged in the Italian Renaissance and that had found continental scope in Bourbon France attained perhaps their fullest and highest expression as an instrument of strategy. The Habsburgs followed in the footsteps of the Bourbons in treating diplomacy as an arm of state power and in grasping that its elevated application could bring advantages in great-power competition. But to an even greater extent than the French, the Austrians needed adroit diplomacy to compensate for the inadequacy of the military instruments at their disposal and stay alive in Europe's most dangerous neighborhood.

There is a whiff of the Byzantium about Habsburg Austria—a vulnerable frontier empire, forever fading yet enduring, whose leaders were forced, as it was once said of Metternich, to substitute "cunning for strength." The extraordinary demands of Austria's geography drove her diplomats to pursue the balance of power to its highest logical expression. It was in their attempts to render the European equilibrium more stable, by enmeshing it in a web of treaty obligations, that Austria pioneered the transition from the "conspiracy for loot" that had characterized European diplomacy in Kaunitz's time to the 19th-Century congress system.[86]

When Austria's eclipse came, it was after a new generation of leaders discarded the seemingly antiquated methods of Metternich and tried to achieve security through offensive military power. Lashing out in a series of short, sharp wars in the reign of Franz Joseph, Austria found herself ranged against multiple rivals without a single ally—precisely the conditions that Kaunitz and Metternich had labored for so long, successfully, to avoid. Ejected from Germany and Italy and shorn of her centuries-old buffers, Austria quickly fell to the status of a second-rate power.[87]

It may be true, as one German historian has written, that "one [who] has a weak heart should not go mountaineering."[88] But the genius of Habsburg diplomacy was that it surrounded a weak-hearted Austria with so many willing sherpas and sturdy belays that a fall was impossible without pulling the other climbers into the chasm with her. That Austria would, with the passage of time, lose many of the supports that held her in place for so long was inevitable; that she would willingly throw them away and leap into the chasm on her own accord was not. The results for Austria and for Europe were as predictable as they were catastrophic.

CHAPTER SIX

The Punching Doll

Peoples and men, folly and wisdom, war and peace, come and go like waves and the sea remains. Our states and their power and honor are nothing to God but ant-heaps and beehives which are trampled by an ox's hoof or snatched by fate in the shape of a honey gatherer.

—OTTO VON BISMARCK

The Germans never forget that Russia is looking at them.

—LORD SALISBURY

NEARLY A THIRD of a century after Metternich's death, it looked as if the great war that Europe's diplomats had labored for generations to avoid had finally arrived. In the closing days of 1887 and into the following year, reports circulated in Berlin that Russian troops were massing on Austria's eastern frontier. For months, Germany's two eastern neighbors had been squabbling over yet another Balkan problem, this time involving the fate of the fledgling kingdom of Bulgaria. Hardly a day passed without the newspapers in St. Petersburg calling on the tsar to lead a crusade of Slavs against Austria-Hungary. By degrees the Russian Empire seemed to be mobilizing her gargantuan army. Austria too was now arming as quickly as her rickety structures would allow. And because it was widely assumed that the Habsburg monarchy would lose the coming war, the generals in Germany, Austria's closest ally, were on edge.

Germany was not in an ideal position to fight a war, should it need to do so. Despite her reputation as Europe's greatest military power, the new German state possessed an army that was barely half the size of its Russian counterpart. If the two went to war, it could reasonably be assumed that France, Germany's bitter enemy, would attack her from the west. The result would be a two-front war of the kind that Kaunitz had engineered against Frederick II in the previous century, but on a much larger scale.

Germany's general staff had a remedy for this problem. Rather than wait for her enemies to coalesce, they reasoned, Germany should strike first, knock out Russia, and then turn her full attention to France. Bold strokes of this kind were becoming something of a German specialty. Just a few years earlier, the Prussian army had used similar methods to inflict humiliating defeats on Denmark, Austria, and France and, in the process, had laid the foundation for a unified German state.

Standing in the generals' way was Germany's leading statesman, the formidable Prince Otto von Bismarck, chancellor of the Second Reich. At first glance, Bismarck was an unlikely character to play the part of a dove. A towering figure with a stormy disposition and walrus mustache, usually depicted in a *pickelhaube* helmet and military jacket, he looked the very picture of a warlike Prussian Junker. Over the preceding decade and a half, he had transformed Germany from a group of bickering small states into an empire that was well on its way to becoming the mightiest force in Europe.

Yet better than anyone, Bismarck knew just how vulnerable his new creation was. His recurring nightmare was that Germany's neighbors would combine to strangle the young empire in its cradle. Since becoming chancellor in 1871, he had operated an intricate system of alliances designed to avoid that scenario and give Germany the space she needed to develop as a great power. The centerpiece was a tenuous, three-way friendship with Russia and Austria that isolated France diplomatically. Bismarck likened it to a punching doll, with Germany providing ballast at the base: as long as Germany didn't pick sides, the doll stayed upright, and Europe didn't go to war. Now, all of that seemed to be collapsing, as Germany's generals—the "demigods," as Bismarck called them—poured over maps, mobilization plans, and railway schedules.

But Europe's war would have to wait. For unbeknownst to the general staff, Bismarck had for months been skillfully at work, creating secret new arrangements to keep his punching doll upright and avert a two-front war. In so doing, Bismarck was unknowingly entering what would become the last and perhaps greatest act of his career, and giving Europe one final, golden generation of peace before Armageddon.[1]

Rise of the Iron Kingdom

Bismarck had good reason to want peace. Compared to Europe's other big states, geography had been conspicuously unkind to Germany. Where France and Austria both enjoyed at least partial protection in the form of encircling seas or mountains, Germany sat exposed on the North European Plain, a featureless expanse that runs from the North Sea to the river Vistula in modern-day Poland.

Germany's location stunted her development as a great power. For centuries, Germany was more a geographic expression than a state—a motley assortment of princely estates, bishoprics, and free cities organized under the gauzy appellation of "Holy Roman Empire of the German Nation." Metternich's reorganization of Germany along federal lines at the Congress of Vienna had changed the structure of this mosaic, but not its fundamental identity. Within the confederation, Austria held pride of place while Prussia, the largest of the north German states, was accorded a privileged-but-junior position.

For a while, Austria was able to keep Prussia in its box. But friction was inevitable. By the middle years of the 19th Century, the two were engaged in a running fight for leadership of Germany. The feud came to a head in 1866. At Sadowa in the modern-day Czech Republic, not far from the site of Frederick the Great's first great victory in the previous century, a Prussian army bottled up and defeated a larger Austrian force.[2] Afterward, Metternich's German Confederation was dissolved and, in its place, a new North German Confederation was formed with Prussia at the helm. With astonishing speed, Austria's long dominance of Germany ended and the Habsburg monarchy became a second-rate European power.

It was inevitable that France and Prussia would come to blows next—as they did in the brief but catastrophic war of 1870–1871.[3] At Sedan on the French frontier, Prussian forces encircled and decisively defeated the main French army under Napoleon III. Within days the French Empire had collapsed and been succeeded, after a short interlude, by a new French Third Republic. Four months later in the Hall of Mirrors at Versailles, the assembled princes of Germany proclaimed the Prussian king Wilhelm I emperor of Germany.[4]

Europe's Juvenile Giant

The salient attribute of the new German Empire was its mass. In size, it was a third larger than today's Federal Republic of Germany, with territories that stretched from the Ardennes to the Russian border, and from Switzerland to the waistline of the Jutland peninsula. At the moment of its inception, the empire had a bigger population than any other European power except Russia and a gross domestic product (GDP) greater than any but Britain. It produced two and a half times more coal per year than France, and forty-five times as much as Russia. In pig iron and steel

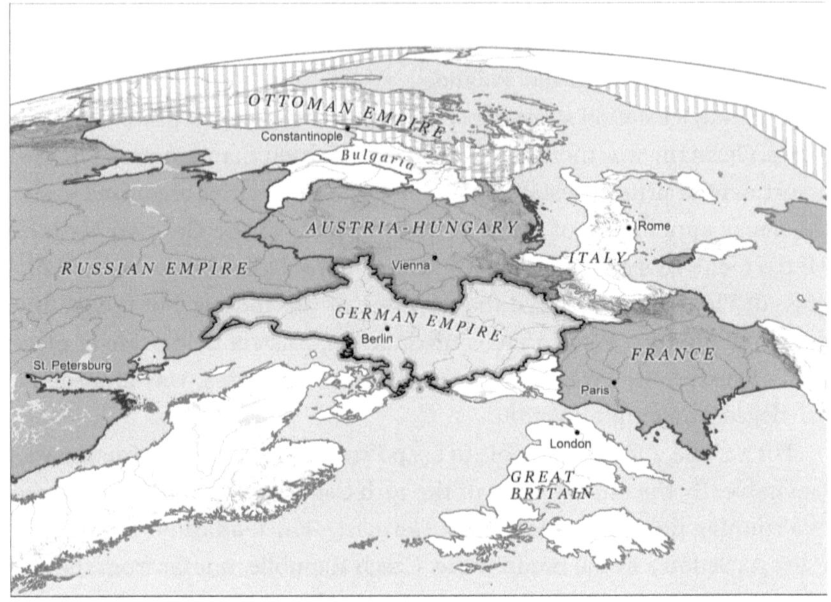

FIGURE 6.1. The German Empire in 1887 (Credit: Andrew Rhodes)

production—the critical metrics of power in this era—it was second only to the British Empire.[5]

It would be hard to overstate how dramatically the appearance of this powerful new giant changed European diplomacy.[6] For ages, German weakness had been a defining feature of European politics. The absence of a strong force at Europe's center had set the rhythms of its conflicts. It's what had enabled Europe's flanking powers, France and Russia, to exert such a preponderant role; allowed Austria, despite her innumerable pathologies, to remain in the first rank of the great powers; and allowed Britain to hang offshore and intervene episodically, in the sure knowledge that she would find allies among Germany's pocket-sized states who shared her interest in preserving the European status quo. These realities had given the old balance of power its force and logic.

All of that was swept away when the Second Reich appeared. It wasn't only the new Germany's immense power potential that changed the game so dramatically; it was the principle on which that power had been constructed. In Metternich's old dispensation, a premium had been placed on legitimacy and treaty rights. The new Germany embodied the violent negation of those tenets and the triumph of the power principle, in the service of the national idea—"the notion," as Henry Kissinger writes, "that relations among states are determined by raw power and that the mighty will prevail."[7]

The Demigods

The combination of Germany's latent strength and vulnerable geography decisively shaped her military culture.[8] Whereas Austria's protective geography had encouraged a defensive attitude toward warfare, Germany's exposure created incentives to strike out and defeat enemies through maneuver and firepower. The spectacular success of the unification wars, with their limited scope, short duration, and decisive political effects, seemed to confirm the outsized potential for using force in this fashion.

The father of these successes was Field Marshall Helmuth von Moltke, chief of the German general staff. Cerebral and taciturn, Moltke had come of age in the period after the Napoleonic Wars when Carl von Clausewitz was superintendent of the Prussian military academy.[9] Clausewitz held that war was a chaotic, primordial act of violence that states use to impose their will on one another. Learning from Napoleon's campaigns, he counseled the state to harness this destructive force in single-minded determination against a central object—the enemy army—until it was annihilated.

Moltke imbibed deeply from this new gospel and, in the emerging technologies of the Industrial Revolution, saw the means for realizing Clausewitz's ideal of decisive battle.[10] Moving quickly along Prussia's centralized railway networks, Moltke's armies descended like a swarm of mechanized insects to bottle up and destroy enemy forces. Using these methods, Moltke led Prussia to victories against Denmark, Austria, and France that were showpieces of Clausewitzian warfare.

In one crucial respect, however, these wars showed that Moltke differed from his master. Whereas Clausewitz thought that civilian leaders should retain firm control even during wartime, Moltke believed that they should shut up once the fighting started. As the chaos of violence manifested itself, only the military professionals could devise the right expedients. The job of politicians was to get out of the way.

In a multifront war, Moltke reasoned, Germany could deal with her attackers in the same way that Frederick had dealt with them: by taking the offensive. In the period immediately after unification, Moltke was convinced that Germany could deal with France and Russia *simultaneously*.[11] In the years that followed, he modified these plans to embrace a sequential approach. Germany would make a quick strike at France before pivoting to deal with Russia. But by the early 1880s, he had begun to reverse this strategy in favor of hitting Russia first while retaining a defensive force in the west to keep an eye on France's forts.

The idea of offensive action had a seductive logic, of choosing the timing and location of confrontation and achieving something like comprehensive security for the state through bold initiative and decisive, violent action. The young officers on Moltke's staff who developed the plans held a godlike status in German society that made them the rough equivalent of professional athletes in our own time.[12] While Moltke himself respected civilian power, at least in peacetime, his younger subordinates viewed Germany's civilian leaders with contempt and longed to use the awesome instruments at their disposal to finish what they had begun in the unification wars and set the new empire on surer foundations.

An Unlikely Peacemaker

That Germany's generals didn't have their way is largely due to the efforts of a domineering, childish, narcissistic genius named Otto von Bismarck-Schönhausen.[13]

At the moment of Germany's unification, Bismarck was fifty-five and at the pinnacle of a career that would span the reigns of four monarchs. Descended from an old family of Junkers—the squirarchy of Protestant landowners who formed the upper echelons of the Prussian army and civil service—he first appeared on the scene as an energetic supporter of the Hohenzollerns during the upheaval of 1848. Bismarck's ascent in the years that followed was swift, with stints in the Landtag (Prussia's parliament) and as an obstreperous delegate to the federal diet in Frankfurt before joining the diplomatic corps as ambassador in St. Petersburg and then Paris. Following his appointment as minister-president and foreign minister in 1862, Bismarck promptly became the mainspring of Prussian politics, exercising dominance over both the parliament and the king.

The German Empire was Bismarck's creation. He was the chief engineer of Prussia's sequential victories over Denmark, Austria, and France. He drafted the Constitution of the North German Confederation, which became the foundation for the constitution of the new Reich. And he served as the empire's first chancellor, a post he would retain for nearly two decades before his abrupt dismissal by Wilhelm II in 1890.

Bismarck didn't look or act like a diplomat. At six foot three, he cast an intimidating shadow in an age when most men were a foot shorter. Like Metternich, he could be charming—when he wanted. But Bismarck was no polished creature of the salon; he was a man of stormy extremes and unplumbed insecurities. If Metternich personified the Enlightenment ideals of reason and equipoise, then Bismarck embodied the full range of emotions idealized by Germany's Romantic poets. At the core of his personality was a demonic energy fueled by obsessive political rivalries. He nursed elaborate, decades-long grudges and was known to persecute enemies after they had retired or even died.[14] If Metternich's idea of revenge, as his wife said, was to invite an enemy for dinner, Bismarck's idea of revenge was to *eat* his enemy for dinner: to systematically destroy the person's career, reputation, and finances. The more public the humiliation, the better. It's not hard to see why more than one contemporary thought he might be the literal Devil.[15]

Most politicians draw energy from human interaction; a few from introspection. Bismarck was of the latter variety. For one of history's most successful practitioners of diplomacy, he was curiously allergic to the human intercourse on which that profession subsists. He would retire to his country estate at Varzin to brood and strategize, then emerge with a force and focus that astonished observers. In every direction, he saw enemies. He regarded Germany's liberals with suspicion, as unwitting agents of instability, and its conservatives with condescension, as reactionary bumpkins. A political loner, he shunned the normal bonds of party and had few friends or confidants.

What made Bismarck tick was power. This he gained, like Cardinal Richelieu, Kaunitz, and Metternich, through a close relationship with his ruler, Wilhelm I, who was eighteen years his senior. But to a far greater extent than earlier characters in this book, Bismarck dominated his royal master. This was mainly by force of personality. But it was also by design. In crafting the constitution, Bismarck had deliberately concentrated executive power in the hands of the federal chancellor, who was in sole command of most government functions and answerable to the kaiser alone.[16] As one biographer puts it, "Bismarck designed [the constitution] for Bismarck," building a "fragile structure not only to suit himself but also to suit an arrangement in which a strong chancellor bullies a weak king."[17]

And bully him he did. Where Metternich had used politesse and indirection to "manage upward," never fully overcoming the emperor Francis's jealously guarded prerogatives, Bismarck used emotional manipulation and blackmail to almost always get his way. The tone for the relationship was set early on, when Wilhelm, having promised his wife Augusta not to hire Bismarck, was bowled over by the Junker's charisma and hired him on the spot.[18] In the twenty-six-year partnership that followed, Bismarck developed reliable, if not altogether scrupulous, techniques for

FIGURE 6.2. Unlikely peacemaker: Otto von Bismarck
(Credit: Peter Horree / Alamy)

overcoming Wilhelm's objections to his plans. These ranged from subterfuge and childlike tantrums to feigned illnesses and threats of resignation, which Bismarck employed with great flourish and frequency in response to even mild opposition from his sovereign.[19]

Some historians have detected in Bismarck the absence of coherent political principles other than the aggrandizement of his own power. Certainly, he defied easy ideological categorization and was capable of infinite tactical flexibility in the pursuit of his objectives. As he once said to the Reichstag:

> Liberal, reactionary, conservative—those I confess seem to me luxuries. . . . Give me a strong German state, and then ask me whether it should have more or less liberal furnishings. . . . I've no fixed opinions; make proposals, and you won't meet any objections of principle from me. Many roads lead to Rome. . . . There are no eternal rules.[20]

The North Star for Bismarck was Germany, as an extension of Prussian power. Bismarck's philosophy was Realpolitik: the service of the state as an end in itself.[21] He was perfectly willing to ally with whatever faction or foreign power the circumstances required, as long as doing so advanced that end. "When I have been asked whether I was pro-Russian or pro-Western," he said, "I have always answered: I am Prussian. . . . as soon as it was proved to me that it was in the interests of a healthy and well-considered Prussian policy, I would see our troops fire on French, Russians, English or Austrians with equal satisfaction."[22]

Bismarck's "System"

Like Richelieu and Metternich, Bismarck left his mark on his country's diplomatic institutions. The new Foreign Office of the Second Reich was formed on the foundation of the Prussian Ministry of Foreign Affairs. It was structured in the conventional French fashion, with three divisions corresponding to the functional requirements of diplomacy (political, commercial, and legal), presided over at the top by a state secretary who reported to the chancellor.[23]

To a much greater extent than Metternich, Bismarck distrusted the bureaucracy—the "boa constrictor," as he called it. He saw the Foreign Office as an incubator for liberalism and a source of constraints on his own power.[24] Like Richelieu, he relied on a small circle of well-placed deputies that included his son, Herbert, who would eventually become state secretary.

Bismarck's conception of diplomacy was a natural outworking of his political philosophy. The first and last object of policy must be the state—and what most threatened the state was war on many fronts.[25] The necessity of avoiding a "Kaunitzian" coalition dictated what Bismarck defined as the guiding principle of diplomacy, that Germany must always be "*à trois* in a world governed by five powers."[26] The quickest way to bring about a hostile coalition would be to behave aggressively. This was the heart of Bismarck's disagreement with the generals: rather than making Germany more secure, he believed that military buildups and preventive war would bring about the very catastrophe they were meant to prevent.[27]

Bismarck set down his thoughts on Germany's predicament in the summer of 1877 while vacationing at the Bavarian spa town of Bad Kissingen. "A French newspaper said recently about me that I suffered from '*le cauchemar des coalitions,*'" he wrote. "This sort of nightmare will last for a long time, and maybe forever, an entirely justified worry for a German minister." To avoid this nightmare, Bismarck believed that Germany needed to adhere to a diplomatic strategy premised on eschewing territorial expansion and promoting "an overall political situation in which all the powers except France need us and are held apart from coalitions against us by their relations to each other."[28]

Bismarck's tactics for achieving this goal would shift over time. But a handful of basic principles would remain constant throughout the remainder of his career. These were: the preservation of Austria-Hungary, the isolation of France, and friendship with Russia.

The first may come as a surprise, given the lengths to which Bismarck had gone to orchestrate Austria's defeat in 1866. But Bismarck saw that it was in Germany's interest to prop up the Habsburg monarchy, lest it collapse and create a power vacuum inviting expansion by Russia, a far more capable rival.[29] At Gastein in 1871, he engineered a rapprochement between the German and Austrian emperors. Eight years later, he formalized the link with a defensive alliance under which the two powers pledged to aid one another if either was attacked by Russia. The so-called Dual Alliance (expanded to include Italy in 1882) would become the cornerstone of Bismarckian foreign policy, comprising the German Empire's most serious, durable, and consequential foreign commitment.

France was a different animal entirely. By herself, the French Third Republic wasn't a mortal danger to Germany; what made France dangerous was her desire for revenge and motivation to organize an encircling coalition against Germany. Bismarck's diplomacy was geared to preventing that outcome by keeping France isolated. He sought conciliation with France wherever possible, as long as it did not involve the return of the contested territories of Alsace-Lorraine. To this end, Bismarck enthusiastically encouraged French colonial expansion, while resisting pressure from German merchants and industrialists to build an overseas empire of Germany's own.[30] As Bismarck once said, "Here lies Russia and here lies France, and we are in the middle. That is my map of Africa."[31]

The crux of Bismarck's system was the maintenance of amiable ties with Tsarist Russia. "The secret to politics," he once said, is to "make a good treaty with Russia."[32] As long as such a basis existed, Bismarck had a good chance of achieving his other goals; without it, anything was possible. There were ample bases on which to ground such a friendship. The German emperor Wilhelm I was Tsar Alexander II's uncle. German bonds financed Russian railways; the Russian army bought weapons from German manufacturers. By the 1880s a fifth of all German investment in Europe was going to Russia, and the German central bank was home to more than half of all externally held Russian securities.[33]

The problem was the inherent tension between the Austrian and Russian planks of Bismarck's diplomacy. Paradoxically, Germany's eviction of Austria from Central Europe had directed its attention to the southeast, in the direction of the Balkans, which brought it into increasing competition with Russia. Bismarck's method for averting a clash between the two eastern empires was to pull both powers closer to one another, and to

Germany. In May 1873 he formed a secret military convention with Russia, committing the two powers to aid one another in the event of an attack by a third party. This was capped, a month later, with a treaty at Schönbrünn committing the three empires to "consult one another so that differences between them do not prevail over considerations of a higher order."[34] The resulting arrangements, which would come to be known as the League of the Three Emperors, would be refined over time into a three-way pact for preserving peace in the Balkans.

Viewed in toto, Bismarck's system wasn't all that different than Metternich's. At its center stood an Austro-German core similar to Metternich's central "dike," only with Berlin in charge and Vienna in a subordinate position. Bismarck buttressed this core with an arrangement in the east—the "triangular rampart," as Bismarck called it—that performed a function similar to the old Holy Alliance in Metternich's time. As long as these components held, Austria and Russia would be restrained, France would be denied the opportunity to launch a war of revenge, and Germany would be protected from Bismarck's nightmare of a war on two fronts.

The Pax Teutonica

It didn't take long for storms to form that tested the resilience of Bismarck's system. The first came in the spring of 1875, when the removal of Germany's remaining occupation forces from France and the initiation of a rearmament program in Paris sparked what would come to be known as the "War in Sight" crisis.[35] France attempted with some success to convince Russia and England that Bismarck was preparing to launch a war of aggression. The incident subsided when it became apparent that Bismarck had no such intentions. But it had a lasting effect in demonstrating the suddenness with which an encircling coalition could materialize, should Germany ever actually embrace a logic of expansion.[36]

An even more severe test came in the Balkans. By the mid-1870s the "Eastern Question," as it was known at the time, was reaching fever pitch as the Turks struggled to hold onto their remaining European territories. In 1875 a series of uprisings, first in Bosnia-Herzegovina, then in Bulgaria, Serbia, and Montenegro, brought the matter to a head. The unrest attracted attention from Russia, where pan-Slav elements whipped up support for the region's mostly Slavic and Orthodox Christian populace.

Bismarck saw no direct German interest in any of this. But he feared that the situation would lead to a war between Russia and Austria, each of which would expect Germany to take its side. His first recourse was to invoke the provisions of the Three Emperors' League—this being, after all, precisely the kind of problem that that grouping was designed to address. In May 1876 Bismarck met in Berlin with his Austrian and Russian counterparts to devise a joint position. They produced a diplomatic note, known as the Berlin Memorandum, which called on Turkey to cease hostilities or risk military intervention.

It didn't work; indeed, the fighting intensified, especially in Bulgaria, where Turkish authorities unleashed paramilitary units on the Christian population that committed mass atrocities in which thousands of civilians were killed. A conference convened among the major powers in Constantinople met with similar failure, and the following spring Russia declared war on Turkey. In the campaign that ensued, Russian forces inflicted a string of decisive defeats on their Ottoman counterparts. European concern quickly swung from sympathy for the Bulgarians to concerns that Russia would shortly dominate the entirety of the Balkan peninsula and make it all the way to Constantinople.

For a moment, it looked like the situation might spark a European war. Fearing an imminent Russian attempt to break up the Ottoman Empire, the British government under Prime Minister Benjamin Disraeli sent a Royal Navy squadron into the narrow passageway separating the Turkish capital from the Asian mainland.[37] Russian forces stopped just shy of the Bosphorus and made peace with the Turks at San Stefano in March 1878.

The resulting agreement did little to allay European anxieties about Russian domination of the Balkans. Under its provisions, a new Bulgarian state was created that outstripped its neighbors in size, stretching across the width of the peninsula from the Black Sea to the Aegean. Though nominally independent, it was widely assumed to be a Russian cat's-paw that would enable the tsar to extend his reach to the Mediterranean. In response, Britain called up her reserves and began deploying ships to the eastern Mediterranean in anticipation of war.

It was at this juncture that Bismarck entered the scene in what would become one of the most memorable episodes of his career. In the summer of 1878 in Berlin, he convened a conference of the major powers to find a peaceful resolution to the Bulgarian imbroglio. In agreeing to get involved, Bismarck's goal was to prevent a European crisis that could threaten German security. To keep France from exploiting the situation, he needed to defuse it in a way that prevented Russia from succeeding in her conquests without appearing to place Germany in the scales against Russia. Bismarck spelled out his approach in a speech to the Reichstag: "The adjustment of peace does not, I believe, consist in our playing the arbiter. . . . Peace is brought about, I think, more modestly. Without straining the simile which I am quoting from our everyday life, it partakes more of the behavior of the honest broker, who really wishes to bring about a bargain."[38]

To bring about this "bargain," Bismarck worked behind the scenes to formulate an agreement that would allow Russia to back down without losing face. He carefully meted out help to each side, generally favoring Russia in the eastern Balkans, Austria in the western Balkans, and Britain in the Mediterranean—acting, in other words, in accordance with what he saw as the traditional interests of each.[39] He then used the conference to multilateralize, and thus legitimize, what had already been agreed in principle behind closed doors.[40]

When the Berlin Congress concluded, the immediate issue that had brought Britain and Russia to the brink of war had been resolved. The Ottoman Empire was preserved. Bulgaria was divided into three parts, with an "autonomous principality" in the north, a semi-autonomous province called Eastern Rumelia in the south, and the rest reverting to Turkish rule.[41] As compensation, Russia got Southern Bessarabia, Austria-Hungary was allowed to occupy Bosnia-Herzegovina, and Britain got Cyprus.

Coming on the heels of the "War in Sight" crisis, the Berlin Congress demonstrated, as few other things could have done, that Germany was a status quo power committed to preserving the peace of Europe, and that she was willing to use her considerable good offices to that effect. Against such a power, it could be said, there was no need to form Kaunitzian coalitions; to the contrary, the congress seemed to suggest that Germany's central location could be an asset.

Losing Russia

It was ironic, given the lengths to which Bismarck had gone to avoid alienating Russia at the Berlin Congress, that the leaders of that country would come to regard its proceedings as a national defeat and resent the man who had convened it. The Russians were disappointed that they had so little to show for their recent victories against Turkey. Rather than blaming themselves for diplomatic ineptitude or blaming Britain for depriving them of just gains, they blamed Bismarck for not working harder on their behalf.[42]

The fallout in Russo-German relations was felt almost immediately. The tsar took on a frosty tone in his correspondence with the kaiser. Russian newspapers mounted a sustained attack on Bismarck's character. The Russian army ramped up armaments and pushed its cavalry pickets closer to the German frontier. And Russia's diplomats, egged on by the media, began a conspicuous courtship of France.

It was in reaction to these events, and still with the nightmare of encirclement in mind, that Bismarck inked the Dual Alliance with Austria in the fall of 1879. He stepped up outreach to the Disraeli government, on the correct assumption that Britain would be positively inclined toward an alignment aimed at countering what were, after all, that country's two chief rivals, France and Russia.[43]

In parallel, Bismarck worked to breathe new life into the Three Emperors' League. In 1881 the treaty was renewed and strengthened. The first article obliged all three signatories to remain in a position of friendly neutrality if any found itself at war with a fourth party. The second article explicitly addressed the Balkans, pledging to safeguard the status quo in that region only by mutual agreement.[44] Three years later the agreement was renewed with great fanfare in Skierniewice in modern-day Poland, with all three emperors in attendance. Bismarck, it seemed, would be able to have it both ways: he would reinforce his "triangular rampart" in the East while rebuilding a Central European "dike" in case the rampart collapsed.

Bulgaria Unravels

The sequence of events that would bring Bismarck's elaborate system to the brink of collapse began in the same Bulgarian mare's nest that the Treaty of Berlin had been intended to untangle. Developments in that country following the conclusion of the Berlin Congress illustrate the ageless truth that diplomatic agreements that result in political outcomes detached from local realities are destined to fail. At Berlin, the British had imagined that the Bulgarians would be content to have a small state rather than no state at all, while the Russians had imagined that the Bulgarians would be grateful to the tsar for giving it to them. Both were wrong. The Bulgarians chafed at Russian patronizing and rejected the division of their nation as unnatural.

The year after the congress met, the parliament of the principality of Bulgaria offered its throne to a German prince, the twenty-two-year-old Alexander of Battenberg, son of the Grand Duke of Hesse. Upon arrival in Bulgaria, Battenberg found a powder keg of local feuds, set against the backdrop of a hastily conceived constitution that failed to delineate the prerogatives of the executive and legislative branches. Real power in the country lay in the hands of a coven of Russian "advisors" with a mandate from the tsar to run the country like a suburb of St. Petersburg.

Because he was the Russian tsarina's nephew, it was assumed that Battenberg would go along with this arrangement. But the young prince proved to be more independent-minded than either the Russians or the Bulgarians had anticipated. He was willing to see Bulgaria become a Russian satellite, but not if it meant he had to be a puppet to the tsar's generals. In his bid to throw off their tutelage, Battenberg mobilized Bulgarian national feeling, which was now turning decidedly anti-Russian. Showing surprising spunk for a foreign transplant, he evicted the generals, defeated an attempted invasion by Serbia, and, in the fall of 1885, presided over his principality's unification with Eastern Rumelia to form an enlarged Bulgarian state, thereby achieving by main force a large measure of what had been proscribed at Berlin.

These events set in motion dangerous subterranean shifts in European diplomacy. The problem was not that Bulgaria had unified; this scenario had been anticipated by Bismarck, who had included contingencies for managing it into a secret addendum to the 1881 treaty with Austria and Russia.

Rather, the problem was the character of the new state that had suddenly formed. Instead of the Russian satellite that Europe had long feared, the new Bulgaria was a western protégé that resented Russian influence. The battlelines that had formed at the Berlin Congress now flipped: it was Russia that was disadvantaged by a big Bulgaria, and Britain and Austria-Hungary that favored it.[45]

All of this came as a painful jolt to Russia. "Seldom, surely," as George Kennan later wrote, "has a Great Power been required to drink a more bitter cup of gall." The tsar placed the blame for the Bulgarian calamity squarely on Bismarck's shoulders. The only remedy was to resume the quest to take the Ottoman capital and finally realize Russia's destiny to dominate the Balkans. To do that, Russia needed to deal decisively with Austria-Hungary, which could only occur if she was separated from Germany.

It was by this line of reasoning that the tsar and his advisors arrived at what would be two fateful decisions for the future of Europe: The first was not to renew the League of the Three Emperors when it lapsed in June 1887. The second was to begin to explore in earnest a Russian alliance with France, prevention of which had been the central obsession of German diplomacy since 1871.

System Breakdown

Going into 1887, it appeared that Bismarck's intricate system would collapse and that war would come in its wake. That system had been designed with one overarching danger in mind: that a crisis in the Balkans would enmesh Germany to a degree that enabled France to launch an attack on the Rhine.

This danger seemed to be about to come true. Just as Russia was coming unhinged, France was in the grips of its most serious war fever yet.

Since the start of the previous year, France's War Ministry had been in the hands of a nationalist firebrand, General Georges Boulanger, who advocated for a war of revenge against Germany. At Boulanger's direction, the French army had been working feverishly to strengthen its forward positions on the German frontier.[46] With Russian forces making similar preparations in the east, the ingredients seemed to be present for Bismarck's "nightmare" to become a reality.

Bismarck would spend the next several months trying to put the genie back in the bottle. Tellingly, his first step was to shore up German military power. It will be remembered that he had long sought to avoid building up the army to a point that Germany's neighbors felt intolerably threatened by it. While continuing to abide by this principle, he took steps to improve his empire's defenses. In November 1886 he proposed legislation in the Reichstag to expand the size of the army from 427,000 to 468,000 men.[47] German forces would still be outmatched by the French and Russian armies.[48] But the bill sent a clear signal that Germany was alive to the situation and capable of defending itself.

Bismarck drove the point home in a speech to the Reichstag on January 11, 1887. In words clearly intended for consumption in St. Petersburg, he made clear he wanted to preserve "friendship with Russia" but was committed to preserving Austria. To France, he said that Germany had "neither the reason nor the intent" to seek confrontation. And to the German and Austrian generals, he said that preventive war was off the table.[49]

The message was clear: Bismarck planned to continue his old formula of giving Russia a free hand in Bulgaria while backing Austria only in extremis so that he could concentrate German military power against France. This concentration, in turn, strengthened Germany's deterrent in the west, making war less likely.

Yet the fact remained that Germany could shortly find herself in exactly the position that Bismarck had long sought to avoid, of being shackled by to a weak Austria while fending off simultaneous military moves from Russia and France.

To deal with this problem, Bismarck made a determined effort to draw Britain more closely to Germany's side. Rather than try to coax her into a formal alliance, which would complicate Germany's relationship with Russia, Bismarck had the good sense to appeal to Britain's own interest in working with Italy and Austria-Hungary, which shared British apprehension of French and Russian designs on North Africa and Turkey respectively.[50] By these methods, Bismarck gradually nudged Britain and Italy into an informal alliance in February 1887, whereby they agreed that "the status quo will be maintained to the extent possible in the Mediterranean."[51] A month later, Austria-Hungary was brought into the arrangement via an exchange of notes that effectively extended its provisions into the Black Sea.

The First Mediterranean Agreement, as these pacts would collectively become known, hemmed in France while ensuring that if Austria-Hungary and Russia came to blows, Bismarck could count on Britain and Italy to bear the burden of defending that country.[52] The Anglo-Italian alignment meant that in the event of war, France would have to stretch her military power in two directions *other than* the German frontier. The Anglo-Austrian alignment meant that in the event of war, Russia would have to dispatch armies in opposite directions hundreds of miles apart (the Balkans and British India), in addition to whatever spot on the Baltic or Black Sea coast the Royal Navy decided to strike. By mobilizing Britain as a factor in the European scales, Bismarck alleviated Germany's two-front dilemma while activating the two-front dilemmas of its main rivals.

The Reinsurance Treaty

If things got out of hand, the Mediterranean Agreement shielded Germany from having to choose between Austria and Russia. But it did not address the danger that Russia and France might form a formal alliance against Germany. The search for a hedge against this latter scenario produced the final grand diplomatic maneuver of Bismarck's career, the so-called Reinsurance Treaty with Russia.

This secret treaty, hashed out over a seven-day period in May 1887 between Bismarck and the Russian ambassador to Germany, Paul Shuvalov, was in its essentials a recapitulation of the main terms of the Three Emperors' League in bilateral form.[53] The first article pledged to "maintain benevolent neutrality" and to "localize the conflict" if either power "should find itself at war with a third Great Power"—*unless* the war in question came about because Russian attacked Austria or Germany attacked France. The second article committed Germany to recognize Russia's "preponderant and decisive influence in Bulgaria." A secret amendment committed Germany to assist Russia in achieving her desired outcomes in Bulgaria and to support Russia if she found it "necessary to assume the task of defending" the Bosporus.[54]

It didn't take long for this new framework to be tested. In early July, the Bulgarian parliament offered the country's recently vacated throne to another Germanic candidate, Ferdinand of Saxe-Coburg (or "Foxy Ferdy" as the well-fed, well-coiffed prince was known), a blue-blood

Austrian army officer with close ties to the Habsburg court. In St. Petersburg it was widely assumed that the entire affair, coming on the heels of Bulgaria's rejection of a Russian candidate, had been orchestrated by Vienna. In keeping with the third article of the Reinsurance Treaty and the spirit of the secret annex, the Russians expected that Bismarck would intervene energetically on Russia's behalf to oppose these designs.

Bismarck was happy to play the part—to a point. His conception of order in the Balkans had long been a separation of spheres of influence in which Russia would enjoy sway over the eastern half, and Austria-Hungary the western half, of the peninsula. But the Foxy Ferdy episode, and the eagerness with which the Russians now importuned Germany to act on their behalf, underscored a critical deficiency in Bismarck's increasingly elaborate arrangements: the possibility that Russia would be drawn into a war by an act of *Austrian* provocation, in which case Germany would be obligated to take Russia's side.

Bismarck's response to this danger was to fine-tune the Mediterranean Agreement so that it would be better able to bear the direct burden of protecting Austria. So far, the three parties to that arrangement—Britain, Italy, and Austria—had only agreed to cooperate in the Mediterranean. This left open the possibility that Britain would pocket cooperation in North Africa, where French provocations were intensifying, while striking a deal with Russia to avoid open conflict over the Turkish straits. The only remedy was to tie Britain and Italy more explicitly to the defense of Austrian interests in the Balkans.

In October, Bismarck sent his son Herbert to London with a proposal for Britain to join Italy and Austria in guaranteeing the Ottomans against a Russian attack. Lord Salisbury, British prime minister since 1885, was quick to see the danger of this plan, which would expose Britain to far greater risk than she had accepted under the looser agreement earlier in the spring.[55] Before proceeding with new guarantees, Salisbury asked the obvious question: How exactly would *Germany herself* respond if Austria were attacked by Russia?

In response, Bismarck penned an extraordinary letter aimed at reassuring Salisbury of Germany's defensive intentions. "The German Empire," Bismarck wrote:

> has three great powers for neighbors, and its borders are exposed. It therefore must not lose sight of the question of coalitions that could form against it. If Austria were to be vanquished, weakened or become an enemy, we would be isolated on the Continent of Europe in the presence

of Russia and France and face the possibility of a coalition of these two powers. . . . [A]s long as we aren't certain that we've been abandoned by the powers whose interests are identical to ours [Britain and Austria], no German Emperor can follow a political policy other than defending the independence of friendly countries [Britain and Austria] who are like us satisfied with the current state of Europe and ready to act without hesitation and without weakness when their independence is threatened.[56]

Along with the letter, Bismarck transmitted a copy of the Dual Alliance of 1879, outlining for the first time the extent of Germany's guarantee of Austria.* This showed that Bismarck's promotion of the Mediterranean Agreements wasn't just a cynical ploy; Germany, too, had skin in the game.

By opening a window into Germany's diplomatic logic, couched in a convincing review of its overall grand strategy, Bismarck was able to persuade Salisbury to take the (for Britain) highly unusual step of entering into a security commitment on the continent.

The Second Mediterranean Agreement came into being three weeks later, via an exchange of notes between the British, Italian, and Austrian governments. Article 1 committed the three powers to the "maintenance of the status quo in the Orient"; Article 4 committed them to support the "independence of Turkey, as guardian of important European interests"; and Article 5 forbade Turkey from "her suzerain rights over Bulgaria to any other Power" nor abdicating her status as "guardian of the Straits."[57]

What all of this amounted to, in effect, was a hedge against Russian encroachments into the Balkans of the sort that would threaten either Turkey or Austria. Even if an Austro-Russian collision came about because Austria initiated it, Germany stood a fair chance of staying out of the conflict as long as this "Near Eastern Triplice" did its job. With this final piece in place, Bismarck's elaborate rewiring of European diplomacy to compensate for the collapse of the Three Emperors' League was complete.

Securities and Cigarettes

Remarkably, even with the Reinsurance Treaty and Second Mediterranean Agreement in place, the march to war continued as Europe headed into the winter of 1887–1888. Russia blamed Austria for Foxy Ferdy's acceptance of the Bulgarian throne. In this ongoing saga, the Russians

---

* Bismarck had already told the Russians about the Austrian treaty during the negotiation of the Reinsurance Treaty.

looked to Berlin for assistance and, in so doing, exposed the obvious tension in Bismarck's designs—to wit, that the Dual Alliance and Mediterranean Agreements conflicted in certain respects with the provisions of the Reinsurance Treaty. The former two instruments assured Austria of the support of Europe's "saturated powers," including Germany, while the latter assured Russia of Germany's support and, in its most secret parts, even seemed to encourage Russian designs on the Bosporus of the kind that would trigger a military response from Britain.

With a more stable climate in St. Petersburg, these tensions might have been managed. But the direction of Russian policy remained, from Bismarck's perspective, an open question. The Russian press kept things stirred up, and French agents stoked Russian suspicions that they were being misled and manipulated by Berlin. In this environment, it was entirely possible that Russia would use the Reinsurance Treaty to play for time while she prepared for war.

In a last-ditch effort to defuse the situation, Bismarck employed what today would be called financial warfare. At the same time that he was aligning the pieces for the Second Mediterranean Agreement, he instructed the German Reichsbank to stop accepting Russian bonds as collateral for loans. This sent a message to financial markets that the German government, which held more than half of all Russian state debt, had lost confidence in tsarist credit.[58] The resulting sell-off, coming at a moment when Russia was attempting to stabilize its currency, undercut the Russian army's ability to undertake large-scale offensive action and drove home to Russia's leaders the impossibility of a policy of confrontation with Berlin.

Bismarck launched the attack on Russian securities just days before a meeting with the tsar, who stopped off in Berlin in mid-November 1887 on his way back from a trip to visit his in-laws in Denmark. One can imagine the scene in this tense meeting as a visibly agitated Alexander III chain-smoked cigarettes and accused Bismarck of double-dealing in Bulgaria, while his towering host rebutted the accusations and protested Germany's fidelity.[59] Bismarck used the occasion to lodge his own complaints about the anti-German tenor of the Russian press and remind the tsar of Berlin's obligations to defend Austria.

The interview appears to have had a salutary effect in planting seeds of doubt in the mind of the tsar about the reliability of the counsel he was receiving from hawks in the Russian press and army. Whether it was because of Bismarck's persuasive powers or the sell-off of Russian debt, or both, the temperature in Russo-German relations improved from this point forward—at least in the short term. Longer term, the Russians drew the conclusion that they needed a more reliable economic and military partner than Germany, driving them toward an alliance with France.[60]

The Valkyries Mount

These herculean efforts notwithstanding, there remained yet a final danger: that the German army would launch an offensive war on Russia. None made the case more forcefully than General Albrecht von Waldersee, a Moltke protégé who would soon succeed his master as chief of the general staff. Like many in the German army, he believed that Bismarck's diplomacy—the policy of the "see-saw," as he called it—was beneath the dignity of a great empire. Through the network of military attachés at German embassies, he ran what amounted to a parallel foreign policy. Using this network, late in 1887, Waldersee initiated staff talks with the Austro-Hungarian high command aimed at planning for a joint war against Russia.[61]

As Bismarck's system teetered in the early months of 1887, Waldersee saw his chance. Bolstering his case for war was the fact that the German army had recently completed a big modernization program while the Russians were just embarking on a similar process that would take years to complete.

Here was the proverbial window of opportunity. And like all such windows, it seemed to be closing before it had opened. Already, as Waldersee explained to the emperor in a memorandum dated November 7, 1887, Russia's deployable manpower was greater than it had ever been. "Since spring," Waldersee wrote, "there have been repeated signs that Russia is making preparations for a warlike state of affairs in the not-distant future."[62] The scale of these preparations—comprising, in effect, a stealth mobilization—would inevitably erode whatever edge Germany had in mobilization speed. It was time to act, or face a war on much less favorable terms down the road.

Waldersee's legendary boss Moltke, now pushing ninety, agreed with his assessment. "Only if we take the offensive," the old *Feldmarschall* wrote to the emperor, "will our chances be favorable."[63] Better to attack in the winter, while the ground was hard with frost, than to wait for spring. With good reason, Waldersee thought he had checkmated Bismarck: "The Chancellor still hopes to avoid the war with Russia," he confided in his diary on Christmas Eve 1887, "[but] nothing he does will avail, for we are heading for war, and it will come in the Spring."[64]

Defeating the Hawks

Bismarck moved decisively to keep control of foreign policy. His main tactic was to awaken in the mind of the cautious Wilhelm I a healthy fear of what war would bring about for Germany. So effectively did he prevail upon the ninety-year-old monarch that the old man was supposedly overheard by servants late at night feverishly reciting from Bismarck's memoranda.[65]

While thwarting the generals' counsel, Bismarck also worked to augment Germany's military deterrent. A few days after the tsar left Berlin, he proposed a bill that would increase the army's reserves by 600,000 men. He urged the army to strengthen its forces on the eastern frontier, signed a new military convention with Italy, and stepped-up intelligence-sharing with Britain—even going so far as to provide Salisbury's government with detailed information on France's Atlantic ports.[66]

At the same time, Bismarck made it clear to the hawks that none of this would be used to support an offensive war. "As long as I am minister," he declared, "I will not give my consent to a prophylactic attack on Russia."[67] To undercut the preparations for war, on February 3, 1888, Bismarck published the text of Germany's secret treaty with Austria-Hungary.[68] To the German and Austrian generals, who remarkably still didn't know the exact details of their countries' alliance, the treaty's text made clear that nothing short of an outright attack by Russia would suffice as a casus foederis for drawing Germany into war on Austria's side. To Russia's leaders, the fact of the treaty's publication underscored Germany's defensive intentions and the essentially restraining function that Bismarck was attempting to play vis-à-vis Austria in Bulgaria.

To put a punctuation mark on the matter, a few days later Bismarck made one of his most famous speeches, aerating, once again, the outlines of his diplomatic strategy. Addressing the Reichstag, he reminded everyone why Germany had tied itself to Austria's security in the first place, while underscoring the treaty's defensive nature. He expressed confidence in the tsar's good word and peaceful intentions while sounding enough of a note of warning to douse whatever bellicose embers still burned in St. Petersburg. "We Germans fear God, and naught else in the world," Bismarck said in closing, "[and] it is this fear of God which makes us love and cherish peace."[69]

Bismarck's peroration was greeted rapturously in the chamber and on the streets outside.[70] The scene was not unlike the one that would greet Neville Chamberlain following his return from Munich in 1938. Except that in Bismarck's case, the euphoria was warranted, for the peace at hand would prove to be authentic and durable.

Bismarck in the Dock

Bismarck's February 6 speech would come to be seen as a bookend to the Bulgarian crisis. As Europe entered the spring of 1888, tensions among the great powers abated. The armies didn't march. The general staffs reluctantly stood down. The newspapers found new topics to write about.

That Europe didn't go to war in 1887 or 1888 was primarily due to Bismarck's diplomacy. In the space of a little more than a year, he renewed, brokered, or midwifed no fewer than five bilateral or multilateral agreements, while fending off an attack on his domestic power base by the German general staff, winning a general election, and getting two major military spending bills through parliament. These would be impressive feats for any leader. But for a man in his seventies who suffered from creeping rheumatism, could hardly chew his food, and could only sleep with the aid of morphine, they are astounding.[71] It's hard to disagree with Otto Pflanze's assessment that it was the work of Bismarck, "more than any other factor," that "preserved the fragile peace of Europe in the greatest and most complex international crisis since 1815."[72]

Some modern historians have offered a more critical appraisal, arguing that there was never really a very serious risk of war, and that Bismarck simply manipulated international events to strengthen his domestic power base. Most recently, Jonathan Steinberg has suggested that Bismarck's maneuvers were driven by paranoia, that Germany could easily have defeated Russia and France in a two-front war, and that it therefore "had no need of these subtle and secret agreements" in the first place.[73]

At the time, however, it was far from obvious that Europe wouldn't go to war. Lord Salisbury, a phlegmatic leader not given to exaggeration, wrote in 1888, "We are at this moment on the sharp ridge that separates the slopes toward war and peace. . . . a very slight push either way will decide the issue."[74] Plenty of onlookers were ready to provide the "slight push" toward war, including large segments of the political and military leaderships in France and Russia, as well as most of the German and Austrian generals.

Nor is it obvious that Germany would have prevailed in a two-front conflict. France had undergone a substantial modernization since its defeat in 1871. Russia had the largest army in the world. Together, they fielded more than three times as many troops as Germany. Only with the benefit of hindsight, and the horrors of trench warfare, would the extent of the advantage of the defensive in the mechanized era become so obvious. The assumption that Germany would be playing at a disadvantage in a protracted two-front struggle was baked into the planning of Moltke's staff, which is why they favored the offensive.

The idea that Bismarck was an "unprincipled warmonger" also doesn't hold up to scrutiny.[75] There *were* warmongers in the German general staff at this time who would gladly have implemented a program of military expansion. It is a reflection of Bismarck's political skills that they didn't get the chance to test their well-oiled war plans, and a testament of his diplomatic skills that the generals in Austria, Russia, and France didn't get a chance to implement theirs either.

What distinguished Bismarck from the generals is that he was enough of a realist to see that the German Empire would not be able to attain a lasting security by primarily military means. For Bismarck, European peace and German security were intimately intertwined.[76] The motivation to preserve the state that stood at the core of his political philosophy found its logical outworking in a policy of carefully calculated war avoidance. At an earlier stage of his career he had been perfectly willing to use offensive force, when it suited the state's needs. But once Germany was united and "satiated," that ceased to be the case, and diplomacy rather than war became the instrument of choice.

The web of agreements that Bismarck made to compensate for the collapse of the Three Emperors' League preserved peace by tilting the gameboard against any power that opted for aggression. If either Russia or Austria launched an offensive war, they would find Germany arrayed on the other side. These arrangements were favorable for German national security because they were good for the cause of peace—in that order. The Mediterranean Agreements allowed Germany's leaders to keep her military forces concentrated against the most likely threat—France—on the reasonable assumption that Russia would be restrained by other powers in the event of an eastern war. This concentration, in turn, strengthened Germany's western deterrent, further reinforcing peace.

In both cases, military power was a crucial enabler to Bismarck's diplomatic success. The two army bills that Bismarck pushed through parliament during the period of the Bulgarian crisis increased German military power, while stopping well shy of the kinds of numbers that would have made Germany threatening to its neighbors. The timing of these bills wasn't a coincidence; coming at moments of peak international tension, they sent a message about Germany's capability to act militarily, should diplomacy fail.

Would a different kind of system have been more effective at keeping the peace? Probably not. A hands-off foreign policy of the kind Bismarck probably preferred would have left Germany isolated and vulnerable to an encircling coalition. Eschewing a hard commitment to Austria-Hungary could have led to that old empire's collapse, leaving behind a patchwork of small ethnic states that would have tempted Russian expansion. Backing Austria too far, however, could have exposed Germany to war against Russia and France, as indeed would be the case in 1914. Avoiding these negative outcomes required a juggling act of astonishing dexterity, lubricated by agreements that conflicted with one another in spirit, if not letter. Yet it should not be concluded on the basis of this complexity that a more advantageous course was available at the time. The ultimate metric of Bismarck's methods' success is that, at the moment of his dismissal by Kaiser Wilhelm I in 1890, they were working. Germany was secure against the most plausible near-term danger at an acceptable cost in effort and defense spending.

The German Legacy: The Diplomacy of Control

Like the great powers examined in earlier chapters, the role of diplomacy in German strategy was heavily conditioned by geography. Like Austria, the German Empire occupied a central location; what set Germany apart was the extent of military and economic power at her disposal for coping with that predicament. To a far greater extent than even the Bourbon kings of France, German leaders could conceive of achieving security by military-offensive means alone. From the moment of her birth, the unified German state had the makings of a potential European hegemon. Her advantages over rivals in population, territory, and industry made such a course seem plausible, while simultaneously generating so much opposition from Europe's other great powers as to make it impossible.

These realities generated an enduring paradox of strategy for Germany: the more she sought security by military means, the less secure she would become. Rarely has a state in history faced a more intense security dilemma.[77] For Germany's generals, who had experienced the victories at Sadowa and Sedan, it was only natural to look to military means for breaking out of the "nightmare" of encirclement. That prospect seemed all the more viable in an era when new technologies appeared, for a moment, to make warfare more capable of achieving decisive political outcomes than ever before.

What made Bismarck so unique was that he correctly saw the perils of this seductive solution. His insight was to realize that a rising power can choose economic growth and political influence or military strength—but not all three.[78] He chose the first two, and stuck to that choice from 1871 until his dismissal, not because he was a pacifist but because he saw the futility of the alternative path despite the evidence provided by the three wars of unification that he himself had engineered.

Choosing to eschew military hegemony did not excuse Germany from the hard work of securing herself; indeed, in some ways it made it harder. Even if she did not pursue an expansionist course, she had no choice but to follow a politically interventionist one, in the sense of thickly entangling herself with her neighbors so that their interactions with one another did not develop in a direction that would endanger Germany. The essence of this policy was building alliances as instruments of management, restraint, and control, in order to shape the behavior of rivals in ways that would benefit Germany.[79]

LIMITING RIVALS' OPTIONS

Using alliances to manage the range of options available to a rival was not new. Metternich constructed the Quadruple Alliance in large part to restrict France's room for maneuver and hijacked the Holy Alliance into a mechanism for restraining Russia. But Austria's ability to use alliances in this fashion was always limited by her relative military weakness, which constantly put her in the position of either having to tag along or risk being bypassed. Bismarck, by contrast, presided over a great power that was capable of providing very meaningful assistance or resistance to her neighbors in the attainment of their desired objects. This created leverage, which Bismarck applied ingenuously, if not always scrupulously, to control neighbors.

Virtually every agreement to which Germany was a party or encouraged during Bismarck's tenure was centered on some form of control. The Three Emperors' League sought to bind Austria and Russia to obligations that limited their range of maneuver in the Balkans; the Dual Alliance gave Bismarck de facto veto power over Austrian policy in that same region; the Reinsurance Treaty restrained Russia's options vis-à-vis Austria; and the Mediterranean Agreements limited Britain's and Italy's options for aligning with France or Russia. What Germany got most through her treaties was the ability to exercise influence over other powers' actions while maintaining flexibility in her own. Short of being an island like Britain, this was the closest that a great power could get to a noncommittal foreign policy.

DEFLECTION PAR EXCELLENCE

Bismarck succeeded in a diplomacy of control because he consistently worked with, rather than against, the interests of other powers. His aim was not to see rivals defeated outright, which would only produce resentment, but to see their ambitions deflected to other objects that, while still desirable to themselves, were less threatening to Germany.

As we have seen, earlier great powers in history also used diplomacy to deflect rivals. But Bismarck brought these methods to a new level of ambition. His objective was to reorient Germany's neighbors outward from the European core and toward the periphery. To that end, he supported Russia in Central Asia, Britain in Egypt, and France in North Africa, while not allowing Germany to be pulled too deeply into this game. Deflection played to Germany's strength as a central power, in that she could offer something of value to her neighbors (protecting their continental flanks) so that they could turn attention elsewhere. Bismarck was perfectly willing to see Russia, Britain, and France come into colonial conflict as a result. But his primary aim was to divert Europe's antagonisms to areas that would be less consequential to the European balance of power. If there was going to be a fire, it was better that it occurred in Germany's back garden rather than her front parlor.

DIPLOMATIC BURDEN-SHIFTING

Bismarck excelled in the art of marshaling other states' efforts against a common enemy and thereby reducing risk for Germany. This was an especially useful discipline for a central power to master. What made the Mediterranean Agreements so extraordinary was that they effectively shifted the burden of defending Austria away from Germany—her main ally—toward two other states (Britain and Italy) with a less direct stake in Austria's preservation.

Germany's international interlocutors could see the burden-shifting logic of these arrangements as well: it was on that basis, after all, that Salisbury demanded an exposition of Germany's intentions toward Austria as a precondition to inking the Second Mediterranean Agreement. The reason the scheme succeeded is that when his bluff was called, Bismarck could produce convincing evidence, in the form of the text of the Dual Alliance, to demonstrate that Germany was *not* playing a double game. Bismarck's gambit worked, in other words, because it was rooted not in deception but in a genuine harmonization of interests. If it had been anything less, the arrangement would never have materialized.

THE LIMITS OF CONTROL

The pursuit of control that lay at the heart of Bismarck's diplomacy entailed both an inward-facing and outward-facing program. Bismarck used addresses to the Reichstag as a bully pulpit on matters of foreign policy to affect domestic politics and specific pieces of legislation, and to send messages to Germany's own generals as well as leaders in other capitals. In Bismarck's attempts to mold public opinion, we see the growing importance of media in an era of mass literacy, nationalism, and democracy. Bismarck's efforts to manipulate the press ultimately backfired, as foreign capitals came to reflexively discount anything emerging from government-friendly sources, even when it turned out to be an attempt at genuine strategic signaling.[80]

Secrecy was an outworking of control. It's obvious why Bismarck would favor secret diplomacy, given the complexity of arrangements that while perhaps not mutually contradictory in the deep particulars, would certainly seem to be so to the publics of Germany's rivals. Yet ironically, this very secrecy often worked to the disadvantage of his diplomacy. Had the terms of the Reinsurance Treaty been revealed to the generals at the time of its creation, it might have given pause to the war party in Vienna. Had the terms of the Dual Alliance been known to Britain, Salisbury might have been willing to enter into more specific commitments to Austria earlier than he did. Had Russia known about the Mediterranean Agreements, she might not have persisted with its war preparations in the fall of 1887. And had the nature of the casus foederis in Germany's alliance with Austria been known to both countries' own military men, they probably wouldn't have spent so much energy planning for a preventive war, with all of the attendant risks to European peace.

The biggest downside of Bismarck's diplomacy of control was the distrust that it bred among Germany's neighbors. Statesmen in other capitals could see Bismarck coquetting with one another but had a partial view, at most, of the aims of these maneuvers. In international affairs it is necessary to assume the worst. The extreme complexity and secrecy of Bismarck's machinations naturally begat fear.[81] This suspicion never fully went away, even after Bismarck's peaceful intentions were made manifest, and would only grow in the years after he left the scene.

The tragedy of Bismarck is that his efforts to keep the peace without resorting to military buildups and war ultimately fueled the dynamics that would lead to those outcomes. Bismarck's realism consisted in seeing that this tragedy was to some extent inevitable yet still preferable, for

Germany's security, to building a powerful military. His unrealism consisted in thinking that Europe's other powers could be manipulated by his cunning methods to such an extent that they would not react to his empire's underlying power potential. In this, Bismarck was, like Metternich, ultimately playing against the clock, not because he was leading a weak empire that would eventually be sidelined or subsumed, but because he was leading a *strong* empire that was probably bound to eventually unite everyone against herself. His "nightmare" of encircling coalitions could be deferred but not avoided. The accomplishment of his statecraft was to delay this outcome as long as he remained in power, which is the most that a statesman of any generation can hope for.

Bismarck's triumph following the Bulgarian crisis would be short-lived. Within a month of his February 6 speech to the Reichstag, Wilhelm I was dead. He was succeeded, after a short interval, by the strutting and insecure Wilhelm II. The same constitution that Bismarck had designed to make his position exclusively dependent upon the will of a decent and long-suffering emperor now subjected him to the whim of an emperor who was neither. Here at last was the menacing military empire that Europe had feared would arise from German unification. In response, Bismarck's "nightmare" quickly materialized, as Europe's great powers banded together to counterbalance German strength. When war finally came in 1914, Germany found herself embroiled, for the first time since Frederick the Great, in a war on two fronts.

In the history of diplomacy, Bismarck's Germany marks the arrival of a new kind of actor, capable of harnessing power politics to the national principle on a continental scale. Bismarck retained Metternich's methods of balancing and congress diplomacy but wielded them in the service of no higher end than the state. He demonstrated that, even in an era when military power promised to deliver previously unimaginable political outcomes, diplomacy could hold its own as an instrument of strategy alongside a bureaucratically empowered military, and that it was capable of securing the state at an affordable cost, even in the era of bolt-action rifles, telegraphs and railways. He reconfirmed that diplomacy's core function remained conservative and defensive in an age of changing politics, technologies, and power relationships.

It was probably inevitable that a great power of Germany's vast latent strength, impetuous generals, and anchorless political class would elicit a defensive reaction from her neighbors. But it was not inevitable that Germany's leaders would throw away the advantages of Bismarck's system so abruptly and choose offensive war as the solution to their country's dilemmas. In the end, Bismarck's system failed not so much because his successors didn't understand it but because they rejected it, opting instead for a simpler and seemingly more dignified military-intensive security. That Bismarck's successors didn't succeed in dominating Europe is largely due to the successors of Lord Salisbury, to whom our attention now turns.

CHAPTER SEVEN

The Octopus

Ententes may vanish—battleships remain the surest pledges this country can give for the continued peace of the world.

—ADMIRAL JACKIE FISHER

I am gradually coming round to the opinion that we must alter our foreign policy, and throw our lot in, for good or bad, with some other Power. . . . Our interests being so extended makes it almost impossible for us to concentrate sufficiently, in any one direction, the pressure and power of the Empire so as to deter foreign nations from trying to encroach upon our interests in that particular quarter.

—LORD GEORGE HAMILTON

A FEW DAYS before Christmas 1901, Britain's aging prime minister, Lord Robert Cecil, third Marquess of Salisbury, notified King Edward VII that his government would shortly conclude a treaty of mutual defense with the Empire of Japan. The prospect of entering into the country's first peacetime alliance in ages did not fill Salisbury with joy. For years, the famously reclusive Tory statesman had presided over an avowedly noncommittal foreign policy. When it came to alliances, Salisbury once explained to a German diplomat, the British were an altogether more slippery kind of animal: *"Nous sommes des poissons"*—we are fish.[1]

But times were changing. As the 19th Century drew to a close, Britain found the geopolitical gameboard increasingly tilted against her. The country's main rivals, France and Russia, had recently formed an alliance. The new German Empire had embarked upon an ambitious program of shipbuilding and colonial acquisition. And further afield, the United States and Japan were emerging as major players in their own right, with blue-water navies and aspirations to dominate their respective regions.

Individually, none of these powers was a match for the British Empire. But collectively, they outstripped it in industrial and naval power. With the British army bogged down in a long and grinding war in South Africa, Britain's rivals had ample opportunity to scheme against her in other quarters. Even if they never congealed into a hostile bloc, the presence of so many powerful states at so many points on the compass created the prospect of a multifront dilemma well beyond the country's ability to manage.

Britain, in short, needed friends. And to achieve that, she would have to move away from Salisbury's old approach. Already, Britain had negotiated a new treaty with the United States that allowed her to draw down naval strength in the Western Hemisphere. The proposed treaty with Japan, it was hoped, would similarly lighten Britain's defensive burdens in the Far East. There was even talk of reaching an understanding with one or more of the European great powers.

Salisbury had mixed feelings about all of this. A pessimist to the core, he foresaw a dark future in which Britain would find herself bound by inflexible treaties that would suck her into other countries' wars. "There is no limit: and no escape," he wrote. "We are pledged to war."[2]

But Salisbury's time was passing. A new generation of British leaders was coming onto the scene, determined to push him aside, end Britain's "isolation," and embark upon a more vigorous foreign policy aimed at shoring up Britain's defenses and safeguarding her vulnerable empire. Within a few months, Salisbury would step down as prime minister, and a year after that he would be dead. With astonishing speed, the men who replaced him would alter the course of British policy, engineering a diplomatic revolution every bit as daring as Kaunitz's had been, but on a worldwide scale. In the space of just six years, they would convert four of their empire's five rivals, including two of its oldest enemies, into partners or allies. As a result of their labors, it would be Britain's most dangerous adversary, Germany, that would be encumbered with the dangers of a multifront war, when the long-expected global conflagration finally came.

Empire of the Sea

A time traveler to Salisbury's day would have been surprised to learn that Britain needed help of any kind, from anyone. The maps that adorned the walls of English primary schools showed a planet painted pink in British territories. These radiated outward from the British home islands like the tentacles of a huge octopus: westward across the Atlantic to Canada and the Pacific; southward, down the spine of Africa to Natal and the Southern Ocean; and southeast, through the Mediterranean and the Suez Canal to India, Singapore, and Australia.[3]

In the final years of Queen Victoria's reign, the British Empire ruled a quarter of the world's people and almost as high a proportion of its surface area. Its population was larger than those of the next four great powers combined, it accounted for nearly a quarter of global trade, and it produced more steel than all of mainland Europe. The volume of securities on the London Stock Exchange exceeded those of the New York and Paris exchanges combined. British companies owned more than half of the world's shipping, two-thirds of its telegraph cables, and a large proportion of its railways.[4]

Backing Britain's position was the world's most powerful fleet. By the late years of the 19th Century, the tonnage of warships in the Royal Navy outmatched those of France, Russia, and the United States together. From 1889 onward, British governments adhered to a formal policy—the so-called Two Power Standard—maintaining a navy at least as big as those of the next two most powerful states combined. By 1900 an astonishing 40 percent of capital ships worldwide flew under the British ensign, backed by a globe-girdling array of overseas ports and coaling stations and the 125,000 native troops of the Indian Raj.

Britain's accumulation of this formidable maritime empire had been possible because her leaders carefully limited the country's involvement in the affairs of the nearby mainland. When a powerful neighbor attempted to conquer Europe, Britain would use her navy and vast wealth to organize coalitions among the Continent's weaker powers and restore the balance of power. But when each war ended, she would return her focus to empire-building. By doing so, Britain had been able to avoid the costs of maintaining a large standing army and grow rich on her overseas territories.[5]

By Victoria's reign, this strategy was at its peak. The long decades of peace under Klemens von Metternich's congress system allowed Britain to expand her holdings in Africa and Asia without worrying about a major threat closer to home. Under Lord Salisbury, Britain was said, not altogether accurately, to abide by a policy of "splendid isolation."[6] Salisbury had been a young foreign secretary at the time of Otto von Bismarck's Berlin Congress in 1878. Over the succeeding three decades, he led three governments, in two of which he held the posts of premier and foreign minister concurrently.[7]

Salisbury was no isolationist. He was a realist who believed in a vigilant, if circumspect, promotion of the national interest. What he objected to

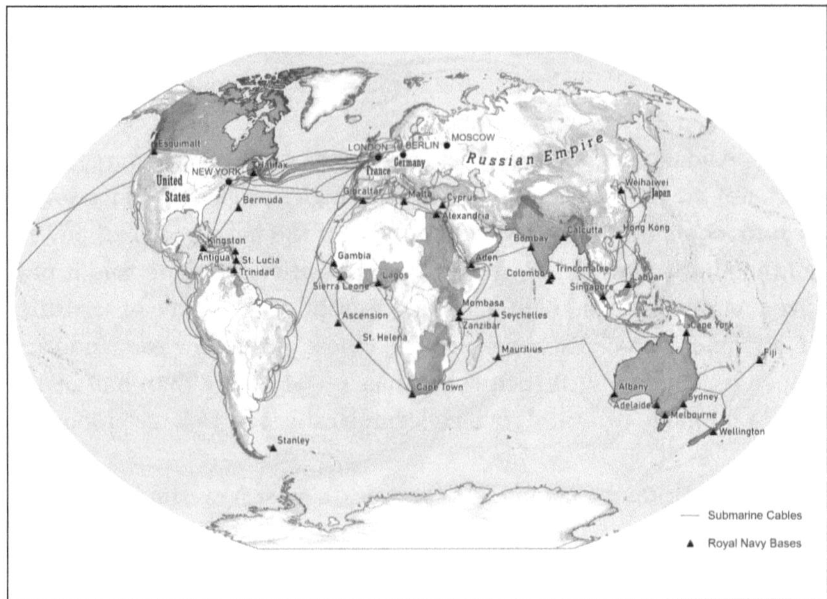

FIGURE 7.1. The British Empire in the reign of Edward VII
(Credit: Andrew Rhodes)

was not international commitments per se, but speculative undertakings that tied Britain's hands with respect to future events that were inherently unknowable. Glacial, dyspeptic, and aloof, he had a studied preference for inaction. "Whatever happens will be for the worse," he once remarked, so "it is in our interests that as little should happen as possible."[8]

Salisbury's instincts aligned well with the traditional tenets of British grand strategy. Over a two-decade period, he conducted a conservative program of diplomacy that adroitly managed—and exploited—European rivalries. His signature technique was to appease France and Germany with concessions in regions that held low value to British strategic interests.[9] Through such methods he had been able to support a stable balance in Europe without allowing Britain to be pulled into either of the continent's hardening alliance blocs.

Salisbury's diplomacy brought the British world system to its pinnacle. During his tenure, Britain stayed out of successive European crises while acquiring 4.25 million square miles of new territories and roughly doubling her overseas assets.[10] All of this was achieved while maintaining a low burden on British taxpayers, with government spending not exceeding 10 percent of the gross national product or taxes going over a shilling on the pound.[11]

The Edwardian Predicament

Britain's heyday didn't last. By the final years of Queen Victoria's reign and the early years of her son Edward VII's, there were growing signs that the favorable conditions the empire had long enjoyed were giving way to a more crowded, complicated, and dangerous international situation.

Some of the problems were old and familiar. The empire's main rivals, France and Russia, were expanding their navies and seeking new colonial acquisitions. Imperial Germany was quickly catching up in industrial output and, in 1898, took the first in a series of steps toward building a blue-water navy. But new forces were also appearing on the scene. Across the Atlantic, the United States was beginning to shift her energies from the conquest of America's western frontier to international power projection. And in the Far East, Japan was emerging from her long period of feudal introspection to become a major regional power.

Britain had faced fluid power environments before. But this time was different. The world's great empty spaces were "filling up," and everyone suddenly seemed to want a bigger navy.[12] In 1890 a U.S. naval officer named Alfred Thayer Mahan wrote an influential book arguing that a large fleet was a prerequisite to global power status.[13] A few years later, a British geographer named Harold Mackinder wrote an article warning that Britain would find it harder to maintain maritime dominance against Eurasian competitors who were capable of pulling huge land mases under their control.[14] Unlike in previous eras, Britain in the early years of the 20th Century would be faced with continent-sized rivals possessing fleets as big as, or possibly bigger than, her own.

The dangers of Britain's position were driven home by her involvement, from 1899 onward, in a vexing colonial war in South Africa. What began as an attempt to quell an insurrection by Dutch farmers in the Transvaal morphed into a prolonged ordeal that would absorb the attention of half a million British and imperial troops. Comparable in its effects on Britain's psyche to the later American experience in Vietnam, the Boer War brought Britain's traditional system of strategy to the breaking point.

Coming at a time of escalating dangers worldwide, the Boer War showed just how thinly stretched British power had become. Should Russia decide to attack India or France make a determined push up the Nile, Britain would be hard-pressed to repel them. Worse, the war created the possibility that the major powers of Europe might combine their navies to threaten the British home islands. In any of these scenarios, a major move by one rival was almost certain to inspire others to follow suit, with the potential for simultaneous crises in multiple regions that would be well beyond the navy's capacity to handle.

Faced with these dilemmas, British leaders had two options: they could either expand the size of the navy so that it could handle the threat of three or even four major opponents, or they could find a way to reduce the number of active rivals against which the navy had to contend.[15]

The first path was Britain's initial instinct. But it was also the least practical. As the first lord of the Admiralty, Lord Selborne put it bluntly at the beginning of 1901:

> Hitherto the policy of this country has been stated to be so to build battleships as to maintain an equality of numbers with the combined battleships of the two powers possessing for the moment the largest fleets. It does not seem to me that this basis of calculation is one that will any longer serve, considering that within the last five years three new navies have sprung into existence—those of the United States, Germany and Japan. It is certain that it would be a hopeless task to attempt to achieve an equality with the three largest navies; but I go further, and say that, if the United States continue their present naval policy and develop their navy as they are easily capable of developing it if they choose, it will be scarcely possible for us to raise our navy to a strength equal to [even] that of France and the United States combined.[16]

The reason for Selborne's pessimism was money. Already, in keeping with the two-power standard, Britain maintained a fleet of twenty-two capital ships against a combined French-Russian total of fifteen. To keep pace with the United States and Germany, Britain would at a minimum have needed to expand its main battle fleet by an additional six ships, which would have required a budget increase of more than 40 percent.[17] The costs in the long run would have been considerably more than Britain was accustomed to spending and beyond what her politicians envisioned as a reasonable tax burden.[18] Adopting "a four-power standard or three-power standard" was not only undesirable, Selborne wrote to the cabinet, it was "impossible."[19]

In these circumstances, the only viable option was to alleviate the pressures on the Royal Navy by diplomatic means. Selborne and other senior naval officials were outspoken proponents of doing exactly that. In a letter dated September 2, 1901, Admiral Walter Kerr, the first naval lord, wrote:

> It has been pressing itself upon me for some time past, that with the immense growth of navies that is now going on and the great strides being made on all sides in creating naval power, that our hitherto

followed policy of "splendid isolation" may no longer be possible and that great as the disadvantages in other ways may be, an understanding with other Powers may be forced upon us. . . . The strain which is being put upon our naval resources with all our wide world interests is, in view of the feverish developments of other nations, being subjected to a heavier strain than they can well bear . . . and any relief that can in reason be obtained would be most welcome.[20]

That same fall, Selborne wrote to the cabinet that he was "strongly in favor of concentrating" Britain's naval strength "as far as possible," even if that meant finding partners to take up the slack in the Far East.[21] The following spring, the Admiralty communicated a similar message to Britain's Colonial Office, noting that "in view of the great development which is taking place in certain Foreign Navies, it has become necessary . . . to concentrate more than is the case at present the Naval force in commission."[22]

The Admiralty's logic was impeccable: if the navy could no longer safely assume numerical superiority over Britain's foreseeable opponents, then it needed to focus its strength on the places that mattered most, which were the British home islands and the Mediterranean. To do that, the country would have to accept greater risks in other, less vital places, and the job of British diplomacy would be to mitigate those risks. The end of Britain's diplomatic "isolation," in other words, followed axiomatically from the end of her worldwide naval supremacy. To cope with the dangerous new world situation, Britain would have to do what her leaders had effectively avoided in preceding decades: they would have to pick sides.

The "Little Man"

In making the case for using diplomacy to lighten the navy's burdens, Britain's top sailors were pushing on an open door. The country's civilian leaders were increasingly of the same mind. The "khaki" election of 1900 elevated the voices of a new generation of leaders who were determined to jettison Salisbury's cautious method and take a fresh approach to foreign policy.[23] These included members of a breakaway faction from the Liberal Party, known as the Liberal Unionists, who had been in coalition with the Conservatives since 1895 and now found themselves heavily represented in the new cabinet.[24] Selborne was part of this group of hawks, as was the illustrious colonial secretary, Joseph Chamberlain, a self-made industrialist and former mayor of Birmingham who, it was widely assumed, would someday be prime minister.[25]

The member of this group who would do the most to shape the new course in Britain diplomacy was the least remarkable of the lot. The selection of Charles Henry Keith Petty-Fitzmaurice, 5th Marquess of Lansdowne, to succeed Salisbury as foreign secretary in the fall of 1900 came as a surprise to the British establishment.[26] A shy, anemic-looking man in his mid-fifties, Lansdowne had served as secretary of state for war during the worst disasters of the Boer War. Queen Victoria hadn't liked him, and neither did her son Edward VII, who described Lansdowne as "not a clever man . . . not clever at all."[27] The idea that such a person could fill the shoes of the great Salisbury was met with derision in the British newspapers, which called Lansdowne's appointment a "first-rate joke" and ran cartoons depicting him as an effeminate fop whose only qualifications were "a knowledge of French and an amiable disposition."[28]

With his appointment as foreign secretary, Lansdowne was stepping into British officialdom's most exclusive club. The Foreign Office at the turn of the century was an elite institution that reflected, in its composition and mindset, the attributes of a mature world empire in its late prime.[29] By the end of Salisbury's tenure, the Foreign Office's political section consisted of around fifty personnel divided into six departments corresponding roughly to the world's major regions.[30] At the top stood the powerful permanent undersecretary, the ranking civil servant, and beneath him, three assistant undersecretaries with authority over one or more of the regional bureaus.

What made the Foreign Office so powerful was not its size but its culture and knowledge base. Foreign Office officials had gone to the same top schools, were members of the same clubs, and shared a similar worldview. The resulting institution was traditional in outlook, rigid in procedure, and highly literate in expression. Critics called it the "Foreign Office mind." But it equipped Britain with a "way of thinking" with which to detect dangers and opportunities in "the fast-flowing stream of international politics."[31] More than a collection of paper-pushers, the Foreign Office represented Britain's accumulated institutional memory as a great power: the "digestive organ" by which events could be conceptualized against the basis of Britain's past experiences, and translated into practical policy.

Foreign secretaries enjoyed considerable autonomy in the formulation and execution of foreign policy.[32] At the time Lansdowne assumed his post, the Foreign Office still bore the imprint of Salisbury's long years of dominance in British foreign policy, which had been characterized by neglect of day-to-day details and a certain degree of detachment from events in the further reaches of the empire.[33] One individual who had flourished in this permissive environment was Sir Francis Bertie, a smart but irascible career bureaucrat who had amassed a greater degree of influence over British foreign policy than his nominal boss, the undersecretary, Sir Thomas Sanderson. Churlish, territorial, and domineering, Bertie disliked Lansdowne—the "little man," as he called him—and had very different conceptions of how the Foreign Office should be run, both with respect to personnel and policy.[34]

Despite the challenges arrayed against him, however, Lansdowne would prove to be a surprisingly effective foreign secretary. The same quiet reserve and lack of ego that made him a laughingstock in the press also made him a good listener and, as it turned out, leader and diplomatist.[35] By the time he became foreign secretary, Lansdowne had served as governor-general of Canada and viceroy of India—postings that gave him insights into just how vulnerable the empire had become at its outermost frontiers.[36]

These experiences made Lansdowne more capable than most of his cabinet colleagues of taking in the big picture. It is under Lansdowne's tenure that the Foreign Office would become more deeply integrated into what would today be called an interagency process with Britain's defense and intelligence establishments.[37] Lansdowne saw in diplomacy an instrument for alleviating Britain's global burden, not by joining one of Europe's alliance networks outright but by ameliorating difficulties with as many rivals as possible. As he would remark late in his tenure, "In these times, no nation which intends to take its part in the affairs of the civilized world can venture to stand entirely alone."[38]

The End of "Isolation"

Like his colleagues, Lansdowne was determined to reexamine Salisbury's approach to the world. It wasn't only the dangers that had been revealed by recent crises or the navy's urgent appeals for diplomatic relief. It was the old man's style. Time and time again, Salisbury was willing to give ground to Britain's rivals without getting much in return. In previous years, he had sat by while the French scooped up Madagascar and the Germans grabbed a chunk of East Africa. Channeling the frustrations of other hawks in the cabinet, Lord Curzon, Britain's viceroy in India, compared Salisbury's methods to "throwing bones to different dogs to keep them quiet" while the dogs "devoured the bones and snarled for more."[39]

This was appeasement, and it was not a new thing in British foreign policy.[40] As far back as the 1860s, British statesmen had engaged in the practice of managing foreign disputes by "admitting and satisfying

FIGURE 7.2. The "little man": Lord Lansdowne (Credit: Hum Images / Alamy)

grievances through rational negotiation and compromise, thereby avoiding the resort to an armed conflict which would be expensive, bloody, and possibly very dangerous."[41] This had been Salisbury's main method, and that of Gladstone before him, for avoiding confrontations in far-off parts of the world and, in particular, for preserving Britain's precarious position in Egypt.[42]

Lansdowne and his colleagues were not averse to appeasement in principle; indeed, their subsequent methods continued the tradition. What they objected to was a policy of appeasement that did not yield lasting strategic benefits by alleviating the multifront pressures bearing down on Britain. What they wanted, to use Curzon's canine analogy, was to tame some part of the pack of "dogs" circling their empire so that Britain could focus her attention on the most dangerous predators.

The question was which animals to collar and which to confront.[43] Lansdowne's preference was to befriend Britain's most powerful European rival. Coming into office, his one "preconceived idea" was that Britain "should make every effort to maintain, and, if we can, to strengthen" relations with Germany.[44]

British leaders had been flirting with this idea for a while. Two months before Lansdowne came to office, Britain's outspoken colonial secretary, Joseph Chamberlain, had circulated a memo arguing that Britain should reach an understanding with Germany in the Far East, paid for by British territorial concessions, with a view to an eventual alliance.[45] With time, he hoped to develop similar understandings with the United States and Japan. The resulting three-legged stool, with Britain as the center, would allow her to reposition warships from western and eastern waters to the Mediterranean in the assurance that German land power would pin down Russian and French forces in the event of a European war.

After arriving at the Foreign Office, Lansdowne eagerly took up the task of courting Germany while working on parallel secret tracks to improve ties with the United States and Japan.

The first of these was a particular priority for Lansdowne. Anglo-American relations were strained by a number of old boundary disputes in North America.[46] Lansdowne directed Britain's diplomats to resolve these disagreements, even if it meant making the bulk of the concessions. These efforts bore early fruit in the Hay-Pauncefote Treaty, signed in November 1901, which formalized Britain's recognition of exclusive U.S. control of the Isthmus of Panama. The significance of this agreement was that it signaled, in effect, Britain's abandonment of the Western Hemisphere as a strategic concern and acknowledgement of U.S. supremacy over nearly half of the world's surface area.[47]

Lansdowne's efforts with Japan proceeded at a similarly expeditious pace. His first instinct was to engage Japan jointly with Germany, but he was brought around to the idea of a bilateral Anglo-Japanese defensive pact by advocates in the Admiralty, Treasury, and Foreign Office.[48] As Francis Bertie argued at the time, "If we do nothing to encourage Japan to look to us as a friend and possible ally against Russia and France, we may drive her to a policy of despair, in which she may come to some sort of terms with Russia."[49]

Lansdowne's talks with Japan's man in London, Baron Tadashu Hayashi, yielded a draft agreement that was presented to the cabinet in early November and, after some modifications to limit Japan's scope for offensive action, resulted in a formal agreement between the two countries in January 1902.[50] The treaty committed both countries to neutrality in the event that either was attacked by a single opponent and mutual aid if there were two attackers. This formula favored Britain, insofar as it met the central requirement of supplementing British naval strength in eastern waters without obliging it to come to Japan's aid in the not-so-unlikely event that she went to war with Russia over Korea. In effect, Lansdowne had outsourced the security of the British Empire's most exposed Far Eastern possessions to a non-European power.

No Third Leg

Lansdowne had less success improving ties with Germany. The obstacles to this goal were less obvious than they would become in later years, once the effects of the steady buildup of naval power that Germany initiated a couple of years earlier began to be felt.[51] Early signs were positive, as the two countries had little difficulty reaching an agreement to coordinate policy in China. Under the Yangtze Agreement of October 1900 Britain and Germany pledged "not to take advantage of the present complications to obtain for themselves any territorial advantages in China," including by ensuring that the ports and rivers of the country's coastal areas remained "free and open to trade."[52]

For a moment it looked like this agreement might pave the way to something more ambitious. But it was not to be. The first indication of trouble came when the German chancellor, Bernhard von Bülow, declared in the Reichstag in March 1901 that Germany had no intention of honoring its commitments to Britain in the East, for fear of upsetting Russia.[53]

Unfazed, Lansdowne continued his quest for an understanding of some kind. He found a willing co-conspirator in the new German ambassador to England, Count Hatzfeldt, who in May of that year intimated to Lansdowne that Britain should join the German-led Triple Alliance. In the confused conversations that followed, it quickly became apparent that Hatzfeldt was ahead of his skis. The underlying impediment was not the question of the geographic scope of a deal or what should constitute its casus foederis but the nature of the power relationship between the two parties. Surveying Britain's global predicament, German leaders concluded that Britain needed an alliance much more than Germany did, and that the island power's difficulties would only raise the price that Berlin could demand as time passed.[54]

The German mindset was reflected in Hatzfeldt's conversations with Lansdowne. As Lansdowne described one such interaction to the cabinet:

> Were we, he asked, prepared to continue our present *"isolement"*? We must be alive to the dangers which it invoked. If we recognized them, it was for our interest to join one of the two great groups into which the European Powers were divided. We might try Russia if we liked, *"mais cela vous coutera cher"* [it will cost you dearly]. As for Germany, if nothing should come of these overtures, she might find herself obliged to look elsewhere for alliances. He begged that I would not consider that when he said this he was using the language of menace.[55]

Instead of whetting London's appetite for a deal, these tactics had the opposite effect. The problem wasn't only one of style; German diplomats had overplayed their hand. "The liability of having to defend the German and Austrian frontiers against Russia is heavier than that of *having to defend the British Isles against France*," Salisbury wrote in a last blast of forensic vigor. "Even, therefore, in its most naked aspect the bargain would be a bad one for this country."[56] Building on this theme, Bertie wrote a lengthy memorandum demolishing Berlin's analysis of the underlying power dynamic:

> The German government lay stress on the danger to England of isolation, and enlarge on the advantages to her to be secured by an alliance with Germany . . . but in considering offers of alliance from Germany it is necessary to . . . bear in mind the position of Germany in Europe as regards France and Russia. . . . Germany is in a dangerous situation in Europe. She is surrounded by Governments who distrust her and people who dislike or at all events do not like her. . . . In these circumstances it is essential for the German Government to endeavor to obtain the certainty of armed support from England for the contingency of an attack on Germany by France and Russia combined, for if England be not bound to Germany and His Majesty's Government come to a general understanding with France and Russia . . . the position of Germany in Europe will become critical.[57]

Bertie's reasoning was sound. Both Germany and Britain faced the problem of a future war on more than one front. But Germany would feel this pressure much more acutely because she was a land power. Losing in Asia or Africa would hurt Britain much less than losing on the Rhine or Vistula would hurt Germany. The astute assistant undersecretary had put his finger on the central flaw in German diplomatic strategy, which was predicated on the assumption that Britain lacked alliance options if Germany said no. But Britain's options were manifest in Germany's own predicament. If Britain said no, what were Germany's options?

Courting Old Foes

Lansdowne was disappointed by the failure of his "one preconceived idea," but he remained determined to alleviate Britain's global burden.[58] While the arrangements with Japan and the United States had eased demands on the Royal Navy, there was still a real danger that Britain could find herself in a war across multiple regions against Russia and France simultaneously. Lansdowne wanted to go straight to the source and broker a thaw with Russia, but mounting tensions between her and Japan, Britain's new ally, made that difficult.[59]

That left France. The value of defusing tensions with Britain's ancient foe grew more apparent in the early 1900s as both countries worried about being pulled into a war with one another in the event that their respective allies, Japan and Russia, came to blows in the Far East.

The sequence of events that led to the Anglo-French entente cordiale began with a visit by King Edward VII to Paris in May 1903. By summer, Lansdowne and his French counterpart, Théophile Delcassé, were in talks about ameliorating a broad range of colonial disputes. The mood was amicable from the start, with Lansdowne telling the French that if they would "put their cards upon the table and say what they wished to obtain, and what they were prepared to concede with that object, we should be ready to meet them in a similar spirit."[60]

What began as separate tracks of talks on Newfoundland fisheries, the Moroccan constitution, and Siamese rivers merged into an effort at a "comprehensive settlement."[61] By the end of the year—about the same amount of time it had taken for Anglo-German talks to collapse—the contours of a grand bargain had been reached. In the resulting agreement, signed on April 8, 1904, Britain and France recognized one another's positions in Egypt and Morocco respectively and agreed to resolve a slew of old boundary disputes in West Africa, the Atlantic, and Southeast Asia.[62]

One reason things moved so quickly was that Lansdowne's effort enjoyed the support of the bureaucracy. Francis Bertie and other "young Turks" in the Foreign Office saw the deal with France as a way to counterbalance Germany.[63]

Not surprisingly, the French felt the same way. As Lansdowne reported at the end of one conversation, his French interlocutor "expressed his belief that . . . a good understanding between France and England was the only means of holding German designs in check, and that if such an understanding could be arrived at, England would find that France would be able to exercise a salutary influence over Russia and thereby relieve us from many of our troubles with that country."[64]

The episode highlights the difference in negotiating styles between Germany and France. France's diplomats formulated a desired end point corresponding to their chief need—relief from the German danger—and worked toward that object indirectly, by emphasizing their ability to help Britain with *her* chief problem, which was the danger from Russia. Germany's diplomats proceeded from the premise that Britain's position was inherently unsustainable and sought to frighten Britain away from Russia without bothering to posit an attainable end point.

In the event, Russia's defeat in the long-awaited war with Japan, which broke out while Anglo-French talks were underway, transformed the prospects for an Anglo-Russian understanding. The destruction of the Russian fleet at Tsushima in May 1905 dramatically altered the naval balance of power, effectively removing Russia from the ranks of top-tier sea powers.

The danger was that in Russia's fragile condition, she might be sucked into Germany's orbit. Writing to Lansdowne in the final phases of the Russo-Japanese war, Britain's ambassador in St. Petersburg noted with alarm the "restless spirit and feverish energy" with which Kaiser Wilhelm was courting the tsar.[65] The remedy, as diplomats from both countries could see, was to develop an "all-round settlement of outstanding questions" on the Anglo-French model, with a particular emphasis on reducing tensions in Central Asia.[66]

It was under the subsequent Liberal government and during the tenure of Lansdowne's successor, Sir Edward Grey, that the two empires finally settled their accounts. The Anglo-Russian Convention, signed in August 1907, was essentially a bundle of compartmentalized territorial deals corresponding to the two powers' main areas of disagreement in Central Asia. Persia was divvied up into spheres of influence, while both powers foreswore expansion in Tibet, and, most importantly from Britain's perspective, Russia acknowledged Afghanistan as an exclusively British concern.[67] While Lansdowne did not stay in office long enough to see the outcome, it was the outworking of his policy of sustained, constructive diplomatic engagement with Britain's rivals.

Lansdowne's Tally

It would be hard to exaggerate what British diplomacy accomplished, or set in motion, during Lansdowne's tenure. In the space of about seven years, Britain concluded agreements with four of the five powers that had worried her leaders at the time of the Boer War. The treaties with the United States, Russia, and France addressed decades-old disputes in a dozen regions across three continents. Two of the powers in question were Britain's oldest rivals, with pedigrees of hostility stretching back a century (in Russia's case) and a millennium (in France's case).

The benefits for Britain's strategic position were immediate. First and most consequentially, Lansdowne's diplomacy facilitated the concentration of naval power that Selborne had argued was imperative without undertaking ruinous financial outlays. The deals with the United States allowed Britain to shutter three of her nine overseas naval stations, while the one with Japan allowed Britain to pare back her fleet assets in Far Eastern waters and reorient strategic attention to the European theater. It was thanks to these arrangements that a new first sea lord, Sir Jackie Fisher, was subsequently able to implement his famous worldwide redistribution of British naval power in the period leading up to World War I.[68] Without Lansdowne's diplomacy, that would not have been possible.

Less commented upon, though no less significant, is the salutary effect that Lansdowne's diplomacy had in actually keeping Britain out of a multifront war in this period. It was far from clear at the time, for example, that Britain would avoid a military confrontation with the United States; indeed, such a clash between rising and declining powers was logical to assume on the historical pattern. More obviously, the deals with France and Russia addressed what had been the most vexing ulcers of late Victorian grand strategy: Egypt and Central Asia, both of which had generated serious war scares in years prior. The Anglo-French entente ensured that the Russo-Japanese war remained localized, while the Anglo-Russian understanding helped reduce tensions in Central Asia that remained elevated even after Russia's defeat by Japan.[69]

Britain derived these benefits without, at least initially, taking on onerous new commitments. The deal with Japan was carefully framed to keep Britain out of that country's subsequent war with Russia. In the Russian and French cases, the template that Britain used for cementing cooperation was something more than an exchange of diplomatic notes but less than a formal military alliance. An entente was like a public flirtation, a whispering in the ear and wink of the eye, attended by the salving of old wounds—or as Lansdowne conceived it, "a declaration of common policy and a desire to maintain close diplomatic relations."[70] Such a formula could be pursued without an unmanageable contradiction with the goal of also trying to alleviate tension with Germany, as indeed Lansdowne attempted to do throughout his tenure.

Yet inevitably for diplomacy on such a scale, Lansdowne's deals carried costs. Each came at the expense of British concessions. In North America, Britain lost any hopes of stopping the Panama Canal, which its naval planners rightly foresaw would forever alter the balance of power in the Atlantic. In the Far East, Britain tacitly conceded the status of top naval power to an Asiatic state without a long-term plan for regaining her position there. With France, Britain gave up any hopes of becoming the dominant power in a large swath of northern and equatorial Africa. With Russia, she foreswore suzerainty over Tibet, long an object of British desire, and, as Curzon later complained, "handed over to Russia not only the trade route from Baghdad but also the important marts of Isphahan and Yezd."[71]

This ledger of debits has led some modern historians to wonder if Britain's diplomacy of this period didn't in fact get it wrong. One scholar has argued that by coming to terms with Russia and France, Britain abnegated her vocation as conservator of the tottering Austro-Hungarian and Ottoman empires, thereby undermining the stability of the European system.[72] Another holds, more damningly, that by operating on the logic of appeasing those rivals most capable of threatening its Empire, Britain gave up her historic role of holding the balance of power, estranging Germany and setting the stage for World War I.[73]

These critics ask too much of British diplomacy, insofar as they expect statesmen at the time to have been more concerned with long-term questions of order than the immediate needs of British national security. That dictated that the number of active threats facing the empire be reduced to a number that could be managed with available naval and financial resources. Britain had to free up bandwidth to focus on the preservation of her most vital interests; to have done otherwise would have courted disaster. For what would it profit the world's greatest empire if she held the "marts of Isphahan and Yezd" but lost the Mediterranean or North Sea? Developing an achievable framework for safeguarding the latter at a reasonable cost in places like the former was the central requirement of British diplomacy, and achieving it was no mean feat. In this, Lansdowne's deals must be judged a success.

Lansdowne never abandoned the aim of friendship with Germany. "I wish to raise my voice against the assumption," he told a group of young conservatives in one of his last speeches as foreign secretary, that "there must necessarily be an estrangement between ourselves and [Germany]. This suggestion seems to me to proceed upon the altogether untenable theory that the stock of international good will . . . is so limited that if a certain amount of it has been served out there is none left for any of those who may afterwards apply for it."[74] A diplomat to the end, he believed a deal could and eventually would be reached as long as goodwill prevailed.

Subsequent events would show that Lansdowne put too much stock in British goodwill and perhaps too little in German steel production. Once constructed, the German high seas fleet would, by itself, require all of Britain's considerable energies to handle. When war came in 1914, Britain was able to concentrate on this preeminent danger only because peace had been made with her other rivals. The fact that, at this moment of peril, Britain was spared the burden of a war against rivals on multiple fronts, and that her adversary was afflicted, and doomed, by that same burden is a testament to the skill of Lansdowne's diplomacy. The fact that the foreign secretary achieved that effect without giving up on his hope of improved ties with Germany is a testament to his humanity.

Appeasement Redux

Lansdowne's nobleness of spirit was palpably present a generation later, when another British leader, just as humane but a good deal more cheeseparing, returned home from a mission of peace that hinged on the logic of appeasement. The situation facing the British Empire in the autumn of 1938 was much bleaker than it had been in Lansdowne's time, but the strategic circumstances were depressingly similar. Once again, Britain was confronted with the prospect of a global war on multiple fronts. Once again, rumors of war in the Far East raised doubts about the Royal Navy's ability to safeguard the tenuous sinews connecting England with her empire. Once again, British diplomats found themselves across the table from a coy and menacing Germany, now filled with hateful animus and much further along in war preparations. And once again, the world appeared to be heading into another great conflagration.

This time, however, it seemed that diplomacy would save the day. Today we remember the piece of paper that Neville Chamberlain waved on the tarmac at the Heston Aerodrome after returning home from his meeting with Adolf Hitler in Munich as a symbol of craven surrender and the prelude to the greatest conflict in human history. But it didn't appear that way to onlookers at the time. To the British public, most of whom had lost menfolk in the Great War, the Munich Agreement seemed to promise salvation from a second carnage. To Britain's elite, it seemed to offer redemption for the harsh terms that they regretted imposing on Germany after the previous war. Most of all, the Munich Agreement seemed to show that the eminently English virtues of fair play and reasonableness could indeed bring about "peace in our time."

Chamberlain's efforts to appease Hitler were welcomed by most of Britain's top military men, for the same reason that their predecessors had welcomed Lansdowne's diplomatic deals two decades earlier. Unlike the pacifists, British strategists weren't motivated by guilt, nor were they under any illusions that Nazi grievances could be satiated. Rather, like Selborne in his day, they hoped that diplomatic maneuver could relieve the multifront pressures on their beleaguered empire—perhaps not on as grand a scale as the 1904 and 1907 ententes, but with a similar logic, of allowing Britain to husband her strength for the eventual, inevitable struggle. What Britain needed from her diplomats in 1938, even more than in Lansdowne's era, was time. And that's exactly what Chamberlain's mission to Munich seemed, for a glimmering but transient moment, to have achieved.

Postwar Pinnacle

The dystopian landscape facing Britain in the fall of 1938 was a far cry from the world that had seemed to be taking shape just two decades earlier, in the aftermath of World War I. Like all the major combatants, Britain had suffered horrendously in that conflict. But more than any other Allied nation, she had benefited from the peace that followed.[75]

Under the terms agreed at the Paris Peace Conference in the summer of 1919, the German and Ottoman empires were disassembled, and big chunks, including choice portions of Africa and the Middle East, were transferred to Britain. A year earlier, the German High Seas Fleet and the bulk of the German merchant fleet had been handed over, like poker winnings. At war's end, the Royal Navy possessed forty-two dreadnoughts, while the rest of the world combined had forty-four—giving Britain the widest margin of naval superiority in her history.[76]

On paper, Britain's strategic situation had never been better. Virtually all of the old imperial dilemmas were abated. France was too weak to ever again mount a bid for European hegemony. Russia was paralyzed by civil war and incapable of threatening India. Critically for a world switching from coal to petroleum, Britain now controlled the planet's richest oil-producing lands. In Europe, friend and foe alike were debtors to the Bank of England.[77]

More than anyone, Britain had her fiery liberal prime minister, David Lloyd George, to thank for the outcomes at Paris.[78] Lloyd George didn't like or trust diplomats. The war, he believed, had shown that only elected leaders—men of the people, like himself—could be entrusted with the execution of foreign policy. Sidelining the Foreign Office, he restricted consultations at Paris to a small circle of advisors and proceeded to cut deals directly with the other Allied heads of state.[79]

Lloyd George was not alone in his views. Publics on both sides of the Atlantic placed much of the blame for the preceding four years of bloodshed on what they saw as the incessant backroom scheming of monocled diplomats. During the war, the Foreign Office was relegated to a position of nonimportance in British policymaking, and its core functions were outsourced to other departments.[80] Out of a total British delegation of four hundred at Paris, only eighteen were professional diplomats.[81]

The "New" Diplomacy

In place of the old methods, Lloyd George believed the time had come for a "new" diplomacy in which nations would sort out their differences in the light of day, the same way that political parties did in parliament. Instead of exchanging diplomatic notes via embassies, leaders would hash things out at big confabs with the press in tow. The result, it was widely thought, would be a more democratic form of statecraft better suited to the modern world, that would allow countries to resolve their disagreements before they escalated into conflict.

The chief advocate for this new way of doing things was Lloyd George's American counterpart, President Woodrow Wilson.[82] Where Lloyd George thought the old diplomacy was ineffectual, Wilson thought it was downright pernicious. In his famous Fourteen Points, delivered to the U.S. Congress the year before, Wilson outlined a radical postwar blueprint in which traditional diplomacy would be replaced by world government. His first point called for the end of secret treaties in favor of "open covenants, openly arrived at," his fourth for wholesale disarmament, and his fourteenth for creating a peace organization at which nations of all sizes would have their disputes settled by arbitration in much the same way that domestic feuds are settled in a court of law.[83]

These ideas were not entirely new; what *was* new was to hear them espoused as a practical policy program by the elected head of a country of America's enormous latent power. The breathtaking scope of Wilson's agenda reflected the boundless potential of an ambitious, adolescent nation as-yet uninured to the exigencies of great-power status. Where extollers of world peace since Kant had treated the balance of power as a foundation from which international law could grow over time, Wilson saw it as the source of war itself. "There must be," he told the Senate in January 1917, "not a balance of power, but a community of power; not organized rivalries, but an organized common peace."[84] The "organized peace" he had in mind would be governed by a new League of Nations that abolished alliances and policed itself through communal action.

Wilson's nostrums were a tonic to Britain's younger diplomats.[85] Harold Nicolson, a junior Foreign Office official attached to the British delegation in Paris, later wrote:

> There was in his pronouncements a slight tinge of revivalism, a touch of Methodist arrogance, more than a touch of Presbyterian vanity. . . . He felt that those myriad eyes looked up to him as to a prophet arisen in the West; as to a man chosen by God to give to the whole world a new message and a more righteous order. . . . It is not a sufficient explanation to contend that President Wilson was conceited, obstinate, nonconformist and reserved. He was also a man obsessed: possessed.[86]

Problems with Wilson's grandiose plans didn't take long to appear. How was the new community of peace to be organized? Who would enforce its dictates? How should the principle of national self-determination operate in a world of multinational empires? Did it apply to all of the great powers, including those among the vanquished who might grow larger as a result? How was the new program of disarmament to be carried out without inviting new acts of aggression?

Wilson had, at best, hazy answers to these questions. "Never before had such revolutionary goals been put forward," as Kissinger later wrote, "with so few guidelines as to how to implement them."[87] Having carried a radical gospel to Europe, Wilson proved incapable of organizing the de minimis requirements for its practical implementation. His refusal to make even modest concessions to ensure the ratification of the Versailles Treaty in the Senate doomed the League of Nations at its inception, rendering America an indifferent onlooker to a venture of which it had been a chief progenitor.[88] The resulting structure was a toothless giant that was incapable of adjudicating even minor disputes among its members, much less abolishing human conflict.

It wasn't only the League of Nations that miscarried at Paris. The very premise of the new diplomacy—that democratizing negotiations would produce better results—was quickly shown to be wrong. The politicians brought their profession's pathologies to the game: vanity, impatience, and spin over substance. At Paris, Wilson had grown bored of his own ideas.[89] He and the other leaders were distracted by politics back home and ignorant of the matters they were deciding. "Who are the Slovaks?" Lloyd George was overheard to say. "I can't seem to place them."[90]

Where the old diplomacy had operated on the rule that "conferences only succeed when their results are arranged beforehand," the new diplomacy left everything to be settled *at* the conference, in a compressed timespan.[91] The public nature of the gatherings put pressure on leaders to have something glitzy to show for their labors, with the predictable result being elaborate communiques that masked disagreements and left the underlying problem to be resolved at a later date.

The results could be disastrous. At Spa in 1920, Lloyd George, on a whim, issued what seemed to be verbal security guarantees to Poland that almost dragged Britain into war with Russia.[92] At Sèvres that same year, he endorsed a hair-brained scheme by Greek nationalists to resurrect the Byzantine Empire, igniting a regional bloodbath that left half a million people dead and almost ended in armed confrontation between Britain and Turkey. At Paris, divergent domestic pressures led Allied politicians to defer the explosive question of how much Germany should pay in war reparations.[93] After twelve conferences failed to resolve the issue, France took matters into her own hands, launching an invasion of Germany's coal-rich Ruhr region that brought Europe to the brink of war.

Diplomacy, it turned out, was a good deal harder than the politicians had imagined.

Empire on the Cheap

Many of Britain's professional diplomats warned of the dangers of allowing the country's affairs to be determined by amateur leaders reacting to the public mood. In 1917 Sir Ernest Satow, one of the Foreign Office's leading Asia hands, published a guide to diplomacy that extolled the profession's classical arts and cautioned against the allurement of new formats that left "no time for reflection or consultation, and demand an immediate and often a hasty decision on matters of vital importance."[94] Two years later, F. A. Whyte, a junior diplomat of the Foreign Office delegation at Paris, published a translation of the writings of François de Callières with an introduction that called on Britons to "leave such transactions undisturbed in the hands of the expert."[95]

These criticisms of the new diplomacy proved prescient. In the years after the Paris peace conference, the Foreign Office was called upon to devise a series of "band-aids" for the problems created by the politicians. At the London Conference of 1924, British diplomats worked quietly with U.S. counterparts to defuse the standoff in the Ruhr and broker a compromise, known as the Dawes Plan, that helped restart the flow of U.S. loans to Europe.[96] A year later at Locarno, British diplomats midwifed an agreement on postwar borders that made it possible for Germany to join the League of Nations.[97] And at Lausanne in the summer of 1923, they brokered a replacement to the disastrous Treaty of Sèvres that helped restore stability to the Near East.[98]

For Britain the greatest service of the old diplomacy in this period came in her relations with the United States and Japan. The main strategic danger facing Britain in the years immediately following World War I was that she would face one or both of these powers in a war at sea.[99] In particular, British leaders worried about an ambitious new U.S. shipbuilding program, which threatened to plunge the two Atlantic powers into a naval arms race.

In response, British diplomats promoted an arms control framework aimed at capping fleet sizes among the world's top navies.[100] At the Washington Naval Conference of 1921–1922, the major powers instituted a ten-year "holiday" on building capital ships, prescribed a schedule for scrapping existing ones, and placed limits on total warship tonnage with a ratio of five British ships and five American ships for every three Japanese ones.

These arrangements didn't require the Royal Navy to give up much. It had already abandoned the two-power standard two years earlier in favor of a one-to-one metric to keep pace with the United States.[101] But by enshrining this new standard, the new naval treaty gave Britain an assurance that America would not develop a fleet *far outstripping* her own. This came at a cost to Britain of jettisoning her old alliance with Japan, the continuation of which would have complicated London's efforts to preserve the all-important relationship with Washington. But this was a price worth paying for the prize of preserving Britain's fragile naval position, while laying the foundation for joint Anglo-American management of international security problems.[102]

Together with the improvised fixes in Europe and the Middle East, Britain's engagement with the United States and Japan alleviated the empire's strategic burdens and allowed Britain to scale back defense spending and focus on policing the empire.

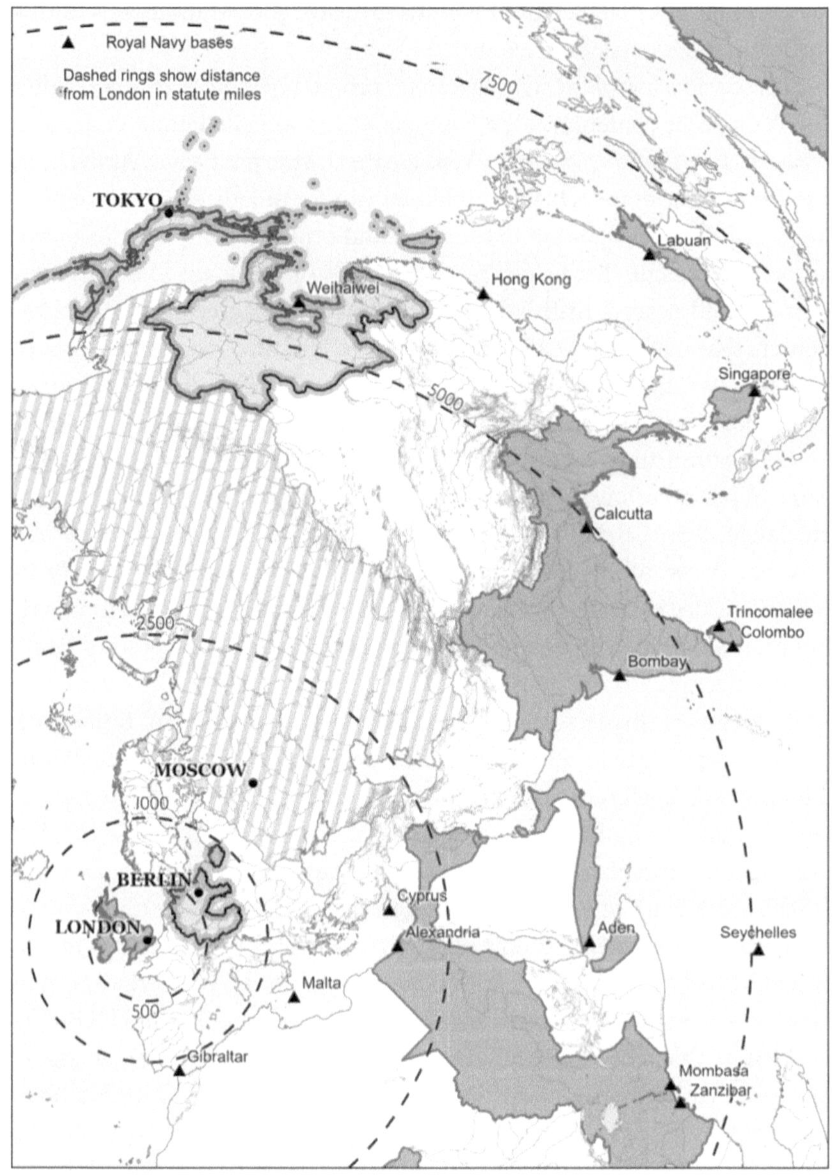

FIGURE 7.3. The British Empire in 1938 (Credit: Andrew Rhodes)

A Menagerie of Predators

Diplomatic improvisations, however, could only do so much to sustain Britain's global position. The immediate postwar environment had been rendered artificially benign by the general exhaustion prevailing among most of the major powers. But cyclonic forces were gathering force that would soon bring about the collapse of the post–World War I order.

By the 1930s, Britain's relative economic position was much weaker than it had been in Edwardian times.[103] After the war, the country's gross domestic product (GDP) grew at a slower pace than any great power except France. Meanwhile, America's economy swelled to gargantuan proportions; even after the carnage of the Great Depression, it was larger than those of Britain, Germany, and Japan combined. During these same years, Russia's national income increased fourfold and Japan's GDP grew by an astonishing 260 percent, overtaking the economies of France and Italy. Germany's economic recovery proceeded at a faster pace than expected; by the mid-1930s her steel production was twice that of Britain's, and her manufacturing output was already on track to surpass those of Britain and France combined.

As this global power redistribution accelerated, revisionist powers saw the Paris settlement as a shackle to be cast off at the earliest opportunity. Germany and Russia both pined to regain lost territories in Eastern Europe. Italy wanted the Mediterranean territories it had been denied at Paris. Japan wanted territory in China and nearby island chains. All of these countries viewed the Versailles settlement as a British scheme to deprive them of the critical resources needed to become global powers.[104] By the early 1930s, all were gripped by revolutionary ideologies that defined national objectives in zero-sum terms. The Fascist leaders who came to power in Italy in the early 1920s saw themselves as nationalist saviors charged with resurrecting the Roman Empire. The Nazi leaders who came to power in Germany in 1933 saw themselves as Arian exemplars destined to build a thousand-year empire. And the militarist-nationalist leaders who controlled Japanese foreign policy from the mid-1930s onward saw their country as a racial paragon with a mandate to dominate Asia.

While these enemies were growing stronger, Britain's defenses were weaker, in relative terms, than they had been in many generations. Under the so-called ten-year rule, introduced in 1919 and renewed automatically each year, Britain's military budget was gutted and her fighting services pared to the bone. By the early 1930s, the Royal Navy possessed about a quarter of the world's battleships (compared to 40 percent in the early 1900s), British shipbuilding had shrunk to 7 percent of pre-1914 levels, and British aircraft production ranked sixth among the major powers.[105]

It wasn't only British material strength that suffered in these years; the country was spiritually sapped as well. At a moment when the populaces of Germany, Italy, and Japan were working themselves into hysterias of national revenge, the British public remained mired in a postwar funk of exhaustion and guilt. A nationwide survey in 1934 found that nine out of every ten Britons supported an "all-round abolition" of the armed forces.[106] Most believed that the Paris treaties had treated Germany unfairly and should be amended. Like Britain's admirals, they saw diplomacy as the best hope for keeping Britain out of a new world war that it was in no position, either psychologically or strategically, to fight.

Umbrella Man

The man who would attempt to fulfill these expectations was Arthur Neville Chamberlain.[107] A latecomer to politics, Chamberlain was sixty-eight years old when he became prime minister in May 1937, just as the European kettle was starting to boil. His father was the great Birmingham tycoon Joseph Chamberlain, mentioned earlier, and his half-brother was Austen Chamberlain, who had won a Nobel Prize for negotiating the Locarno treaties in the previous decade.

With the passage of time, Chamberlain's name has come to symbolize temporizing weakness and indecision. The popular image is of a feeble man with a librarian's demeanor who lacked nerve and allowed himself to be swayed by events. Nothing could be further from the truth. Neville Chamberlain was a forceful and energetic leader who was supremely confident in his own abilities and knew exactly where he was going. Hardworking and athletic, he rose early, worked late, and maintained a muscled abdomen into his sixties.[108] Since entering Parliament in 1918, he had quickly risen through the ranks to become the brightest star in the Conservative Party.

Chamberlain's stuffy attire concealed a modern and, by the standards of his party at the time, progressive, politician. His passion was social reform. As minister of health in the 1920s, he abolished workhouses for the poor and laid the foundations for the British welfare state.[109] As chancellor of the exchequer in the early 1930s, he brought Britain through the Great Depression while paying down the country's war debts and cutting unemployment in half.[110] A savvy communicator, he was the first British leader to master the use of mass media as a tool of politics in the age of radio.[111]

As prime minister, Chamberlain exercised an iron grip on power. He enforced a rigid discipline around his priorities, ruthlessly sidelining critics and even wiretapping their phones. "I tell you that I am not dictatorial, I am not autocratic," he was once overheard shouting to subordinates at Number Ten Downing Street. "You are all wrong wrong wrong[!]"[112]

Chamberlain's interest in details extended into the realm of defense policy. His vision wasn't all that different from Lloyd George's in 1919, in that he wanted to maintain Britain's empire at the lowest cost possible in order to prioritize domestic prosperity.

Chamberlain had no illusions about the growing danger abroad. As chancellor of the exchequer, he discarded the ten-year rule and instigated a series of increases to the defense budget.[113] Chamberlain didn't just throw money at the problem; he closely followed defense policy debates of the time and applied himself to the particulars of military strategy. His views were influenced by the writings of Basil H. Liddell Hart, a retired British army officer who believed that Britain had erred by sending large armies to Europe in World War I and advocated for a revamped version of Britain's traditional maritime strategy that would emphasize economic warfare and imperial defense while maintaining a limited commitment to the European mainland.[114]

Hart's ideas jived with Chamberlain's conception of an affordable empire. He was especially worried about the threat posed by long-range bombers, which in the event of war threatened to launch a "knockout blow" on the British home islands.[115] Bucking the conventional wisdom, Chamberlain prioritized the modernization of the Royal Air Force (RAF), and in particular the development of a strategic bombing force. Altogether by the time the Munich crisis broke out in 1938, spending on the RAF had increased by nearly 700 percent, while spending on the Royal Navy was up 130 percent.[116] Had it not been for Chamberlain's efforts as chancellor of the exchequer, Britain would have been much less ready for World War II.

Chamberlain's Grand Strategy

More than most leaders, Chamberlain had a clear conception of an overarching strategy for handling the dangers arrayed against his country. He "conceived himself able to comprehend the whole field of Europe," Churchill later wrote, "and indeed the world."[117]

Chamberlain's starting point was the recognition that Germany was the main danger facing Britain. While this may seem obvious now, for much of the 1930s Japan had appeared to be the greater threat. Like in Edwardian times, Britain could not defend her possessions in the Far East while also protecting the home islands. As early as 1934, the Admiralty had told the cabinet that "we cannot simultaneously fight Japan and the strongest European naval Power."[118] By the time Chamberlain took office, these concerns were at fever pitch. At the end of 1937, the Chiefs of Staff warned that the empire's military resources were woefully insufficient for fighting Germany, Italy, and Japan concurrently and implored the cabinet to "reduce the number of our potential enemies."[119]

Chamberlain's preferred solution was to renew the alliance with Japan—a course of action that enjoyed the support of Britain's military

FIGURE 7.4. Confident statesman: Neville Chamberlain
(Credit: Shawshots / Alamy)

establishment.[120] The problem was that, unlike in Edwardian times, Japan was now in full-blown expansion mode and had designs on British territories in the Far East, including especially the naval base in Singapore. Since Japan also threatened the Pacific territories of the United States, any new treaty between the two island powers risked alienating the one country whose support Britain would need most if it found herself at war again with Germany again.

Britain's other diplomatic options were similarly fraught. The impotence of the League of Nations had been laid bare by its inability to stop Japan's attack on Manchuria in 1931. Efforts at coordination with the United States were going nowhere; even a modest British proposal in late 1937 to make a joint show of naval power in the Pacific had met with a cool reception in Washington.[121] And while Churchill and others correctly argued for resurrecting the World War I–era alliances with Russia and France, Chamberlain distrusted the Soviets and believed that coquetting too heavily with Paris might bring about the very conflict he wanted to avoid.[122]

It is a mark of Chamberlain's self-confidence as a strategist that he was undaunted by these challenges. The same mastery of economic data that had made him an effective social reformer convinced him that Germany could not afford a long war. It might outproduce Britain in planes and tanks in the short term. But if Hitler actually used those weapons, Chamberlain reckoned, he would trigger an Anglo-French-U.S. coalition whose industrial powers far outstripped those of the Reich. Hitler surely saw these same facts and would, the thinking went, choose to avoid war if he could attain satisfaction by other means.

Thus, the crux of Chamberlain's grand strategy was to identify and meet Germany's de minimis demands and, in so doing, buy time for Britain to deal with Japan.[123] The need for such an arrangement was driven home in December 1937 by an interim report on Britain's defenses, which found that the country had "arrived at a position . . . in which we were faced by the possibility of three enemies at once."[124] By appeasing Hitler, Chamberlain believed he could sequence the strategic dangers facing the country while avoiding a military buildup on a scale that would overwhelm Britain's fragile economy. His aim was to husband Britain's resources and "remove the danger spots one by one"—or, as one historian put it, conduct a "strategy of shuffle."[125]

Crucially for his overall strategy, Chamberlain thought that Hitler could be appeased at a reasonable price to Britain.[126] Hitler's desires seemed to amount to a few strips of territory populated by ethnic Germans, in a region (East-Central Europe) that was well outside Britain's historic sphere of influence.[127] Nor did he believe that appeasing Hitler would damage Britain's reputation; to the contrary, he thought that it would show that Britain was a humane and enlightened country committed to finding a lasting peace on the basis of "the rule of law and order, of reason and good faith."[128] All that was needed was to sell the idea to the Nazis—and that, Chamberlain thought, would require a more imaginative diplomacy than Britain had been pursuing.

Chamberlain's Diplomacy

In executing his strategy, Chamberlain, like Lloyd George before him, tended to work around the Foreign Office and do as he pleased in diplomacy.[129] He relied on amateur intermediaries to convey messages to

Hitler and set up a side channel to the Italian duce Benito Mussolini. Anticipating the practice of later American presidents, he established a direct line to Britain's pro-German ambassador in Berlin, Sir Neville Henderson, and retained a foreign-policy aide, Sir Horace Wilson, outside the formal reporting chain.[130] From the outset, Chamberlain established that he would pursue his vision, on his terms.

As Central Europe simmered in the early months of 1938, Chamberlain grabbed the initiative by signaling his intention to reach a new general settlement, underwritten with an offer to discuss a transfer of overseas colonies. Hitler shrugged off the idea and, shortly thereafter, annexed Austria. At this stage, the Foreign Office wanted to take a firmer stance and warn Germany against similar moves in next-door Czechoslovakia.[131] But Chamberlain dismissed this advice, for fear that it would make the situation worse. When Germany concocted a border incident and began making threats of invasion, he reluctantly allowed his foreign secretary, Lord Halifax, to send a diplomatic note to the effect that Britain would back France if the latter intervened. That seemed at first to do the trick. But when Hitler addressed the Nuremburg Rally in early September, he made it plain that Germany was preparing to take military action in the Sudetenland.

It was at this juncture that Chamberlain embarked on the first of his ill-fated efforts to "save the situation" through direct negotiations with Adolf Hitler.[132] On September 15 he flew to meet with the führer at his mountaintop retreat at Berchtesgaden, in the Bavarian Alps. It's a sign of Chamberlain's determination that the sixty-nine-year-old prime minister boarded an international flight for the first time in his life in order to attend this meeting, and a sign of his desperation that he was willing to then take a train the additional three hours from Munich to Hitler's lair.[133]

Most negotiators enter into a parley by formulating demands that are somewhat in excess of what their interlocutor is likely to accept, in the expectation of meeting somewhere in the middle. Chamberlain did the opposite. He tried to anticipate the maximum demand that Hitler would want and make *that* his opening offer. He had already established with the cabinet prior to his departure that he intended to give Hitler the Sudetenland and that he would apply pressure only to the Czechs, who were expected to make all of the concessions.[134] Once at Berchtesgaden, he agreed in principle to the Führer's desire—the cession of the Sudeten territories and placement of Czechoslovakia under international stewardship so as to negate its alliances with France and Russia—on the sole condition that the transfer receive a veneer of legitimacy by being preceded by a plebiscite.

A week later, Chamberlain flew back to Germany to report, in errand-boy fashion, that he had persuaded the French and Czechs to go along. Smelling blood, Hitler responded by upping the ante and demanding the immediate surrender of the Sudetenland, without plebiscite. Chamberlain balked at first, but caved after Hitler provided a written statement of his demands and offered to extend his deadline to October 1. Once again, it fell to Chamberlain to sell Hitler's plans to the French and Czechs.

It was after this second meeting that Chamberlain began to encounter real resistance at home to his policy of appeasement. The doubts extended to the Foreign Office, where officials worried about the consequences for British credibility.[135] Even the normally pliant Halifax now began to have second thoughts; it felt, he wrote, as if Hitler was now "dictating terms, just as though he had won a war but without having had to fight."[136] On September 26, to Chamberlain's dismay, the Foreign Office released a statement warning Germany that if it molested the Czechs it was likely to meet with resistance from Britain, France and Russia.

At this juncture, it looked for a moment as if sanity—and the balance of power—would prevail. Stiffening his spine, Chamberlain sent Horace Wilson to tell Hitler that Britain would respond to aggression against the Czechs by standing with the French, and, when no response was forthcoming, he mobilized the British fleet.

But as the clock wound down, Chamberlain's fears got the better of him. The Chiefs of Staff encouraged his misgivings by emphasizing what they saw as the impossibility of the Czechs' position.[137] Henderson sent bloodcurdling descriptions from Berlin of the horrors that would befall the Czechs if Hitler's threats went unheeded. And leaders from around the world, including U.S. president Franklin Roosevelt, urged Chamberlain not to give up in his quest for peace.

Most decisively, Hitler continued to string Chamberlain along by hinting that he was ready to compromise. Not long after the order went out to mobilize the fleet, Hitler sent a telegram suggesting that he would be willing to scale back his demands and accept the original concessions made by the Czechs after Berchtesgaden until a plebiscite could be arranged. Clutching at this "last tuft of grass on the verge of the precipice," Chamberlain immediately replied that Hitler would "get all essentials without war and without delay. . . . I cannot believe that you will take the responsibility of starting a world war, for the sake of a few days' delay in settling this longstanding problem."[138]

Hitler's response came later in the day, as Chamberlain was delivering an emotional address to the House of Commons. It contained an invitation for the prime minister to attend an emergency meeting the next day in Munich. This prompted the chamber to erupt in applause, and within hours Chamberlain was boarding another plane for his fateful, final meeting with Hitler.

Munich and Its Aftermath

The meeting in Munich on the last two days of September 1938 would go down as perhaps the most destructive twenty-four hours in the modern history of diplomacy. The images are indelibly stamped on the Western psyche: a haggard Chamberlain and his demoralized French counterpart Édouard Daladier, standing alongside the wolflike, uniformed figures of Hitler and Mussolini. On paper, the Western leaders gave away nothing more that day than they had already sacrificed: Germany got possession of the Sudetenland, only in ten days instead of one; the Czech population was forced to evacuate without their possessions; the fate of adjacent regions was assigned to a multilateral commission.

Chamberlain was greeted rapturously when he got home. British newspapers proclaimed "PEACE," and the *New York Times* lauded the prime minister's conduct as "Christlike."[139] More than forty thousand letters of gratitude poured in from around the world; dolls were made in Chamberlain's likeness, and a new song was added to Anglican hymnals in his honor.[140]

The euphoria didn't last. Czechoslovakia after Munich was not a viable state. By stripping its frontiers, Chamberlain had taken away the fortifications upon which it depended for self-defense. In March 1939, German troops occupied what remained of the country. Inspired by the scavenging, Mussolini grabbed Albania. Joseph Stalin drew his own conclusions from the debacle; unimpressed by Britain's performance at Munich, the Soviet leader decided to join the revisionists and entered into an alliance with Germany in August 1939.

Within a year of Munich, Hitler had turned his attention to Poland, where Chamberlain finally drew the line. That Hitler continued to doubt Britain's resolve to fight to the very end is a reflection of the timorous impression that Chamberlain had created in their meetings. When war finally came, it was as Chamberlain had predicted: a long war that Germany could not sustain. But it came at the cost of eighty million lives and the ultimate demise of the British Empire.

The decades that followed have brought innumerable postmortems of what went wrong at Munich.[141] The diagnoses have ranged from vanity and self-delusion to excessive idealism and faulty intelligence.[142]

Everyone generally agrees that Chamberlain had noble intentions and that he underestimated Hitler. Most agree that he faced bad options, summed up in James Levy's line, "too many enemies, too few resources to keep them all at bay," and that his diplomacy bought time for Britain to rearm.[143]

Viewed as a component of grand strategy, however, Chamberlain's diplomacy must be judged a failure. His aim had been to quiet Europe in order to concentrate attention on Asia. He achieved the opposite, emboldening Germany and thereby *reducing* the bandwidth that Britain could devote to Japan. Whereas Lansdowne's appeasements had involved places in the outer world where British interests were secondary, Chamberlain's appeasement focused on the critical theater that had the potential to produce a mortal threat to the home islands. By attempting to mollify Hitler, he signaled the permissibility of revisionism to predators large and small. Hitler just happened to be the readiest beast to explore that invitation to its fullest logical extent.

What's surprising is how little has been said about the defects of Chamberlain's practice of diplomacy as such. Chamberlain's actions were characterized by improvisation and reaction. Over and over again, he allowed Hitler to set the pace and parameters of negotiations. At Munich, Hitler determined the timing of the meeting (one day's notice), its location (the Führer's private study), and its composition (the Czechs were excluded, as were the Russians). Before the meeting even occurred, Chamberlain had already conceded the essential point, leaving only the speed of the fulfillment of the other side's desires to be determined. He went into the room astonishingly ill-prepared: without extensive study of the matters at hand, usually accompanied by one unqualified aide, and without even attempting to coordinate goals with his French ally. Once in the room, he allowed himself to be controlled by his opponent's emotions, accepting Hitler's aims as the basis for negotiation and abandoning his own positions at the slightest indication of displeasure.

While Chamberlain styled himself a realist, his diplomacy was distinctively unrealistic. The end he pursued was not a balance of power but the much more nebulous object of altering the mindset of a mercurial foreign ruler. He proceeded from the specious premise that problems in international relations are the result of misunderstandings that can be cleared up like disagreements between individuals.[144] In doing so, he effectively discarded the advantages that British diplomacy should have possessed in treating with the dictators. Whatever Chamberlain's personal feelings about the justness of the Versailles settlement, the fact is that that framework benefited Britain by positioning her to rally international opinion behind the protection of the status quo. This Chamberlain resolutely refused to do. By insisting on being the hero of the hour, he excluded diplomatic formats that would have been more effective for actually achieving his purpose.[145] By positioning himself as the instigator of revision to the post-1919 order, Chamberlain made Britain an unwitting participant in the destruction of an edifice that she herself had constructed. By standing on the principle of peaceful change, he conveyed legitimacy to Hitler's aims while relinquishing the moral advantage of standing for Western democracy against ethno-nationalist autocracy.

Could Britain's professional diplomats have done any better? Probably so. The very qualities that made the Foreign Office so unbearable to Chamberlain—its traditionalism and red tape—were advantages in parleys with a dictator who gained an edge by cornering a desperate old man and using the clock against him. And while the bureaucracy was as susceptible to error as anyone, the fact is that at the time Chamberlain undertook appeasement, the Foreign Office remained committed to preserving the independence of Czechoslovakia, through the use of alliances, on the basis of the balance of power.[146] Chamberlain sidelined these voices and created a bubble around himself and Horace Wilson, both amateurs at diplomacy.

Maybe what makes us so uncomfortable about appeasement is that it was nurtured by certain pathologies that are congenital to liberal democracy. Chamberlain was pursuing what he understood to be the public will—perhaps excessively so.[147] His worldview reflected the modern liberal belief that conflicts arise not because the other side's interests collide with one's own but because he is misunderstood, and the corollary, that conflict can be avoided through the patient application of reason and goodwill. His practice of diplomacy bore all the marks of that profession's democratization. In both method and aim, it was a natural extension of the "new diplomacy" inaugurated at the Paris Peace Conference in 1919. Like Wilson and Lloyd George, Chamberlain believed that grand things could be accomplished when charismatic leaders got together and cut big deals, without the blinkers and fetters of the bureaucrats. His peregrinations were simply a continuation of the diplomacy by conference that had been pursued to such disastrous effect in the 1920s, only on a more intimate scale and with vastly more calamitous results. It is unfortunate for the world that his interlocutor was better equipped to exploit the potentialities and contradictions of the new diplomacy than he was.

The British Legacy: Global Diplomacy

What sets Britain apart from earlier maritime great powers is the size of the canvass on which her diplomacy operated. At any given moment, British leaders had to have reasonable plans for defending possessions on as many as six continents connected by long and tenuous lines of communication through the world's seas and oceans. The resulting power gradient was vicious in the extreme. Where Venice in her time had to worry about outposts a few hundred miles from her lagoons, Britain's furthest territories were seven thousand miles from the Thames estuary. Even with the advent of steam power and aeroplanes, Britain was never able to conquer distance on the scale required to cover her liabilities by military means.

The global nature of Britain's power shaped how her leaders used diplomacy. The chief instrument by which Britain maintained her position, naval power, was highly mobile but incapable of generating lasting positions of strength deep in the interior of the world's major regions. Diplomacy offered a natural expedient to manage the resulting gaps between means and ends and thereby preserve the empire at an affordable cost to the home country. Salisbury's manipulation of continental rivalries, Lansdowne's ententes, Lloyd George's harnessing of the League of Nations to British imperial interests, and Chamberlain's "strategy of shuffle" all proceeded from this same hard-nosed logic.

Britain's diplomatic culture and institutions evolved to support the country's worldwide role. Global strategy requires global knowledge, systematically curated and integrated with politics. The practice of concentrating diplomatic strategy in the hands of a talented supremo like Richelieu or Bismarck would not work in Britain; the breadth and variety of places that had to be taken into account when formulating strategy was too great. The Foreign Office was an expression of this reality; in its heyday, it acted as a gearbox where the complexities of interaction with numerous rivals on a global stage could be converted into high policy.

THE ART AND PERIL OF APPEASEMENT

Britain's global commitments pushed her leaders toward a diplomatic logic of conciliation.[148] Appeasement was a logical strategy for a maritime power attempting to manage trade-offs on such a vast scale. No other conceivable expedient could have allowed Britain to square the circle of resources and responsibilities so quickly and efficiently.

However, the same unforgiving power gradient that made appeasement so tempting also made it dangerous for Britain. Distance and oceans erode resolve. If a Byzantine emperor appeased the Sassanids in order to effect a pivot to another frontier, his rivals could assume that the legions would eventually return. But with Britain no such presumption existed. The empire's far-flung outposts, sprinkled along the rimlands of Eurasia, conveyed something other than permanence. If Britain ever retreated from these places, it wasn't clear if she would return.

The dangers of appeasement became more apparent as British power waned. Lansdowne sought localized understandings with rivals in outer regions involving secondary British interests against a baseline of still-impressive British strength. Chamberlain sought a general understanding with the main adversary in a region involving primary British interests against a baseline of relative weakness. In between lay three decades of decline not only materially but spiritually, in Britons' willingness to bear the burdens of empire. Technology heightened the problem by presenting new weapons like the strategic bomber that allowed an opponent to place the British home islands at risk in a more direct way than had been possible in preceding eras. These factors conspired to confirm a predisposition for appeasement when the better bet would have been to use Britain's ancient method of recruiting on-shore allies to uphold the European balance of power. The wages of this miscalculation were ruinous for Britain, her empire, and the world.

PISCATORIAL CREDIBILITY

For most of her history, Britain's geography afforded her that rarest of luxuries in great-power competition: the ability to choose. But it also placed limits on the reach of British diplomacy, which could go only as far inland as British sea and expeditionary power could penetrate. This reality often undermined British credibility in dealings with other powers. In this sense, the problem facing British diplomacy was the opposite of that facing Imperial Germany. Where Germany's enormous strength made other states suspect that her conciliatory gestures cloaked an instinct for predatory expansion, the diffuse nature of Britain's power—and the island nation's reputation for aloofness—made other states wonder if she could or would act in a moment of crisis.

Credibility lies at the heart of effective diplomacy. The ability of other states to count on a great power's follow-through is integral to the value of the diplomat's spoken word and a precondition to the success of those treaties into which he enters. The art of diplomacy for a power in Britain's position was to communicate sufficiently credible resolve so as to affect the calculations of other states in the desired way at the decisive moment, without promising more than Britain could actually deliver or tying her leaders' hands to such a degree as to prevent them from changing course if circumstances dictated. This was easier said than done, and it grew much harder as British power eroded over time.

British diplomacy consistently sought a calculated ambiguity that would leave its options open until the very last minute. The entente format was perhaps its most elegant expression: more than a friendly gesture, less than a full embrace. When it worked well, it gave Britain the benefits of balancing at a rebate in risk. But Britain's ambivalence could also have catastrophic consequences. Belgium in 1914 and Czechoslovakia in 1938 are both examples of friendly states that were left guessing about Britain's intentions until the last minute. In these instances, Britain's hesitancy deprived her of effective diplomacy's most powerful byproduct: deterrence.

MORAL EXPECTATIONS

To a greater extent than earlier great powers, Britain's diplomacy was infused with moral expectations. Even if often unfulfilled in practice, Britain's image was that of a great liberal power that stood up for the underdog, at least in Europe. Foreign secretaries could expect to be vigorously challenged on the basis of how their policies squared with the country's highest ideals. Public pressure could mount for action on strictly moral grounds and gain real force through the party-political process. Diplomatic efforts that seemed to violate British ideals, like treaties of alliance with a despotic power, could subject governments to opprobrium in a way that would have seemed strange to Richelieu or Kaunitz.

British diplomatic culture was a by-product of those ideals. Britain's diplomats were motivated by "public-school decency" and sought to apply standards of fair play and common sense to dealings among states.[149] It came naturally for such leaders to embrace the precepts of the "new diplomacy" and league system. Appeasement, too, was an outworking of the democratic conception of order as a by-product of compromise. A.J.P. Taylor's comment that Chamberlain stood for "all that was best and most enlightened in British life" could as readily be applied to Lansdowne and Lloyd George. Whatever his failings, Chamberlain embodied the diplomacy of a humane and civilian power that genuinely sought peace. The problem was that the gap between Britain's enlightened ideals and the real extent of her power was very wide. When Britain seemed to fall short of the principles on which the nation's political institutions were built, the disappointment was greater for her people, and the consequences steeper for her reputation, precisely because of what the country was seen to stand for. Yet when the chips were down, Britain's leaders, like those of other great powers across the ages, consistently put survival and the national interest above all other considerations.

In the annals of grand strategy, Britain occupies a category of her own, as the world's first and last insular great power of global reach. Like the Republic of Venice, she seemed to defy the possible. On the basis of armed might alone, Britain could never have amassed an imperium spanning much of the earth's surface while thwarting successive attempts at hegemony in Europe. That she was able to do so is as much a testament to dexterous diplomacy as it is to skill in commerce and naval warfare. Like the Venetians, the British were consummate evaluators of timing and risk. Their diplomats excelled at augmenting Britain's advantages in money and ships with onshore allies to alleviate the pressures of Britain's exposed position. The result in Britain's heyday was the best of all worlds geopolitically: immense wealth and influence at a fraction of the cost.

In the history of diplomacy, Britain forms the connective tissue between the classical European states-system and the global power blocs of the 20th Century. Britain was the last mistress of the balance of power and the first operator of worldwide collective security. British institutions represented the culmination of the post-Westphalian revolution in diplomatic administration and technique, harnessed to the strategic outlook of a world power. In her championing of the League of Nations, Britain anticipated the United Nations system of the later 20th Century; in her attempt to integrate state interests and democratic ideals, she anticipated the dilemmas of American power in the Cold War. That era would bring new actors capable of organizing resources on a continental scale, far beyond those that Britain ever commanded. The country that would inherit Britain's role and the burdens it entailed was her colonial offspring across the Atlantic Ocean, where our attention now turns.

CHAPTER EIGHT

Chaos under Heaven

We have the Soviet Union to the north and the west, India to the south, and Japan to the east. If all our enemies were to unite, attacking us from the north, south, east, and west, what do you think we should do? . . . Didn't our ancestors counsel negotiating with faraway countries while fighting with those that are near?

—MAO ZEDONG

History suggested that it was usually more advantageous to align oneself with the weaker of two antagonistic partners, because this acted as a restraint on the stronger.

—HENRY KISSINGER

IN EARLY FEBRUARY 1969, Mao Zedong, chairman of the Chinese Communist Party and founder of the People's Republic of China, asked an old friend, Marshal Chen Yi, to take a fresh look at the country's grand strategy. "Who is the main enemy, US or USSR?" Mao asked. "And, is war likely?"[1]

These were extraordinary words to hear from the leader of the world's most populous Communist power and the doyen of the international Marxist movement. For much of his career, Mao had looked up to the Soviet Union as an ideological big brother. In 1950, at Mao's urging, the two Eurasian giants had signed a treaty of friendship that was meant to last a generation. In the years that followed, Soviet loans and technical support had kept China's economy afloat while Mao tightened his bloody grip on power.

In addition to a shared collectivist ideology, Moscow and Beijing were united by a common enemy: the United States. In the early 1950s they had fought together against U.S. forces in Korea. Now, they were both assisting Ho Chi Minh in his ongoing struggle against the United States in Vietnam.

But Mao had reasons to worry about his neighbor to the north. In 1968, Soviet premier Leonid Brezhnev proclaimed a new doctrine under which Moscow reserved the right to intervene in the internal affairs of other Communist states as it saw fit. In the months that followed, Soviet troops began massing on the Chinese border. Like the toad in Aesop's fable, Mao was starting to realize he had a scorpion on his back.

Mao wasn't the only one reconsidering his options. Half a world away, a similar process was playing out in the capital of China's ideological arch-enemy. Eleven days before Mao tasked his generals with conducting their review, Richard Nixon asked the staff of the National Security Council (NSC) to make a study of American strategy in Asia. The newly elected president wanted to know how U.S. objectives toward China squared with those of Russia, as well the alternative options for U.S. policy, and the "risks and costs" associated with each.[2]

Nixon's reappraisal was, in its own way, just as revolutionary as Mao's. Nixon was an ardent anti-Communist with a long history of criticizing Red China. At the time of his election in November 1968, the consensus in Washington held that China was a more ideologically hidebound and strategically unpredictable adversary than the Soviet Union. An NSC assessment the year before Nixon took office concluded that China was America's "biggest headache," and would likely remain so until Mao died.[3]

But in America, too, perspectives were shifting. The Vietnam War was entering its fifth year and exacting a steep price in American blood and treasure. Anti-war protests were at a fever pitch, the economy was headed for recession, and U.S. credibility was at a low ebb. With half a million troops bogged down in Indochina, the United States was in no position to counter Soviet thrusts in Europe or the Middle East—thrusts that Brezhnev's new doctrine seemed to make more likely by the day.

Like their counterparts in Beijing, the Nixon team had compelling reasons to rethink their nation's grand strategy. And to cerebrate these complex matters, the president had a formidable intellectual weapon, in the person of his new national security advisor, Dr. Henry Kissinger, who was determined to put his own, very distinctive stamp on U.S. foreign policy.

For all their obvious differences, Mao and Nixon shared a common problem, of needing to alleviate adversarial pressures on multiple fronts. In a curious synchronicity, the world's leading disciple of Karl Marx and the conservative Republican from California would conduct parallel reflections largely unaware, at least initially, of one another's cogitations. Their reappraisals would follow a similar logic, rooted in Realpolitik rather than ideology, and converge on the same bold idea, of using diplomacy to break the stalemate of Cold War blocs.

The result would be one of the most famous gambits in the history of diplomacy, as grand in conception as Britain's colonial rapprochements in the previous century, but involving continent-sized superpowers that counted their strength in hydrogen bombs rather than dreadnoughts. The geopolitical earthquake that followed would see the United States flip one of her two adversaries into a fair-weather partner, create the breathing space she needed to recover from the nightmare of Vietnam, and help lay the foundation for America's eventual triumph in the Cold War.

A Superpower Like No Other

The country that elected Richard Nixon president on November 15, 1968 was a superpower of immense wealth and might, the likes of which the world had never seen. Since her emergence as a cluster of British colonies on the eastern seaboard of North America, the United States had grown in the space of less than two centuries to become the strongest power on earth.

America shared many traits with her British mother country. Wide oceans shielded the United States from danger and gave her the interests and outlook of a maritime power. As had been true for Britain and Venice, insular geography encouraged the development of seafaring commerce and republican institutions. But unlike previous sea powers, America combined the advantages of insularity with the resources of a large land mass, roughly the size of Europe. She also differed in political formulation. In contrast to earlier great powers that had been created on the basis of the blood ties of an ethnic group or the territorial claims of a ruling dynasty, the American republic was founded on a political creed, which held that power derived from the consent of the governed. The claims set out in the Declaration of Independence were stated in universal terms, extending ostensibly to all humankind.

America's unique circumstances shaped the way that her leaders thought about diplomacy.[4] While the young Republic faced serious challenges from birth, her environment was much more conducive to state-building than the narrow confines of Europe, where states of all sizes strove and struggled in constant turmoil, cheek-by-jowl. America's founding generation distrusted traditional diplomacy as an instrument of Old World intrigue—"the pest of the peace of the world," as Thomas

Jefferson called it.[5] Early U.S. diplomats shunned ambassadorial titles and trappings, presenting themselves as citizen-emissaries who didn't play Europe's dirty games.

Yet for all that, the new country proved ruthlessly effective at employing diplomacy as an instrument of grand strategy. Three of the founding fathers served as ambassadors abroad, and the Department of State was America's first federal agency. While spurning military alliances on the European mold, Americans were adept at using diplomacy to outmaneuver European rivals and lock-in overseas advantages in trade. From an early point, U.S. leaders saw diplomacy as a tool for buying time to coalesce as a nation, in the sure knowledge that the American continent's vast resources would eventually enable her to surpass even the strongest of rivals.[6]

A policy of true isolationism was never a viable option for a country dependent on outside trade.[7] But for more than a century after her founding, America's energies were directed primarily inward, to the conquest of her own hinterland.[8] She was able to do so in large part because of the supremacy of the Royal Navy in the Atlantic, which kept other powers from dominating Europe and turning their full attention to North America. It was only as the United States completed this process that she began to turn her energies outward and take on the attributes of a true great power. By the presidency of Teddy Roosevelt, America was capable of holding her own against Europe's great powers. Using a combination of naval power and skillful diplomacy, Roosevelt established the United States as the preeminent power in the Western Hemisphere and created an overseas empire in the Caribbean and Pacific.[9]

America's rise was propelled by economic growth on a much grander scale than anything seen before. Between the closing of the Western frontier in 1890 and the outbreak of World War I, America's population increased by 54 percent, her steel production by 240 percent, and her warship tonnage by 310 percent. In 1913, the year Nixon was born, the U.S. stock market accounted for 20 percent of global equity market capitalization; on the day he became president, the number was 70 percent. In 1914, U.S. GDP was already four times that of Imperial Germany; by the eve of World War II, it was larger than all the other major powers combined.[10]

The immensity of America's power, when harnessed to the principles of her founding, created the ingredients for an idealistic mission of global proportions. As we saw in the previous chapter, America's leaders treated the negotiations at the Paris Peace Conference in 1919 as an opportunity not to restore the balance of power but to replace it with a world peace organization. The collapse of Woodrow Wilson's plans heralded America's withdrawal not only from the League of Nations but also from the Western alliance that was meant to undergird it. In the years that followed, the United States didn't retreat entirely from world affairs, but she kept them at arm's length, reverting to her earlier focus on commerce and managing the Western Hemisphere.

While Wilson's experiment failed, it underscored a fundamental difference between America and every great power that had come before her. The continent-sized republic could imagine using diplomacy on a stupendous scale, to either transcend geopolitics or, with equal self-assurance, retire from it. While neither extreme was ever truly viable, the point is that America could even contemplate such options. Only a country of unplumbed resources, unbounded confidence, and unfettered ideals could conceive of using diplomacy this way.

Cold War Diplomacy

America's first instincts after World War II were similar to those of Woodrow Wilson twenty-five years earlier. Like Wilson, President Franklin Delano Roosevelt believed he could rewire the international system to prevent future wars. Learning from the mistakes of the League of Nations, he envisioned a collective security organization in which the United States, Britain, Russia, and China—the so-called four policemen—would underwrite peace while the rest of the world disarmed. With such a structure in place, America would be able to bring her troops home, get on with the Soviet Union, and refocus her energies on the Western Hemisphere.

Roosevelt's methods replicated aspects of the "new diplomacy" introduced at Paris in 1919. He engaged world leaders directly, relied on amateur envoys, and sidelined the State Department. Like earlier 20th-Century Western statesmen, he believed that he could reason with totalitarian interlocutors using the political methods that worked inside a democracy. Roosevelt's unrequited attempts to placate Joseph Stalin unwittingly facilitated Soviet efforts to extend Communist control over large portions of Eastern Europe and North Asia, thus placing the United States at a disadvantage in the early phases of the Cold War.[11]

Soviet behavior presented the United States with a grand strategic dilemma. Since its founding, the country had been able to count on Britain to prevent hostile powers from dominating Europe. But as British power receded, American leaders faced a choice between either shouldering Britain's role, with all the burdens that entailed, or consenting to the aggregation of a large share of the world's resources under the control of a Eurasian hegemon whose authoritarian system of government was diametrically opposed to its own.

The dangers of the latter scenario were spelled out in an embassy cable dated February 22, 1946, by a young U.S. chargé d'affaires in Moscow named George Kennan. The time had come, Kennan argued, to see that Soviet Russia was a mortal enemy with whom there could be "no permanent modus vivendi." Only through a policy of "firm and vigilant containment," he wrote in an anonymous article for *Foreign Affairs* the following year, could Russia's "expansive tendencies" be checked. With such a foundation in place, America could use diplomacy to shape Soviet behavior, in the assurance that the country's insolvent economic system would eventually collapse upon itself.[12]

Kennan's meditations provided the framework around which America would form an answer to the dilemmas created by Britain's decline. His insights were given practical form by Dean Acheson, who served as secretary of state to Roosevelt's successor, President Harry S. Truman. Urbane and cerebral, Acheson was one of a new generation of U.S. diplomats who were skeptical of Roosevelt's approach and determined to learn from Wilson's mistakes in Paris.[13] Rather than chasing after the Russians for a political settlement, Acheson believed that the United States needed to focus her diplomacy on first creating "situations of strength in the free world"; only then would there be any basis for serious diplomatic interactions with Soviet Russia.[14]

What Acheson had in mind were peacetime alliances linking America to Western Europe and East Asia. Standing U.S. military commitments would replace Britain's guardianship of the balance of power, backed by U.S. financial aid to thwart Communist subversion and a new international monetary system, brokered at Bretton Woods, that established a gold-backed U.S. dollar as the paramount global currency and created mechanisms to prevent currency wars between the United States and her allies.[15]

This new framework came together with astonishing speed. In 1947 Truman announced that the United States would assist any country resisting Soviet inroads; the same year, he unveiled a large aid program, later known as the Marshall Plan, to rebuild foreign economies shattered by the war, and two years later, his administration signed the North Atlantic Treaty, under which America committed to defend Western Europe from Soviet attack on a standing basis going forward.

The logic of Truman's grand strategy was spelled out in NSC-68, a secret memo written in the spring of 1950 under the direction of Paul

Nitze, director of the State Department Policy Planning Staff. Nitze accepted Kennan's diagnosis of Soviet aims but envisioned a more assertive response, underwritten by a dramatic expansion of U.S. military power. Diplomacy's role in this scheme would be to "create such political and economic conditions in the free world, backed by force sufficient to inhibit Soviet attack, that the Kremlin will accommodate itself to these conditions, gradually withdraw, and eventually change its policies drastically." Until that happened, Washington should be "ready to take the initiative at times in seeking negotiation," but only "as a tactic" to "gain public support" and to "minimize the immediate risks of war."[16]

Nuclear Diplomacy

The presidents who came after Truman generally hewed to its admonition to focus U.S. diplomacy on creating situations of strength rather than seeking a general settlement with the Soviets.

Following Truman's example, Dwight D. Eisenhower spurned Soviet offers to discuss the future of Germany and rebuffed nudges from Churchill to leverage the U.S. nuclear advantage to bring Moscow to the table on terms favorable to the West.[17] Eisenhower's interactions with Nikita Khrushchev established a pattern whereby U.S. and Soviet leaders used meetings to recite talking points without expecting a breakthrough.[18] While John F. Kennedy came to office in 1961 intending to pursue a more vigorous diplomacy, his interaction with Khrushchev in Vienna in 1961 devolved into an ideological brawl that initially confirmed the pattern.

What eventually shook things loose was atomic weapons. The Soviet Union's development of a nuclear arsenal capable of threatening North America gave U.S. leaders a compelling reason to engage in substantive diplomacy with Soviet counterparts.[19] This was partly because of the change that these weapons brought to the overall military balance. But the shift also had to do with the nature of nuclear weapons themselves. These were not normal instruments of war. The hydrogen bombs that America and Soviet Russia possessed by the mid-1950s could generate destruction many times greater than Hiroshima. By the 1960s, both superpowers had enough of these weapons to survive an initial attack and launch a second strike on the other. The result was a stalemate in which a nuclear onslaught by one side would result in the destruction of both. For the first time in history, as the early nuclear strategist Bernard Brodie observed, the objective of armies was not to win wars but to avoid them.[20]

All of this had significant implications for diplomacy. At face value, nuclear weapons made diplomacy more necessary than ever, as a means of ensuring state survival and, indeed, that of the entire human species. Yet they also made diplomacy more difficult. For millennia, the task of diplomats had been to convert the potential for violence into political outcomes without bloodshed. Implicit in these exertions was the possibility that a failure of negotiations could result in war. It was the desire to avoid that outcome, more than any abstract love of peace, that led states to compromise. This logic broke down, however, against a nuclear-armed state. If negotiation failed, nuclear weapons made war less likely than before, which in turn weakened the necessity to compromise.[21]

Among the first to recognize these realities was a young Harvard professor named Henry Kissinger. In an influential 1956 book entitled *Nuclear Weapons and Foreign Policy*, he contended that the advent of nuclear weapons made it harder to harness war to political ends in the way Carl von Clausewitz had envisioned. To escape this dynamic, Kissinger argued that the United States had to create a way of pursuing limited objectives against the Soviets. The task of U.S. diplomacy, he wrote, was to create options "other than all-out war or inaction" by devising "a framework in which the question of national survival is not involved in every issue."[22]

Kissinger's point was vividly illustrated by a string of crises that brought the two superpowers to the nuclear precipice. The most dangerous of these occurred in 1962, in a standoff that followed in the wake of the deployment of Soviet nuclear weapons in Cuba. War was averted, but only through eleventh-hour negotiations that left both sides rattled.[23]

The Cuban Missile Crisis had two long-lasting effects on Cold War diplomacy. One was to prod the superpowers to get serious about using diplomacy to limit the chances of nuclear war.[24] Efforts in this direction had been underway for some time without success. Cuba broke the logjam, leading to the creation of a hotline between the two superpowers and, in October 1963, the signing of the Partial Nuclear Test Ban Treaty. This was followed by a long series of diplomatic attempts to curb the arms race, including the Treaty on Non-Proliferation in 1968, the Strategic Arms Limitations Treaties (SALT) and anti-ballistic missile (ABM) treaty of 1972 and 1979, and the Strategic Arms Reduction Treaties (START) of 1991 and 1993.

Cuba's other effect was to focus the superpower rivalry outward, to areas of the global chessboard outside the two antagonists' spheres of influence.[25] For the United States, Cuba heightened the perception that new demonstrations of resolve were needed to restore the credibility of American power. The place where Kennedy chose to draw the line was Vietnam.

The Path to Détente

Defeat at the hands of insurgents has a way of sobering even the greatest empires. The reverses that the Boers inflicted on the British army in South Africa in the early 1900s forced the Salisbury government to take stock of Britain's global position and contemplate changes to her grand strategy that would have been unthinkable even a few years earlier.

Vietnam had a similar effect on the United States. Since Truman, U.S. strategy had been predicated on the notion that America would outlast the Soviet Union through a gradual process of containment. Wherever Soviet influence popped up, the United States would apply the tourniquet, using superior military and economic power to bleed the Russians dry until their system collapsed.

Vietnam seemed to do the reverse. Instead of sapping Soviet strength, the war devolved into a Boer War–style ulcer that drained U.S. resources and resolve. From a handful of advisors at the beginning of the decade, the American presence swelled to more than half a million troops by 1969. Altogether, over nearly a decade of fighting, the war would consume more spending than World War I and the Korean War combined and cost the country more than fifty thousand lives.[26] The longer it dragged on, the less popular it became at home, generating immense pressure for successive presidents to bring it to an end.

As had been true for Edwardian Britain, America's travails in Vietnam coincided with an inauspicious moment on the world scene. Japan and Germany had recovered from their postwar slumps and were beginning to compete with America for international markets. A weakening dollar led to a rush on U.S. gold reserves that spelled trouble for Bretton Woods. The Soviets seemed to be getting stronger in every domain, from industrial output to military spending and space exploration.

The cascade of crises converged in the election year of 1968. While protestors clashed with riot police in cities across America, the North Vietnamese launched the Tet Offensive and the Soviets invaded Czechoslovakia. U.S. defense planners worried that Moscow might be planning to exploit the country's preoccupation with Vietnam to make move on West Berlin.[27] That spring, Acheson, Nitze, and other aging architects of containment warned President Lyndon Johnson that the country was on the brink of catastrophe. America could not continue with business as usual; a dramatic course correction was needed, and urgently.

The correction came in the unlikely form of Richard Milhous Nixon.

By the time of the 1968 election, Nixon had been out of public office for nearly a decade. He had risen to prominence as an outspoken anti-Communist in the Senate in the 1950s before serving two terms as Eisenhower's vice president. His subsequent losses, first to Kennedy in the 1960 presidential election, and then to the incumbent Democrat in the 1962 California gubernatorial race, had seemed to herald a permanent exit from politics. But in 1968, Nixon roared back into the spotlight, fending off attacks from a young Ronald Reagan to become the GOP nominee and beating the Democrat candidate Hubert Humphrey by a razor-thin margin of less than 1 percent.

Nixon was an unusual man. Shy, cerebral, and calculating, he was a brooder by nature who seemed better suited to case law than to campaign rallies and kissing babies. Raised a Quaker, Nixon had abandoned his faith as a young man following the loss of two brothers to tuberculosis. Through the school of hard knocks, he had developed a tough shell of realism that helped him succeed in politics but left little space for sentimentality. Ideals weren't meaningless for Nixon; to the contrary, and paradoxically, he saw himself as an idealist in the mold of Woodrow Wilson. But their value was mainly instrumental, in the motivation they gave individuals and nations to push ahead in the game of survival.[28]

Perhaps because of his melancholy personality, Nixon understood the public mood in 1968 better than any other American politician. He ran on a law-and-order ticket of restoring national dignity after years of foreign war and domestic turmoil. That included getting out of Vietnam—but in a way that preserved America's honor. Writing in *Foreign Affairs* the year before the election, Nixon warned that America could no longer be the "world policeman."[29] But neither should she give heed to the calls to turn inward. "Weary with war, disheartened with allies . . . dismayed at domestic crises," the country needed a new course, better aligned to new realities. These were words that a country exhausted by Vietnam wanted to hear.

The Power Couple

In earlier chapters of this book, transformative diplomacy was usually the result of an effective partnership between two individuals. Richelieu and Louis XIII, Kaunitz and Maria Theresa, Metternich and Francis I, Bismarck and Wilhelm I: all were power duets that combined the elements of intellectual creativity and executive power.

Richard Nixon found his intellectual sparkplug in Henry Kissinger.[30] When Nixon asked him to become national security advisor in

November 1968, Kissinger was a forty-five-year-old academic known mainly for his writings on nuclear weapons.[31] For two decades, he had incubated at Harvard, first as a student of philosophy, then as a faculty member, and finally, from 1959 onward, as a tenured professor.

Like Nixon, Kissinger was an outsider. Although a registered Democrat, he had never been accepted into the inner circle of the Kennedy administration, where he was seen as a brilliant but untrustworthy climber.[32] From the sidelines, he had advised the luckless Republican governor of New York, Nelson Rockefeller, through three failed presidential campaigns. After the last of these in 1968, Kissinger surreptitiously transferred his colors to Nixon, but continued advising both candidates until the election clarified who his new boss would be.

Like Metternich, Kissinger was an immigrant. His family fled to America from Bavaria on the eve of World War II. But Kissinger had no patrician pedigree to smooth his path to power; the son of a schoolteacher, he cut his own trail using a remarkable combination of brains, hustle, and grit. Of the dozen or so central characters examined in the fifteen hundred years covered by this book, he is one of the only commoners, one of only two self-made men (the other is Nixon), and the only Jew.*

He is also, arguably, the only philosopher. Like many other Europeans of his generation, the war had robbed Kissinger of religious faith; like many other American academics of the time, the war's aftermath focused his mind on the potentialities of U.S. power in the atomic age.[33] The result was a lifelong fascination with order—how it is built, how it holds together, and where it is ultimately moving—that would captivate Kissinger from his student days until his death at age one hundred in 2023.

At first, Kissinger looked to metaphysics for answers. He was especially drawn to Immanuel Kant, the 19th-Century German idealist who believed that history was progressing toward a golden age in which human societies would coexist in perpetual harmony. Kissinger was enthralled by this vision. "Peace," he wrote in his undergraduate thesis, "is man's noblest task, humanity's ultimate purpose." But he was troubled by the lack of evidence for it in nature or history. If anything, things seemed to be going in the opposite direction, toward greater barbarism. How was humanity to achieve its "ultimate purpose" if society degenerated so easily into bouts of entropy?[34]

---

* Chrysaphius was probably not a blue blood. Disraeli was Jewish (baptized into Christianity) but is not a major character in the book. The Chamberlains were wealthy merchants, not nobles. Mao was violently self-made. Even Zhou Enlai, as a descendent of prosperous mandarins, came from a more privileged background than Kissinger.

Kissinger found his answer in diplomacy. At a moment when America's top international relations scholars believed traditional diplomacy was dead and needed to be replaced by world government, Kissinger's inquiries led him more deeply into the classical European states system.[35] What he found there deviated widely from Kant's liberal ideals. Where Kant had put his faith in democracy and commerce, Kissinger's reading led him to see the balance of power as a reliable, if imperfect, source of stability in human affairs. In his doctoral dissertation he described how European diplomats after the Napoleonic wars built a durable peace on the principles of reason and equilibrium. This achievement was the result not of inexorable historical forces, but of the efforts of morally flawed individuals striving to create stability amid the chaos of events.

Kissinger's studies produced a worldview similar to Nixon's. Both were realists who thought in terms of power. Nixon, the career politician, had an instinctive grasp of the mechanics of power honed through years of Washington horsetrading. Kissinger, the intellectual, was uncomfortable with American democracy and drawn to higher-level questions of order. This he described as a combination of power and "legitimacy," which he saw as arising not from regime type but from agreements between states "about the nature of workable arrangements and about the permissible aims of and methods of foreign policy."[36]

From different starting points, Kissinger and Nixon arrived at the same conclusion: that containment was not a viable strategy. Nixon doubted its political and fiscal sustainability; Kissinger thought it was simply too rigid to provide stability. "By attempting to achieve situations of strength at each point around the Soviet periphery," he wrote in 1951, "we in effect allow the Soviet General Staff to deploy our forces and to lure our Armed Forces into endless adventures."[37] Instead, Kissinger believed that the superpowers needed to find a modus vivendi that would keep competition within certain bounds. Doing that, he wrote in 1968, would require a "new burst of creativity" to build the "concepts which will enable us to contribute to the emergence of a stable order."[38]

The New Machinery

Nixon and Kissinger shared a deep distrust of bureaucracy. Nixon's contempt for the State Department can be traced to his earliest days in Congress, where he came to believe that it was a hotbed of Communist sympathy.[39] Kissinger's critique was more cerebral: bureaucracy, he believed, was antithetical to the creativity, finesse, and boldness required for enlightened statecraft.[40]

Before entering office, the two formed a pact to sideline the State Department and make important decisions about foreign policy in the White House. The mechanism by which they would do so was the National Security Council.[41] This had been formed by Congress in 1947, along with the Central Intelligence Agency, Joint Chiefs of Staff, and Department of Defense, to equip the U.S. government with a standing peacetime machinery to compete with the Soviets.[42] But whereas the importance of these other entities had grown over time, that of the NSC had diminished. Successive presidents either treated it as a staff of glorified research assistants or saw it get hijacked by wily cabinet secretaries who used it to feed precanned options to the Oval Office.

Nixon's first three executive memos, circulated on the day of his swearing-in ceremony, made clear his determination to use the NSC as an arm of executive authority with Henry Kissinger at its head.[43] Under plans drawn up with the help of a systems analyst from Harvard, Kissinger revised the structure and workflow of the NSC in ways designed to augment his own power.[44] He abolished the so-called Senior Interdepartmental Group, a kind of steering committee chaired by the undersecretary of state that filtered the policy options going to the president, and replaced it with a new Review Group with himself as chair. He instituted a system of formalized taskings, known as NSSMs,* whereby he would dole out orders to the various departments. And he implemented a complex system of interlocking committees with himself at the helm.

Nixon enhanced Kissinger's power by selecting easy-going personalities for cabinet roles while surrounding himself and Kissinger with "hard-edged ethnic" types who excelled in bureaucratic trench warfare.[45] For secretary of state, Nixon tapped William Pierce Rogers, an establishment lawyer who he judged unlikely to fight for the prerogatives of that post.[46] For secretary of defense, Nixon chose Melvin Laird, a congressman from Wisconsin who he assumed, incorrectly, would be similarly passive. Both men clashed with Kissinger. Nixon rarely intervened in these struggles, but when he did, it was usually in Kissinger's favor. Kissinger ruled his roost with consummate skill, guarding access to Nixon, managing the media, and keeping the bureaucracy on its back foot. From day one, the two men were at war with much of their own administration.

---

* National Security Study Memorandum.

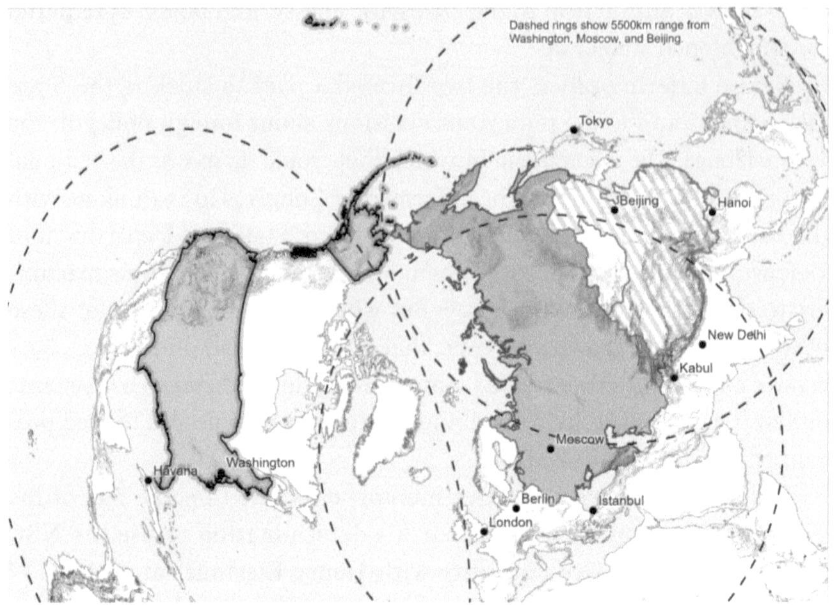

FIGURE 8.1. The Cold War, 1969 (Credit: Andrew Rhodes)

The New Course

Richard Nixon's view of the global situation as he was sworn into office in January 1969 wasn't all that different from the view of the Liberal Unionists who came into Lord Salisbury's cabinet following the "khaki" elections in the fall of 1900. His point of departure was that the framework that had guided American strategy since the late 1940s was insolvent and needed to be replaced. The U.S. nuclear monopoly was gone, America's rivals were more numerous, her allies were richer, Vietnam was bleeding the country dry, and her deteriorating balance of payments position threatened the basis of the postwar Bretton Woods system.

Like the Edwardians, Nixon wanted to bring his nation's commitments in line with the new realities not in order to abnegate its global position but to preserve it.[47] At the time he took office, America maintained a 2.5 war standard, whereby the Pentagon was required to maintain forces capable of fighting two major adversaries and handling a smaller contingency in a third theater. To sustain this level of effort, the country was spending $80 billion a year (about 8 percent of GDP) on defense and had 1.1 million troops under arms, of which 70 percent were in Asia.[48] To win in Vietnam and handle contingencies in Europe or the Middle East, U.S. military planners estimated they would need 200,000 additional troops, at a cost of $10 billion.[49]

Nixon's solution was to reduce U.S. effort in Asia and refocus it on the place that mattered most for U.S. security, which was Europe. In his first year in office, he dropped the 2.5 war standard and replaced it with a 1.5 war formula. Preempting the Democratic-controlled Congress, he introduced a FY70 defense budget that cut outlays by $3 billion, in addition to $4.2 billion in planned spending from the previous administration.[50] More cuts followed, eventually bringing military spending and force levels back to levels not seen since before the Korean War.[51]

To offset this reduced U.S. effort, Nixon planned, as the British had done, to make better use of regional allies. He outlined his new approach to a group of journalists during a layover on the island of Guam in July 1969, on his first presidential trip to Asia. The Nixon Doctrine, as it would come to be called, consisted of two principles: that America would honor her commitments to allies, and that they would be expected to handle internal threats to their security.[52] Over the next three years, Nixon's administration would walk a careful tightrope, admonishing allies to take on more of the burden for conventional defense while reassuring them that the United States would not desert them as it withdrew from Southeast Asia and shifted focus back to Europe.

Also like the Edwardians, Nixon wanted to reduce tensions with U.S. rivals. The first plank of this policy was already in place, in the form of a process of U.S.-Soviet détente, begun under Johnson, that was aimed at reducing nuclear tensions. Nixon could expand on this policy without taking political risks, accepting credit for success or blaming failure on his predecessors.

The second plank—an opening to China—was much riskier.[53] For years, Nixon had been a firm backer of the Nationalist Chinese government under Chiang Kai-shek on the island of Taiwan, and had long advocated a policy of maximum pressure against the Red Chinese state established under Mao Zedong in 1949. But during his wilderness years, Nixon had come around to the view that engaging with Beijing in some fashion was necessary for U.S. interests.[54]

This idea had been circulating for some time.[55] The problem was that, while plenty of people could see the logic for a policy change, no one could figure out how to make it work. The two countries had no formal diplomatic relationship. They had already fought one war in Korea in 1950 and almost fought another over Taiwan in 1958. In 1963 Kennedy went so far as to propose a U.S.-Soviet strike against China's nuclear program.[56]

An NSC assessment the year before Nixon came to power concluded that China would remain hostile toward the United States until Mao died.[57]

Nixon had good reasons to challenge this consensus. Politically, he needed to find a way to launder his reputation as a hawk in the eyes of a peace-minded public. Like many at the time, he also thought that China might hold the key to America's dilemma in Vietnam. Efforts to end the war were deadlocked, mainly because the North Vietnamese saw that Washington wanted to withdraw and had no reason to let it out easily. Beijing, Nixon thought, might be able to pressure Hanoi to change its stance, thereby allowing U.S. forces to leave in an orderly fashion.[58]

There was also the Soviet factor. In later years, Kissinger would claim that he intended from the outset to use Chinese rapprochement as a fulcrum to nudge Soviet cooperation on other matters in a policy of "triangulation."[59] In a 1968 speech for Rockefeller, he had written that the United States should seek "a subtle triangle" with the two countries in order to "improve our relations with each."[60] But once in office, Kissinger appears at first to have dropped the idea. He was initially skeptical of Nixon's plan to engineer a thaw with Beijing and only returned to the idea of triangulation much later, after rapprochement had begun to bear fruit.[61]

Rather than a sophisticated game of triangles, Nixon was driven by an instinctive desire to reduce military and fiscal burdens anywhere possible. An attempt at containing China and the Soviet Union simultaneously would have required enormous exertions at a time when the U.S. economy was strained and the country was war weary. Diplomacy was a logical way to lighten these burdens, even if Nixon wasn't sure exactly what fruit he expected it to bear at the beginning.

Nixon moved quickly in implementing his new approach. Just days after taking office, he directed the NSC to take a fresh look at China policy, drawing on "alternative views and interpretations of the issues involved."[62] The response was a mix of new- and old-think. The State Department's Asia Bureau argued that the status quo was untenable and the time had come to try an opening. The CIA stuck to its long-standing position that China was unlikely to change its behavior until Mao died. The State Department's intelligence office was similarly skeptical; the chances of a "theatrical *ménage à trois*" leading to a "serious rapprochement," it warned, were "remote."[63]

The outcome of this process was never in doubt. At a Senior Review Group meeting in May 1969, three options were tabled: "(a) continue present course, (b) intensify containment, and (c) reduction in tension."[64] But the decision had already been made to attempt something more dramatic.

In a preview of how Nixon and Kissinger would operate, they used these debates to float ideas but not to make policy. Over the next three years, they would wage an inspired but also tortuous and obsessively secretive campaign to bring about rapprochement with China. The question was not whether Nixon would attempt to turn the page with China, but how fast he could do so—and whether Beijing would be singing from the same hymnal.

Ally with the Wu to Oppose the Wei

Creative diplomacy often succeeds because of mistakes on the part of the enemy. Kaunitz's efforts to woo Louis XV might never have succeeded had Frederick the Great not grown impatient and entered into an impetuous alliance with England.

The same was true of the U.S. opening to China. For all of Nixon and Kissinger's creativity, their policy might have miscarried had it not been for the unwisdom of Soviet Russia. For during the same period that the Americans began making overtures to Beijing, Moscow was waging its own aggressive and clumsy effort to deal with its large southern neighbor.

The split between the Soviets and the Chinese had been growing for some time. Its origins lay in the ideological schisms that emerged following the death of Joseph Stalin fifteen years earlier. But the disagreement was never primarily about ideology. The Chinese feared Soviet aggression and wanted to expand their own influence in the Communist world.[65] The Soviet invasion of Czechoslovakia in 1968 and subsequent proclamation of the Brezhnev Doctrine showed that Moscow was willing to use force to cement its authority within the Communist bloc.[66]

Tensions boiled over in early March 1969 in a series of clashes on the Sino-Soviet border, which the Chinese almost certainly initiated. When fighting renewed that August, it quickly escalated, to the point that it looked as if the Soviets were preparing a preemptive nuclear strike on Beijing.[67] A hastily arranged meeting between Zhou Enlai and Alexei Kosygin, chairman of the Soviet Council of Ministers, staved off a larger war. But tensions would remain high for a long time to come.

These incidents showed the Chinese how serious their multifront dilemma had become. While fighting the Russians in the north, Beijing also had to keep a wary eye on U.S. forces in Korea and Japan to the east, as well as Vietnam to the southwest and India to the west, where tensions continued to mount in the border regions of the Himalayas. All of this acted as a powerful stimulant for China's leaders to reassess the fundamentals of their country's grand strategy at exactly the same moment that Nixon and Kissinger were doing the same in the United States.

The man in charge of China at this moment was every inch the strategist, in addition to probably being the biggest mass murderer in history. Mao Zedong was seventy-three years old when Nixon was elected in 1968 and already in a state of advanced physical decay. Over the preceding half-century, he had transformed the Chinese Communist Party from a rag-tag insurgency into a mass peasant movement that defeated first the Japanese and then the Chinese nationalists to become the most powerful force in Asia.[68] In the years that followed, Mao consolidated his rule in a series of brutal suppressions that, altogether, resulted in the deaths of around sixty-five million people.[69]

Like the Qing emperors of old, Mao enjoyed the prerogatives of a god on earth. Ensconced in Beijing's Zhongnanhai compound, a complex of gardens and palaces to the southwest of the Forbidden City, Mao ruled in paranoid isolation, attended by a retinue of teenage female attendants who indulged his sexual whims like modern-day concubines.[70] A consummate manipulator, he played courtiers against one another with effortless skill and issued pronouncements that were treated as poetry-edicts by his Chinese followers and innumerable left-wing votaries in the West.

As tensions with the Soviets mounted, Mao asked his old comrade Chen Yi to make a study of the situation. Chen's instructions were not that different from those that Kissinger was receiving from Nixon at almost exactly the same moment. Chen and three of his fellow generals were to think creatively and "not be confined to the established views and conclusions."[71]

The resulting document, known as the Four Marshals Report, is a classic study in realist logic.[72] It looked at the map from the standpoint of China's two main enemies, the United States and the Soviet Union, and concluded that the latter was the bigger threat. "The United States and China are separated by the vast Pacific Ocean," the marshals wrote. America's "strategic emphasis" lay in Europe, and Vietnam was a costly distraction. "The last thing the U.S. imperialists want to see is involvement in a war against China, allowing the Soviet revisionists to take advantage of it."

Drawing on history, the marshals argued that China should use diplomacy to reduce the number of active opponents arrayed against her. They cited Stalin's 1939 nonaggression pact with Adolf Hitler as one example and, as another, China's own Three Kingdoms period, when the realm had been divided into feuding states. China should follow the policy of the kingdom of Shu Han, they wrote, which "All[ied] with the Wu in the east to oppose the Wei in the north."

The upshot was that Mao should ease tensions with the United States. He should "make full use of time and strengthen preparations in all respects," the marshals wrote, "adopt[ing] a military strategy of active defense and a political strategy of active offense." In a subsequent report, the marshals went further, arguing that Beijing should "take the initiative" and hold talks with the Americans at a senior level.

By early the following year, Chen's counsel had gone from conjecture to policy, as Mao instructed his premier, Zhou Enlai, to look for ways to engage diplomatically with the United States. Had the Soviets not been so short-sighted in attacking the Chinese, it's unlikely that Mao would have embraced Chen's advice.[73] But after the nuclear scare, Mao was willing to embark on a bold new course, even if it carried risks.

Mandarin Seductions

When Kaunitz made his initial approach to Louis XV, he chose to go through the king's mistress, Madame de Pompadour, in order to bypass the French king's bureaucrats, whom he knew would impede the effort. When Kissinger set out to engineer a rapprochement with Mao Zedong, his main concern was to bypass the bureaucrats of *his own* government.

To achieve this secrecy, Kissinger used the good offices of Romanian president Nicolae Ceaușescu and Pakistani president Yahya Khan, two petty tyrants who, like Pompadour, had close links with the enemy leadership and were eager to use them to improve their own stations. Over a twenty-month period between the summer of 1969 and the spring of 1971, Kissinger used both channels to ferry messages to Beijing while keeping the State Department in the dark.

His efforts paid off in early December 1970 when the Pakistanis delivered a message that Mao was willing to meet with Nixon.[74] After a series of frenzied huddles in which Nixon wickedly dangled the prospect of sending an emissary other than Kissinger, it was agreed that the national security advisor should secretly travel to meet with the Chinese premier, Zhou Enlai. When the Chinese accepted this arrangement on June 2, Nixon and Kissinger opened a bottle of Courvoisier and drank a toast "not to ourselves" but "to generations to come who may have a better chance to live in peace."[75]

Kissinger's first trip to China took place the following month. To preserve secrecy, Kissinger traveled surreptitiously through Pakistan, where he feigned illness and, while supposedly recuperating, slipped across the Himalayas in a Pakistani government plane to China.

Before leaving, Kissinger wrote a memo for Nixon in which he speculated that the Chinese would treat him like a barbarian, "com[ing] to pay tribute to the center of culture and politics."[76] This was a well-grounded assumption. Over the millennia, the Chinese had developed effective methods for dealing with visitors like Kissinger. When faced with a backward but martially superior opponent, they would bribe and seduce them into becoming supplicants to the Chinese emperor.[77]

The barbarian-handler who met Kissinger in Beijing was among the most sophisticated in the trade. The arrival of Zhou Enlai in Kissinger's memoirs has all the drama of a main character appearing for the first time in a novel. He "moved gracefully," was "urbane, infinitely patient, extraordinarily intelligent" and possessed an "inner serenity" and a "special human quality."[78]

There was something undeniably bewitching about Zhou. Reared in the twilight of China's Qing dynasty, he descended from a long line of mandarins in Zhejiang Province, whose notables included a prominent Confucian scholar of the Song dynasty.[79] From childhood he was steeped in Tang poetry and Chinese classical literature. Unlike most others in Mao's inner circle, he had lived and studied abroad and gained exposure to Western ideas. He had glammed onto Mao early in the revolutionary struggle and served as a loyal retainer until his death in 1976.

Zhou's quiet manner and philosophic bent belied a hardened core of the kind that one finds in people accustomed to having to survive under a brutal and arbitrary regime. For all his diplomatic finesse, it must be remembered that he was the committed lieutenant of one of history's most ruthless killers, and that he himself had ordered the deaths of many innocent people.[80] True to the revolutionary ethos of the Maoist state, Zhou saw diplomacy as an arm of warfare against China's enemies. "In the life of a nation," he once told a graduating class of Chinese foreign service officers, "it must be ready at all times to wage two kinds of war—a war of words and a war of swords. The war of words includes both spoken and written words. Diplomacy falls within the province of the war of words. . . . As sure as day turns into night, there will be a constant war of words, every day of the year."[81]

Zhou quickly took the measure of his American guest. After their first day of meetings, he reported to Mao that Kissinger was willing to make a surprising number of concessions to secure a presidential visit. Mao's instruction was to go back the second day and "brag" to Kissinger about the "big strategic picture."[82] Doing so would give Zhou a chance to sound off on Maoist talking points but also, one assumes, feed Kissinger's desire to talk about great matters of state—and thus his ego.

The Chinese had read their man well. They saw that, for Kissinger, Nixon's trip was itself the deliverable. This gave Zhou leverage, which he used to probe the outer reaches of what China might be able to get. The test came in the form of the wording of the trip communiqué, which Zhou waited until the last minute to spring on Kissinger, just before his plane was scheduled to depart. The document portrayed Nixon as a supplicant, coming to Mao like the barbarians of old, to discuss the item of maximum interest to China (Taiwan), the resolution of which would precede a normalization of ties.[83] When Kissinger balked at the draft, Zhou folded, reserving harder negotiations for a later day.

These interactions succeeded in securing a presidential visit, which was set for some time before May 1972. The most important result of Kissinger's first trip to China, he later wrote, was the "comprehension by each side of the fundamental purposes of the other."[84] For the Chinese, however, its most important result was that it showed the barbarians were willing to pay for Nixon to come to Beijing. As Mao said at the time, "It would take time for a monkey to evolve into a human. They are now at the stage of an ape."[85] All that remained was to work out the details of this "evolution."

Linkages and Triangles

Diplomatic successes often turn on cost-benefit calculations. When Kaunitz proposed an alliance to the Bourbon court, the reaction was initially negative but improved when it became apparent that Vienna was willing to barter something tangible, in the form of the Austrian Netherlands. Conversely, when Lord Lansdowne pursued his "one preconceived idea" of improved ties with Germany, the mood was initially positive but soured as it became clear the Germans would expect a higher price for the courtesy of friendship than Britain was prepared to pay.

What was America willing to pay for rapprochement with China, and what did it hope to get in return? The bureaucracy had its own answers to these questions. An interagency memorandum in February 1971 listed potential benefits as preventing a clash over Taiwan, recruiting China into a nuclear arms control agreement, and forestalling a Sino-Soviet "offensive alliance."[86] The Asia hands at the State Department thought Nixon should be willing to give political and trade concessions—but that he should go slowly, conditionally, and in coordination with U.S. allies. The Pentagon was more cautious still; whatever direction things took, it believed that the United States should not cede her military position in Taiwan without exacting significant Chinese concessions in return.[87]

For Nixon and Kissinger, Vietnam was top of mind. When Kissinger received Zhou's invitation in April, his first reaction was to say to the president, "If we get this thing working, we will end Vietnam this year."[88] In addition, by this stage both men had begun to think more intently about how to use the opening to China to America's advantage in dealings with the Soviet Union.[89] For months, these had been stuck in a rut, as Moscow exploited Congressional clamoring for an arms control deal to pressure the administration for various concessions and refused to commit to a presidential summit. In a memo to Nixon before his trip, Kissinger listed "Chinese perceptions of the Soviet Union" alongside the more concrete goal of getting Mao to exert "some moderating influence on Indochina."[90] Both objectives, however, ultimately took a back seat to an overarching political goal—which, as Kissinger later wrote in his memoirs, was to "succeed in arranging the cherished summit."[91]

Chinese objectives revolved primarily around Taiwan. In his first message to Washington, Zhou had made it clear that the only purpose of any visit must be "to discuss the subject of vacation of China's territory, called Taiwan."[92] Zhou elaborated on Chinese aims in a presentation to the Politburo. Out of eight "principles," the first four dealt with Taiwan, including removal of U.S. forces from the island, affirmation that Taiwan "is China's territory," and preventing any U.S. move toward a policy of "two Chinas" or "one China and one Taiwan.[93]

Kissinger's method for convincing China to help in Vietnam was to link it to U.S. concessions on Taiwan. This was consistent with the administration policy of "linkages," whereby Washington would condition U.S. action on matters of concern to a foreign power on the other side's attention to U.S. concerns. By intimating a willingness to withdraw U.S. forces from Taiwan, Kissinger hoped to elicit Chinese pressure on Hanoi to negotiate, which in turn would ease America's departure from Vietnam. This was a logical strategy, especially given that a large portion of the U.S. troops stationed in Taiwan were there to assist with operations in nearby Vietnam.

How much was Kissinger willing to concede on Taiwan? Apparently quite a lot. A Europeanist at heart, he probably believed that Taiwan's return to mainland rule was a historical inevitability; as he told Nixon at one point, "It's a tragedy that it has to happen to Chiang at the end of his life, but we have to be cold about it."[94] Nixon was more cautious; an old Cold Warrior, he worried that giving away too much would expose him to attacks from the conservative wing of the Republican Party, where prominent figures like Ronald Reagan were sure to denounce any deal as a sellout. He was willing to scale back U.S. commitments to Taiwan, but he wanted to give ground sparingly, in return for Chinese concessions. He told Kissinger to play it cool and not concede anything on Taiwan "until it was necessary to do so."[95]

Kissinger did the opposite. In his first meeting with Zhou, he declared that he had "no strong opinion" about Taiwan, and that America had no plans to adopt a policy of "two Chinas," or "one China, one Taiwan," or to support a Taiwanese independence movement, aid the island in an attack on the mainland, or use it as a base for U.S. operations.[96] The only thing he couldn't give was formal recognition of the People's Republic. But he hinted that that too would come, along with more concessions on Taiwan, if Nixon won reelection—which a Beijing trip would help to ensure.

Given this approach, it's not hard to see why the Vietnam-Taiwan linkage never materialized. Later events would show that Beijing did not possess the leverage over Hanoi that Nixon and Kissinger supposed it did. But the fact is that the Chinese had already obtained a lot of what they wanted on Taiwan without having to pay for it. In the first few minutes of their first meeting, Kissinger gave significant ground on two of the first four items on Zhou's list. From the Chinese perspective, this was the key that unlocked everything that followed.[97]

Kissinger was more successful in using rapprochement to prod the Soviets. When, four days after returning from Beijing, he met with the Soviet ambassador Anatoly Dobrynin, he found that Moscow had suddenly become more pliable than in previous interactions. "For the first time in my experience with him," he wrote, Dobrynin was "totally insecure."[98] Kissinger exploited the situation to secure a presidential trip to Moscow and give fresh impetus to efforts at a new arms control agreement. As Dobrynin later conceded, the Soviets had been "outplayed" and knew it; going forward, Brezhnev had little choice but to embrace the logic of U.S.-Soviet détente in order to "neutralize any collusion between Washington and Beijing."[99]

Kissinger's trip brought a dramatic turnaround in Nixon's political fortunes. Even if he hadn't made progress on Nixon's top priority (Vietnam), he had delivered on the promise to inaugurate an "era of negotiations." Before Kissinger's trip, Nixon had no summits on the calendar; after it, he had two. The only question was how well the two men would use these openings in the sixteen months that remained before the 1972 election.

Keeping Old Friends

Diplomatic rapprochements always come with costs. When Byzantine emperors sought détente with the Persians, they had to watch that the Bedouin did not switch sides. When Venetian doges and Valois kings signed treaties with the Ottoman sultans, they were accused of betraying Christ. When the British Empire cut a deal with the Russians in 1907, clients from the Persian shah to the tribes of the Hindu Kush suddenly wondered about British credibility.

Nixon's opening to China was no different. The president's televised announcement on July 15, 1971 that he would travel to Beijing shocked U.S. allies. Whatever the merits of the extreme secrecy that Kissinger required to develop his policy, it meant that even America's closest friends were kept in the dark, with all the risks that entailed.[100] Twenty-four hours before Nixon's trip was announced, the president of Pakistan knew more about what was happening than did the leaders of America's Asian allies, the U.S. State Department, or even the vice president of the United States. Taipei's ambassador to the United States, found out twenty minutes before the president's TV broadcast; the Australian ambassador, James Plimsoll, had forty-five minutes' notice.[101] The Japanese prime minister, Sato Eisaku, was told as he was leaving a cabinet meeting, while the U.S. ambassador to Tokyo heard the news on the radio as he was having his hair cut.[102]

For allied leaders, the shock was strategic and political—but also personal. Many had taken political risks to align with Nixon after he came to office and were now subjected to withering attacks at home. Sato, who had just concluded intense negotiations with Washington over Okinawa, told a visitor, "I have done everything they have asked," and "they have let me down."[103] Australian prime minister William McMahon was blunter. "You should know," he wrote to Nixon, "we were placed in a quandary by our lack of any foreknowledge of what is certainly a dramatic step in the foreign policy of the United States."[104]

The situation was especially bad for the Taiwanese, who had been fighting a losing battle to prevent mainland China from gaining a seat in the United Nations. Nixon had been walking a tightrope on this issue, pretending to help Taiwan but not doing anything to jeopardize the opening to China. Kissinger's trip gave the game away, leading Taipei to wonder whether it could still count on American support in the UN—or, for that matter, might be bartered away as collateral. The betrayal stung; this "is not the kind of thing a friend and ally should do," Shen told the U.S. press. The Taiwanese National Assembly warned of "serious consequences" for the relationship, and Taipei even considered offering naval basing rights to Soviet vessels in retaliation.[105]

Allied frustrations bled over into U.S. domestic politics. Conservative Republicans had long championed the cause of Taiwan, with support from a powerful network of donors, operatives, and advocacy groups known as the "China Lobby." They and their allies in Congress lambasted Kissinger's trip as a sellout to Red China.[106] California governor Ronald Reagan ramped up the pressure on Nixon to defend Taiwan's UN seat, while New York senator James Buckley announced that he was rallying a group of GOP renegades to oppose the president's foreign policy.

These factions required careful handling.[107] Nixon and Kissinger made phone calls to placate Reagan and Buckley while Secretary Rogers (who had also been kept in the dark) was deployed to buck up Asian allies. Nixon asked Reagan to fly to Taipei as his special emissary to tell Chiang Kai-shek that America would not abandon Taiwan. It was an inspired idea, but its logic was undercut by the fact that Kissinger was simultaneously maneuvering to ensure that Taiwan lost the UN vote.[108] Even as he sought to reassure critics, Nixon remained firmly focused on developing the China opening to the fullest extent possible.

Coup de Maître

Elected leaders can do a lot of harm when they try to conduct diplomacy without adequate preparation. Lloyd George's improvisations at Sèvres sowed the seeds for one of the worst wars in Middle Eastern history. Neville Chamberlain's freelancing at Berchtesgaden convinced Hitler to increase his demands on Czechoslovakia. And Franklin Roosevelt's freewheeling with Stalin inadvertently spurred the spread of Soviet influence in Eastern Europe.

Richard Nixon suffered from no such deficiencies when he went to see Mao Zedong in February 1972. His trip was probably the most exhaustively prepared in U.S. presidential history. Four months before the visit, Kissinger had traveled to Beijing for a second set of meetings with Zhou, this time in public, to arrange the agenda, communiqué, and media component in advance. Altogether by the time Nixon arrived, Kissinger had spent more than forty hours with Zhou Enlai, spread across sixteen meetings and eight days, in addition to numerous casual interactions.[109]

Nixon continued to contemplate U.S. goals all the way up to the last minute. On the flight over, he wrote on his yellow legal pad:

WHAT THEY WANT:

1. Build up their world credentials
2. Taiwan
3. Get U.S. out of Asia

WHAT WE WANT:

1. Indo China (?)
2. Communication—To restrain Chinese expansion in Asia
3. In Future—Reduce threat of confrontation by China Super Power

WHAT WE BOTH WANT:

1. Reduce danger of confrontation & conflict
2. A more stable Asia
3. A restraint on USSR.[110]

Nixon's interactions with Mao and Zhou demonstrate his skills as a statesman. He knew his brief, was honest about what he could and couldn't do, and didn't lose track of his objectives. Like Kissinger, he had a sense of the historical importance of the moment and tried to see things from the Chinese perspective. Unlike Kissinger, Nixon doesn't appear to have been seduced by his hosts.

Nixon's method was also different from Kissinger's. Where Kissinger had started by intimating America's willingness to address China's grievances and worked his way up to the big picture, Nixon started with the big picture and worked his way down to particulars. He had a unique way, probably developed from long experience in Washington deal-making, of putting his finger on his interlocutors' greatest fears and then showing how what he wanted would help them deal with those problems. Why did the Soviets "have more forces on the border facing you than they do on the border facing Western Europe?" he asked Mao shortly after they met. "Which danger does the PRC [turn to] face? Is it the danger of American aggression—or of Soviet aggression?"[111]

Mao didn't play along. Employing the tactics he had used during the Long March, he retreated when the enemy advanced. China wasn't worried about being attacked by anyone, and, besides, these kinds of things were Zhou's responsibility; the chairman would stick to "philosophical questions."[112] This deflection denied Nixon the leverage his line of questions was aimed at achieving, while also subtly putting Mao on a different plane, above Nixon.

FIGURE 8.2. Cold War power broker: President Nixon with Chairman Mao
(Credit: CPA Media Pte Ltd / Alamy)

Nixon made a final attempt to solicit Chinese help on Vietnam on the second day of the trip, but Zhou didn't budge; he countered by suggesting that America simply get out of Vietnam, like the French had gotten out of Algeria—and stay out.[113]

Nixon found easier sledding when the discussion moved to the Soviet Union. When he told the Chinese that he worried about the speed of the Soviet nuclear buildup, Zhou noted with alarm that the Soviets had shifted "the main body of their forces" from Europe to the Far East.[114] This was the glue of rapprochement. Zhou shifted from the traditional Chinese stance of opposing U.S.-Soviet arms control talks by supporting the SALT negotiations but sought to preserve trade space by insisting that any statements coming out of the summit be framed in a way that appeared "anti-Soviet."[115]

The most tangible by-product of the visit was the communiqué, which was released to the world in Shanghai on the last night of the trip. Much of the verbiage had already been worked out on Kissinger's second trip. In those talks, the Chinese had insisted on a dual structure by which areas of agreement would be stated in language agreed by both sides while areas of disagreement would be dealt with in separate sections of text, reflecting the divergent views of the two capitals.

Taiwan fit very much into the latter category. After arriving in Beijing, Nixon confirmed Kissinger's earlier concessions; the question, he told the Chinese, was how to convey this policy shift in a way that "would not stir up the animals" back home.[116] The two remaining questions were how to characterize Taiwan's relationship to the mainland and what the nature of the U.S. military presence on the island would be going forward.

Kissinger's clever formula for handling the first was to say that "the United States acknowledges that all Chinese on either side of the Taiwan Strait maintain there is but one China and that Taiwan is a province of China. The United States does not challenge that position." He refused a Chinese request that the United States say it "hope[d]" for a peaceful solution on Taiwan as well as a demand that it commit to a timetable for withdrawal. But he made an important concession on the second matter, by stating that America's "ultimate objective" was withdrawal, and that it would "progressively reduce" its forces as tensions abated.[117]

The communiqué nearly fell apart at the last minute when the State Department raised a number of objections about the wording of the text. This was the inevitable result of Kissinger's long battle to exclude Secretary Rogers from China policy. Rogers pointed out that the final draft mentioned America's defense pacts with Japan and South Korea but not the one with Taiwan. The last time such an omission was made, in a 1950 speech by Dean Acheson, the result had been a major war on the Korean Peninsula.[118] The text therefore had to be reopened, to the dismay of the Chinese. Rather than adding Taiwan to the list of countries mentioned as having defense treaties with America, Kissinger opted to dilute the references to South Korea and Japan.

The resulting document is a stately pastiche that holds a number of contradictory principles in unrelieved tension. In a pregnant clause intended for Soviet consumption, the two parties agreed to "oppose" attempts by "any other country" to seek hegemony in Asia. Beyond that, there isn't much of a shared outlook. America affirmed her commitment to "individual freedom and social progress." The Chinese recited the liturgy that Marxism is the "irresistible trend of history." The disagreement on Taiwan is laid out in detail, with the Chinese restating their long-standing position that the island is a "province of China," while the U.S. language marks a noticeable shift from old positions. The communiqué ends with nebulous promises to encourage "people-to-people contacts," "facilitate the progressive development of trade," and "stay in contact" going forward.

On the last night of the trip, Nixon spoke at a banquet in Shanghai in which, as Kissinger puts it, the *mao-tai* (a stout sorghum liquor) "flowed like water." In a demonstration of why the old French diplomatist François de Callières warned against mixing alcohol and diplomacy, Nixon hinted that America would defend China if it were attacked by an outside power.[119] Kissinger tells us the president drank late into the night, seeking "reassurance" from his aides that he had done the right thing by going to China, and wondering how history would view it all. Kissinger was ready to give reassurance, for he intended to shape history's judgments about what had been done there.

Aftermath

Nixon's trip to China was well-received back home. When Nixon landed at Andrews Air Force Base, he was met by fifteen hundred well-wishers, one of whom described the experience as "sort of like seeing the astronauts coming back from the moon." Seventy percent of Americans thought the trip was worthwhile. Most of Congress, the media, and academia viewed the trip favorably. Even some conservative critics were caught up in the moment; Reagan congratulated the president and joked that he should turn the story of the trip into a TV mini-series.[120]

America's Asian allies were less enthused. While the administration continued to reassure Taiwan of U.S. support, its actions showed that the relationship had indeed changed; over the next two years, Nixon withdrew half of U.S. troops, along with nuclear-capable fighter aircraft, U-2 spy planes, and nuclear weapons.[121] Japan was also unhappy about the summit. Sato's government collapsed in July; a meeting between Nixon and the Japanese emperor improved the atmosphere, but relations would be damaged for years to come. Adapting to the new circumstances, Tokyo cut its own deal with Beijing in September, followed by Australia, New Zealand, and the Philippines. Nevertheless, none of these allies broke politically from the United States, and most of them increased defense spending.

The trip also acted as a fillip to U.S.-Soviet relations. Kissinger's push for détente bore fruit when, three months after visiting Beijing, Nixon made the first-ever visit by an American president to Moscow. During the summit, he and Brezhnev concluded the Strategic Arms Limitations Agreement (SALT I), a five-year arrangement capping U.S. and Soviet land- and sea-based ballistic missile arsenals, and a separate treaty limiting the construction of anti-ballistic missile systems. Both treaties suffered from the extreme secrecy and propensity for upfront concessions that characterized Kissinger's China diplomacy.[122] But they were wildly popular in Congress (which ratified SALT by a vote of 88–2) and among the public (74 percent of whom approved of it).[123]

In parallel, Kissinger used the momentum from Nixon's China trip to U.S. advantage in the Paris peace talks. While neither Beijing nor Moscow would (or could) exercise the kind of restraint on Hanoi that Nixon had hoped, outreach to both powers helped isolate the North Vietnamese at a key moment when the administration was escalating the conflict to force Hanoi's hand.[124] By October, Kissinger was able, with some exaggeration, to announce that "peace is at hand."[125] After the Christmas bombing of 1972, Hanoi reluctantly agreed to suspend hostilities long enough for U.S. forces to leave the country. The resulting agreement was signed in January 1973, and, two months later, the last U.S. combat units left Vietnam.

While promoting peace abroad, Nixon continued to advance an economic program of fiscal restraint. Under a deal worked out in the summer of 1971, the United States jettisoned the gold standard, thereby staving off an unsustainable run on the nation's dwindling bullion reserves. The move, along with government spending cuts, wage-price controls, and a 10 percent surcharge on imports, effectively devalued the dollar and gave a boost to U.S. industry.[126] All of this came as yet another shock to allies but was popular with the American electorate. Unemployment fell, exports increased, and U.S. stocks enjoyed the biggest spike in history to that point.[127] Nixon's approval rating, which had stood at 49 percent at the beginning of 1972, shot up to 62 percent by midyear.

In the 1972 election campaign, Nixon could credibly claim that he had delivered on his 1968 campaign promises. He was on the cusp of brokering peace in Vietnam, had struck a new bargain with allies that protected American jobs and kept the nation out of new imbroglios, relaxed tensions with China and the Soviets, and negotiated two nuclear treaties.

The result was one of the biggest landslides in U.S. political history. Nixon won the 1972 election with a whopping 60 percent of the vote, sweeping every state except Massachusetts and collecting 520 out of 538 electoral votes.[128] In a little over a year, Nixon had gone from what he called "the lowest point" of his presidency to the pinnacle of his career. Kissinger's diplomacy had been a major, if not indeed the decisive, factor in bringing about this astonishing turnaround.

Kissinger in the Docket

The foreign-policy accomplishments of Nixon's first term tend to be overshadowed by the scandals of his second term.[129] In the decades since, Kissinger's diplomacy has been attacked from all sides. From the right, he is criticized for doing deals with America's enemies over the heads of her allies, as summed up in Pat Buchanan's quip after Beijing that he had "sold out to the bastards." From the left, he is criticized for a callous disregard for human rights, as summed up in Christopher Hitchens's comment that he is "a war criminal, a liar . . . responsible for murder."[130]

Yet even Kissinger's harshest critics acknowledge that he and Nixon revolutionized American foreign policy. Over a four-year period, the two men implemented a series of initiatives that extricated the United States from Vietnam and demonstrated beyond any doubt that the country had not lost the capacity for bold strokes on the world stage.[131] Their opening to China resuscitated American statecraft at a time when it had grown sterile and showed that diplomacy could be wielded for strategic effect, even in the age of global ideologies and atomic weapons.

How does Kissinger stack up to other great diplomats across the ages? His task with China was easier than Kaunitz's with France, in the sense that the opponent he was attempting to woo had recently been attacked and *wanted* to be courted. There is some truth to Kissinger's claim that, like Bismarck, he maintained better relations with his country's rivals than they maintained with each other, though Bismarck's system was more complicated, and he presided over it for a much longer span than Kissinger. Kissinger was more effective than Lansdowne in courting two antagonists simultaneously, though he exaggerates when he characterizes U.S. ties with China as a "quasi-alliance" on par with Britain's 1904 entente with France.[132]

The obvious comparison, and the one Kissinger probably liked the most, is with Metternich.[133] Nixon's big moves, Kissinger tells us, brought about an entirely new world order, built on a recalibrated balance of power and a shared set of agreements about the way the world should work.[134]

This is a bit of a stretch. Even at its height, Kissinger's "triangular" system of diplomacy never possessed the characteristics of order as Kissinger himself defined it. Without doubt, the world was brought into greater balance, in the sense that Chinese and American power was redirected toward the shared Soviet threat. One could even say that this brought stability, in that it lowered tensions at a moment when the world was tending to conflict.[135]

But the resulting state of affairs lacked the vital component of agreed rules of the road—"legitimacy," as Kissinger called it—that would be necessary to call it a functioning political order. Even while lowering tensions, the rivals continued to bleed and harass one another wherever possible. All three just happened to desire a period of strategic rest, or *recueillement*, to regain strength before resuming the contest on more favorable terms.[136] To call this an "order" would be like saying that three gunslingers who find themselves reloading at the same moment are somehow a shooting club.

Kissinger is on especially shaky ground when he imputes a motive of order-building to Mao.[137] Chinese documents describe rapprochement as a gambit to "aggravate the contradictions" between the Americans and Soviets, to "divid[e] up enemies and enhanc[e] ourselves."[138] Even if one accounts for the ideological nature of such statements, they are consistent with Chinese actions. Mao, after all, was at least as much a driver to rapprochement as Nixon. It's more probable that he and Zhou were applying the imperial Chinese logic of "ally[ing] with the Wu to oppose the Wei" than that they were attempting to play Talleyrand to Kissinger's Metternich.[139] When Mao crowed that "all under heaven is in great chaos," he wasn't lamenting the absence of order but exulting in the opportunities it presented for advancing China's interests.

Was Kissinger a good negotiator? It's an important question, not least because Kissinger sold himself, above all, as such. He denigrated traditional U.S. negotiating methods, saying that Americans put too much emphasis on "goodwill and facility for compromise." By treating what "the other side will accept," as an end in itself, he wrote, Americans allow rivals to sit tight and "discover what else we might offer." By contrast, the Chinese were pros: They stood on principles and avoided getting pulled into the weeds. They got to their preferred position in "one jump" and then stuck to it, come what may.[140]

The funny thing is that Kissinger's dealings with the Chinese look an awful lot like the conciliatory methods he so vociferously criticized. In his opening meeting with Zhou, he essentially gave Beijing, if not everything it wanted, then enough to undercut his own leverage later in the process. As one Chinese scholar writes, Zhou "immediately realized that, to pave the way for Nixon's China visit, Kissinger had already made critical concessions on Taiwan."[141] Why didn't Kissinger try harder to extract reciprocal concessions? Because for him, Nixon's trip to Beijing was the chief deliverable. The Shanghai communiqué was part of the payment for that trip; almost all of the concessions in the document were on the American side. Even the stagecraft of Nixon's trip, with the president going like a supplicant to Mao, bespoke a China-tilted power dynamic; as Zhou later said, "It is not we who need something from them, but they who need something from us."[142]

It is only when Kissinger's diplomacy is taken out of the weeds of the Shanghai communiqué or the nebulous realm of global order and viewed where it belongs, in the context of strategy, that its value to the United States can be properly appraised. The goal of Nixon's grand strategy was to alleviate the military and fiscal burdens on the United States *without forfeiting the overall U.S. position.* He wanted to effect a controlled reduction of effort in Asia in order to refocus resources on the place that was most important to U.S. national security, which was Europe. The point of all this was to preserve U.S. power and influence, not diminish it. As one historian put it, Nixon wanted "military retrenchment without political disengagement."[143]

This, and not some generic lowering of tensions, is what Kissinger's efforts were meant to support—and he largely succeeded in that task. Put simply, his diplomacy made the shift from a 2.5 to a 1.5 war standard possible. Engaging with China bought breathing space for the United States to shift focus to Europe without hazarding the loss of Asia. The Nixon Doctrine supported this pivot; while it did not achieve the degree of burden-sharing the president hoped, it did prompt most Asian allies to accept more responsibility for local defense without rupturing relations.[144] The combined effect was to enable the United States to significantly lower defense spending on the reasonable assumption that her adversaries would not be able to seize the moment to their advantage.

Nixon's pivot was not an end in itself; it was meant to give America an edge against her main opponent, the Soviet Union. Kissinger's diplomacy forced the Soviets to bear the full brunt of their own two-front dilemma. Prior to Nixon's adjustments, 70 percent of U.S. forces worldwide were in Asia and 30 percent were in Europe; afterwards, the ratio was reversed.[145] Freed from the U.S. threat on their seaward flanks, the Chinese were able to devote more military attention to their border with the Soviet Union. SALT, for all its flaws, supported the goal as well; recent scholarship shows that Nixon and Kissinger saw arms control as a device to buy time for the United States to replenish its strength and "compete as hard as possible."[146]

Détente, of course, also benefited the Soviets, who we now know needed to reduce spending on armaments at least as much, if not more, than the United States (even if they ended up doing the opposite).[147] But, at the time, their ability to continue producing missiles seemed limitless, while the United States was in no shape, politically or economically, to enter into a new arms race. At base, Nixon's strategy can therefore be seen as resting on a competitive wager that the characteristics of the U.S. system would enable it to make better use of a period of rest than its main opponent. The Soviets themselves realized this; as Dobrynin later reflected, Nixon's efforts at détente "disguised a policy of strength."[148]

Nixon's wager turned out to be correct. His policies allowed America to get her second wind spiritually as well as strategically, at a moment when it might have turned inward.[149] In part because of his redirection of military effort away from Southeast Asia, the United States was able from the mid-1970s forward to direct more resources toward new R&D programs—the so-called Second Offset—that resulted in a range of breakthrough technologies that the Soviets could not match.[150] More broadly, the gradual entry of China as a trading nation into the world economy heightened the Soviet Union's isolation as a failing command economy.[151]

The full payoff to Nixon's bet would come several years later, under the presidency of one of his harshest critics. Despite his long-standing criticism of Nixon, Ronald Reagan adopted many elements of his approach, including a modified form of linkages and arms control, and grafted them into a framework grounded in the traditional logic of containment.[152] Coming at a moment when America's morale and resources had recovered from the post-Vietnam torpor, Reagan was able to capitalize on Nixon's earlier reconcentration of effort to Europe. The man who had denounced détente as surrender wielded it as a competitive tool while regaining the moral high ground and tightening the screws on a financially depleted Soviet Union.

China played an underappreciated role in Reagan's strategy. Even as he exposed the evils of the Soviet system, Reagan continued to quietly buck up Communist China as a counterweight to that system.[153] When Reagan's CIA began supplying weapons to mujahideen fighters resisting the Soviets in Afghanistan, they did so using mules that were supplied by the Chinese.[154] Here perhaps was the ultimate irony of Kissinger's diplomatic legacy: that policies he and Nixon had viewed as transcending the logic of containment ended up strengthening the efficacy of that very strategy. Far from prolonging the Cold War, as some critics allege, Nixon helped shorten it. The consequences of his administration's deepening of ties with China, both for good and for ill, remain with us to this day.[155]

The American Legacy: Federal Diplomacy

Like every other great power in this book, America's approach to diplomacy has been shaped by geography. The United States combines the protective features of earlier maritime great powers like Britain with the mass of continental empires like Germany but on a far larger scale. The same providential location that allowed America to congeal as a great power nurtured the growth of a republican-democratic polity of a size not seen in history. The result was a paradox: A super-republic of immense might that could go, within the space of a few years, from trying to stand apart from the world to trying to remake the world in its own image.

Yet, as this chapter shows, the same laws of geopolitics encountered by every other society in history also apply to the United States. Even a superpower of America's strength and ideals has been confronted by the reality of limited power that has compelled humans from the beginning of time to embrace the discipline of strategy. By the early 1970s, the pressures on the American global position were severe; like every other great power in this book, the country faced a choice between growing her military to cover expansive liabilities or rebalancing her international portfolio and reducing the number of threats requiring military attention.

Like earlier successful great powers, America chose the second option. Faced with two powerful adversaries beyond their country's immediate ability to manage, U.S. leaders used diplomacy to alleviate fiscal burdens and refocus military resources on the main threat. However novel at the time, the basic contours of their approach are as old as time. Yet even as they charted this "new" course, Nixon and Kissinger found their diplomacy constrained as well as advantaged by a diplomatic mindset and set of institutions that were distinctively American.

FEDERAL DIPLOMACY

To an even greater extent than in earlier republics, power in the American state is divided among multiple actors. The executive branch's authority over foreign affairs is shared with the Senate and sifted internally, among various organs that vie for influence over policy. The American public participates energetically in debates about foreign policy. And the professional bureaucracy attending to these matters has taken a life of its own in the decades since World War II, reaching a size and scale of influence that far outstrips those of earlier great powers. These traits give U.S. policymaking a federal character, which affects diplomacy in two ways.

First, it means that American leaders must be as much or more inwardly focused as they are outwardly focused in conceiving and executing diplomatic enterprises. A Metternich-type figure exercising wide sway over external policy for a period of decades while being largely detached from domestic issues would never be possible in the U.S. system.[156] Bold strokes in diplomacy are harder because the complexity of the U.S. federal system rewards consensuses that, once locked in, are difficult to alter. The dynamic is the opposite of that in Imperial Germany, whose system and circumstances continually pulled leaders toward dramatic or even rash acts of improvisation that only a domineering figure like Bismarck could counter. In the U.S. case, the natural tendency is toward the reverse: long periods of inertia that can only be broken by a big jolt. This can be beneficial in stable stretches of history but, as with the case of containment, become an impediment to creativity when the country needs to change course. As Nixon and Kissinger showed, "bursts" of innovation in policy require highly focused leadership that is willing to devote primary attention to foreign policy and able to rewire aspects of the U.S. system to chart a new course.

Second, the nature of U.S. power affects the way Americans negotiate. The U.S. political and economic systems are inherently competitive and meritocratic. They tend to produce self-made individuals who rise to prominence on the basis of brains rather than bloodlines. Men like Nixon and Kissinger would not have been possible even in the comparatively open systems of Venice or Britain. Of the two men, Nixon was the better negotiator precisely because of his long experience in political dealmaking and the private sector. Kissinger was limited by his dislike for and inability to understand American democracy. Nixon by contrast instinctively utilized features of that system to drive change in foreign policy and enhance his negotiating position vis-à-vis the Chinese. Looming elections and noise from the "animals" in Congress gave both men a paradoxical leverage and ability to create time pressure in negotiations that were credible precisely because of the divided nature of power in the U.S. system.

ALLIANCE MANAGEMENT

America possesses more alliances than any previous great power. U.S. alliances also tend to involve much deeper commitments, in the form of binding treaties that are approved by the Senate and considered to have the force of law. This gives American power a quality more on par with the Amphictyonic leagues of ancient Greece or even the confederal structures of the Holy Roman Empire than the fly-by-night arrangements of Venice and Britain.

The special characteristics of America's alliances influence how it conducts diplomacy. On one hand, alliances enhance U.S. diplomatic leverage by positioning the country to act as a kind of spokesperson for a large grouping of states that, more often than not, will tend to follow her lead in world affairs. On the other hand, the enormous power disparity between the United States and even her most significant allies creates a perverse incentive for allies to free-ride that, over time, can erode the strategic value of these relationships, which hinges on allies being active participants in the maintenance of a stable balance of power within their regions. This generates a perpetual dynamic in U.S. diplomacy of trying to both reassure and motivate allies that would have been familiar to Bismarck from his dealings with Austria, but on a much bigger scale.

The experiences of Nixon and Kissinger show that the United States has a larger margin of error in alliance management than is perhaps commonly assumed. They undertook the boldest outreach to U.S. adversaries of the modern era while attempting to jolt allies into greater self-help—and largely succeeded in both tasks. In many cases, the former aided in the success of the latter. The "shock" of Nixon's China gambit prompted many U.S. allies in Asia to increase defense spending while making their own, carefully bounded overtures to Beijing. There were always limits to how far those overtures could go; however much allies may chafe at U.S. outreach to rivals, the fact is that, then as now, they lack viable alternatives to the U.S. market and security umbrella. Only a country of America's unusual qualities—sufficiently powerful to credibly offer protection, sufficiently distant to credibly threaten withdrawal—could attempt diplomatic experimentation on this scale with a fair prospect of success.

MORAL PURPOSE

More than any previous great power, Americans have tended to invest their diplomacy with a moral purpose that transcends geopolitical expediency and relates its ends to the good of humanity as a whole. This impulse has given America a propensity, unique in the history of diplomacy, to champion utopian causes at the global level. The attempts at world governments after both world wars were largely of American origin and impetus. Even when these have failed, as invariably they have, U.S. leaders have felt a need, rooted in the country's DNA, to relate their foreign policies to a set of ideals above the national interest.

Nixon was no exception. In his reports to Congress, there are unmistakable accents of Wilsonian idealism. Diplomacy was needed, not just to bring the boys home but to promote peace and "social justice" for all humankind. The same was true, ironically, for Kissinger; as one biographer argues, realism for Kissinger was not a rejection of morality but the "best way to pursue the stable world order that he believed was the ultimate moral imperative, especially in the nuclear age."[157] After leaving office, he made a decades-long effort to retrospectively tether his policies to an overarching Kantian purpose, of building a world where nations worked together to "affirm individual dignity," advance democratic governance, and devise "agreed-upon rules."[158]

All of this is important, not because it suggests Nixonian policies were idealistic but because it shows the extent to which idealism permeates the American worldview. Even the most realist practitioners of statecraft in modern U.S. history felt a reputational need to anchor their policies in loftier substrate than Realpolitik.

At the same time, Nixon's successes demonstrate that realist precepts are compatible with republican government. Much as Roosevelt had allied with Stalin against Hitler, Nixon could align with Mao against Brezhnev when the circumstances made it necessary. While the ideological character of the Cold War did not preclude these alignments, it did put limits on how far or deep they could go. To a greater extent than the Valois-Habsburg rivalry, the republican and Communist systems of government were in irreconcilable tension. Détente and rapprochement were bound to be short-lived affairs; both were modi vivendi that allowed America to tread water and regain her strength.

Nixon was able to pull this off not because he was antagonistic to democracy but, to the contrary, because he was considered an exemplar of that system's most belligerent advocates. The reason that "only Nixon could go to China" was because his background as an ardent anti-Communist gave him credibility with voters and allies. His political genius was to channel the mood and needs of the electorate to a constructive outlet without abnegating America's reputation as leader of the free world. He was arguably more successful in this task than Mao, whose image as a revolutionary in many parts of the Communist world never recovered from rapprochement.

✦

The United States is the first country in history, and the only democratic republic, to practice diplomacy on a global scale backed by the resources of a continent-sized landmass. In American diplomacy we see the concept of state sovereignty that emerged from Westphalia harnessed to a set of ideals that, in scope if not in substance, recall the universalist creeds of pre-Westphalian empires.

America's unusual combination of ideals and power has created periodic temptations to either retreat from the world or transform it in the country's image. Yet when push comes to shove, the United States has shown that it can wield strategic diplomacy with a high degree of dexterity to thwart even the most threatening combinations of adversaries. Viewed as a whole, U.S. diplomacy has been immensely successful, building the largest array of military-commercial alliances in history, enabling the country to grow richer than any other to date, and winning its fiercest global competition to date without having to fight a nuclear war.

The 20th Century is strewn with many U.S. diplomatic tombstones, including Wilson's conference diplomacy and Roosevelt's four policemen. But it also saw the triumph of a uniquely American variety of hard-nosed diplomacy that blended aspects of British maritime strategy, continental realism, and homegrown meritocratic pragmatism. At its heart is a concept of using diplomacy as a tool of strategy to outlast powerful enemies that would have been recognizable not only to the classical European statesmen whom Kissinger so admired but also to the descendants of the Chinese emperors who would now succeed the Soviet Union to become the American Republic's greatest adversary.

CHAPTER NINE

The Necessity of Diplomacy

Diplomacy is one of the highest of the political arts. In a well-ordered commonwealth it would be held in the esteem due to a great public service in whose hands the safety of the people largely lies.

—A. F. WHYTE

EVERY GROUP OF leaders in this book faced an "Archidamus moment," when a great war loomed on the horizon beyond the state's immediate ability to win by force alone. All were proud states still in their prime, with a history of martial excellence and a civilizing mission that imbued their statecraft with a sense of purpose transcending mere power accumulation. Defeat, whether by subjugation or surrender, meant not only the possibility of losing territory but national influence, honor and identity as well.

We should therefore not be surprised that the allure of the military option—which is to say, that of attacking the enemy *tout de suite*—was very strong for most of the great powers surveyed in this book. The counsel of the militant Spartan Sthenelaidas echoes across the ages. Theodosius's Gothic generals find their counterparts in the valorous knights of Francis I's entourage and Waldersee's number-crunching Prussian staff officers. That Archidamus's counsel prevailed in each case was the result of a higher computation by political leaders: that the state's available military resources were insufficient to the threats at hand and thus that pursuit of diplomatic options to recalibrate the strategic ledger was necessary.

The law too exercised a powerful pull across these pages, less so than the soldiers, but with its own special appeal. The Italian friar Simone da Camerino and his Augustinian brothers find secular analogues in Klemens von Metternich and Woodrow Wilson. The Italian League, Vienna system, and League of Nations were all, at base, attempts to codify agreements among nations that would prevent war for as long as possible. Each lost utility as the underlying balance of power that had made it possible shifted. None provided a realistic option when new enemies appeared on the horizon.

For every group of leaders in this book, the diplomat offered a service that neither the soldier nor the jurist could provide: the possibility of rearranging power in space and time to the state's advantage, so that it did not face tests of strength beyond its ability to bear. In every case, the starting point of creative diplomacy was a recognition of the necessity of tradeoffs. Diplomacy's role in strategy was to create political expedients with which to temporarily bridge finite means and seemingly infinite ends, either by augmenting the resources at the state's disposal externally or by reducing the number of enemies requiring immediate attention, or both.

Diplomacy's functions in strategy bring it into the realm of high policy. Long before Anatolius arrived at Attila's camp or Starhemberg stepped into the boudoir of Madame de Pompadour, diplomacy as a policy was well underway. It begins in the cabinet room, in the minds of leaders, who consider its potentialities alongside and in conjunction with other instruments of state power. Every group of leaders in this book had an Archidamus at the table, whether in the form of a diplomat-chancellor like Kaunitz or Bismarck, or an advisor like Chrysaphius or Chen Yi, who made the case for diplomacy as a strategic option in the state's highest councils.

Strategies of Diplomacy

These voices prevailed in strategic debates not because they were uniformly brilliant but because they could point to diplomatic courses of action that would tangibly improve the state's position in competition when other options would not avail. From the examples in this book, we can identify three basic templates of diplomatic strategy that recur across the ages.

Strategies of conciliation use diplomacy to try to avert confrontation with an adversary by satisfying it in some way. This can take different forms. One is *deflection*, whereby a great power essentially bribes an opponent in hopes that it will turn its attention to another target, as the Byzantines attempted with the Huns and the Venetians attempted with the Turks. Another is *appeasement*, whereby a great power gives an opponent what it wants, usually in the form of territory, on the calculation that it will be satisfied, as Lansdowne and Chamberlain tried to do with Britain's rivals. A third is *détente*, whereby two great powers look for a mutual lowering of temperature, as Kissinger and Zhou both sought for their respective nations.

Strategies of enmeshment use diplomacy to pull a rival closer, usually through some combination of trade ties and shared political priorities. It is most common after a major war, when states need a period of strategic rest and economic recuperation. Most of the examples of enmeshment in this book involved a relatively weak power looking for ways to lighten the load of defense expenditure and maintain empire on the cheap. Venice after the Peace of Lodi, Austria after the Vienna Congress, and Britain after Versailles all derived important military and economic advantages from pulling other powers into regular systems of consultation, designed to head off crises diplomatically before they morphed into major wars.

Strategies of isolation use diplomacy to build coalitions that aggregate military and economic resources to oneself while denying them to an opponent. This can take a couple of different forms. When war is on the horizon, it is an urgent business of cobbling together states of all shapes and sizes to throw at the opposing power. It is in these moments that states are most likely to set aside differences with other, less menacing foes, as Theodosius did with Persia and Kaunitz did with France. Alternatively, isolation can mean playing the long game. This usually involves some combination of using standing alliances to tourniquet an opponent externally while amplifying certain pathologies inherent to its domestic situation. Cardinal Richelieu's *guerre couverte* vis-à-vis the Habsburg Empire is one example; Harry Truman's strategy of containment is another.

No matter how brilliantly conceived, none of these strategies offers any assurance of success, of course. Embarking on a diplomatic strategy at a moment of danger is fraught with risk. In most of the examples in this book it was not a first choice but rather a necessity that was foisted upon a great power by geopolitical and financial exigencies. Like a military campaign, a diplomatic gambit may fail for all kinds of reasons, including ineptitude, canny adversaries, or simply bad luck. Diplomats as a tribe are no wiser than generals, and diplomacy can be just as flawed in conception or execution as military plans. Even when conceptually sound, a diplomatic strategy may miscarry. Leaders may miscalculate their leverage, misjudge the moment, or misread an opponent. The consequences can be calamitous, and in the worst case may even hasten the advent of the very war that the great power was trying to delay or avoid.

Skill in diplomacy therefore matters. Like war, diplomacy is an enterprise that rewards study. But where military affairs are sometimes referred to as a science, diplomacy lies firmly within the realm of art. Its methods, being inherently less technical, are much less subject to change over time than modes of war fighting. Its chief media—the motives and expedients of the human mind and heart—cannot be as readily reduced to mathematical variables or counters on a tabletop.[1]

Perhaps that is why skill in diplomacy has always gone hand-in-hand with the study of history. Knowledge of the past has always been the best resource available for understanding the behavior of states and individuals. Diplomacy's institutions emerged expressly for retaining that knowledge, as a way of gaining an advantage in the present. Diplomacy's greatest chroniclers, like Callières, Satow, Nicolson, and Craig, looked to the past for inspiration and continuity. And its great practitioners, like Richelieu, Kaunitz, Metternich, Bismarck, Salisbury, Kissinger, and Zhou, all made a point of studying history to understand their own states' strengths and flaws, as well as those of their opponents.

Studying diplomatic history does not provide pat lessons for the present any more than military history does. Circumstances change from one situation to the next, and formulas that work in one moment may fail in another. Nevertheless, just like the study of war, the study of diplomacy contains plenty of wisdom for anyone willing to look. Glancing back across the chapters of this book, it's possible to identify a handful of basic principles that have stood the test of time and hold merit down to the present day.

DIPLOMACY CONCENTRATES POWER

By far the most important and enduring strategic application of diplomacy is to concentrate one's own power while diluting that of an opponent. Concentration, as Clausewitz wrote, is the key thing in strategy; diplomacy helps achieve it by brokering political arrangements that allow the state to reduce its exertions in one place and increase them in another, more critical location without incurring the full risk that that would otherwise entail.

Concentrating power enables a state to stagger the main dangers arrayed against it, and thereby get a grip on the factor of time in competition. A sequential logic lay at the heart of most of the diplomatic strategies in this book. Byzantines conciliated Persians to focus on Huns; Venetians made peace with Milanese to concentrate against Ottomans; Valois turned off disputes with Tudor to prioritize Habsburg; Habsburg allied with Bourbon to mass against Hohenzollern; Germans aligned with Russians to concentrate against French; Brits quieted French and Russians to beef up against Germans; Americans and Chinese both sought détente with the other to concentrate against Soviets.

There is no hard rule as to which rival a state concentrates against. In most instances it's true, as Kissinger observed, that great powers tilt toward "the weaker of two antagonistic partners" to counterbalance the stronger. But not always. There are plenty of examples of leaders in this book—Theodosius (with Persia), Kaunitz (with France), Lansdowne (with the United States)—who aligned with what, on paper, was the stronger rival against a weaker but mutually threatening opponent.

In these and other cases, the adversary that states prioritized was not necessarily strongest in overall military and economic terms but rather the one that was the most immediately and determinedly threatening.[2] Compared to Attila's rampaging "wolves of the north," the cataphracts of Persia were a faraway concern. Frederick the Great's legions were a stone's throw from Vienna, while those of France's lay beyond the Alps. Britain worried less about the growing U.S. navy across the Atlantic than the Imperial Germany fleet next door. Effective diplomacy, in other words, takes account of the enemy's aims and ability to act on those aims, not just its overall capabilities.

EFFECTIVE DIPLOMACY CONSTRAINS OPPONENTS

Diplomacy is a conservative and defensive enterprise. Its role in strategy is not to enable conquest or aggrandizement but to place limits on how far others can go down those paths. Any state's freedom of action is naturally hindered by all kinds of things: geography, fear from other nations, economic inadequacies, the limited reach of military technology. Effective diplomacy works with the grain of these constraints to narrow the options for profitable aggression and stack the deck in favor of stability.

Diplomacy's constraining function differentiates it from two modern conceptions of the profession. One is the idea that diplomacy's job is to uncover good intentions on the part of an adversary, on the assumption that the only real obstacle to peace is misunderstandings that can be cleared up with persistence and good faith. The other is the notion that the job of diplomacy is to transform opponents internally, on the assumption that the obstacle to peace is the existence of incompatible systems of government.

Historically, diplomacy's assumptions have been much more pessimistic than the former, and its aspirations altogether more modest than the latter. Classical diplomacy assumes the worst about human nature. It doesn't attempt to remove the causes of conflict, which are endemic to the human species, but to form combinations that make aggression more difficult. Diplomacy embraces compromise as the inevitable by-product of an imperfect and competitive world. As an enterprise, it is free from illusions about permanent solutions. Its aims are always temporary, because power is fluid and fleeting. Diplomacy's promise is to use knowledge of power's nature to limit it, not to change the nature of power or of mankind.

CONCILIATE TO CONSTRAIN, NOT TO APPEASE

Every great power in this book tried to conciliate a big opponent at some point in its history. Those that succeeded used diplomacy to shape an opponent's incentives by constraining its options; those that failed lost sight of diplomacy's constraining function and tried to change an aggressor's motives.

To see the point, compare the diplomatic strategies of Theodosius the Younger and Neville Chamberlain. For all its seeming fecklessness, Byzantine diplomacy was grounded in a ruthless assessment of the Huns' vulnerabilities. Attila's captaincy depended on the support of lesser chieftains, who conditioned their loyalty on the uninterrupted flow of loot. His battlefield prowess depended on large numbers of well-fed horses, which meant he couldn't stray too far from the grazing lands of the Pannonian Plain. Byzantine diplomacy worked to amplify both constraints: gold tethered Attila's authority to the Byzantine state; reduce the gold, and the lesser chieftains might revolt—as indeed they eventually did. Keep the game going long enough, and the Huns would eventually choose easier targets in the West, where grass was in greater abundance than in the rocky terrain of the Balkans.

Chamberlain's diplomacy might have embraced a similar logic, but it didn't. Like Attila, Hitler faced constraints, in the form of domestic opposition and the desire of neighboring states to balance against German power. But instead of using diplomacy to strengthen those constraints, Chamberlain tried to remove the sources of conflict by giving Hitler what he wanted, and, in so doing, weakened them. Where Theodosius gave gold to the Huns to deflect them away from territory, Chamberlain gave territory to Germany in hopes of satisfying its hunger.

The tragedy of Munich was not only what was given up in Czech territory and British honor, but what was needlessly sacrificed in the way of natural advantages that a traditional balance-of-power strategy might have exploited. In place of the age-old logic of constraints, Chamberlain thought in the modern logic of misunderstandings. By trying to clear up the latter, he ultimately undermined the former. He lost sight of diplomacy's core function, which is to check power, not enable it.

ENMESH TO RESTRAIN AN OPPONENT, NOT YOURSELF

There is a fashionable modern notion that enlightened states use diplomacy to wrap themselves in layers of commitments that restrict their own freedom of maneuver and thereby win the trust of other states. Doing so, the reasoning goes, softens the edges of competition by rendering the state in question more benign and inviting reciprocity on the part of adversaries.[3]

In fact, successful great powers have used enmeshment the same way they have used other diplomatic strategies: to restrict an opponent's range of options for conducting aggression. Pulling a rival closer to oneself offers an opportunity to foster economic dependencies that make a revisionist military agenda harder to pursue down the road. As with conciliation, the goal is not to transform an opponent but to shape its behavior in ways that enhance one's own ability to prevent or, if necessary, wage war.

This principle is on display in the attempts at collective security examined in this book. Venice used the Italian League to negotiate limits on the armies of her mainland rivals and collect financial contributions for maintaining a large navy to guard the *terraferma*. Austria used the Vienna system to tie down her main rivals, expand the Habsburg resource base, and enlist Europe's help in managing the empire's tenuous buffers. Britain used the league system and interwar naval treaties to lighten the load of security in Europe and concentrate scarce naval and military resources on policing her overseas empire.

Closer to our own time, Communist China has used the economic enmeshment occasioned by Nixon's opening and confirmed by post–Cold War U.S. presidents to create dependencies that translate into constraints on the United States in wartime, while the U.S. side has been much less adept, until recently, at using these arrangements to its advantage.

In all of these cases, successful great powers were those that accepted a certain degree of reciprocal restraint while working to ensure that they were the net beneficiary of the resulting arrangement. They cooperated with rivals in ways that enhanced their own security, not because they sought order as an end in itself. As power relationships shifted and the likelihood of war grew, enmeshment lost its utility.

ISOLATE AN ENEMY TO PREVENT WAR

Another idea that has gained traction in recent years is that using diplomacy to encircle an opponent with countervailing coalitions is a dangerous activity that makes war more likely. Backing a rival power into a corner, the thinking goes, is a surefire way to make it lash out and start the very offensive wars that diplomacy is supposed to prevent.[4]

The examples in this book suggest that the opposite is usually the case. Using diplomacy to isolate an opponent tends to make war less likely, for the simple reason that it forces a would-be aggressor to diffuse its military attention in multiple directions, therefore reducing its chances of success through conquest.

This point is illustrated by numerous examples throughout the book. Francis I's alliances with Lutherans and Turks forced Charles V to forgo his planned humiliation of France and laid the groundwork for the longest period of peace in the Habsburg-Valois rivalry. Richelieu's cultivation of alliances with Sweden and the German states allowed France to delay entry into the Thirty Years' War for nearly two decades. France's attempts to build alliances in Eastern Europe in the 1930s might have dissuaded Germany from the path of conquest had Chamberlain not wasted the opportunity. And both Kissinger and Zhou promoted Sino-U.S. rapprochement on the grounds that it would remove an opening for easy Soviet aggression in Europe or Asia respectively, as indeed turned out to be the case.

In all of these cases, encircling coalitions presented incentives for an aggressive state to pursue its aims through diplomacy rather than conquest. The reason is not that it liked being encircled but because doing so made the military option more difficult to pursue with a reasonable chance of success. Indeed, it could be said with little exaggeration that the sine qua non of strategic diplomacy is to foist the multifront burden back onto an opponent in order, as Richelieu put it, to "keep your enemies so busy everywhere that they could not win anywhere."

INTERESTS OUTWEIGH IDEOLOGY

For every great power in this book, diplomacy with rivals sometimes involved actions that were at odds with religious or ideological principles that its society held dear. Without exception, states chose to put what Archidamus called the "law of self-preservation" above all other considerations.

There is a modern conceit that holds that leaders could make such decisions more easily in the past because the ideological stakes were lower. In an era of "democracy versus autocracy," the reasoning goes, diplomacy carries a heavier moral freight than it did in the era of kings and potentates. But this greatly understates the costs of compromise for past societies. For a Byzantine emperor to cut deals with pagan Huns and Sassanids, or a Valois prince to parlay with Ottoman infidels and Lutheran heretics, was to subject their peoples to the wrath of God and potentially jeopardize their own souls. Even in the supposedly cold-blooded era of the classical European states system, the reputational stakes of adversarial diplomacy were often much higher than they seem in retrospect.

The force that repeatedly led bitter enemies to find common cause was fear of a shared enemy. Historically, that has consistently trumped the dictates of conscience, faith, or creed. What's remarkable is not that states made such a choice, or that doing so produced a retrospective soul-searching, but that diplomacy made it possible in the first place. If, as FDR said of his alliance with Joseph Stalin, "It is permitted you in time of grave danger to walk with the devil until you have crossed the bridge," then diplomacy is what states used to get across the bridge.[5]

EFFECTIVE DIPLOMACY IS IMBUED WITH A HIGHER MISSION

It should not be concluded from the foregoing text that diplomacy is simply the science of fear. Every great power in this book pursued a mission that transcended power politics and bespoke a higher cultural, civic, or religious aspiration that was precious to its own people and attractive, or at least not repellant, to at least some of its neighbors. Even when forced to temporarily subordinate those ideals to interests, great powers did not abandon their overarching mission as a great power.

Mission is not "soft power." It is identity. A nation's mission infuses its diplomacy with an attractant force that is at once unique to itself and relatable beyond its borders. The persuasive power of a Byzantine envoy lay not only in the gold that he could promise but also in the civilizing effects of Roman law, the salvation of the Christian Church, and the marvels of Constantinople that made neighboring tribes want to imitate Byzantine ways. Habsburg diplomats represented an ancient Catholic dynasty committed to legitimacy and treaty rights. And American diplomats in the Cold War had at their back a great democratic republic grounded in the humanizing ideals of the U.S. Constitution.

Order is the ultimate by-product of national mission. The wider and deeper the attraction of a great power's mission, the more durable and mutually beneficial the order that stems from that sense of mission is likely to prove. Many of history's most disastrous breakdowns of order occurred when a leading state discarded time-proven missions in favor of the power principle. The shift from the conservative equipoise of Richelieu to the expansionism of Louis XIV is one example; the transition from Bismarck's alliance system to Kaiser Wilhelm's *Weltpolitik* is another; and Chamberlain's relinquishing of Britain's historic mission as protector of small state liberties and upholder of the balance of power is a third.

Conversely, a durable and credible mission can lead other states to remain committed to a great power even when it shifts policies in ways that negatively affect them in the short term. Kaunitz and Kissinger were both able to engineer radical reorientations in their nation's foreign policies without sacrificing long-standing alliances with smaller states because the great powers they represented were understood to be committed to a mission that was preferrable to those of other great powers. A compelling mission, in other words, increases diplomacy's margin of error. Even when they prioritize stark self-interest, successful great powers use diplomacy to manage the contradictions that arise between principle and necessity.

THE LITTLE GUYS MATTER

The idea that big powers discard allies, especially small ones, with impunity doesn't find much support in history. To the contrary, successful great powers across the ages have devoted considerable energy to retaining the friendship of comparatively weak and vulnerable actors, often over very long stretches of time.

The reason is not charity but self-interest, rooted in the recognition that these asymmetrical relationships, if properly managed, convey important advantages to the big guy. Small allies fill gaps in their patron's military capabilities, as Hungarians and Turkomen did for Venice and Britain's continental allies did for the Royal Navy. They guard important geography, as Bulgars, Ghassanids, and Arabs did for Byzantium and as Saxons, Poles, and Italians did for Austria. And when located in the rear area of an opponent, they force it to divert attention and resources away from its intended area of concentration, as Sweden did for France against the Habsburgs and as Albanians did for Venice against the Ottomans.

There is a particular glue to these kinds of relationships: the big power's desire to check a rival overlaps with the little guy's desire to keep his independence from that same opponent. That bond comes under strain when a great power enters into détente with the shared rival. But rather than throwing old friends to the wolves, successful great powers use diplomacy to retain them even as they engage with the rival power. Metternich's efforts to maintain the independence of Saxony and Poland while conciliating Prussia and Russia, Bismarck's efforts to reassure Austria-Hungary while keeping close to the tsar, and the Nixon administration's attempts to allay Taiwanese and Japanese fears about rapprochement with China are all examples.

Great powers go to these great lengths not out of nostalgia but because the loss of old allies could call into question the cost-benefit ledger of the new alignment. The whole point of conciliation with a major rival is to find temporary advantage for oneself *without* conceding long-term advantages to that rival in the process. Neglect of this principle has often ended badly, with small states either joining, or being absorbed by, the rival. Successful great powers therefore work to make détente palatable for the little guys who are adversely affected by it. Diplomacy, in other words, is not a zero-sum affair but the instrument by which states attempt to have it both ways.

IN NEGOTIATIONS, CULTURE COUNTS

States care about similar sorts of things, but the way they go about seeking advantage at the negotiating table varies according to the geography, history, and culture of a given society, as well as what its people see as wise and acceptable bargaining behavior. Skillful diplomacy recognizes these particularities and bases its methods on a careful read of what makes the other side "tick."

Diversity in negotiating styles is itself a major theme throughout the book. The Byzantines combined flattery and emoluments with the patient accumulation of leverage over long periods of time. The Venetians sought reciprocal advantage through shrewdly contrived contracts, backed by back-channel lobbying. The Austrians formulated their objectives as legal principles that allowed them to set the terms of the negotiations. The Edwardian British used what might be called the good-faith model, of putting all the cards on the table and looking for areas of pragmatic overlap.

Successful great powers modify their negotiating style to reflect the characteristics of an opponent. The Byzantines used conventional treaty diplomacy with the Persians, a literate cosmopolitan civilization like themselves, but used methods of barter and intrigue when dealing with a nomadic, ego-driven culture like the Huns. Louise of Savoy's emissaries appealed to Christian virtue and seigneurial duty when treating with Charles V but adopted a more solicitous posture in approaching Suleiman. Zhou instructed Chinese diplomats to imitate the Russian cultural traits of rudeness and excessive demands when dealing with the Soviets while assuming a more relaxed and complimentary attitude with the pragmatic Americans.

Great powers that failed to adapt their negotiating styles to the culture of opponents have often not fared well. Wilhelmine Germany's attempt to use the Prussian method of menace to frighten Britain into an alliance disastrously misread Britain's fair-play culture and pushed that country toward France. Chamberlain and FDR both made the mistake of assuming that their autocratic interlocutors would negotiate on the basis of consensual give-and-take of the kind that characterized their democratic systems at home, with negative results.

These examples illustrate that diplomacy is not a one-size-fits-all activity. This runs against a modern view that holds that states and individuals operate more or less like private-sector firms on the basis of cost-benefit calculations. States may be rational actors, but how they define cost and benefit, and approach bargaining, are conditioned by culture. Effective diplomacy takes those local particularities into account and approaches bargaining through the eyes of one's interlocutors rather than only one's own.

SUPERIOR DIPLOMACY FACILITATES SUPERIOR TECHNOLOGY

There is a modern tendency to view diplomacy as an antediluvian force that is essentially retrogressive in its aims and methods. In fact, states have used diplomacy across the ages to gain a competitive edge against opponents in the race to develop and field war-winning technology.

First, diplomacy allows states to build a larger innovation base than would otherwise be possible by propelling commercial friendships that enable wealth generation and technology sharing. Second, it creates security alliances that enable states to specialize in, and therefore get better at, a certain range of technologies that are the most vital for its unique geographic situation. Diplomatic pivots and military-technological recalibrations often went hand-in-hand in the examples covered in this book. Edwardian Britain's development of the dreadnought would have had much less efficacy had British diplomacy not first created the combinations that allowed it to shift resources away from the fleets of older vessels kept at far-flung naval stations. America's "second offset," which produced the technologies that helped win the Cold War, was facilitated by Nixon's deceleration of effort in Southeast Asia.

In both cases, diplomacy helped enable critical technologies without the budgetary strains they would have entailed absent a reduction on other fronts. The value of this role cannot be overstated. If the defining challenge for great powers is to manage the inherent tension between the imperative of safety, which requires ever-more-expensive military capabilities, and the imperative of avoiding burdens that would sap national economic vitality, then diplomacy must be seen as among the most crucial instruments at the state's disposal.[6]

MONEY IS MORE EFFECTIVE AT ATTRACTION THAN DETERRENCE OR COMPELLENCE

A staple of modern statecraft is the idea that financial power has largely removed the need for classical diplomacy. States can shape an opponent's behavior quite efficiently, the thinking goes, by using sanctions to deny it access to capital and thus depriving it of the financial means for aggression. The resulting coercive potential would seem to reduce the need for violence—but also for compromise.

History doesn't provide much evidence to support this thinking. There are plenty of examples in this book of states using money to get someone to do something helpful *for* them, but few of states using money successfully to prevent someone from doing something harmful *to* them. The Byzantine diplomats used cash to succor the enemies of their enemies. Venetians brought the practice to an art form in the Balkans and Anatolia. And the British used financial diplomacy on a prodigious scale to keep Europe's small states alive and thus stymie attempts at continental hegemony. In all of these cases, money had the effect of arming and abetting vulnerable actors who were already inclined, for very personal reasons, to want the thing that their patron wanted.

When states do try to use money coercively, the results can be unpredictable. Thucydides tells us that Athenian sanctions against Megara had the effect of stiffening the latter's resolve to go to war. The most dramatic example in this book is Bismarck's attack on Russian state bonds at the high point of the 1887–1888 crisis. Instead of dissuading Russia, the move proved decisive in pushing it into France's arms and limiting Germany's diplomatic options down the road. By stoking passions and hastening conflict, sanctions can actually work at cross-purposes with diplomacy's efforts to keep control of the clock. Using money coercively, in other words, may change someone's behavior, but not necessarily in the way one intended.

EFFECTIVE DIPLOMACY DEPENDS ON DISCIPLINED INSTITUTIONS

Bureaucracy emerges in the story of diplomacy as a response to the pressures of competition. The Byzantines built a bureau of barbarians to give their envoys insider information about the tribes around their borders. The Venetians gave as much care to building a cadre of well-trained ambassadors, backed by an archive of *relazione*, as they did to outfitting their navy. The French kings tied far-flung embassies to a centralized secretariat that could direct diplomatic strategies on a continental scale.

At each stage, bureaucracy grew to meet the demands of an administrative state that needed to organize ever-larger resources for war. The result was a paradox: states developed bureaucracy to gain an edge in competition, yet the larger the bureaucracy became, the more it took a life of its own and stifled diplomatic creativity.

Effective bureaucracies are those that stay laser-focused on diplomacy's core functions while staying in lockstep with the will of the executive. Those functions include the maintenance of a specialized knowledge of foreign situations and skill in negotiations, but also the ability to formulate policies that relate both of those things back to the state's strategic needs at a given moment. Great powers need not just Frangipanis and Starhembergs to negotiate good deals but Chrysaphiuses and Berties to conceptualize those deals through the prism of high policy. The job of diplomatic bureaucracy is to provide both types and to instill in them an ethos of consummate skill in the service of the state and its foremost interests.

Diplomatic institutions do not automatically stay focused on these core functions; like all large bureaucracies, they seek to expand their own resources and increase their independence from the executive. But when these tendencies collide with strategic exigency, the latter invariably wins out. With remarkable consistency, almost every leader in this book wrangled the bureaucracy into alignment with his or her will at moments of international danger, either by creating parallel structures or by radically overhauling the bureaucracy, or both. Skill in diplomacy, in other words, requires continual renewal of institutions that underwrite its most important functions. Successful great powers cultivate diplomacy as an instrument of national-strategic excellence—and pull it back to its raison d'être when bureaucracy strays.

DEMOCRACY DOESN'T GUARANTEE SUCCESS

There is a modern tendency to believe that democracies are destined to triumph over all other forms of government. Their inherent superiority as purveyors of human liberty, the thinking goes, enables them to dispense with old-fashioned diplomacy and aspire to an altogether more ambitious agenda, of converting opponents into foreign versions of themselves and paving the way for Kant's vision of perpetual peace.

Democracy does convey some important advantages in diplomacy. Republics tend to be more skilled at commerce and coalition-building than autocracies. They have greater domestic stability over the long haul and are animated by national missions that tend to be more attractive to other states. Legislatures and election cycles create favorable time pressure when making deals, as Nixon and Kissinger discovered. Even hardboiled realists like Niccolò Machiavelli and Bismarck acknowledged that democracies are more likely to stick to treaty commitments than autocracies.[7] All of this enhances credibility, which is the foundation of effective diplomacy.

But like any system of government, democracy comes with its own special challenges. The "new" diplomacy of the post–World War I era is an example of the kind of fever that can grip democratic electorates from time to time. Some of the greatest disasters in this book came about when elected leaders tried to conduct diplomacy on the basis of progressive notions about the way the world should work. Woodrow Wilson's fantasy at Versailles, Lloyd George's improvisations of the 1920s, Neville Chamberlain's debacle at Munich, and Franklin Roosevelt's blunders with Stalin all shared a rejection of diplomacy's historic logic of constraint in favor of liberal ideas that enjoyed broad public support.[8] The most successful elected leader to practice diplomacy in this book, Richard Nixon, was attuned to popular pressures but harnessed them to a realistic policy agenda that was effective precisely because it reverted to diplomacy's classical ends of equipoise and restraint.

Being a democracy, in other words, does not allow a great power to transcend power realities or exempt it from the tradeoffs that lie at the heart of effective diplomacy. Democracies are as liable to hubris as any other form of government, and a good deal more susceptible to popular fads. If anything, their propensity to mood swings and tendency to view the world in missionary terms mean that their leaders have to be more deliberate about sustaining a focus on the national interest and nurturing the classical repertoire of skills that comprise diplomacy's professional core, lest these be subsumed by fashionable causes.

SUCCESSFUL DIPLOMATS RARELY GET THANKED

There are plenty of statues of the West's most famous generals and admirals, but very few of its great diplomats. At its heart, diplomacy is about managing the contradictions that arise from the pursuit of survival in a world of shifting power. Success is rarely rewarded with national gratitude, for to do so would be to acknowledge that nations must often settle for less than their highest aspirations.

Almost every leader in this book was blamed for betraying the ideals that his or her society held dear—even when their policies were successful. Pulcheria's denunciation by Chrysaphius as a practitioner of unmanly intrigue plays out over and over across the ages.* Francesco Foscari, Francis I, and Richelieu were all accused of heresy for dealing with infidels. Metternich was called a Mephistophelian schemer, and Bismarck was thought by some to be Satan incarnate.[9] Lansdowne and his successors were criticized in Parliament for abandoning liberal traditions when they sought a pact with the autocratic tsar. Nixon and Reagan were castigated for abnegating America's democratic ideals when they negotiated with Communists. Even Zhou Enlai was denounced by Communist hardliners for "rightist capitulationism."

So consistent is this pattern that it may be said that the diplomat, like the prophet, is "not without honor, but in his own country." Unlike the noble soldier or the righteous jurist, the diplomat by definition works in the medium of accommodation. Yet in performing this function, the diplomat is providing a national benefit that neither the soldier nor the jurist can bring about. Carrying the onus that comes with adjusting principle to power is part of the service that diplomacy ultimately renders. The casualty of esteem may not be as great as that which occurs on a battlefield, but it is sacrificial nevertheless, and just as essential for that highest of state ends: survival. Without survival, even the noblest mission is nothing but a mirage.

Rediscovering Diplomacy

Every few generations, Western societies seem to rediscover the necessity and potential of diplomacy. This invariably comes about because of the failure of military force or law to live up to their promise of providing

---

* It's curious to note the frequency with which great diplomats have found themselves at odds with their boss's spouse. Chrysaphius's feud with Eudocia is replicated in Richelieu's rivalry with Louis XIII's lovers, Kaunitz's jousts with Maria Theresa's husband Francis Stephen, Metternich's tiffs with the emperor Francis's wives, Bismarck's epic clashes with Wilhelm I's wife and daughter-in-law, Kissinger's strained relationship with Pat Nixon, and Zhou Enlai's turf wars with Mao's wife Jiang Qing.

safety without the messy anguish of compromise. That failure is usually accompanied by a sense of disillusionment about what were thought to be heroic potentialities for either technology or ideals. The realization that something as timeworn as diplomacy holds relevance for the seemingly novel problems of the present always comes as a revelation.

The most timeless restatements of diplomacy's potential have come about in such moments. François de Callières wrote his *Art of Negotiating with Sovereign Princes* to caution warlike Bourbon kings against the allure of wars of conquest and alert them to the comparative advantages of that could be obtained at much less expense and bloodshed by a well-furnished diplomacy. The rearticulations of diplomacy in the early 20th Century by Satow, Whyte, and Nicolson were meant to shake Western leaders from the conceits of legalism, amateurism, and pacifistic naivety. The renaissance of diplomatic thinking in the early Cold War from scholars like Hans Morgenthau and Kissinger was driven by a quest for tools of survival that did not rely on the uncertain, perilous extremes of international tribunals and nuclear blackmail.

At each of these junctures, the impetus to rediscover diplomacy as an instrument of strategy came as a result not of historical sentimentality but of geopolitical necessity. We are at a similar juncture today. To a much greater extent than after 1919 or 1945, the diplomat's status has depreciated since 1991. More than ever, it is tempting to believe that human societies have finally found a winning recipe for safety and tranquility that does not depend on the antique methods of classical diplomacy. But this conceit is likely to once again prove premature, for two reasons.

First, systemic war has returned as a very present and pressing possibility in relations between great powers. Despite the hopes of the post–Cold War period, liberalism manifestly did not expunge geopolitics from the human story. After an interlude, the normal mode of history has returned, in a resurgently vicious form. Uneven growth rates have brought what they always bring: new accumulations of power to challenge the old. The key actors are big states, and the objects of their jockeying are allies, territory, wealth, and prestige. Once launched, wars take on all the old chaotic elemental savagery that Clausewitz foresaw, only with recourse to more destructive weapons that make annihilation a more obtainable object than ever.[10] Leaders still need some way of reining in these forces, bridging gaps between national-security means and ends, and keeping war's costs and aims subordinate to politics.

Second, no substitute has emerged to supplant diplomacy's function in strategy. All the international institutions in the world cannot stop a great-power war from breaking out, or bridle its severity, length, or outcome. Nor can we assume that nuclear weapons will prevent such wars from occurring and escalating. Indeed, in an age of shifting military balances, mutual nuclear vulnerability, and proliferating conventional military technologies, revisionist powers have a more reasonable prospect of getting what they want the old-fashioned way, through conquest and subjugation, than at any point since before the advent of the atomic age.

No fancy gizmo is going to suddenly replace the diplomat. Social media may provide a constant stream of unfiltered information about what's happening in a foreign country, but it is no substitute for the textured appraisals that forward-deployed diplomats can make about underlying realities on the ground. Zoom makes it easier to have long-distance meetings, but compromise is still best achieved in the thrust-and-parry of personal interactions. Artificial intelligence can provide instantaneous interpretation, organize mountains of data, or even outline optimal trade-offs.[11] But it cannot formulate preferences or provide the finesse and interpersonal skill that have always constituted the X factor of success in negotiations.

The paths that 21st-Century diplomacy may take cannot be predicted. But it's safe to assume that they will more closely resemble the diplomacy of bygone eras than the marginalized forms it has assumed since the end of the Cold War. As in the past, those great powers that can heed Archidamus's advice and keep a grip on their own illusionary reflexes are likely to gain command over the temporal and spatial elements of strategic competition. Those that can mobilize effective coalitions and hold them together over long stretches, concentrate scarce military resources in the critical theater, and, when necessary, convert old foes into temporary allies are sure to hold the decisive advantage in the geopolitical contests of the 21st Century.

The nations of the West should have a competitive edge in wielding diplomacy in this fashion. It is in the West that the tradition of using political combinations to thwart hegemonic accumulations of power finds its richest and fullest expression. By such methods, all three attempts at world supremacy in the modern era—by Imperial Germany, Nazi Germany, and the Soviet Union—were prevented from succeeding.

But it's not a foregone conclusion that that will be the case a fourth time around. Diplomacy is not the exclusive preserve of any one nation. To a greater extent than any of those earlier powers, 21st-Century China is adept at using diplomacy to win friends and influence people. Its leaders have demonstrated the mixture of political acumen, ideological flexibility, and patience that typically characterize successful great powers. It too is animated by a sense of national mission and destiny in the world, and has economic and civilizational benefits to attract smaller states. And it is showing sobriety and self-discipline in cultivating the habits and institutions of strategic diplomacy.

Meeting this challenge will be the organizing task of U.S. diplomacy for the foreseeable future. The path to doing so begins with jettisoning the fallacies that have grown up since the end of the Cold War. One is the idea that the United States should aspire to transform rather than constrain our rivals. Another is the notion that international order rather than national safety and prosperity should be the American diplomat's primary object. The former flows from enlightened pursuit of the latter, not vice versa.

But the biggest fallacy is the conceit that humankind is progressing toward an apotheosis in which brave new ideas and technology will free us from the age-old dictates of geography, history, and human nature. Effective diplomacy proceeds from a sober recognition that human events tend to tragedy, that the quest for power is endemic to the species, and that the job of strategic statecraft is to set sturdy, if transient, limits to how far that quest can go. Diplomacy seeks not to transcend struggle but to carve out islands of stability amid its dangers and contradictions. The ultimate paradox of diplomacy is that by seeking that most selfish of ends—state survival—it has made possible the greatest moments of prosperity and peace in the human story. That task remains as difficult, but also necessary, in the 21st Century as it was in bygone eras.

NOTES

Preface

1. There are several serviceable introductions to diplomacy. Paul Gordon Lauren, Gordon A. Craig, and Alexander L. George, *Force and Statecraft: Diplomatic Challenges of Our Time* (Oxford: Oxford University Press, 2021) is a good starting point. The writing of G. R. Berridge is consistently excellent; his *Diplomatic Theory from Machiavelli to Kissinger* (coauthored with Maurice Keens-Soper and T.G. Otte; London: Palgrave Macmillan, 2001) provides a digestible account that is the best of its kind. Sir Harold Nicolson's *Diplomacy* (New York: Galaxy Books, 1964) and *The Evolution of Diplomacy* (New York: Collier Books, 1966) remain fashionable classics. See also Jeremy Black, *A History of Diplomacy* (London: Reaktion Books, 2010); Joseph M. Siracusa, *Diplomatic History: A Very Short Introduction* (Oxford: Oxford University Press, 2021); and Keith Hamilton and Richard Langhorne, *The Practice of Diplomacy: Its Evolution, Theory and Administration* (New York: Routledge, 2011).

2. Chester A. Crocker, Fen Osler Hampson, and Pamela Aall, eds., *Diplomacy and the Future of World Order* (Washington, DC: Georgetown University Press, 2021), 4.

3. See Monica Duffy Toft and Sidita Kushi, *Dying by the Sword: The Militarization of U.S. Foreign Policy* (New York: Oxford Academic, 2023).

4. A sample: Richard Langhorne, "Current Developments in Diplomacy: Who Are the Diplomats Now?," *Diplomacy & Statecraft* 8, no. 2 (July 1997); Shaun Riordan, *The New Diplomacy* (Cambridge: Polity Press, 2003); Andrew F. Cooper, "The Changing Nature of Diplomacy," in Cooper et al., *The Oxford Handbook of Modern Diplomacy* (Oxford: Oxford University Press, 2013), 35–53; Aaron David Miller, "The End of Diplomacy?" *Foreign Policy*, February 3, 2010; and Brian Patrick Bolger, "The Age of Diplomacy Is Over," *The National Interest*, December 4, 2023.

5. See, for example, Graham T. Allison, *Destined for War: Can America and China Escape Thucydides's Trap?* (New York: Mariner Books, 2018); and Elbridge A. Colby, *The Strategy of Denial: American Defense in an Age of Great Power Competition* (New Haven, CT: Yale University Press, 2021).

6. Quoted in Peter W. Dickson, *Kissinger and the Meaning of History* (Cambridge: Cambridge University Press, 1978), 3.

Chapter One: The Lost Art of Diplomacy

1. Robert B. Strassler, ed., *The Landmark Thucydides* (New York: Simon & Schuster, 1996), 48. It should be kept in mind, of course, that Thucydides's account was at best a reconstruction of events whose exact details are lost to history.

2. Donald Kagan points out that a large amount of time passed between the assembly's deliberations and Sparta's entry into the war, and posits that Archidamus's reasoning had a greater impact on Spartan actions than Thucydides had been prepared to concede. See Kagan, *The Outbreak of the Peloponnesian War* (Ithaca, NY: Cornell University Press, 1969), 300–316.

3. Peter Paret and Michael Howard, *Carl von Clausewitz: On War* (Princeton, NJ: Princeton University Press, 1984), 204.

4. Sir Ivor Roberts, ed., *Satow's Diplomatic Practice*, seventh edition (Oxford: Oxford University Press, 2017), xxix.

5. For a succinct overview of diplomacy's history from the earliest times to today, see Roberts, 6–19.

6. Henry Kissinger's definition ("the art of restraining power") probably drew on David Jayne Hill's 1905 formulation, "deliberately formed conventions in restraint of force." The various definitions of diplomacy tend to stress either process or outcome. Examples of the former include Harold Nicolson ("the process and machinery by which . . . negotiation is carried out") and Martin Wight ("the system and the art of communication between powers"). Examples of the latter include Robert Strausz-Hupé ("the adjustment of differences through negotiations") and Hans Morgenthau ("the promotion of the national interest by peaceful means").

7. Berridge, Keens-Soper, and Otte, 3.

8. Lauren, Craig, and George, 5.

9. Martin Wight, *Power Politics* (New York: Continuum, 2002), 115.

10. Joshua 9:4, King James Version. Remarkably, the Israelites honored the treaty despite Gibeon's deception. See Joshua 9:1–18 and 10:1–11.

11. A. F. Whyte, *The Practice of Diplomacy* (London: Constable & Co., 1919), vii.

12. Nicolson, *Evolution*, 88; Kissinger later made a similar point in *White House Years*, 746–747.

13. Quoted in Berridge, Keens-Soper, and Otte, 34.

14. Henry Bertram Hill, *The Political Testament of Cardinal Richelieu* (Madison: University of Wisconsin Press, 1961), 94.

15. René Albrecht-Carrié, *A Diplomatic History of Europe since the Congress of Vienna* (New York: Harper & Brothers, 1958), 7.

16. Lauren, Craig, and George, 5.

17. Joseph Nye defines "soft power" somewhat nebulously, as "the ability to affect others to obtain preferred outcomes by the co-optive means of framing the agenda, persuasion, and positive attraction." Berridge convincingly argues that "'soft power' is nothing more than influence." See his blog entry dated January 17, 2014, at https://grberridge.diplomacy.edu/soft-power-is-nothing-more-than-influence/.

18. See Nicolson, *Evolution*, 16; and Morgenthau in Berridge, 20.

19. Quoted in Maurice Keens-Soper and Karl W. Schweizer, eds., *François de Callières: The Art of Diplomacy* (New York: Leicester University Press, 1983), 75.

20. Whyte, v–vi. See also Hans Morgenthau, *Politics among Nations* (New York: Alfred A. Knopf, 1960), 139.

21. Robert Strausz-Hupé, William R. Kintner, and Stefan T. Possony, *A Forward Strategy for America* (New York: Harper & Brothers, 1961), 210. See also Mark A. Stoler, "War and Diplomacy: Or, Clausewitz for Diplomatic Historians," *Diplomatic History* 29, no. 1 (January 2005): 1–26.

22. John Lewis Gaddis, *What Is 'Grand Strategy'? American Grand Strategy after War* (2009), Triangle Institute for Security Studies and Duke University Program on American Grand Strategy, unpublished, 7.

23. Strassler, 46.

24. Paret and Howard, 92–93.

25. "To be isolated," as Walter Lippmann wrote, "is for any state the worst of all predicaments. To be the member of a combination which can be depended upon to act together, and, when challenged, to fight together, is to have achieved the highest degree of security which is attainable in a world where there are many sovereign national states." See Walter Lippmann, *U.S. Foreign Policy: Shield of the Republic* (New York: Little, Brown and Company, 1943), 105.

26. Paret and Howard, 605–610.

27. Strausz-Hupé, Kintner, and Stefan T. Possony, 218.

28. Gordon A. Craig and Felix Gilbert, eds., *The Diplomats 1919–1939* (Princeton, NJ: Princeton University Press, 1981), 22.

29. Strassler, 48.

30. Henry W. Lucy, ed., *Essays by the Late Marquess of Salisbury* (New York: Dutton, 1905), 11–12.

31. "The nature of things in this world," as the 16th-Century Italian diplomat Francesco Guicciardini wrote, "is such that nearly everything contains some imperfections in all its

parts." See the discussion on negotiation as the embrace of imperfection in G. R. Berridge's essay on Guicciardini in Berridge, Keens-Soper, and Otte, 41.

32. Dickson, 53.

33. See Fredrik Logevall and Kenneth Osgood, "The Ghost of Munich: America's Appeasement Complex," *World Affairs* 173, no. 2 (July/August 2010).

34. The work of Gordon Craig, cited throughout this book, can be seen as an extension of the Satow-Nicolson tradition into the post–World War II era. See Sir Ernest Satow, *A Guide to Diplomatic Practice, Vol. I*, second edition (London: Longmans, Green & Co., 1922); Whyte, *The Practice of Diplomacy*; and Harold Nicolson, *Diplomacy*, third edition (New York: Oxford University Press, 1964). See also the chapters on Callières, Satow, and Nicolson in Berridge, Keens-Soper, and Otte, 106–124, 125–150, and 151–180.

35. See Hans Morgenthau, "Diplomacy," *Yale Law Journal* 55, no. 5 (August 1946): 1067–1081.

36. See, for example, Barry Steiner, *Bernard Brodie and the Foundations of American Nuclear Strategy* (Lawrence: University of Kansas Press, 1991), 30.

37. It was around this same time that Thomas Schelling began using behavioral economics and game theory to show how nuclear weapons could be used to change an opponent's behavior without resorting to force. While his research offers many insights, Schelling's main interest was violence rather than diplomacy as such, so is not covered extensively in this book. See Thomas C. Schelling, *Arms and Influence* (New Haven, CT: Yale University Press, 1966) and the overview of coercive diplomacy in Lauren, Craig, and George, chapter 10.

38. See Niall Ferguson's compelling reappraisal, *Kissinger 1923–1968: The Idealist* (New York: Penguin Press, 2015).

39. Kant quoted in Henry Kissinger, *World Order* (London: Penguin Books, 2014), 40. Kissinger was not alone in his preoccupation with order. As Paul Schroeder, perhaps the most talented diplomatic historian of his time, put it, "The central problem for IR theory, one often hears, is understanding order rather than power, devising a viable principle of international order for the control and management of conflict." See Schroeder, "Alliances, 1815–1945: Weapons of Power and Tools of Management," in *Systems, Stability and Statecraft: Essays on the International History of Modern Europe*, ed. David Wetzel, Robert Jervis, and Jack S. Levy (New York: Palgrave MacMillan, 2004), 196.

40. Kissinger, *World Order*, 327.

41. See the gloomy statistics in Hal Brands, "The Triumph and Tragedy of Diplomatic History," *Texas National Security Review* 1, no. 1 (December 2017): 138–139.

42. Most importantly: G. R. Berridge, Paul Lauren, Gordon Craig, Alexander George, Maurice Keens-Soper, and T. G. Otte. Also notable is the work of Brendan Simms, Andrew Erhardt, and John Bew. See also David Milne, *Worldmaking: The Art and Science of American Diplomacy* (New York: Farrar, Straus and Giroux, 2015).

43. See, for example, William J. Burns, *The Back Channel: A Memoir of American Diplomacy and the Case for Its Renewal* (New York: Random House, 2020); Stuart Eizenstat, *The Art of Diplomacy: How American Negotiators Reached Historic Agreements That Changed the World* (Lanham, MD: Rowman & Littlefield, 2024); and Nicholas Kralev, *Diplomatic Tradecraft* (London: Cambridge University Press, 2024).

44. See, for example, Andrew F. Cooper, Jorge Heine, and Ramesh Thakur, eds., *The Oxford Handbook of Modern Diplomacy* (Oxford: Oxford University Press, 2013); and Crocker, Hampson, and Aall, eds., *Diplomacy and the Future of World Order*.

45. The field originated with Edward Luttwak's seminal work, *The Grand Strategy of the Roman Empire from the First Century A.D. to the Third* (Baltimore: Johns Hopkins University Press, 1976). Other classics include Luttwak's *The Grand Strategy of the Byzantine Empire* (Cambridge, MA: Belknap Press, 2009); John P. LeDonne, *The Grand Strategy of the Russian Empire, 1650–1831* (Oxford: Oxford University Press, 2003); Geoffrey Parker, *The Grand Strategy of Philip II* (London: Redwood, 2000); and Paul Rahe, *The Grand Strategy of Classical Sparta: The Persian Challenge* (New Haven, CT: Yale University Press, 2015). For a sample of recent work in this field, see Hal Brands, ed., *The New Makers of Modern Strategy: From the Ancient World to the Digital Age* (Princeton, NJ: Princeton University Press, 2023).

For a recent panoramic, see Christopher J. Fettweis, *The Pursuit of Dominance: 2000 Years of Superpower Grand Strategy* (Oxford, UK: Oxford University Press, 2023).

46. There are exceptions. Edward Luttwak reflects on the role of diplomacy in strategy, mainly in wartime, in his book *Strategy: The Logic of War and Peace* (Cambridge, MA: Harvard University Press, 2002), 269ff. Williamson Murray and Richard Hart Sinnreich examine patterns of diplomatic and military history in *The Shaping of Grand Strategy: Policy, Diplomacy, and War* (Cambridge: Cambridge University Press, 2011)—see especially chapter 9. Lawrence Freedman offers valuable insights on the role of diplomacy in nuclear warfare in *Strategy: A History* (New York: Oxford University Press, 2013), chapter 12.

47. Francis Fukuyama, *The End of History and the Last Man* (New York: Free Press, 1992).

48. See, for example, Joseph S. Nye, "Public Diplomacy in a Changing World," *Annals of the American Academy of Political and Social Science* 616 (March 2008): 94–109; and Eric Schmidt, "Innovation Power: Why Technology Will Define the Future of Geopolitics," *Foreign Affairs*, March/April 2023.

49. See, for example, Jorge Heine, "Club to Network Diplomacy," in Cooper, Heine, and Thakur, 54–67.

50. As Martin Wight (117) shows, revisionist regimes from the French Revolution to the Nazis and Bolsheviks have tended to twist diplomacy's functions and treat it as a weapon for promulgating their political gospels and undermining opponents abroad.

51. David Jayne Hill, *A History of Diplomacy in the International Development of Europe, Volume I: The Struggle for Universal Empire* (New York: Longmans, Green & Co., 1905), ix.

52. Andrea Bartoletti argues that two-front war has posed "the greatest threat to state survival from ancient times to contemporary international politics." See his innovative book *Escaping the Deadly Embrace: How Encirclement Causes Major War* (Ithaca, NY: Cornell University Press, 2022).

53. Not much has been written on time in strategy. For a smart appraisal, see Nadia Schadlow, "The Forgotten Element of Strategy," *The Atlantic*, June 22, 2023.

54. The key source is Richard E. Neustadt and Ernest R. May, *Thinking in Time: The Uses of History for Decision-Makers* (New York: Free Press, 1986).

55. Dickson, 2–3.

Chapter Two: The Eunuch and the Barbarian

1. Following the empire's division by Diocletian in the 3rd Century AD, it was reunited by Constantine the Great, only to be divided again, this time permanently, by Theodosius I in 395, when he left a partitioned inheritance to his two sons, Arcadius and Honorius. The two halves maintained a dynastic link well into the 5th Century. Eastern emperors and officials referred to themselves simply as "Roman" and continued to view the western lands as part of the broader Roman universe, or *oikouménē*, that made up their notional inheritance long after the western half of the empire had fallen to the barbarians. The term "Byzantine," originally intended as a slur to denote the Orthodox Church's inferior status to Roman Catholicism, did not appear until the 16th Century. "Byzantine" and "Eastern Roman" have been used interchangeably by scholars since the 17th Century and is how I use them in this book.

2. The fragments that remain of Priscus's writing can be found in John Given, *The Fragmentary History of Priscus: Attila, the Huns and the Roman Empire, AD 430–476* (Merchantville, NJ: Evolution Publishing, 2014). The excerpt here is from Fragment 13. Priscus is among a handful of contemporary sources available from the 5th Century. The dearth of first-hand evidence for this era has tended to deter historical investigation. See C.D. Gordon, *The Age of Attila: Fifth Century Byzantium and the Barbarians* (Ann Arbor: University of Michigan Press, 2013), 27–28. In addition to Priscus, this chapter draws wherever possible on the writings of other contemporary and subsequent chroniclers, including Olympiodorus, Candidus, John of Antioch, Theophanes, and John Malalas.

3. Priscus, Fragment 14.

4. The essential source is Edward Luttwak, *The Grand Strategy of the Byzantine Empire* (Cambridge, MA: Belknap Press, 2009). See also Jonathan Shepard and Simon Franklin, eds.,

Byzantine Diplomacy: Papers from the Twenty-Fourth Spring Symposium of Byzantine Studies, Cambridge, Society for the Promotion of Byzant, March 1990 (Aldershot, UK: Variorium Reprints, 1992); Dimitri Obolensky, "The Principles and Methods of Byzantine Diplomacy," in *Byzantium and the Slavs* (Crestwood, NY: St. Vladimir's Seminary Press, 1994); Charalampos Papasotiriou, *The Role of Diplomacy in Byzantine Grand Strategy*, Discussion Paper, Centre for the Study of Diplomacy, University of Leicester, 1996; and Anthony Kaldellis, *The New Roman Empire: A History of Byzantium* (Oxford: Oxford University Press, 2023).

5. I use the term "barbarian" not to suggest that the Huns lacked cultural sophistication but rather in the way that the Byzantines used it, to denote a pagan who did not fall within the Roman-Christian *oikouménē*. For a discussion of this term's various uses, see Jakub J. Grygiel, *Return of the Barbarians: Confronting Non-State Actors from Ancient Rome to the Present* (Cambridge: Cambridge University Press, 2018), 8–11.

6. The Huns appeared in the space between the Volga and Don Rivers sometime in the mid-3rd Century. Little is known about their origins. Two classic sources are E. A. Thompson, *The Huns* (Oxford: Blackwell, 1996); and Otto J. Maenchen-Helfen, *The World of the Huns: Studies in Their History and Culture* (Berkeley: University of California Press, 1973).

7. See Maenchen-Helfen, 3–9; and Thompson, chapter 2. The quote from Ammianus comes from Thompson, 28–29. For a description of Attila's impact on Byzantine strategic thinking, see Warren Treadgold, *A History of the Byzantine State and Society* (Stanford, CA: Stanford University Press, 1997), 93–95; and Luttwak, 49–52.

8. For many years historians erroneously dated this battle to 443 due to a flawed sequencing of fragments from Priscus's manuscript. For the correct chronology, see Maenchen-Helfen, 114–124.

9. Maenchen-Helfen, 25.

10. For a succinct overview of the empire's main strategic theaters, see Mark Whittow, *The Making of Byzantium* (Berkeley: University of California Press, 1996), 38–53.

11. For a detailed breakdown of Byzantine military commitments by theater, see Treadgold, 105–107. His figures are for the period about fifty years after the arrival of the Huns and thus perhaps somewhat higher than they would have been in Theodosius's time, before the acceleration of the crises of the Western Empire.

12. Whittow (50) describes the Balkans as a "a zone of defense-in-depth" for the Byzantines.

13. A good source for Theodosius II's reign is Fergus Millar, *A Greek Roman Empire: Power and Belief under Theodosius II 408–450* (Berkeley: University of California Press, 2006). See also Treadgold, 78–148.

14. John Malalas, *The Chronicle of John Malalas*, trans. Elizabeth Jeffreys, Michael Jeffreys, and Roger Scott (Leiden: Brill, 2017), 195.

15. See John of Antioch, Fragment 194, in Gordon, 27–28.

16. This paragraph draws on Millar, 193 and Treadgold, 117.

17. Chamberlains usually presided over a set of portfolios in the empire's domestic or foreign affairs. Chrysaphius was one in a line of powerful chamberlains that included his father's servant Eutropius and later Anastasius, chamberlain to the emperor Zeno. See Treadgold, 117.

18. For an analysis of the role of eunuchs in Byzantine society, see Keith Hopkins and M. K. Hopkins, "Eunuchs in Politics in the Later Roman Empire," *Proceedings of the Cambridge Philological Society* 189, no. 9 (1963): 62–80; and Shaun Tougher, *The Eunuch in Byzantine History and Society* (London: Routledge, 2008).

19. Malalas, 198.

20. Luttwak (51) puts the size of this force at between 30,000 and 50,000 men—a significant number when one considers that the entire Byzantine garrison for Thrace and the Balkans at this time was probably around 45,000 men.

21. See the examples of the Huns exploiting Byzantine distractions in Thompson, 79.

22. Treadgold, 79–82.

23. Thompson, 83.

24. We don't know the exact amount of gold promised in this treaty, but Maenchen-Helfen (117) reckons it at fourteen hundred pounds on the basis of the arrears demanded by the Huns.

25. The German historian Rudolf Helm traced the roots of Byzantine diplomatic structures and notions of protocol and rank to ancient Rome. See Evangelos Chrysos, "Byzantine Diplomacy, AD 300–800: Means and Ends" in Shepard and Franklin, eds., 30; and Fergus Millar, "Government and Diplomacy in the Roman Empire during the First Three Centuries," *International History Review* 10, no. 3 (August 1988): 345–377.

26. Treadgold, 113 and 119.

27. The Skrinion Barbaron gathered intelligence about barbarians, but probably not in the sense of modern-day spying, which appears to have fallen under the jurisdiction of the Byzantine postal service. The interpreter named Vigilas who was involved in the attempted assassination of Attila during the diplomatic mission of 449 would probably have been attached to the Skrinion Barbaron. Thompson (109) points out the unusual difficulty that the Byzantines had in finding interpreters with a sufficiently advanced knowledge of the Hunnic language to accompany diplomatic missions.

28. For more on Byzantine strategic literacy, see Luttwak, 235–321.

29. Thompson, 94.

30. Thompson, 108.

31. For more on these factions and debates, see Treadgold, 94–98.

32. See John of Antioch, Fragment 194, in Gordon, 28. It should be kept in mind that many of the negative assessments of Theodosius by later Byzantine writers have roots in the theological debates of the time and should therefore be taken with a grain of salt.

33. Nestorius was echoing the criticism of Jerome, who saw the practice of paying for peace with the barbarians as sinful, and anticipating the criticism of Procopius, who would later accuse the emperor Justinian of allowing "all the barbarians [to become] masters of all the wealth of the Romans." See Prokopios, *The Secret History: With Related Texts*, ed. Anthony Kaldellis (Indianapolis, IN: Hackett, 2010), chapter 19.

34. See Edward Gibbon, *The Decline and Fall of the Roman Empire* (New York: Alfred A. Knopf, 1993), 3:392–425; John Julius Norwich, *Byzantium: The Early Centuries* (New York: Viking Press, 1989), 419–420; and Georg Ostrogorsky, *Geschichte des byzantinischen Staates* (München: Verlag C. H. Beck, 1975), 31.

35. Zosimus, *New History*, Vol. 2, trans. Ronald T. Ridley (Brill: Leiden, Boston, 2017), 114.

36. Owen Lattimore, *Inner Asian Frontiers of China* (Boston: Beacon Press, 1962), 465–466.

37. Luttwak, 33.

38. Luttwak, 38.

39. Priscus, Fragment 8.

40. I use the term appeasement here to refer to the practice whereby a state makes concessions to another to dissuade it from aggression. Papasotiriou (10ff.) argues convincingly that the Byzantines differentiated their tribute policies, which were intended to create dependencies and therefore leverage, from appeasement, which as he points out was usually "reserved for use as a measure of last resort."

41. Priscus, Fragment 6, emphasis added.

42. Treadgold, 81.

43. Maenchen-Helfen, 117.

44. See Treadgold, 88, 90, and 95.

45. See the discussion in Alexander Kazhdan, "The Notion of Byzantine Diplomacy," in Shepherd and Franklin, 13–15.

46. For an up-to-date account of Byzantine-Persian relations in this period from the Persian perspective, see Michael J. Decker, *The Sasanian Empire at War: Persia, Rome, and the Rise of Islam* (Yardley, UK: Westholme, 2022), chapter 5. See also Z. Rubin, "Diplomacy and War in the Relations between Byzantium and the Sassanids in the Fifth Century AD," in *The Defense of the Roman and Byzantine East: Proceedings of a Colloquium Held at the University of Sheffield*, ed. Philip Freeman and David Kennedy (Oxford: British Institute of Archaeology at Ankara, April 1986), 677–695.

47. Obolensky, quoted in Chrysos, 28.

48. The intention was sincere, but largely instrumental. Chrysos (25ff.) challenges the German historian Ekkehard Eickhoff's claim that Christianity was the animating force of Byzantine diplomacy, arguing that "the prospect of an absolute ecumenical domination was never discussed seriously in the empire." In a similar vein, Kazhdan (10–11) acknowledges that Byzantine diplomacy was informed by Christian universalism, rooted in the imperial notion of *oikouménē*, but argues that this universalism "was conservative rather than expansionist . . . [and] predominantly defensive." See also Luttwak, 113–123.

49. Obolensky (14) points out that the success of Christian missions can be seen as a barometer for the success of the empire's foreign policy. See also Alexander Borislavov Angelov, "Conversion and Empire: Byzantine Missionaries, Foreign Rulers, and Christian Narratives (ca. 300–900)" (PhD diss., University of Michigan Library, 2011), https://deepblue.lib.umich.edu/handle/2027.42/89651.

50. The veracity of these accounts has been challenged—see Maenchen-Helfen, 262ff.

51. Maenchen-Helfen, 269ff.

52. See John Lydus cited in Chrysos, 30–31.

53. Chrysos, 34.

54. Chrysos, 33ff.

55. Priscus, Fragment 1.1. See also Thompson, 82; and Chrysos, 34.

56. See Papasotiriou, 13.

57. See the uses of Constantinople's marvels in Byzantine diplomacy in Obolensky, 17–18; and Luttwak, 124–25.

58. Priscus, Fragment 7.

59. For more on the Byzantine imperial hierarchy and conception of world order more broadly, see George Ostrogorsky, "The Byzantine Emperor and the Hierarchical World Order," *Slavonic and East European Review* 35, no. 84 (December 1956): 1–14. For a breakdown of the empire's methods for ranking neighbors, see Kazhdan, 14; and Papasotiriou, 12–13. For an elaboration on this concept's application in later Byzantine history, see Franz Doelger, *Byzanz und die Europaeische Staatenwelt* (Ettal, Germany: Buch-Kunstverlag, 1953), especially the section entitled "Familie der Könige," 34ff.

60. Obolensky, 10.

61. Kazhdan, 16.

62. Obolensky (16) notes three uses of titles vis-à-vis barbarians: to flatter, to bind, and to signify their standing in the *oikouménē*. This system reached an apogee in the reign of the emperor Zeno, when the Ostrogothic leader Theodoric was named *magister militum praesentalis* (master of soldiers in the emperor's presence) and consul. See Treadgold, 161.

63. For more on the various uses of gold in Byzantine diplomacy, see J. Iluk, "The Export of Gold from the Roman Empire to Barbarian Countries from the 4th to the 6th Centuries," *Münstersche Beitraege zur antiken Handelsgeschichte* 4 (1985): 79–103; C. D. Gordon, "Subsidies in Roman Imperial Defense," *Phoenix* 3 (1949): 60–69; R. C. Blockley, "Subsidies and Diplomacy. Rome and Persia in Late Antiquity," *Phoenix* 39, no. 1 (Spring 1985): 62–74.

64. See Gabriela Simonova, "Byzantine Diplomacy and the Huns," *Macedonian Historical Review* 2 (2011): 82.

65. As Thompson (98) points out, the Byzantines understood that plunder was a "social necessity" for Attila. Gordon ("Subsidies," 60) sees three strategic uses of tribute by the Byzantines: "buy[ing] alliance and active military help against more formidable enemies," "buy[ing] immunity from attack," and "creat[ing] division among the enemies of the empire so as to maintain the frontiers intact." Blockley (62) identifies two types of subsidies: "reward of good behavior," which was "paid from strength," (backed by credible military alternatives), and "rental of good behavior," which was "paid from weakness."

66. Treadgold, 88.

67. Priscus, Fragment 8.

68. An indication of how widely the act of orchestrating an assassination attempt under the cover of a diplomatic mission departed from established norms of diplomacy even in this era can be seen in the otherwise uncouth Attila's protestations to that effect, and in the fact that the plot was concealed from the ambassador leading the mission.

69. The amount of annual tribute agreed in 443 was roughly equal to the sum that the Byzantine navy around this time paid on an annual basis to its oarsmen (see the breakdown in Treadgold, 145). Luttwak (54) calculates that even the larger tribute of 448 was equivalent to the combined annuities of six senior court officials. Altogether, Iluk (94ff.) estimates that successive Byzantine emperors remitted around 53,000 pounds of gold to the Huns in the 5th Century; for a frame of reference, he notes, the emperor Leo spent 65,000 pounds of gold and 700,000 pounds of silver on a single military campaign.

70. Papasotiriou (3–4) points out that the use of tribute in the north ultimately made more sense than force because of the continually shifting nature of barbarian threats there, which meant that "victories tended to be only ephemeral since a vanquished enemy was liable to be replaced by others."

71. Thompson, 157.

72. Thompson (148, 203–224) is one of the few historians prior to Luttwak to mount a defense of Theodosius's policies.

73. As Luttwak (3) observes, Chrysaphius "has as good a claim as any to the invention of Byzantium's new strategy, whereby the direct use of military force to destroy enemies was no longer the first instrument of statecraft, but the last." Obolensky (3) notes the impact that these early encounters with the barbarians had in laying the foundation for later Byzantine diplomacy: "It was partly in response to the northern challenge that was forged, in the course of centuries, by steadfast faith and lucid thinking, by careful study and observation, by trial and error, that imperial diplomacy which surely remains one of Byzantium's lasting contributions to the history of Europe."

74. Chrysos, 33ff.; and Kazhdan, 17–18.

Chapter Three: Ducats for the Sultan

1. The full content of Marcello's instructions can be found in *Régestes de délibérations du Sénat de Venise concernant la Romanie*, ed. Freddy Thiriet, vol. 3 (Paris: Mouton & Co., 1961). The first message of May 8 is No. 2923; the July 5 message is No. 2932; the July 12 message is No. 2934; and the July 17 message is No. 2935. In addition to Thiriet, sources consulted for this chapter include Samuele Romanin, *Storia documentata di Venezia*, vol. 3, second edition (Venice: Giusto Fuga, 1913); and Riccardo Predelli, *I libri commemoriali della republica di Venezia*: Regesti, vol. 5 (Cambridge: Cambridge University Press, 2012). While there are no extant copies of the famous *relazioni* delivered by returning Venetian ambassadors for the period covered in this book, the earliest of these, from 1492, and many other examples are preserved in full in Eugenio Albèri, *Le relazioni degli ambasciatori veneti al Senato durante il secolo decimosesto*, series 1, vol. 4 (Firenze: Società Editrice Florentina, 1860).

2. The key source on Mehmed II is Franz Babinger, *Mehmed the Conqueror and His Time*, ed. William C. Hickman, trans. Ralph Manheim (Princeton, NJ: Princeton University Press, 1978).

3. Nicolò Barbaro, *Giornale dell'assedio di Costantinopoli, 1453* (Vienna: Libreria Tendler & Co., 1856), 59–65.

4. Reinhold C. Mueller, *The Venetian Money Market: Banks, Panics, and the Public Debt, 1200–1500* (Baltimore: Johns Hopkins University Press, 2019), 211ff.; and Dennis Romano, *The Likeness of Venice: A Life of Doge Francesco Foscari 1373–1457* (New Haven, CT: Yale University Press, 2007), 240–241 and 244–245.

5. The classic source is Paul Wittek, *Rise of the Ottoman Empire* (London: Royal Asiatic Society, 1938). See also Halil Inalcik, "The Rise of the Ottoman Empire," in *The Cambridge History of Islam*, ed. P. M. Holt, Ann K. S. Lambton, and Bernard Lewis. (Cambridge: Cambridge University Press, 1970), 295–323; and Marc David Baer, *The Ottomans: Khans, Caesars, and Caliphs* (New York: Basic Books, 2021), chapter 1.

6. There are a number of excellent general English-language accounts of the Republic of Venice. The most recent is Dennis Romano, *Venice: The Remarkable History of the Lagoon City* (Oxford: Oxford University Press, 2023). See also Frederic C. Lane, *Venice: A Maritime Republic* (Baltimore: Johns Hopkins University Press, 1973); John Julius Norwich, *A History of Venice* (New York: Vintage Books, 1989); William Roscoe Thayer, *A Short History of*

Venice (Boston: Houghton, Mifflin & Co., 1908); William H. McNeill, *Venice: The Hinge of Europe, 1081–1797* (Chicago: Chicago University Press, 1974); J. R. Hale, ed., *Renaissance Venice* (London: Faber & Faber, 1974); D. S. Chambers, *The Imperial Age of Venice 1380–1580* (London: Thames & Hudson, 1970); and Roger Crowley, *City of Fortune: How Venice Ruled the Seas* (New York: Random House, 2013).

7. For a recent articulation of the argument that Venice's republican system of government constituted an advantage in great-power competition, see Matthew Kroenig, *The Return of Great Power Rivalry: Democracy versus Autocracy from the Ancient World to the U.S. and China* (Oxford: Oxford University Press, 2020).

8. John Ruskin divided the political history of the Republic of Venice into two eras: before and after the "final and absolute distinction of the nobles from the commonality." See Ruskin's *The Stones of Venice*, vol. 1, *The Foundations* (New York: John Wiley & Sons, 1880), 2. A good description of the complicated mechanics of Venetian government can be found in Lane, 96–97, 116–117 and 428–429. See also Chambers, 73–107. The estimate of the number of noble families can be found in Stanley Chojnacki, "Social Identity in Renaissance Venice: The Second Serrata," *Renaissance Studies* 8, no. 4 (December 1994): 341–358.

9. For a geoeconomic explanation of Venice's commercial success, see J. Russell Smith, "The World Entrepôt," *Journal of Political Economy* 18, no. 9 (November 1910): 697–713. For an overview of the evolution of Venetian trade, see Lane, 57ff.

10. See Bernard Lewis, *Istanbul and the Civilization of the Ottoman Empire* (Norman: University of Oklahoma Press, 1963), 3–35; and Halil Inalcik, *The Ottoman Empire: The Classical Age, 1300–1600* (London: Weidenfeld & Nicolson, 1973).

11. Historians debate whether the main driver for the Ottoman development of sea power was Venice or Rhodes. See Palmira Brummett, *Ottoman Seapower and Levantine Diplomacy in the Age of Discovery* (Albany: State University of New York Press, 1994).

12. For more on the role of the *bailo*, see Eric R. Dursteler, "The Bailo in Constantinople: Crisis and Career in Venice's Early Modern Diplomatic Corps," *Mediterranean Historical Review* 16, no. 2 (2001): 1–30.

13. Venice was never truly detached from mainland affairs. The acquisition of territory on the *terraferma* had begun decades before the Lombard wars in an earlier contest with Milan. For more on the reasons for this expansion, see Jakub J. Grygiel, *Great Powers and Geopolitical Change* (Baltimore: Johns Hopkins University Press, 2006), 78–83; and Romano, *Likeness*, 12ff.

14. Historians have tended to look dimly on Foscari, with Ruskin going so far as to identify the onset of his reign as the beginning of Venice's decline as a great power. For a more balanced and up-to-date portrait, see Dennis Romano's new biography *Likeness of Venice* (op. cit.).

15. Later generations of Venetians would embellish the jousts between Mocenigo and Foscari. What is clear is that the Venetian elite were divided over how much attention to devote to the affairs of the *terraferma* while keeping the Stato da Mar running smoothly. For the latest scholarship on these debates, see Romano, *Likeness*, 29–32.

16. See Mueller, 214; and Romano, *Likeness*, 257. For a sense of proportion, Lane (426) shows total state revenue around this time at about one million ducats.

17. One historian argues that Venice's prioritization of the *terraferma* was a strategic mistake comparable to Athens' Sicilian expedition. See Andrew Lambert, *Seapower States* (New Haven, CT: Yale University Press, 2018), 123. Lane (235–239) points out that once the mainland wars ended, Venetian tax receipts from the *terraferma* provided the bulk of resources for increasing defense spending to protect the overseas empire.

18. Lane, 238.

19. The key source on Venetian diplomacy is Garret Mattingly, *Renaissance Diplomacy* (New York: Russell & Russell, 1970). See also his essay "The First Resident Embassies: Mediaeval Italian Origins of Modern Diplomacy," *Speculum* 12, no. 4 (October 1937): 423–439; and Wallace K. Ferguson, "Changing Attitudes towards the State," in *Facets of the Renaissance*, ed. Wallace K. Ferguson et al. (New York: Harper & Row, 1963).

20. Daniel Goffman argues persuasively that Italian interactions with the Ottomans in this period contributed much more decisively to the development of the new diplomacy that has commonly been acknowledged. See Goffman, "Negotiating with the Renaissance State: The Ottoman Empire and the New Diplomacy," in *The Early Modern Ottomans: Remapping*

the Empire, ed. Virginia Aksan and Daniel Goffman (Cambridge: Cambridge University Press, 2007), 70–71.

21. Albèri, 1:xvi. See also Donald E. Queller, *The Office of Ambassador in the Middle Ages* (Princeton, NJ: Princeton Legacy Library, 1967), 143.

22. The oldest extant *relazione* is that delivered by Zaccaria Contarini after his return from France in 1492, which can be found in Albèri, 4:2–26. For more on the origins of *relazioni,* see Donald E. Queller, "The Development of Ambassadorial Relazioni," in *Renaissance Venice,* ed. John Hale (London: Faber & Faber, 1974). On the ways in which Venetian *relazioni* differed from those of other Italian city-states, see Queller, *Office,* 175. See also Filippo De Vivo, "How to Read Venetian *Relazioni,*" *Renaissance and Reformation* 34, no. 1–2 (Winter-Spring 2011): 25–59.

23. Albèri, 1:3ff. As Queller puts it (*Office,* 176), when presenting a *relazione,* an ambassador was "not a mere chronicler of events but the painter of a political tableau in broad terms: he depicted the characters of princes and ministers, the attitudes and sentiments of peoples, the strengths and weaknesses of states."

24. The following paragraphs draw on Mattingly, *Renaissance Diplomacy,* 59–108. See also Berridge, *Diplomatic Theory,* chapters 1 and 2; and Lauren, 5–7.

25. It is in this period that, as the Swiss historian Jacob Burckhardt put it, "a new fact appears in history—the State as the outcome of reflection and calculation, the State as a work of art. . . . The deliberate adaptation of means to ends, of which no prince out of Italy had at that time a conception, joined to almost absolute power with the limits of the State." See Burckhardt, *The Civilisation of the Renaissance in Italy* (London: George Allen & Unwin, 1921), 2.

26. Mattingly, *Renaissance Diplomacy,* 71, 76, and 79.

27. For more on warfare in this period and how it affected policymaking, see M. E. Mallett and J. R. Hale, *The Military Organization of a Renaissance State: Venice c. 1400–1617* (Cambridge: Cambridge University Press, 1984). See also Mattingly, *Renaissance Diplomacy,* 62.

28. See Mattingly's description of this transition in Ferguson, 25ff.

29. Nicolson, *Evolution,* 48.

30. See the discussion of Barbaro's treatise, and juxtaposition with the writing of Machiavelli, in Berridge, Keens-Soper, and Otte, 34; and Ferguson, 33–35. Barbaro's writings on diplomacy, which remained undiscovered for centuries, still have not received adequate English-language attention. See Riccardo Fubini, "L'ambasciatore nel XV secolo: due trattati e una biografia (Bernard De Rosier, Ermolao Barbaro, Vespasiano Da Bisticci)," *Mélanges de l'ecole française de Rome. moyen âge* 108, no. 2 (1996): 645–665; and Bruno Figliuolo, *Il diplomatico e il trattatista: Ermolao Barbaro ambasciatore della Serenissimail,* vol. 2 (Naples: Guida, 1999).

31. See the Senate instruction dated July 5, 1453, in Thiriet, 3:2932.

32. The full text of the treaty is recorded by Romanin, 4:528–535.

33. Babinger (111) contrasts the sultan's handling of the Venetians with his brutal treatment of the Genoese around the time.

34. As a frame of reference, the salary of a *bailo* was around a thousand ducats a year. The Venetians were known to pay much larger bribes when circumstances required. See Kenneth M. Setton, *The Papacy and the Levant, 1204–1571,* vol. 2, *The Fifteenth Century* (Philadelphia: American Philosophical Society, 1978), 141; and Romano, *Likeness,* 181.

35. At the moment Constantinople fell, Venice probably had between thirty and thirty-five warships afloat—enough to hurt the Ottomans, but not decisively defeat them. See Renard Gluzman, *Venetian Shipping from the Days of Glory to Decline, 1453–1571* (Leiden: Brill, 2021), 234.

36. For a detailed summary of Simone's negotiations, see the appendices of Margaret L. King, *The Death of the Child Valerio Marcello* (Chicago: University of Chicago Press, 1994), 292–293. The following paragraphs draw on Romano, *Likeness,* 256–266. See also Norwich, 323; Setton, 156–157; and King, 134.

37. The text of this treaty can be found in Jean Dumont, *Corps universel diplomatique du droit des gens* (Amsterdam: chez P. Brunel, R. et G. Wetstein, 1726), 1:202–207.

38. See John E. Law, "The Venetian Mainland State in the Fifteenth Century," *Transactions of the Royal Historical Society* 2 (1992): 60–62.

39. See the entry dated August 30, 1454, in Predelli, 100–101.

40. See Lane, 237.

41. For an overview of Mehmed's campaigns during this period, see Halil Inalcik, "The Ottoman Turks and the Crusades, 1451–1522," in *A History of the Crusades: Volume VI: The Impact of the Crusades on Europe*, ed. Harry W. Hazard and Norman P. Zacour (Madison: University of Wisconsin Press, 1989), 315–325.

42. This and the following paragraph draw on Crowley, 320–321.

43. Setton, 227.

44. Mueller, 189–193.

45. As Crowley (322) put it, the Venetians "bribed heavily and strategically" in the East.

46. For more on the practice of Venetian diplomacy as it related to the Ottomans, see Goffman, 63, 70–71.

47. The Venetians attached a price to Mehmed's head of ten thousand ducats plus a pension of a thousand ducats per annum. See Crowley, 322.

48. Lane, 199.

49. Venetian outreach to Hasan is covered in detail in Babinger, 302–320.

50. Norwich, 347.

51. Mattingly, *Renaissance Diplomacy*, 90.

52. Crowley, 321.

53. Law, 159.

54. See Setton, 201–207; Norwich, 344; and Babinger, 171.

55. Setton, 237.

56. McNeill, 86.

57. Babinger, 306. For a sense of the threat that Uzun Hasan posed to Mehmed, and of the complex jockeying among the various Turkic groups in this period, see Matthew Melvin-Koushki, "The Delicate Art of Aggression: Uzun Hasan's 'Fathnama' to Qaytbay of 1469," *Iranian Studies* 44, no. 2 (March 2011): 193–214.

58. Norwich, 357.

59. Gluzman, 236.

60. See Babinger, 308, 320, and 322.

61. An analysis of the factors in Venice's eventual eclipse as a great power can be found in Grygiel, *Great Powers*, 83–87.

62. See, for example, Alfred Vagts, "The Balance of Power: Growth of an Idea," *World Politics* 1, no. 1 (October 1948): 82–101.

Chapter Four: Black Queen, Red Cardinal

1. Many of the archival documents from Francis's captivity, including Louise of Savoy's diplomatic communications, are reproduced in Aimé Louis Champollion-Figeac, *Captivité du roi François Ier* (Paris: Imprimerie Royale, 1847). Other primary sources consulted for this chapter include *Collection des ordonnances des rois de France: catalogue des actes de François Ier*, 9 vols. (Paris: Imprimerie Nationale, 1907); *Correspondenz des Kaisers Karl V*, 3 vols. (Leipzig: F. A. Brockhaus, 1844); Ernest Charrière, *Négociations de la France dans le Levant: 1515–1547*, 4 vols. (Paris: Imprimerie Nationale, 1848); and Gilbert Jacqueton, *La politique extérieure de Louise de Savoie: relations diplomatiques de la France et de l'Angleterre pendant la captivité de François Ier* (Paris: É. Bouillon, 1892).

2. The best English-language sources remain R. J. Knecht's three works: *Francis I* (Cambridge: Cambridge University Press, 1982); *Renaissance Warrior and Patron: The Reign of Francis I* (Cambridge: Cambridge University Press, 1994), and *Rise and Fall of Renaissance France 1483–1610* (Oxford: Blackwell, 2001). See also John Julius Norwich, *Four Princes: Henry VIII, Francis I, Charles V, Suleiman the Magnificent and the Obsessions That Forged Modern Europe* (New York: Grove Press, 2016); Leonie Frieda, *Francis I: The Maker of Modern France* (New York: Harper Collins, 2018); and Desmond Seward's stylish *Prince of the Renaissance: The Life of François I* (London: Sphere Books, 1974).

3. Seward, 32–33 and 43.

4. Knecht, *Francis I*, 172.

5. Mattingly (*Renaissance Diplomacy*, 133–134) writes, "In the first generation of European power politics, France remained as laggard in diplomacy as she was froward in war."

6. Mattingly, *Renaissance Diplomacy*, 133–137.

7. Louise's instructions to both Frangipani and his luckless predecessor have been lost. See De Lamar Jensen, "The Ottoman Turks in Sixteenth Century French Diplomacy," *Sixteenth Century Journal* 16, no. 4 (Winter 1985): 452. For the text of Suleiman's letter, see Charrière, 116–118. For a recent, playful take, see Christopher de Bellaigue, *The Lion House: The Coming of a King* (New York: Farrar, Straus and Giroux, 2022), 181. The English translation here is available online from the Ottoman Imperial Archives.

8. Seward, 118.

9. Francesco Guicciardini, *The History of Italy* (London: Z. Stuart, 1763), 8: 278.

10. The definitive source is Geoffrey Parker's magisterial *Emperor: A New Life of Charles V* (New Haven, CT: Yale University Press, 2019).

11. The Holy Roman Empire has long been neglected in English-language sources. Two recent correctives are Peter H. Wilson, *Heart of Europe: A History of the Holy Roman Empire* (Cambridge, MA: Belknap Press, 2016); and Barbara Stollberg-Rilinger, *The Holy Roman Empire: A Short History* (Princeton, NJ: Princeton University Press, 2018).

12. Parker, 164.

13. A month before the battle of Pavia, for example, Spain received a cargo of twenty thousand gold pieces from the New World, adding to a haul of sixty thousand pieces from the previous spring. See Parker, 145.

14. Parker, 103.

15. Knecht, *Rise and Fall*, 120. Seward (118) writes that France in this moment was "threatened with extinction." Knecht (177) concurs.

16. The traditional conception of "natural frontiers" is contested nowadays. The emphasis here is not on whether the French as a nation had God-given parameters but rather the strategic benefits that a state occupying this location enjoyed from flanking seas, mountains, and rivers.

17. Alexander V. Avakov, *Two Thousand Years of Economic Statistics: Population, GDP at PPP, and GDP Per Capita* (New York: Algora Publishing, 2017), 1:19.

18. Knecht, *Francis I*, 29–31.

19. Niccolò Machiavelli, *An Account of the Affairs of France* (Hastings, UK: Delphi, 2017).

20. James Fairgrieve, *Geography and World Power* (London: University of London Press, 1927), 156ff. Edward Whiting Fox has commented on the "schizophrenic" nature of French geography that results from being the only European power that straddles the continent's two climatic zones. See also his *History in Geographic Perspective: The Other France* (New York: W. W. Norton & Co., 1971).

21. See Knecht, *Francis I*, 23–24; he notes (133) that the country's size also likely retarded the development of diplomacy there.

22. The historian Michael Roberts famously argued in a 1955 lecture that military technological change in Europe, beginning in the mid-17th Century, drove political centralization. Geoffrey Parker has shown that the process began much earlier, in the Italian wars of the early 16th Century. He points out that the army Francis I had at Pavia was considerably larger than the one Charles VII had taken into Italy a quarter-century earlier (30,000 vs. 18,000). See Parker's seminal article, "The 'Military Revolution,' 1560–1660—a Myth?," *Journal of Modern History* 48, no. 2 (June 1976), especially 206–207, as well as his book *The Military Revolution: Military Innovation and the Rise of the West, 1500–1800* (Cambridge: Cambridge University Press, 1988).

23. Historians debate the extent to which French kingship in Francis I's time was contractual or proto-absolutist. Knecht (*Francis I*, 320–321 and 429–430) convincingly argues for the latter, as does Guérard (130–131), who sees Francis I as the precursor to Louis XIV. For more on this debate, see the discussion in Nannerl O. Keohane, *Philosophy and the State*

in France: The Renaissance to the Enlightenment (Princeton, NJ: Princeton University Press, 1980), 25–82.

24. Mattingly, *Renaissance Diplomacy*, 130.

25. Knecht, *Francis I*, 22.

26. Keohane, 55ff.

27. For a discussion of French political philosophy in this era, see J. H. Hexter, *The Vision of Politics on the Eve of the Reformation: More, Machiavelli and Seyssel* (New York: Basic Books Inc., 1973); as well as Keohane, 25–53; and Knecht, *Francis I*, 21. An English-language translation of Seyssel's work can be found in Claude de Seyssel, *The Monarchy of France*, ed. Donald R. Kelley, trans. J. H. Hexter (New Haven, CT: Yale University Press, 1981). The digitized original of Guillaume Budé's *L'institution du prince* can be found at https://data.bnf.fr/13517089/guillaume_bude_l_institution_du_prince/.

28. Seyssel, 10.

29. Seward, 73.

30. Louise has not gotten her due as a leader and strategist. The most comprehensive biography remains Dorothy Moulton Mayer's outdated *The Great Regent* (New York: Funk & Wagnalls, 1966). For recent scholarship on Louise's life and regency, see Sharon L. Jansen, *The Monstrous Regiment of Women: Female Rulers in Early Modern Europe* (New York: Palgrave Macmillan, 2002). The evolution of Louise's depiction in French historiography and politics is covered in John F. Freeman, "Louise of Savoy: A Case of Maternal Opportunism," *Sixteenth Century Journal* 3, no. 2 (October 1972): 77–98. See also Aubrée David-Chapy, "The Political, Symbolic, and Courtly Power of Anne de France and Louise de Savoie," 43–64, and Laure Fagnart and Mary Beth Winn, "Louise de Savoie: The King's Mother, Alter Rex," 85–114, both in *Women and Power at the French Court, 1483–1563*, ed. Susan Broomhall (Amsterdam: Amsterdam University Press, 2018).

31. Knecht, *Francis I*, 184.

32. Seward, 137.

33. Freeman, 91–92.

34. Guicciardini, 8:279; Mayer, 18.

35. Mayer, 211.

36. The instructions to Tournon, dated April 28, 1525, can be found in Champollion-Figeac, 174ff.

37. Guérard (133) calls Burgundy "the keystone of the realm."

38. Knecht, *Francis I*, 177.

39. Parker, *Emperor*, 156.

40. Louise's reasons for giving up Burgundy seem to have been partly grounded in lessons from an earlier episode in French history—the battle of Poitiers—when France bought peace at too dear a price to ransom a captured king. Her rationale is spelled out in a memorandum dated November 30, 1525, found in Champollion-Figeac, 408ff. See also the discussion in Knecht, *Francis I*, 184.

41. Some of Charles's advisors doubted that Francis would honor the treaty. See Parker's description of the internal Habsburg deliberations and Charles' honeymoon in Parker, *Emperor*, 157–161.

42. The document states that the promise to give up Burgundy was "forced [on him] by the emperor," under penalty of extended "detention and length of prison [time]," and thus the resulting treaty "will remain of no effect and value, as it was done by force and under duress." The original, dated August 22, 1525, can be found in Champollion-Figeac, 303. The protestation was updated and attested hours before the signing of the treaty. See Parker, *Emperor*, 158.

43. Freeman, 95.

44. The document can be found in Champollion-Figeac, 53–57.

45. The French also promised to reign in their Scottish allies and later added commercial privileges for English merchants operating in France. See Knecht, *Francis I*, 185.

46. Knecht, *Francis I*, 186–187.

47. Mayer, 60.

48. Seyssel, 134.

49. Champollion-Figeac, 256.

50. Knecht, *Francis I*, 206–207.

51. The terms were later enlarged to include a trade plank and provision for coordinating on papal matters, cemented by the betrothal of Henry's daughter, Mary, to Francis's younger son. See Knecht, *Francis I*, 213.

52. Guicciardini, 8.

53. Early in Francis's reign, he launched a bid to win the elective title of Holy Roman Emperor. While Charles beat him, the experience demonstrated the potentialities of a strategy of sewing trouble in Germany as a way of draining the emperor's time and money.

54. Wain's sojourn in Germany is documented in Victor-Louis Bourrilly, *Guillaume du Bellay* (Paris: Société Nouveille de Librairie et D'Édition, 1905), 124–126.

55. Rincón's mission is covered in Charrière, 1: 176ff. On a subsequent mission, Rincón was ambushed and murdered by Habsburg agents. See Parker, *Emperor*, 278ff. France's dealings with Hungary and Poland are covered in Charrière, 1:147ff. An analysis of the evolution of France's eastern alliances can be found in Eric Schnakenbourg, "Les tentatives de mediations françaises dans les conflits suédo-polonais du XVII siècle: une diplomatie de la périphérie?" in *La France face aux crises et aux conflits des périphéries européennes et Atlantiques du XVIIe Au XXe siècle*, ed. Eric Schnakenbourg and Frédéric Dessberg (Rennes: Presses Universitaires de Rennes, 2016).

56. There is some debate over whether the *Capitulations* were a formal agreement. Jensen (455–456) argues in the affirmative, while Knecht (*Francis I*, 274–275) is skeptical.

57. Carl J. Burckhardt, *Richelieu and His Age*, vol. 1, *Assertion of Power and Cold War* (New York: Harcourt, Brace & World, 1970), 289. Recent scholarship suggests that French outreach to the Ottomans wasn't all that unusual by the standards of the day. See, for example, Christine Isom-Verhaaren, *Allies with the Infidel: The Ottoman and French Alliance in the Sixteenth Century* (London: I. B. Tauris, 2011).

58. Seward, 198.

59. Parker, *Emperor*, 169.

60. Knecht, *Francis I*, 210; and Parker, *Emperor*, 168.

61. The Ladies' Peace is often described as a victory for Charles, but as Knecht (*Francis I*, 220) points out, "in two important respects it marked a triumph for [Francis's] diplomacy": he kept Burgundy and got his sons back.

62. Freeman, 96.

63. Knecht, *Francis I*, 417.

64. Hamilton and Langhorne, 45. See also Mattingly *Renaissance Diplomacy*, 137.

65. Mattingly, *Renaissance Diplomacy*, 177.

66. Mattingly, *Renaissance Diplomacy*, 174.

67. The old idea that French diplomacy stagnated during this period has been successfully challenged. See, for example, De Lamar Jensen, "French Diplomacy and the Wars of Religion," *Sixteenth Century Journal* 5, no. 2 (October 1974): 25–43.

68. The best modern biography is Jean-Vincent Blanchard, *Éminence: Cardinal Richelieu and the Rise of France* (New York: Walker & Co., 2011). Bronwen McShea's *La Duchesse: The Life of Marie de Vignerot* (New York: Pegasus Books, 2023) examines Richelieu's private life, political career, and relationship to the Catholic Church. See also R. J. Knecht, *Richelieu* (New York: Longman, 1991); D. P. O'Connell, *Richelieu* (Cleveland, OH: World Publishing Co., 1968); and Carl J. Burckhardt, *Richelieu and His Age*, trans. Bernard Hoy, 3 vols. (New York: Harcourt, Brace & World, 1970). For Richelieu's foreign policy, see William F. Church, *Richelieu and Reason of State* (Princeton, NJ: Princeton University Press, 1972); David J. Sturdy, *Richelieu and Mazarin: A Study in Statesmanship* (New York: Palgrave MacMillan, 2004); J. H. Elliott, *Richelieu and Olivares* (Cambridge: Cambridge University Press, 1984); Iskander Rehman, "Sully, Richelieu, and Mazarin: French Strategies of Equilibrium in the Seventeenth Century" in Brands, ed., *New Makers*, 269–294; and the analysis of Richelieu's diplomacy in Berridge, Keens-Soper, and Otte, *Diplomatic Theory*, chapter 4.

69. Hilaire Belloc, *Richelieu: A Study* (Philadelphia: J. B. Lippincott Co., 1929), 17; Kissinger, *Diplomacy*, 58; and Blanchard, 2.

70. Like Louise of Savoy, Catherine de' Medici has not received as much attention in diplomatic history as she deserves. For a fresh appraisal, see Mary Hollingsworth, *Catherine de' Medici: The Life and Times of the Serpent Queen* (New York: Pegasus Books, 2024).

71. Richelieu left a political testament and memoirs, in addition to voluminous correspondence and memoranda. This chapter uses Paul Sonnino's recent translation, *The Political Testament of Cardinal Richelieu* (Lanham, MD: Rowman & Littlefield, 2020), as well as the older translation by Henry Bertram Hill, *The Political Testament of Cardinal Richelieu* (Madison: University of Wisconsin Press, 1961); and M. Petitot, *Mémoires du Cardinal de Richelieu, sur le Règne de Louis XIII,* 10 vols. (Paris: Foucault, 1823). The two key collections of his papers, both of which were consulted for this chapter, are M. Avenel, *Lettres, instructions diplomatiques et papiers d'état du cardinal de Richelieu,* 8 vols. (Paris: Imprimerie Nationale, 1853–1877); and Pierre Grillon, *Les papiers de Richelieu: section politique intérieure, correspondance et papiers d'etat,* 6 vols. (Paris: A. Pedone, 1975–1985). The quotation here is from Richelieu, *Political Testament* (Sonnino translation), 11.

72. For more on Huguenot power in this era, see David Parrott, *Richelieu's Army: War, Government and Society in France, 1624–1642* (Cambridge: Cambridge University Press, 2004), 184–185; and David Parker, *La Rochelle and the French Monarchy: Conflict and Order in Seventeenth-Century France* (London: Royal Historical Society, 1980).

73. Tommaso Campanella, *A Discourse Touching the Spanish Monarchy* (London: Philemon Stephens, 1654), 3, https://quod.lib.umich.edu/e/eebo2/A79588.0001.001/1:1?rgn=div1;view=fulltext.

74. See Klaus Malettke, "French Foreign Policy and the European States System in the Era of Richelieu and Mazarin," in *The Transformation of European Politics, 1763–1848: Episode or Model in Modern History?*, ed. Peter Kruger and Paul W. Schroeder (Munster: Lit Verlag, 2002), 34.

75. Historians debate how much religion, as opposed to state interests, was the primary driver of conflict during the Thirty Years' War. Among a large literature, see Geoffrey Parker, *The Thirty Years' War* (New York: Barnes & Noble Books, 1997), including the biographical essay on 281–303; and Peter H. Wilson, *The Thirty Years War: Europe's Tragedy* (Cambridge, MA: Belknap Press, 2011). The best source for French policy during the Thirty Years' War is G. Pagès, *The Thirty Years War 1618–1648* (New York: Harper & Row, 1970).

76. Burckhardt, *Richelieu,* 3:109.

77. The text of this memorandum, dated January 13, 1629, can be found in Avenel, 3:129ff. The translation here is from Pagès, 118.

78. For an assessment of how Richelieu's management of the Valtelline and Mantuan crises fit into his conception of *la guerre couverte*, see Iskander Rehman, "Raison d'État: Richelieu's Grand Strategy during the Thirty Years War," *Texas National Security Review* 2, no. 3 (June 2019): 52ff.

79. The Valtelline crisis is covered in Parker, *Thirty Years War,* 66, 71, and 76. See also Pagès, 164; Church, 103ff; and John C. Rule, "The Enduring Rivalry of France and Spain 1462–1700," in *Great Power Rivalries,* ed. William R. Thompson (Columbia: University of South Carolina Press, 1999).

80. For more on the drain that the Mantuan crisis placed on Habsburg resources, see Parker, *Thirty Years War,* 106ff. See also David Parrott, "The Mantuan Succession, 1627–31: A Sovereignty Dispute in Early Modern Europe," *English Historical Review* 112, no. 445 (February 1997): 20–65.

81. Burckhardt, *Richelieu,* 3:108ff.

82. Burckhardt, *Richelieu,* 2:274ff. argues that the contours of Richelieu's German policy were already evident in the instructions to Schomberg, which Richelieu helped craft in November 1616. Pagès (96ff.) points out that the strategy was already well-formed by the autumn of 1624, when Richelieu assumed his post. Parker speculates that the inherent complexity of the situation in Germany made Richelieu gravitate toward an Italy-first policy at the start of his tenure. Knecht (*Richelieu,* 95) identifies Richelieu's January 1630 instructions to Marcheville as the earliest indication that he had formulated a coherent policy for Germany. For a cogent overview of the situation in Germany from the French strategic perspective, see the memorandum written in January 1631 by Father Joseph entitled "Memoyre sur

l'estat des affaires d'Alemagne," the full text of which can be found in G. Fagniez, "La mission du père Joseph a Ratisbonne 1630 (Suite et fin)," *Revue Historique* 28, no. 1 (1885): 68–71. The text of Schomberg's instructions can be found in A. Roper, A. Bosvile, and T. Leigh, *Letters of the Cardinal Duke de Richelieu: Great Minister of State to Lewis [sic] XIII of France Faithfully Translated from the Original by T. B.* (London, 1698), 2:150ff.

83. Richelieu, *Political Testament* (Sonnino translation), 24.

84. See Pagès, 95ff.; and Burckhardt, *Richelieu*, 2:164ff.

85. Richelieu's treaty built on and expanded an earlier alliance cemented in the reign of Henry IV. The full text can be found in M. De Wicquefort, *L'Histoire des Provinces-Unies, confirmée & eclaircie par des preuves authentiques*, Book 3 (The Hague: T. Johnson, 1719), 624–627. Over the years that followed, the Franco-Dutch alliance would be renewed three times and French subsidies to the United Provinces would grow to the stunning sum of 2.3 million livres per year. See Richelieu, *Political Testament* (Sonnino translation), 43.

86. Deshayes would later be caught by Charnacé carrying on a parallel diplomacy against the king's interests on behalf of Marie de' Medici, and executed for treason. See Burkhardt, *Richelieu*, 2:356ff.

87. Richelieu worked until the last minute following the Danes' defeat to prevent Christian from coming to terms with the Habsburgs, in order to keep them in the war as long as possible. See Burckhardt, *Richelieu*, 2:347.

88. The key source is Michael Roberts, *Gustavus Adolphus: A History of Sweden 1611–1632* (London: Lowe & Brydone, 1965); and *Sweden as a Great Power 1611–1697, Government, Society, Foreign Policy* (New York: St. Martin's Press, 1968), especially. 134–160.

89. Richelieu mentions Charnacé in his *Political Testament* (Sonnino translation), 25. Charnacé's trip is described in Burckhardt, *Richelieu*, 2:341ff.

90. Richelieu was proud of this diplomatic coup; see *Political Testament* (Sonnino translation), 24.

91. The text of the treaty can be found in Roberts, *Sweden as a Great Power*, 136ff. Historians have come to question the traditional picture of Richelieu drawing Gustavus Adolphus into German affairs; abundant evidence shows that he was driven by opportunism and the need for cash. See, for example, Pagès, 116ff.; For critiques of Richelieu's methods with Gustavus, see Roberts, *Gustavus Adolphus*, 136ff.; and O'Connell, 257.

92. See Parker, *Thirty Years War*, 222.

93. Richelieu, *Political Testament* (Sonnino translation), 42. The French army in Francis I's time was about 40,000 strong; by Richelieu's time it had grown to 150,000. See Parker, "The 'Military Revolution,' 1560–1660," 206–211. See also David Parrott, "French Military Organization in the 1630s: The Failure of Richelieu's Ministry," *Seventeenth-Century French Studies* 9, no. 1 (1987): 151–167.

94. Michael Roberts, *Essays in Swedish History* (Minneapolis: University of Minnesota Press, 1967), 202.

95. The position of principal minister wasn't unique to France; Olivares in Spain and Oxenstierna in Sweden are other examples. See the discussion in Sturdy, chapter 1; and Richard Bonney, *Society and Government in France under Richelieu and Mazarin, 1624–61* (Houndmills, UK: Macmillan, 1988), 26ff.

96. For a comparison of French decision-making in the eras of Francis I and Louis XIII, see Knecht, *Francis I*, 21; and Knecht, *Richelieu*, 18.

97. During the reign of Henry III, one of these had been elevated and given oversight for foreign policy, but the novelty didn't stick. See the overview of French bureaucracy in this period in Hamilton, 77.

98. Bonney, 27ff.

99. The text of the document instituting the change and providing the rationale can be found in Bonney, 39. The French diplomatic corps grew tenfold in the century and a half after Francis's coronation; the ministerial staff mushroomed from five people in Richelieu's time to eighty or more in the reign of Louis XIV. See Nicolson, *Evolution*, 77; and Callières, 24.

100. Richelieu, *Political Testament* (Hill translation), 94, 99. A system of ambassadors was already in place before Richelieu came to power, but he laid greater stress on their competence and alignment with policy. See Hamilton, 77.

101. Richelieu's instructions to ambassadors set a new standard in precision and control. They were often accompanied by memoranda outlining the policy framework guiding France's approach to the country in question and filled with directives that began, "You are to explain . . ." or "You will inform . . ." See, for example, his instructions to du Tour and Marcheville in Burckhardt, *Richelieu,* 2:255 and 334 respectively.

102. Callières, 73.

103. Richelieu, *Political Testament* (Sonnino translation), 34.

104. See the discussion of the downsides to Richelieu's "continuous negotiations" in Berridge, *Diplomatic Theory,* 80–82.

105. See David Parrott, *The Business of War: Military Enterprise and Military Revolution in Early Modern Europe* (Cambridge: Cambridge University Press, 2012); John A. Lynn, "Recalculating French Army Growth during the Grand Siècle, 1610–1715," *French Historical Studies* 18, no. 4 (Autumn 1994): 881–906; and Parker, *The Thirty Years War,* 150.

106. Kissinger, *Diplomacy,* 58.

107. Some scholars question the traditional depiction of Habsburg Spain as an offensive-minded power bent on European hegemony. See, for example, Andreas Osiander, "Sovereignty, International Relations, and the Westphalian Myth," *International Organization* 55, no. 2 (Spring 2001): 251–287.

108. Richelieu seems to have first put this concept forward in 1629, though there is some dispute over the timing and authorship of the memorandum in question. His successor, Mazarin, used the document as the basis for instructions to French diplomats at the Congress of Westphalia. See Andreas Osiander, *The States System of Europe, 1640–1990: Peacemaking and the Conditions of International Stability* (Oxford: Oxford University Press, 1994), 27 and 40–41; Per Maurseth, "Balance-of-Power Thinking from the Renaissance to the French Revolution," *Journal of Peace Research* 1, no. 2 (1964): 123; and Sturdy, 100.

109. Historians debate the extent to which Westphalia marked a turning point in international relations history. The classic statement of the affirmative case can be found in Leo Gross, "The Peace of Westphalia, 1648–1948," *American Journal of International Law* 42, no. 1 (January 1948): 20–41. Osiander, *States System,* 43ff. argues convincingly that the participants saw themselves, not as innovators but as judicious restorationists. For an overview of the debate, see Osiander, "Westphalian Myth," especially 261ff. See also Stephen Krasner, "Compromising Westphalia," *International Security* 20, no. 3 (Winter 1995–1996): 115–151; and Alexander Bick, "Westphalia: Beyond the Myth," in *After Disruption: Historical Perspectives on the Future of International Order,* ed. Seth Center and Emma Bates (Washington, DC: Center for Strategic and International Studies, 2020), 4–10.

110. Blanchard, 2.

111. See Church, 297–299; and Malettke, 33ff.

112. Richelieu, *Political Testament* (Sonnino translation), 35.

113. Callières, 23–24.

Chapter Five: The Spider's Web

1. For more on the role that Pompadour played in European diplomacy at this time, see Eva Kathrin Dade, *Madame de Pompadour: Die Mätresse und die Diplomatie* (Köln: Böhlau Verlag, 2010), especially 89–184.

2. The best modern biography of Frederick II is T.C.W. Blanning's *Frederick the Great: King of Prussia* (New York: Random House, 2016). See also the sketch of Frederick II in Christopher M. Clark, *Iron Kingdom: The Rise and Downfall of Prussia, 1600–1947* (Cambridge, MA: Belknap Press, 2006), 183–189.

3. Tim Blanning, *The Pursuit of Glory: Five Revolutions That Made Modern Europe,1648–1815* (New York: Penguin Books, 2007), 569.

4. The Pragmatic Sanction is explained in Charles W. Ingrao, *The Habsburg Monarchy, 1618–1815,* Second Edition (New York: Cambridge University Press, 2000), 128–129.

5. Reed Browning, *The War of the Austrian Succession* (New York: St. Martin's Press, 1995), 42.

6. Derek Beales, "Joseph II," in *In the Shadow of Maria Theresa, 1741–1780*, Vol. 1 (Cambridge: Cambridge University Press, 1987), 24.

7. Maria Theresa's reign is covered in extravagant detail in Barbara Stollberg-Rilinger, *Maria Theresa: The Habsburg Empress in Her Time* (Princeton, NJ: Princeton University Press, 2021).

8. For more on the Prussian military of this period, see Philip G. Dwyer, "Introduction: The Rise of Prussia," and Rodney Gotlef, "Frederick William I and the Beginnings of Prussian Absolutism, 1713–1740," in *The Rise of Prussia 1700–1830*, ed. Philip G. Dwyer (London: Routledge, 2000). Key sources on 18th-Century warfare include Christopher Duffy, *The Military Experience in the Age of Reason* (New York: Atheneum, 1988); Denis Showalter, *The Wars of Frederick the Great* (New York: Longman, 1996); and Alexander S. Burns, ed., *The Changing Face of Old Regime Warfare: Essays in Honour of Christopher Duffy* (Warwick, UK: Helion & Co., 2022).

9. Maria Theresa to Joseph, May 29, 1778, in Karl Schneider, *Aus Österreichs Vergangenheit, Nr. 11, Aus dem Briefwechsel Maria Theresias mit Joseph II* (Wien: Schulwissenschaftlicher Verlag, 1917), 49.

10. Blanning, *Pursuit of Glory*, 571.

11. Contemporary accounts often refer to Austria as the "Archducal House" or "House of Austria." For simplicity, I use "Habsburg monarchy" and "Austria" interchangeably. I switch to "Austrian Empire" later in this chapter when referring to Austria after Napoleon's dismantling of the Holy Roman Empire in 1806, and I use "Austria-Hungary" in the next chapter to denote the transition to a dualist power-sharing arrangement after 1867.

12. Austria's limitations compared to other great powers are covered in Michael Hochedlinger, *Austria's Wars of Emergence* (New York: Routledge, 2013).

13. For more on the impact that geography had on Austrian strategy, see A. Wess Mitchell, *Grand Strategy of the Habsburg Empire* (Princeton, NJ: Princeton University Press, 2018), 21–51.

14. For an overview of Habsburg leaders' thinking on their empire's various frontiers, see Charles Ingrao, "Habsburg Strategy and Geopolitics during the Eighteenth Century," in *War and Society in East Central Europe*, vol. 2, ed. Gunther E. Rothenberg, Belá K. Király, and Peter F. Sugar (New York: Brooklyn College Press, 1982).

15. See Lothar Höbelt, "The Impact of the Rákóczi Rebellion on Habsburg Strategy: Incentives and Opportunity Costs," *War in History* 13, no.1 (2006): 2–15.

16. These memoranda can be found in Alfred von Arneth, *Geschichte Maria Theresas* (Vienna: W. Braumüller, 1870), 4:262ff. For the minutes of the final session, see Adolf Beer, ed., *Aufzeichnungen des Grafen William Bentinck über Maria Theresia* (Vienna: C. Gerold's Sohn, 1871), 129–142. See also the description of the debate over Habsburg policy at this time in William J. McGill, "The Roots of Policy: Kaunitz in Vienna and Versailles, 1749–1753," *Journal of Modern History* 43, no. 2 (June 1971): 228–244.

17. Kaunitz was promoted to Reichsfürst in 1764 and to Erbländischer Fürst in 1776. Alfred von Arneth, the prolific director of the Austrian archives, published a short biography of Kaunitz's early life in 1900. Grete Klingenstein's *Der Aufstieg des Hauses Kaunitz: Studien zur Herkunft und Bildung des Staatskanzlers Wenzel Anton* (Göttingen: Vandenhoeck & Ruprecht, 1975) deals mainly with his upbringing. In English, the best biography remains Franz Szabo's superb *Kaunitz and Enlightened Absolutism 1753–1780* (Cambridge: Cambridge University Press, 1994).

18. See, for example, Rudolf Graf Khevenhüller-Metsch and Hans Schlitter, *Aus der Zeit Maria Theresias: Tagebuch des Fürsten Johann Josef Khevenhüller-Metsch, 1742–1776*, Vol. 3 (Vienna: Adolf Holzhousen, 1910), 71.

19. See, for example, Karl A. Roider's review of Klingenstein's book in *Austrian History Yearbook* 14 (January 1978): 320–321, as well as Szabo, 20ff.; and Stollberg-Rilinger, 239.

20. Christopher Duffy, *The Army of Maria Theresa: The Armed Forces of Imperial Austria, 1740–1780* (New York: Hippocrene Books, 1977), 20.

21. Excerpts from Kaunitz's memorandum are reproduced in Arneth, 4:272ff. Kaunitz had been mulling Austria's predicament for a while. Shortly after his first posting in Italy in

1743, he wrote a memorandum arguing for a concentrated effort against the Bourbon powers of France and Spain. While he later shifted his argument to focus on Prussia, his logic remained consistent: that the job of Habsburg diplomacy was to amass alliances against the main threat. See Lothar Schilling, *Kaunitz und das Renversement des Alliances: Studien zur Außenpolitischen Konzeption Wenzel Antons von Kaunitz, Historische Forschungen*, Vol. 50 (Berlin: Duncker & Humbolt, 1993), 20ff.

22. Stollberg-Rilinger, 403. The quotation in the previous sentence comes from Arneth, 4:276.

23. The idea of a Habsburg-Bourbon alignment had surfaced occasionally in Austrian strategic discussions since the early 18th Century but never been adopted as policy. See Max Braubach, *Versailles und Wien von Ludwig XIV bis Kaunitz: die Vorstadien der diplomatischen Revolution im 18. Jahrhundert* (Bonn: L. Röhrscheid, 1952).

24. Ingrao, *Habsburg Monarchy*, 158–159.

25. Richard Bassett, *For God and Kaiser: The Imperial Austrian Army, 1619–1918* (New Haven, CT: Yale University Press, 2015), 127. Bear in mind that Francis Stephen was a Lorrainer who "never forgave the French for the loss of his ancestral homeland, the Duchy of Lorraine." See Stollberg-Rilinger, *Maria Theresa*, 166.

26. See Friedrich Meinecke, *Machiavellism: The Doctrine of Raison d'État and Its Place in Modern History* (New Haven, CT: Yale University Press, 1962), especially chapter 12; and F. H. Hinsley, *Power and the Pursuit of Peace* (London: Cambridge University Press, 1963). See also the discussion in McGill, 231 fn11.

27. The next three paragraphs draw on the excellent synopsis in Szabo, 38–48. See also P.G.M. Dickson, *Finance and Government under Maria Theresia: 1740-1780* (Oxford: Clarendon Press, 1987).

28. Kaunitz spelled out his intentions for reform in a letter dated December 1754, which can be found in Hans Schlitter, ed., *Correspondance secrète entre le comte A. W. Kaunitz-Rietberg et le baron Ignaz de Koch* (Paris: E. Plon, Nourrit, 1899), 155ff. See also Stollberg-Rilinger, 240–242.

29. Szabo, 48.

30. Szabo, 46.

31. The memo can be found in full in Adolf Beer, *Archiv für österreichische Geschichte, Denkschriften des Fürsten Wenzel Kaunitz-Rittberg* (Vienna: Karl Gerold's Sohn, 1872), 19–38. Here: 21 and 22.

32. See the debates set in motion by this event in Stollberg-Rilinger, 408ff.

33. The minutes from this meeting can be found in Arneth, 4:387ff. See also McGill, 228–244.

34. See Arneth, 4:439ff.

35. See McGill, 228 fn1; and Szabo, 16–19.

36. I am grateful to Gérard Araud for this insight.

37. Herbert H. Kaplan, *Russia and the Outbreak of the Seven Years' War* (Berkeley: University of California Press, 1968), 122.

38. Karl A. Roider Jr., *Austria's Eastern Question 1700-1790* (Princeton, NJ: Princeton University Press, 1982), 106ff.

39. Stollberg-Rilinger, 405.

40. Martyn Rady, *The Habsburgs: To Rule the World* (New York: Basic Books, 2020), 185.

41. The best source is Franz A. J. Szabo, *The Seven Years War in Europe: 1756-1763* (London: Routledge, 2007).

42. Bassett, 147.

43. See Kaunitz's 1771 memorandum outlining Austria's eastern dilemma in Mitchell, 149–150. See also Saul K. Padover, "Prince Kaunitz' Résumé of His Eastern Policy, 1763–71," *Journal of Modern History* 5, no. 3 (September, 1933): 352–365.

44. The history of the Polish partitions is covered in H. M. Scott, *The Emergence of the Eastern Powers* (Cambridge: Cambridge University Press, 2001).

45. Kaunitz initially tried to prevent the partitions by splintering the Russo-Prussian alliance but quickly shifted to supporting Austrian participation in the scheme when he saw that the outcome was inevitable. See Scott, 217–219.

46. Paul Robert Magocsi, *Historical Atlas of East Central Europe* (Seattle: University of Washington Press, 1993), 70.

47. See Paul Schroeder's analysis of the limitations of balance-of-power logic for ensuring Austrian security in *The Transformation of European Politics 1763–1848* (New York: Clarendon Press, 1994), 14–19. For a smart rebuttal, see Charles Ingrao, "Paul W. Schroeder's Balance of Power: Stability or Anarchy?," *International History Review* 16, no. 4 (November 1994): 681–700.

48. Quoted in Franz A. J. Szabo, "Prince Kaunitz and the Balance of Power," *International History Review* 1, no. 3 (1979): 406–408.

49. See Szabo, "Prince Kaunitz," 406–408.

50. Micheal Clodfelter, *Warfare and Armed Conflicts: A Statistical Encyclopedia of Casualty and Other Figures, 1494–2007* (Jefferson, NC: McFarland & Co., 2008), 183ff.

51. In a large literature, see Harold Nicolson, *The Congress of Vienna: A Study in Allied Unity* (New York: Harcourt, Brace & Co., 1946); Henry Kissinger, *A World Restored: Metternich, Castlereagh and the Problems of Peace 1812–22* (Boston: Houghton Mifflin, 1957); and Adam Zamoyski, *Rites of Peace: The Fall of Napoleon and the Congress of Vienna* (London: Harper Perennial, 2008).

52. Alan Palmer, *Metternich: Councillor of Europe* (London: Phoenix Giant, 1997), 130.

53. For a comparison of the Congress of Vienna to other postwar ordering moments, see Schroeder, *Systems*, 38–57.

54. The best up-to-date biography is Wolfram Siemann's *Metternich: Strategist and Visionary* (Cambridge, MA: Harvard University Press, 2019). See also the new account by Muamer Becirovic, *Clemens Wenzel von Metternich oder Das Gleichgewicht der Mächte* (Hamburg: Osburg Verlag, 2024).

55. Metternich once directed Austrian agents to surreptitiously monitor the ailing Italian composer Donizetti, on the grounds that his continued health was of inestimable value to the world of opera and therefore, presumably, to the national security of Austria. See Desmond Seward, *Metternich: The First European* (New York: Viking Press, 1991), 223–224.

56. Siemann (463–498) argues that Metternich's chief pleasure from these affairs was intellectual rather than physical. See also Zamoyski, 258–259 and 283.

57. Siemann, 691.

58. Clemens Wenzel Lothar Metternich, *Memoirs of Prince Metternich*, ed. Prince Richard Metternich (London: Forgotten Books, 2012), 249–250.

59. The document can be found in Wilhelm Oncken, *Österreich und Preussen im Brefreiungskriege*. Vol. 1. (Berlin: G. Grote, 1876), 640–644.

60. The paragraphs that follow draw on Metternich, *Memoirs*, 249–251 and 36–37.

61. Metternich, *Memoirs*, 36–37.

62. The American political scientist James R. Sofka argues that Metternich was influenced by the writings of the German political philosopher Immanuel Kant while he was a college student in Mainz. See Sofka, "Metternich's Theory of European Order: A Political Agenda for "Perpetual Peace," *Review of Politics* 60, no. 1 (Winter 1998): 115–149.

63. Contra Kissinger's later writing, Metternich preferred to speak of "rights" rather than "legitimacy," as he found the latter term excessively elastic. See Sofka, 128 fn27.

64. Schroeder, *Transformation*, 526.

65. Seward, 139.

66. Paul Schroeder effectively rebuts the notion that Metternich was anything less than, as he puts it, "Austria-first" in outlook. As he points out, Metternich's calculus throughout his career was "simply one of Austrian interests," there being "not a single major aspect of his policy in this period which is not best and most simply understood as an effort to secure power, peace, and internal security for the fragile Austrian monarchy.... His remarkable success in achieving his goals under the guise of European principles, and not the validity or the sincerity of the principles themselves, constitutes his own particular brand of greatness." See Schroeder, *Metternich's Diplomacy at Its Zenith 1820–1823* (Austin: University of Texas Press, 2021), 257.

67. Various strands of this concept can be seen in Metternich's writing as early as 1801, and by 1813 they had congealed into what would be the essence of his policy for the next four decades See Siemann, 171–177; Schroeder, *Zenith*, 8; and Emil Lauber, *Metternichs Kampf um die europäische Mitte: Struktur seiner Politik von 1809 bis 1815* (Vienna: A. Luser, 1939).

68. Mack Walker, ed., *Metternich's Europe: Selected Documents* (London: Macmillan, 1968), 83–84.

69. Siemann (415) argues persuasively that the architects of the Vienna settlement saw themselves as participating in a "reconstruction" or "restitution" rather than a "restoration" of the kind described by Kissinger in *A World Restored*. "Renovation" may be the best description, as it conveys the idea of grafting new components onto a preexisting foundation in an effort to extend the life of the whole.

70. Schroeder, *Zenith*, 5.

71. Isaac Nakhimovsky argues that the Holy Alliance was an example of a federative alternative to the nation-state. See his book *The Holy Alliance: Liberalism and the Politics of Federation* (Princeton, NJ: Princeton University Press, 2024).

72. Sofka, 145.

73. The key modern source on Castlereagh is John Bew, *Castlereagh: A Life* (Oxford: Oxford University Press, 2012). Kissinger treats the death of Castlereagh as the defining event that prompted England's departure from the congress system, while the English historian Walter Alison Phillips sees continuity in the policies pursued by Castlereagh and his successor Canning. For our purposes, it's enough to note that Metternich viewed the ascent of Canning and Chateaubriand, in tandem, as marking the end of the Quintuple Alliance. See Kissinger, *World Restored*, 311–315; and W. Alison Phillips, "The Congresses, 1815–1822," in *The Cambridge Modern History*, vol. X: *The Restoration*, Sir A. W. Ward, Sir. G. W. Prothero, and Sir Stanley Leathes, eds. (Cambridge: Cambridge University Press, 1934), 31–36.

74. A.J.P. Taylor, *The Struggle for Mastery in Europe 1848–1918* (Harmondsworth, UK: Penguin, 1954), 2–3.

75. As it stood, Austria was able to more or less totally ignore this vast frontier—so much so that when, forty years later, she finally found herself involved in a crisis that required significant troop numbers in the eastern provinces of Galicia and Transylvania, there was virtually no infrastructure with which to support the concentration. For the beneficial effects that Metternich's eastern arrangements had on Austrian military-strategic planning, see Gunther Rothenberg, "The Austrian Army in the Age of Metternich," *Journal of Modern History* 40, no. 2 (June 1968): 156–165.

76. Quoted in Schroeder, *Zenith*, 252–253.

77. See inter alia F. R. Bridge, *The Habsburg Monarchy among the Great Powers, 1815–1918* (Oxford: Berg Publishers, 1990), 28.

78. Quoted in Palmer, 202.

79. Historians disagree on the lifespan of the Vienna system. If key aspects of the arrangement (including especially the Holy Alliance) and the method of consultation are included in its definition, then a defensible case can be made that it survived the revolutions of 1848 and was still operating on the eve of the Crimean War of 1853–1856. See Siemann, 423, and Schroeder, *Transformation*, 675–677.

80. See the list in Schroeder, *Systems*, 51.

81. See Rothenberg, 163–165.

82. Bridge, 2.

83. Siemann (422) refers to this as power balancing with a "moral" core.

84. Szabo, *Kaunitz*, 3.

85. The best statement of Austria's logic with respect to buffers is Ingrao, "Habsburg Strategy," in Rothenberg, Király, and. Sugar. See also Schroeder, *Systems*, 77–96.

86. Robert A. Kann, "Metternich: A Reappraisal of His Impact on International Relations," *Journal of Modern History* 32, no. 4 (1960): 333–339.

87. See the analysis in Mitchell, *Grand Strategy*, chapter 9.

88. Otto Brunner quoted in Bridge, 2.

Chapter Six: The Punching Doll

1. This chapter draws on the papers of the German diplomatic service in *Die Grosse Politik der Europäischen Kabinette, 1871–1914*, 40 vols. (Berlin: Deutsche Verlagsgesellschaft für Politik und Geschichte, 1922-1927)—hereafter, *DGP*; Bernhard Schwertfeger, *Die Diplomatischen Akten des Auswärtigen Amtes, 1871–1914*, 5 vols. (Berlin: Deutsche Verlagsgesellschaft für Politik und Geschichte, 1927)—hereafter *DDA*; Horst Kohl, *Die Politischen Reden des Fürsten Bismarck*, 14 vols. (Stuttgart: Cotta, 1894); and Otto von Bismarck, *Gedanken und Erinnerungen von Otto Fürst von Bismarck*, 3 vols. (Stuttgart: Cotta, 1922).

2. The essential source is Geoffrey Wawro, *The Austro-Prussian War: Austria's War with Prussia and Italy in 1866* (Cambridge: Cambridge University Press, 1996). See also Denis Showalter, *The Wars of German Unification*, second edition (London: Bloomsbury, 2015).

3. For a fresh perspective on the Franco-Prussian war, see Rachel Chrastil, *Bismarck's War: The Franco-Prussian War and the Making of Modern Europe* (New York: Basic Books, 2023).

4. By the time this proclamation occurred, Wilhelm was already technically emperor; the title, and the new imperial constitution, had been given legal force by the Bundesrat of the North German Confederation a few days earlier. For more on the structure of the German Empire, see Christopher Clark, *Iron Kingdom: The Rise and Downfall of Prussia 1600-1947* (Cambridge, MA: Belknap Press, 2006), 577ff.

5. The statistics in this paragraph come from: A.J.P. Taylor, *The Struggle for Mastery in Europe: 1848-1918* (Oxford: Oxford University Press, 1988), xxv-xxxi; Albert Carreras and Camilla Josephson, "Aggregate Growth, 1870–1914: Growing at the Production Frontier," in *The Cambridge Economic History of Modern Europe*, Volume 2: *1870 to the Present*, ed. Stephen Broadberry and Kevin H. O'Rourke (Cambridge: Cambridge University Press, 2010), 33–36; and Paul Kennedy, *The Rise and Fall of the Great Powers: Economic Change and Military Conflict from 1500 to 2000* (New York: Vintage Books, 1989), 200–202.

6. For more on the German Empire and its impact on Europe, see Katja Hoyer's excellent *Blood and Iron: The Rise and Fall of the German Empire 1871–1918* (Cheltenham, UK: History Press, 2022); Brendan Simms, *Europe: The Struggle for Supremacy, from 1453 to the Present* (New York: Basic Books, 2013), especially chapter 5; and Clark, chapters 15 and 16. See also Hans Kundnani, *The Paradox of German Power* (Oxford: Oxford University Press, 2015).

7. Henry Kissinger, *Diplomacy* (New York: Simon & Schuster, 1994), 104.

8. See Peter H. Wilson, *Iron and Blood: A Military History of the German-Speaking Peoples since 1500* (Cambridge, MA: Belknap Press, 2023).

9. For a compelling portrait of Moltke's personality and intellect, see Walter Goerlitz, *History of the German General Staff 1657-1945* (London: Westview, 1985), 69–102.

10. See Daniel J. Hughes, *Moltke on the Art of War: Selected Writings* (Novato, CA: Presidio Press, 1993); Eberhard Kessel, *Moltke* (Stuttgart: Koehler Verlag, 1957); and Michael Howard's introductory essay in Paret and Howard, 30–31.

11. Goerlitz, 98–100. See also Graf Moltke and Ferdinand von Schmerfeld, *Die Deutschen Aufmarschpläne, 1870-1890* (Berlin: E. S. Mittler & Sohn, 1929); and Terence Zuber, *German War Planning 1891–1914: Sources and Interpretations* (Martlesham, UK: Boydell Press, 2004). For an analysis of the German obsession with short, offensive wars, see Stig Förster, "Der Deutsche Generalstab und die Illusion des Kurzen Krieges, 1871–1914: Metakritik eines Mythos," in *Militärgeschichtliche Mitteilungen*, vol. 54 (Freiburg: Oldenbourg, 1995), especially 66ff.

12. See Gordon A. Craig, *The Politics of the Prussian Army 1640-1945* (London: Oxford University Press, 1955), 255 and the entirety of chapter 6.

13. The most up-to-date biography is Jonathan Steinberg's polemical *Bismarck: A Life* (Oxford: Oxford University Press, 2011), which devotes less attention to Bismarck's diplomacy than to his psychology and political legacy. Otto Pflanze's three-volume *Bismarck and the Development of Germany* (Princeton, NJ: Princeton University Press, 1990) remains the best overall English-language treatment of Bismarck's life and career. A.J.P. Taylor's 1955 *Bismarck: The Man and Statesman* (London: H. Hamilton, 1985) gives a lively account,

tempered by the author's obvious dislike for his subject. Edward Crankshaw's *Bismarck* (New York: Viking Press, 1981) deals mainly with the political aspects of Bismarck's career. For a sense of how Bismarck's legacy has shifted over time in Germany, see Karina Urbach's "Between Saviour and Villain: 100 Years of Bismarck Biographies," *Historical Journal* 41, no. 4 (December 1998): 1141–1160.

14. See Hoyer, 73–79; Steinberg, 379, 401, 468, and 477; and Crankshaw, 382.

15. Steinberg, 465–470.

16. Articles 11 and 12 placed executive power in the hands of the king of Prussia; Article 15 put the federal chancellor, named by the king alone, at the head of most government functions. See Steinberg, 267–268.

17. Steinberg, 267–268. For an analysis of the constitution and how it privileged Prussia in imperial decision-making, see Hoyer, 59–67.

18. Taylor, *Bismarck*, 51–52. It's a curious fact that Chrysaphius, Richelieu, Kaunitz, Metternich, and Bismarck all had tempestuous relationships with the spouses or lovers of their monarchs.

19. See, for example, Steinberg, 277–280.

20. Taylor, *Bismarck*, 138.

21. For more on Bismarck's philosophy, see Hajo Holborn, "Bismarck's Realpolitik," *Journal of the History of Ideas* 21, no. 1 (March, 1960): 85–86 and 89.

22. Robert K. Massie, *Dreadnought: Britain, Germany, and the Coming of the Great War* (New York: Ballantine Books, 1992), 54.

23. Lamar Cecil, *The German Diplomatic Service, 1871–1914* (Princeton, NJ: Princeton University Press, 1976). See especially 7–20. See also John C. G. Röhl, *The Kaiser and His Court: Wilhelm II and the Government of Germany* (Cambridge: Cambridge University Press, 1994), 152.

24. Holborn, "Realpolitik," 94.

25. There is a large literature on the question of whether Bismarck was motivated primarily by domestic or foreign-policy considerations. A good articulation of the latter can be found in Marcus Jones, "Bismarckian Strategic Policy, 1871–1890," in *Successful Strategies: Triumphing in War and Peace from Antiquity to the Present*, ed. Williamson Murray and Richard Hart Sinnreich (Cambridge: Cambridge University Press, 2014).

26. Bismarck made many repeated references to Kaunitz's coalition against Frederick. See, for example, A. J. Butler, trans., *Bismarck, The Memoirs*, vol. 2 (New York: Howard Fertig, 1966), 255–256; and Kohl, 12:180–181.

27. For more on Bismarck's relationship with the military, see Karina Urbach, "Bismarck: Ein Amateur in Uniform?," in *Die Rückkehr der "Grossen Männer": Staatsmänner im Krieg. Ein deutsche-britischer Vergleich*, ed. Karina Urbach and Brendan Simms (Berlin: De Gruyter, 2010).

28. Quoted in Steinberg, 355. The original text can be found in *DGP*, vol. 2, 153–154.

29. Bismarck meddled shamelessly in Habsburg domestic affairs in a bid to keep Austria aligned with Germany. See Bascom Barry Hayes, *Bismarck and Mitteleuropa* (London: Associated University Presses, 1994).

30. Bismarck momentarily relaxed his opposition to acquiring German colonies when tensions with France abated in the mid-1880s, but it was never the main focus of his grand strategy. See Hajo Holborn, *A History of Modern Germany 1840–1945* (Princeton: Princeton University Press, 1982), 244–46.

31. Holborn, *History*, 294.

32. Taylor, *Bismarck*, 210.

33. Julia Bersch and Graciela Kaminsky, "Financial Globalization in the 19th Century: Germany as a Financial Center," George Washington University Working Paper (September 2008), 29. See also Albert Fishlow, "Lessons from the Past: Capital Markets during the 19th Century and the Interwar Period," *International Organization* 39, no. 3 (1985): 383–439.

34. The texts can be found in *DGP*, 1:202–203 and 206–207 respectively.

35. The "War in Sight" crisis is covered in *DDA*, 1:26ff. Bismarck helped fuel the panic by exploiting French rearmament in a complex effort to outmaneuver the generals and

strengthen his own domestic position. See William Langer, *European Alliances and Alignments 1871–1890* (New York: Vintage Books, 1964), 44–45; and James Stone, *The War Scare of 1875: Bismarck and Europe in the Mid-1870s* (Stuttgart: Franz Steiner Verlag, 2011).

36. Hoyer, 113.

37. Kissinger, *Diplomacy*, 149.

38. Edmund von Mach, trans., "Bismarck as the 'Honest Broker,'" in *The German Classics of the Nineteenth and Twentieth Centuries*, vol. 10, ed. Kuno Francke (Project Gutenberg eBook, 2004).

39. See *DDA*, 1:67; and Kissinger, *Diplomacy*, 157.

40. Before the conference started, the Russians had already agreed to Britain's central demand, that the "big Bulgaria" created at San Stefano be divided into three territories. The problem was that, in spite of this understanding, both sides kept their military assets in-region, prolonging the risk of war. Bismarck pushed the Russians to withdraw their troops without seeing it as a defeat. See *DDA*, 1:57 and 61.

41. Kissinger, *Diplomacy*,154.

42. It didn't help that, the same year as the Berlin Congress, Bismarck introduced tariffs on Russian grain and banned shipments of Russian meat in an effort to shield German farmers from cheap imports.

43. Kissinger (158–159) detects in these moves a shift away from "fluid balancing" toward the goal of "build[ing] a barrier to further Russian expansion." In fact, Bismarck had long aspired to the creation of a defensive Central European barrier to dissuade Russia from attacking Austria-Hungary and forestall the latter from drifting into the arms of France. See, for example, his memorandum from August 1879 in *DGP*, 3:26–36.

44. The text of the 1881 agreement can be found in *DGP*, 3:176–179.

45. This and the following paragraphs draw on George Kennan, *The Decline of Bismarck's European Order: Franco-Russian Relations, 1875–1890* (Princeton, NJ: Princeton University Press, 1979), 131–151.

46. Langer, 379.

47. The German military was funded in seven-year installments known as the "Septennat," the latest of which wasn't set to expire until April 1888. By bringing the bill ahead of schedule, Bismarck was deliberately provoking a deadlock to justify a dismissing the parliament and calling new elections. The domestic dimensions of Bismarck's calculations, however, do not change the fact that there was a genuine crisis abroad requiring a larger army. See Langer, 380–383; and Pflanze, 228–229.

48. France and Russia could field 1.68 million more troops than Germany and Austria. See Kennan, 247.

49. Kohl, 12:175–226.

50. The logic of Bismarck's British diplomacy is spelled out in a letter to the German ambassador in London, Count von Hatzfeldt, dated February 3, 1887. See *DGP*, 4:300ff.; and Pflanze, 247.

51. See *DGP*, 4:311, 315–316, and 319–331.

52. The benefits of the Mediterranean Agreements to German strategy are outlined in a letter by Bismarck's son Herbert, then serving as state secretary, dated March 11, 1887, which can be found in *DGP*, 4:322.

53. The Reinsurance Treaty was the brainchild of Paul Shuvalov's brother, Peter, who had played an important role in helping Bismarck defuse the Anglo-Russian crisis in the lead-up to the Congress of Berlin. The Shuvalovs were part of a faction in Russian foreign policy centered on the foreign minister Nikolay de Giers, who favored preserving the link with Germany against the growing pressure of the nationalists and pan-Slavists at court. For more on the complex debates in the tsar's court at this time, see Kennan, chapter 14.

54. The text of the treaty can be found in *DGP*, 5:253–255.

55. Andrew Roberts, *Salisbury: Victorian Titan* (London: Weidenfeld & Nicolson, 1999), 467–468.

56. *DGP*, 4:376ff.

57. Alfred Franzis Pribram, *The Secret Treaties of Austria-Hungary 1879–1914*, vol. 4 (Cambridge, MA: Harvard University Press, 1920), 125–127.

58. The so-called Lombardverbot incident is covered in *DDA*, 1:161ff. See also Bersch and Kaminsky, 15; Joseph Vincent Fuller, *Bismarck's Diplomacy at Its Zenith* (Cambridge, MA: Harvard University Press, 1967), 255–256; and Langer, 441–442.

59. Pflanze, 270ff.

60. Kennan, 382ff.

61. Goerlitz, 108. For more on the German military's attempts to circumvent civilian foreign-policy structures in this period, see Craig, 255–256; and also Crankshaw, 405–408.

62. Moltke and Schmerfeld, 141.

63. Moltke appears to have had in mind a spoiling attack against Russia, followed by a defensive war in East Prussia, to allow the German army to concentrate primarily on war in the west with France. His letter is reproduced in Moltke and Schmerfeld, 137–138. See also the discussion in Zuber, 51–52.

64. Otto Heinrich Meisner, *Denkwürdigkeiten des General-Feldmarschalls Alfred Grafen von Waldersee*, vol. 1 (Stuttgart: Deutsche Verlags-Anstalt, 1922), 347.

65. See *DDA*, 1:159–160.

66. Roberts, 470.

67. Langer, 445. See Bismarck's message to the German ambassador in Vienna dated December 15, 1887, in *DGP*, 6:25–28.

68. *DGP*, 5:282–290.

69. Pflanze, 272.

70. Pflanze, 272.

71. Pflanze, 263.

72. Pflanze, 274. Paul Schroeder and Katja Hoyer are two notable examples of recent historians with a positive appraisal of Bismarck's legacy. Tellingly, his most vociferous modern critic—Steinberg—devotes more attention to Bismarck's domestic politics than to his foreign policy.

73. Steinberg, 356.

74. Roberts, 480.

75. This claim can be found in Steinberg, 356.

76. Schroeder's judgment is surely correct: "Bismarck's alliances were genuine efforts to give Germany security and to make Europe stable and peaceful, aims that Bismarck recognized to be inseparable. It is difficult to believe that any other device would have worked as well as his did; it is still harder to believe, as some scholars suggest, that in the absence of Bismarck's intrigues and domineering management, the European powers would naturally have settled down to peaceful coexistence without serious crises or tensions." See Schroeder, *Systems*, 208.

77. The key source on security dilemmas is Robert Jervis, "Cooperation under the Security Dilemma," *World Politics* 30, no. 2 (January 1978): 167–214.

78. See the application of this principle to contemporary China in Edward N. Luttwak, *The Rise of China vs. the Logic of Strategy* (Cambridge, MA: Belknap Press, 2012), 39.

79. For more on alliances of restraint, see Schroeder, 210–211. See also Robert E. Osgood, *Alliances and American Foreign Policy* (Baltimore: Johns Hopkins University Press, 1968); and George Liska, *Nations in Alliance: The Limits of Interdependence* (Baltimore: Johns Hopkins University Press, 1967).

80. Langer, 383.

81. As Kissinger (*Diplomacy*, 166) puts it, "Overlapping alliances designed to ensure restraint led to suspicion instead."

Chapter Seven: The Octopus

1. Kissinger, *Diplomacy*, 178.

2. The memo can be found in Kenneth Bourne, *The Foreign Policy of Victorian England, 1830–1902* (Oxford: Clarendon Press, 1970), 476–477.

3. The best recent work is John Darwin, *The Empire Project: The Rise and Fall of the British World-System 1830–1970* (Cambridge: Cambridge University Press, 2009). See Lord Hamilton's "octopus" comparison on 66.

4. The statistics in this and the subsequent paragraph are from Angus Maddison, *The World Economy: A Millennial Perspective* (OECD Development Centre Studies, 2001), 97–99; John Darwin, 115; A.J.P. Taylor, *The Struggle for Mastery in Europe* (Oxford: Oxford University Press, 1988), xxv–xxxi; Paul Kennedy, *Great Powers*, 149, 226, 230; Youseff Cassis, *Capitals of Capital: A History of International Financial Centres, 1790–2005* (Cambridge: Cambridge University Press, 2006), 98; Robert Millward, "Geopolitics versus Market Structure Interventions in Europe's Infrastructure Industries, c. 1830–1939," *Business History* 53, no. 5 (August 2011): 679; Diane Drummond, "Sustained British Investment in Overseas Railways, 1830–1914," in *Across the Borders: Financing the World's Railways in the Nineteenth and Twentieth Centuries* (Aldershot, UK: Ashgate, 2008), 209; and George Modelski and William R. Thompson, *Seapower in Global Politics, 1494–1993* (London: Macmillan, 1988), 230, 238, 266, 293, 309, 314.

5. Historians debate the extent to which Britain prioritized Europe or the empire. Key texts include Julian Corbett, *Some Principles of Maritime Strategy* (London: Longmans Green & Co., 1918); B. H. Liddell Hart, *The British Way of War* (London: Faber & Faber, 1932); and Michael Howard, *The Continental Commitment and The British Way in Warfare: A Reappraisal* (London: Maurice Temple Smith, 1972).

6. Salisbury's foreign policy was never truly "isolationist." See John Charmley, *Splendid Isolation? Britain and the Balance of Power 1874–1914* (London: Hodder & Stoughton, 1999). See also George Monger, *The End of Isolation: British Foreign Policy, 1900–1907* (London: Thomas Nelson & Sons, 1963); Christopher Howard, "The Policy of Isolation," *Historical Journal* 10, no. 1 (1967): 77–88; and Brendan Simms, *Britain's Europe: A Thousand Years of Conflict and Cooperation* (London: Allen Lane, 2016), 134.

7. The best biography is Roberts, *Salisbury: Victorian Titan*. See also E. D. Steele, *Lord Salisbury: A Political Biography* (London: UCL Press, 1999); and John A. S. Grenville, *Lord Salisbury and Foreign Policy* (London: Athlone Press, 1964). This chapter draws on Salisbury's government papers as reproduced in G. P. Gooch and Harold Temperley, eds., *British Documents on the Origins of the War, 1898–1914* (London: H. M. Stationary Office, 1927), hereafter *BD*; as well as Henry W. Lucy, ed., *Speeches of the Marquis of Salisbury* (London: Routledge, 1885) and *Essays by the Late Marquess of Salisbury*.

8. Quoted in Andrew Roberts, "Salisbury: The Empire Builder Who Never Was," *History Today*, October 1999, 48–49.

9. See, for example, Salisbury's handling of the Egyptian problem in Darwin, 75–79.

10. Kennedy, *Great Powers*, 225–226; and Darwin, 116 and 276–278.

11. Prior to 1971, British pounds were subdivided into twenty shillings of twelve pence each, or 240 pence total, so the tax rate would have been about 5 percent. See Keith M. Wilson, *The Policy of the Entente* (Cambridge: Cambridge University Press, 2009), 9.

12. Darwin, 66.

13. Alfred Thayer Mahan, *The Influence of Sea Power upon History, 1660–1783* (Boston: Little, Brown & Co., 1890).

14. H. J. Mackinder, "The Geographical Pivot of History," *Geographical Journal* 23 (1904): 421–437. See also Darwin, 66ff. See Darwin's analysis (66–69) of how changing naval and geopolitical dynamics in this period impacted British strategic options.

15. As the later foreign secretary Edward Grey put it, Great Britain could either adhere to "an absolute standard superior to all other European navies put together" or "adjust [her] foreign policy so that [she] will not at any given moment have combined against you navies which you are unequal to meet." Quoted in Wilson, 8. The key source for British naval debates in this era is Aaron Friedberg, *The Weary Titan: Britain and the Experience of Relative Decline, 1985–1905* (Princeton, NJ: Princeton University Press, 2011).

16. Friedberg, 172–173. The first lord of the Admiralty was the civilian official responsible for the Royal Navy; the first naval lord (changed in 1904 to first sea lord) was its senior-most active-duty officer.

17. Modelski and Thompson, 81.

18. Wilson, 4–16.

19. See Selborne's memorandum entitled "The Navy Estimates and the Chancellor of the Exchequer's Memorandum on the Growth of Expenditure," 16 November 1901, in D. George

Boyce, ed., *The Crisis of British Power: The Imperial and Naval Papers of the Second Earl of Selborne, 1895–1910* (London: Historians' Press, 1990), 133, hereafter *CBP*.

20. See the memorandum from Kerr to Selborne, 2 September 1901, *CBP*, 123.

21. See the memorandum by Selborne, 4 September 1901, *CBP*, 124–125.

22. Quoted in Kenneth Bourne, *Britain and the Balance of Power in North America 1815–1908* (Berkeley: University of California Press, 1967), 359.

23. A "khaki" election is one that occurs during wartime.

24. The Liberal Unionists were so called because they broke with their mother party in supporting the preservation of the union between Great Britain and Ireland. The 1900 government formed "in effect a coalition in which the smaller party, the Liberal Unionists, was proportionately over-represented." See T. G. Otte, "A Question of Leadership: Lord Salisbury, the Unionist Cabinet and Foreign Policy Making, 1895–1900," *Contemporary British History* 14, no. 4 (Winter 2000): 1–26.

25. Joseph Chamberlain never became prime minister but his second son, Neville, did.

26. See the sketch of Lansdowne in T. G. Otte, "Lord Lansdowne, 1845–1927," in *British Foreign Secretaries and Japan, 1850–1990: Aspects of the Evolution of British Foreign Policy*, ed. Anthony Best and Hugh Cortazzi (Amsterdam: Amsterdam University Press, 2018). The best biography is Simon Kerry's accessible and sympathetic *Lansdowne: The Last Great Whig* (London: Unicorn, 2017). See also P.J.V. Rolo, "Lansdowne," in *British Foreign Secretaries and Foreign Policy: From Crimean War to First World War*, ed. K. Wilson (London: n.p., 1987). For a favorable recent appraisal, see John Bew and Andrew Ehrhardt, "The Last Conservative Statesman," *The American Interest*, April 10, 2017. For an analysis of Lansdowne's diplomatic strategy see Andrew Ehrhardt, "Approaches to Strategic Resets in Diplomacy: The Case of the Fifth Marquess of Lansdowne," in *New Perspectives in Diplomacy*, ed. Claire Yorke and Alastair Masser (London: I. B. Tauris, 2021).

27. Kerry, 151.

28. Otte, "Lansdowne," 91.

29. Key sources on the Foreign Office of this period include T. G. Otte, *The Foreign Office Mind: The Making of British Foreign Policy, 1865–1914* (London: Cambridge University Press, 2011); and Zara S. Steiner, *The Foreign Office and Foreign Policy, 1898–1914* (London: Cambridge University Press, 1969).

30. See Kerry, 147 and the description of Foreign Office structure in Steiner, 11. Otte argues convincingly that the same foreign pressures that led Edwardian policymakers to seek a tighter grip on foreign policy also led to reform of the Foreign Office from 1906 onward in search of "national efficiency." See Otte, *Foreign Office Mind*, 240ff.

31. Otte, *Foreign Office Mind*, 5–6.

32. Craig, *The Diplomats*, 16.

33. Darwin, 78.

34. The key source is Keith Hamilton, *Bertie of Thame: Edwardian Ambassador* (Woodbridge, UK: Boydell Press, 1990). See also Monger, 99–103; Steiner, 37; and Kerry, 147.

35. Otte, *Foreign Office Mind*, 241.

36. Otte, "Lansdowne," 92–93.

37. Steiner, 54.

38. Kerry, 182.

39. David Gilmour, *Curzon: Imperial Statesman 1859–1925* (New York: Farrar, Straus and Giroux), 128–129.

40. Kennedy identifies appeasement as a "particularly British form of diplomacy" with moral, political, economic, and strategic roots tracing back to mid-19th Century. See Paul Kennedy, "The Tradition of Appeasement in British Foreign Policy 1865–1939," *British Journal of International Studies* 2, no. 3 (October 1976): 195–215. See also footnote 120 below.

41. Kennedy, "Tradition of Appeasement," 195–199.

42. See the analysis of this dynamic in Darwin, 79.

43. See for example Steven E. Lobell, "Britain's Paradox: Cooperation or Punishment prior to World War I," *Review of International Studies* 27, no. 2 (April 2001): 169–186.

44. Quoted in Charmley, 279.

45. Monger, 15–16. Lansdowne did not share Chamberlain's desire for a general alliance with Germany. What he wanted was probably a "nonobligatory friendship" accompanied by formalized cooperation in the Far East. See Avner Cohen, "Joseph Chamberlain, Lord Lansdowne and British Foreign Policy 1901–1903: From Collaboration to Confrontation," *Australian Journal of Politics and History* 43, no. 2 (April 1997): 129–130.

46. For an overview of Britain's diplomacy toward the United States in this era, see Bourne, *Britain*, especially chapter 9. See also Kori Schake, *Safe Passage: The Transition from British to American Hegemony* (Cambridge, MA: Harvard University Press, 2017); and Lestyn Adams, *Brothers across the Ocean: British Foreign Policy and the Origins of the Anglo-American "Special Relationship" 1900–1905* (London: I. B. Tauris, 2005).

47. The strategic and naval logic of the Pauncefote effort is covered in Friedberg, 169–174.

48. Otte, "Lansdowne," 92–97.

49. Memo by Francis Bertie, 11 March 1901, in *BD*, vol. II, no. 54, 43.

50. *BD*, vol. II, nos. 124 and 125, 113–120. See also Ian Nish, *The Anglo-Japanese Alliance: The Diplomacy of Two Island Empires, 1894–1907* (London: Athlone Press 1966).

51. Scholars disagree on when exactly British leaders began to see Germany's shipbuilding program constituting a mortal danger. As early as 1901, we find Selborne observing to the cabinet that Wilhelm II seemed "determined" to raise German naval strength "so as to compare more advantageously with ours" (*CBP*, 136). Simms argues convincingly that by 1903 "the German threat had replaced the Russian menace as the principal concern for British foreign policy." See Brendan Simms, *Europe: The Struggle for Supremacy, from 1453 to the Present* (New York: Basic Books, 2013), 271. See also Paul Kennedy, *The Rise of the Anglo-German Antagonism 1860–1914* (London: Allen & Unwin, 1980).

52. *BD*, vol. II, 23, and, for text of treaty, 15–16.

53. Otte, "Lansdowne," 95.

54. See, for example, the exchange between Kaiser Wilhelm, Bülow, and Holstein dated 20–22 January 1901, nos. 4982–4986 in *DGP*, vol. XVII, 19–23.

55. Hatzfeldt's suggestion went well beyond Lansdowne's preferred template, which would have involved a narrower set of bilateral commitments, but was supported by some members of the cabinet. Lansdowne went so far as to have a draft treaty drawn up (*BD*, vol. II, 66–67). See Lansdowne memo dated 24 May 1901 in *BD*, vol. II, 64–65; and Monger, 35ff. Hatzfeldt's version of the conversation can be found in *DGP*, vol. XVII, no. 394, 65ff. See also J.A.S. Grenville, "Lansdowne's Abortive Project of 12 March 1901 for a Secret Agreement with Germany," *Bulletin of the Institute of Historical Research* 27, no. 76 (November 1954): 201–213.

56. Memorandum by the Marquess of Salisbury, 26 May 1901, *BD*, vol. II no. 86, 68.

57. Memorandum by Sir Francis Bertie, 9 November 1901, *BD*, vol. II, no. 91, 73–75. It is from this period onward that skepticism toward Germany would grow at the Foreign Office, eventually culminating in the famous Crowe memorandum of 1907. See the discussion in Margaret MacMillan, *The War That Ended Peace: The Road to 1914* (New York: Random House, 2014), 124–126.

58. See the list of obstacles to an Anglo-German understanding in Lansdowne's memorandum dated 11 November 1901 in *BD*, vol. II, no. 92, 76–78.

59. See, for example, *BD*, vol. IV, nos. 181a.–182, 183–188.

60. Lansdowne to Monson, 2 July 1903, *BD*, vol. II, no. 356, 292.

61. Lansdowne to Monson, 29 July 1903, *BD*, vol. II, no. 363, 304.

62. *BD*, vol. II, Appendix, 402–407.

63. Bertie had mixed feelings about the French entente but saw its potential to discomfit Germany. Lansdowne does not appear to have intended the arrangement as an anti-German edifice. See Hamilton, 58; Monger, 100–102.

64. Lansdowne to Monson, 2 July 1903, *BD*, vol. IV, no. 356.

65. Hardinge to Lansdowne, 13 June 1905, *BD*, vol. IV, no. 190.

66. Hardinge to Lansdowne, 30 May 1905, *BD*, vol. IV, no. 189.

67. *BD*, vol. IV, Appendix I, 618–620. See also J.A.R. Marriott, *Anglo-Russian Relations 1686–1943*, second edition (London: Metheun & Co., 1944), 161–162.

68. The classic account is Robert K. Massie, *Dreadnought: Britain, Germany and the Coming of the Great War* (New York: Ballantine Books, 1992). See especially part III.

69. Beryl J. Williams, "The Strategic Background to the Anglo-Russian Entente of August 1907," *Historical Journal* 9, no. 3 (1966): 360–373.

70. Quoted in Lillian M. Penson, "The New Course in British Foreign Policy, 1892–1902," *Transactions of the Royal Historical Society* 25 (1943): 131.

71. Quoted in Harold Nicolson, *Portrait of a Diplomatist* (New York: Harcourt, Brace & Co., 1930). See also Christopher Clark, *The Sleepwalkers: How Europe Went to War in 1914* (New York: Harper, 2014), 158.

72. Schroeder, *Systems*, 137–155.

73. Niall Ferguson, *The Pity of War* (New York: Basic Books, 1999), 55.

74. Kerry, 182.

75. A great deal has been written about Great Britain's approach to the Paris Peace Conference. Early appraisals were shaped by John Maynard Keynes's polemical account in *The Economic Consequences of the Peace* (New York: Harcourt, Brace & Howe, 1920). For a more balanced early appraisal, see H.W.V. Temperley, ed., *A History of the Peace Conference of Paris*, 6 vols. (London: H. Frowde, 1920–1924). For a colorful, if world-weary, retrospective, see Harold Nicolson, *Peacemaking 1919* (New York: Grosset & Dunlap, 1965). For a recent, readable account that captures the pageantry and follies of the proceedings, see Margaret MacMillan, *Paris 1919* (New York: Random House, 2001).

76. Niall Ferguson, *Empire: The Rise and Demise of the British World Order and the Lessons for Global Power* (New York: Basic Books, 2002), 264.

77. Winston S. Churchill, *The Second World War*, Vol. I: *The Gathering Storm* (Boston: Houghton Mifflin, 1948), 30.

78. Keynes's depiction of Lloyd George as a nimble but prevaricating opportunist at Paris has been challenged by later historians. See, for example, Kenneth Morgan, *Lloyd George* (London: Weidenfeld & Nicolson, 1974); and Antony Lentin, "Several Types of Ambiguity: Lloyd George at the Paris Peace Conference," *Diplomacy & Statecraft* 6, no. 1 (1995): 223–251.

79. The Foreign Office's extensive preparations for Paris, most of which were ignored by Lloyd George, are detailed in M. L. Dockrill and Zara Steiner, "The Foreign Office at the Paris Peace Conference in 1919," *International History Review* 2, no. 1 (January 1980): 57–58.

80. Craig, 17ff. See also Roberta M. Warman, "The Erosion of Foreign Office Influence in the Making of Foreign Policy, 1916–1918," *Historical Journal* 15, no. 1 (1972).

81. Craig, 20.

82. The best recent biography is Patricia O'Toole, *The Moralist: Woodrow Wilson and the World He Made* (New York: Simon & Schuster, 2019).

83. The full text can be found at "Address to a Joint Session of Congress on the Conditions of Peace," January 8, 1918, American Presidency Project, https://www.presidency.ucsb .edu/documents/address-joint-session-congress-the-conditions-peace-the-fourteen-points.

84. "An Address to the Senate," 22 January 1917, in Arthur S. Fink, ed., *The Papers of Woodrow Wilson*, Vol. 40 (Princeton, NJ: Princeton University Press, 1966), 535–536.

85. MacMillan, *Paris*, 72.

86. Nicolson, *Peacemaking*, 37, 50, and 52–53.

87. Kissinger, *Diplomacy*, 225.

88. Sigmund Freud later concluded that Wilson's behavior at the Paris conference exhibited the symptoms of the messiah complex. See Patrick Weil, *Madman in the White House: Sigmund Freud, Ambassador Bullitt, and the Lost Psychobiography of Woodrow Wilson* (Cambridge, MA: Harvard University Press, 2023).

89. Nicolson, *Peacemaking*, 52.

90. MacMillan, *Paris*, 42.

91. The quote is from A. L. Kennedy, *Old Diplomacy and New, 1876–1922: From Salisbury to Lloyd-George* (London: Murray, 1922), 359.

92. The episodes in this paragraph are covered in Craig, 25–30ff.

93. Keynes's characterization of the Paris settlement as excessively vindictive has been challenged by historians. See, for example, Marc Trachtenberg, "Reparation at the Paris Peace

Conference," *Journal of Modern History* 51, no. 1 (March 1979); and Sally Marks, "The Myths of Reparations," *Central European History* 11, no. 3 (1978).

94. Satow, *A Guide to Diplomatic Practice*, 157. See also T. G. Otte, "Satow," in Berridge, Keens-Soper, and Otte, 125ff.

95. Whyte, *The Practice of Diplomacy*, xii. See also Maurice Keens-Soper, "Callieres," in Berridge, Keens-Soper, and Otte, 107ff; and Craig, 22ff.

96. Darwin, 365. It would be hard to conceive a more striking contrast to Lloyd George's seat-of-the-pants approach to diplomacy than the extensive preparations that went into the London Conference. See, for example, *Documents on British Foreign Policy*, first series, vol. XXVI (London: Her Majesty's Stationary Office, 1985), nos. 525–526, 645–646. Hereafter *DBFP*.

97. See Austen Chamberlain's exposition of the logic of Britain's approach to European security in the lead-up to Locarno in *DBFP*, first series, vol. XXVII, no. 349.

98. See Lord Curzon's survey of British diplomatic accomplishments at Lasaunne in *DBFP*, first series, vol. XVIII, no. 370. See also Craig, 37ff.

99. Darwin, 369.

100. British diplomats angled the United States into proposing the treaty so that London would not appear to be giving ground. See Harold Sprout and Margaret Sprout, *Toward a New Order of Sea Power: American Naval Policy and the World Scene, 1918–1922* (Princeton, NJ: Princeton University Press, 1943), 127ff.

101. A. D. Baker III, "Battlefleets and Diplomacy: Naval Disarmament between the Two World Wars," *Warship International* 26, no. 3 (1989): 223.

102. For more on this line of argument, see Schake, chapter 10.

103. This paragraph draws on Kennedy, *Great Powers*, chapter 6; and G. C. Peden, *Arms, Economics and British Strategy: From Dreadnoughts to Hydrogen Bombs* (Cambridge: Cambridge University Press, 2007), 129ff.

104. Brendan Simms, "Strategies of Geopolitical Revolution: Hitler and Stalin," in Brands, 616–637.

105. Modelski and Thompson, 575–576; Paul Kennedy, *The Rise and Fall of British Naval Mastery* (London: Macmillan, 1983), 268; and Kennedy, *Great Powers*, 324.

106. Walter Reid, *Neville Chamberlain: The Passionate Radical* (Edinburgh: Birlinn, 2021), 211.

107. The key biography is Keith Feiling, *The Life of Neville Chamberlain* (Hamden, UK: Archon, 1970). See also Robert Self's masterful *Neville Chamberlain: A Biography* (London: Routledge, 2006). Walter Reid's 2021 *Neville Chamberlain: The Passionate Radical* offers a modern reappraisal that challenges the stereotype of Chamberlain as a weak and indecisive leader.

108. Reid, 65.

109. See, for example, Chamberlain's comprehensive national insurance scheme outlined in Feiling, 114ff.

110. Feiling, 283.

111. Reid, 189.

112. Reid, 193.

113. Chamberlain served as chancellor of the exchequer 1923–1924 and 1931–1937.

114. See, for example, the minimal requirements for the British army in B. H. Liddell Hart, *Europe in Arms* (Faber & Faber, 1937), 117. Michael Howard later contested Hart's premise, arguing that British grand strategy had always been much more focused on Europe than he alleged. For an overview of this debate, see Lawrence Freedman, "Alliance and the British Way in Warfare," *Review of International Studies* 21, no. 2 (April 1995): 145–158.

115. Robert Paul Shay, *British Rearmament in the Thirties: Politics and Profits* (Princeton, NJ: Princeton University Press, 1977), 36ff.

116. N. H. Gibbs, *Grand Strategy*, vol. 1 (London: Her Majesty's Stationery Office, 1976), 532.

117. Churchill, 221–222. Chamberlain's hands-on role in formulating strategy is described in Zara Steiner, *The Triumph of the Dark: European International History, 1933–1939* (Oxford: Oxford University Press, 2011), 329.

118. Quoted in Gibbs, 119. Similar assessments by British defense planners in 1935 and 1937 can be found in Michael Howard, 118–119; and David French, *Deterrence, Coercion, and Appeasement: British Grand Strategy, 1919–1940* (Oxford: Oxford University Press, 2022), 331.

119. Quoted in Paul Kennedy, *The Realities behind Diplomacy: Background Influences on British External Policy, 1865–1980* (London: Allen & Unwin, 1981), 287.

120. See, for example, Gibbs, 298; and *DBFP*, second series, vol. XIII, 924.

121. *DBFP*, second series, vol. XXI, no. 464.

122. The entente cordiale was renewed in 1936, but its terms were limited to mutual defense. For Chamberlain's dismissal of reviving Britain's World War I alliances, see Feiling, 347–348; and Robert Self, ed., *The Neville Chamberlain Diary Letters*, vol. 4 (Aldershot, UK: Ashgate, 2000), 305. Hereafter *NCDL*.

123. There is a large literature on appeasement in the 1930s. The best recent treatment is Tim Bouverie, *Appeasement: Chamberlain, Hitler, and the Road to War* (New York: Tim Duggan Books, 2019). For a detailed synopsis of the dynamics behind British policymaking, see John Charmley, *Chamberlain and the Lost Peace* (Chicago: Ivan R. Dee, 1990). For appeasement as an element of strategy, see, for example, Norrin M. Ripsman and Jack S. Levy, "Wishful Thinking or Buying Time? The Logic of British Appeasement in the 1930s," *International Security* 33, no. 2 (Fall 2008): 148–181. For the role that domestic factors played in encouraging appeasement, see Peter Trubowitz and Peter Harris, "When States Appease: British Appeasement in the 1930s," *Review of International Studies* 41, no. 2 (April 2015): 289–311. For the economic factor, see Kevin Narizny, "Both Guns and Butter, or Neither: Class Interests in the Political Economy of Rearmament," *American Political Science Review* 97, no. 2 (May 2003): 203–220. For a defense of appeasement as a tool of strategy, see Daniel Treisman, "Rational Appeasement," *International Organization* 58, no. 2 (Spring 2004): 345–373.

124. *DBFP*, second series, vol. XIX, no. 401.

125. Chamberlain quoted in Feiling, 351, and Darwin, 493.

126. Kennedy defines appeasement as a "policy of settling international . . . quarrels by admitting and satisfying grievances through rational negotiation and compromise, thereby avoiding the resort to an armed conflict." Ripsman and Levy define it "as a strategy of sustained, asymmetrical concessions in response to a threat, with the aim of avoiding war, at least in the short term." Chamberlain's view of what he was doing is closer to Kennedy's definition; he described his method as "the securing of peace by the removal of the *reasonable causes* of war (emphasis added)." See Kennedy, "Tradition of Appeasement," 195; Ripsman and Levy, 153–154; and Charmley, *Chamberlain*, 172.

127. See, for example, Henderson's long memorandum arguing that Germany posed no threat to Britain, dated 10 May 1937, in *DBFP*, second series, vol. XIX, no. 53.

128. Quoted in Feiling, 355.

129. For Chamberlain's negative views of the Foreign Office, see *NCDL*, vol. IV, 279. For his efforts to bring the Foreign Office into alignment with his policy views, see Steiner, *Triumph*, 328–329.

130. For an audit of the damage done by the Chamberlain-Wilson tandem, see Adrian Phillips, *Fighting Churchill, Appeasing Hitler, Neville Chamberlain, Sir Horace Wilson, and Britain's Plight of Appeasement: 1937–1939* (New York: Pegasus Books, 2019).

131. Reid, 231. Unlike the Foreign Office, Chamberlain at this stage still saw Hitler as reasonable. See, for example, *NCDL*, vol. IV, 306–308.

132. *NCDL*, vol. IV, 342.

133. Chamberlain insisted on making the trip in a civilian rather than military aircraft for fear of upsetting the Germans. See Reid, 235.

134. This and the subsequent paragraphs draw on the gripping blow-by-blow account in Bouverie, 247–296.

135. See, for example, the diary entry by Sir Alexander Cadogan, the permanent undersecretary, in David Dilks, ed., *The Diaries of Sir Alexander Cadogan, 1938–1945* (New York: G. P. Putnam's Sons, 1972), 104.

136. Bouverie, 265. See Halifax's telegraph at the time of the meeting at Bad Godesburg in *DBFP*, third series, vol. II, no. 1058. See also Andrew Roberts, *The Holy Fox: The Life of Lord Halifax* (London: Head of Zeus, 2019).

137. Steiner, *Triumph*, 630. Kennedy (*Realities*, 287) points out a pattern throughout the crises of 1937–1938 whereby the Foreign Office advocated for stronger positions to lend credibility to British diplomacy while the Chiefs of Staff argued for more diplomacy to free up military options.

138. Feiling, 372 and 376.

139. Bouverie, 298.

140. Feiling, 379; and Sally Greene, "Peace in Whose Time? Neville Chamberlain's Other Mistake," *Anglican and Episcopal History* 64, no. 2 (June 1995): 141.

141. The classic anti-appeasement case was laid out in "Cato," *Guilty Men* (London: Victor Gollancz, 1940) and elaborated upon in Churchill's writings after the war, culminating in works like Martin Gilbert, *The Appeasers* (Boston: Houghton Mifflin, 1963). Reappraisal began with A.J.P. Taylor's *Origins of the Second World War* (New York: Atheneum 1983) and continues to the present day. For an overview of the evolution of the historiographical debate, see Bouverie, 411ff.; Reid, 275ff.; and Robert J. Beck, "Munich's Lessons Reconsidered," *International Security* 14, no. 2 (Fall 1989): 161–191.

142. See, respectively, Correlli Barnett, *The Collapse of British Power* (New York: Morrow, 1972), 448ff.; Steiner, *Triumph*, 1056; Kissinger, *Diplomacy*, 316; and John Ferris, "Intelligence," in *The Origins of World War Two: The Debate Continues*, ed. R. Boyce and J. A. Maiolo (New York: Palgrave Macmillan, 2003), 322–323.

143. See James P. Levy, *Appeasement and Rearmament: Britain, 1936–1939* (Lanham, MD: Rowman & Littlefield, 2006), 37; and Ripsman and Levy, 176. It's important to note that in the heady days immediately following Munich, Chamberlain believed that his diplomacy's chief accomplishment had not been that it bought time to rearm but rather that it removed the need to continue a defense build-up altogether. See Bouverie, 304–305.

144. See Anthony Adamthwaite, "War Origins Again," *Journal of Modern History* 56, no. 1 (March 1984): 115.

145. These included an offer from France to extend the protection of the entente cordiale to Czechoslovakia, an offer from the Soviet Union to provide trilateral guarantees, and an offer from the United States to convene a conference of all major powers. It's ironic that Chamberlain rejected these proposals as constituting "exclusive groups of nations" while dealing with Hitler in a format that was even more exclusive. See Arthur H. Furnia, *The Diplomacy of Appeasement: Anglo-French Relations and the Prelude to World War II, 1931–1938* (Washington, DC: University Press, 1960), 284–285.

146. As Charmley (*Chamberlain*, 64ff.) points out, the Foreign Office was not a monolith. But it consistently tried to recenter Chamberlain's policy around defense of the status quo.

147. Kissinger, *Diplomacy*, 316.

148. "Whether she clung on in all regions or escaped from some," as Paul Kennedy observes, "[Britain's] stretched global position was an enormously powerful reason for compromise with other states and for the pacific settlement of disputes." See Paul Kennedy, *Strategy and Diplomacy 1870–1945* (London: Fontana, 1983), 18.

149. Barnett, 239.

Chapter Eight: Chaos under Heaven

1. Quoted in Henry Kissinger, *On China* (New York: Penguin Books, 2012), 209ff. The full text of Chen's report can be found in Chen Jian and David L. Wilson, "'All under the Heaven Is Great Chaos': Beijing, the Sino-Soviet Border Clashes and the Turn towards Sino-American Rapprochement, 1968–9," *Cold War International History Project Bulletin* 11, no. 157–175 (Winter 1998): 155–175.

2. "National Security Study Memorandum 14," February 5, 1969, *Foreign Relations of the United States* (hereafter *FRUS*), 1969–1976, vol. XVII, China, 1969–1972 (Washington, DC: United States Government Printing Office, 2006), doc. 4.

3. "Paper Prepared by Alfred Jenkins of the NSC Staff," February 22, 1968, *FRUS, 1964–1968*, vol. XXX, doc. 303.

4. There is a large literature on early American diplomacy. See, for example, Robert B. Zoellick, *America in the World: A History of U.S. Diplomacy and Foreign Policy* (New York, NY: Grand Central Publishing, 2021); Max Savelle, *The Origins of American Diplomacy: the International History of Angloamerica, 1492–1763* (New York: Macmillan, 1967); George C. Herring, *Years of Peril and Ambition, U.S. Foreign Relations, 1776–1921* (New York: Oxford University Press, 2017); Eliga H. Gould, *Among the Powers of the Earth: The American Revolution and the Making of a New World Empire* (Cambridge, MA: Harvard University Press, 2014); and Felix Gilbert, *To the Farewell Address: Ideas of Early American Foreign Policy* (Princeton, NJ: Princeton University Press, 1961).

5. George C. Herring, *From Colony to Superpower: U.S. Foreign Relations since 1776* (New York: Oxford University Press, 2008), 3.

6. Herring, *Years of Peril*, 12.

7. The key source on the foreign policy debates of the early American republic is Walter Russell Mead, *Special Providence: American Foreign Policy and How It Changed the World* (New York: Routledge, 2002). More recently, Stephen Wertheim has shown that isolationism was a concept introduced in the 1940s to support the transition to a more expansive U.S. global role. See his book *Tomorrow, the World: The Birth of U.S. Global Supremacy* (Cambridge, MA: Belknap Press), 2020.

8. For an overview of the early republic's struggles with foreign powers, see Robert Kagan, *Dangerous Nation* (London: Atlantic, 2006). See also Eliot A. Cohen, *Conquered into Liberty: Two Centuries of Battles along the Great Warpath That Made the American Way of War* (New York: Free Press, 2011).

9. The indispensable source is Sean A. Mirski, *We May Dominate the World: Ambition, Anxiety and the Rise of the American Colossus* (New York: Public Affairs, 2023). For an illustration of Roosevelt's skill in strategic diplomacy, see his handling of the Venezuela crisis of 1902–1903 in Edmund Morris, *Theodore Rex* (New York: Modern Library, 2002), chapter 13. See also Howard K. Beale, *Theodore Roosevelt and the Rise of America to World Power* (Baltimore: Johns Hopkins University Press, 1984).

10. Figures in this paragraph are from Kennedy, *Rise and Fall of the Great Powers*, chapters 5, 6, and 7; and *Credit Suisse Global Investment Returns Yearbook 2013*, February 2013, 9.

11. The damage done by FDR's naivety is described in Sean McMeekin, *Stalin's War: A New History of World War II* (New York: Basic Books, 2021), chapters 28 and 32.

12. The text of the "long telegram" can be found in George F. Kennan, *Memoirs 1925–1950* (Boston: Little, Brown & Co., 1967). See also George F. Kennan ("X"), "The Sources of Soviet Conduct," *Foreign Affairs*, July 1, 1947.

13. Ernest May, *"Lessons" of the Past: The Use and Misuse of History in American Foreign Policy* (New York: Oxford University Press, 1973), 21ff. See also Dean Acheson, *Power and Diplomacy* (Cambridge, MA: Harvard University Press, 1958), chapter 1.

14. Dean Acheson, *Present at the Creation* (New York: Norton, 1969), 378–379. The most recent biography of Acheson is Robert L. Beisner, *Dean Acheson: A Life in the Cold War* (New York: Oxford Academic, 2023).

15. See Benn Steil, *The Battle of Bretton Woods: John Maynard Keynes, Harry Dexter White, and the Making of a New World Order* (Princeton, NJ: Princeton University Press, 2014).

16. The full text of NSC-68 can be found in Ernest R. May, ed., *American Cold War Strategy: Interpreting NSC 68* (Boston: St. Martin's Press, 1993); here, 61–62. The up-to-date source on Nitze is James Graham Wilson, *America's Cold Warrior* (Ithaca, NY: Cornell University Press, 2024).

17. Eisenhower rejected NSC-68's formula for rollback but accepted the overall framework of containment and prioritized the creation of positions of strength through alliances. See Robert R. Bowie and Richard H. Immerman, *Waging Peace: How Eisenhower Shaped an Enduring Cold War Strategy* (New York: Oxford University Press, 1998), 189, 202, and 249; and "Report to the National Security Council by the Executive Secretary, NSC 162/2," October 30, 1953, *FRUS, 1952–1954*, vol. II, part 1, 577.

18. Soviet scholars see Ike's 1955 meeting with Khrushchev in Geneva as the moment when the United States began to shift away from an emphasis on situations of strength. See William B. Husband, "Soviet Perceptions of U.S. 'Positions-of-Strength' Diplomacy in the 1970s," *World Politics* 31, no. 4 (July 1979): 495–517.

19. Kennedy in particular believed that the stakes of atomic warfare made direct negotiations with the Soviets necessary. See John F. Kennedy, "On Diplomacy in the Nuclear Age," *International Journal* 29, no. 1 (Winter 1973/1974): 67–70.

20. Bernard Brodie, ed., *The Absolute Weapon: Atomic Power and World Order* (New York: Harcourt, 1946). For an overview of the broader impact that nuclear weapons had on strategy, see Lawrence Freedman, *Strategy: A History* (New York: Oxford University Press, 2013), chapter 12.

21. Robert Gilpin, *War and Change in World Politics* (Cambridge: Cambridge University Press, 1981), 217–218.

22. Henry Kissinger, "Force and Diplomacy in the Nuclear Age," *Foreign Affairs*, April 1, 1956.

23. The key source is Graham T. Allison, *Essence of Decision: Explaining the Cuban Missile Crisis* (Boston: Little, Brown & Co., 1971).

24. John Lewis Gaddis, *The Cold War: A New History* (New York: Penguin Books, 2005), 81.

25. For an analysis of how moves to stabilize the nuclear balance can produce greater instability at lower levels of the gameboard, see Glenn Snyder, "The Balance of Power and the Balance of Terror," in *Balance of Power*, ed. Paul Seabury (San Francisco: Chandler, 1965), 123.

26. Stephen Daggett, "Costs of Major U.S. Wars," *Congressional Research Service*, June 29, 2010. The classic source on the Vietnam War is George Herring, *America's Longest War: The United States and Vietnam, 1950–1975* (New York: Wiley, 1979).

27. Herring, *Colony to Superpower*, 752.

28. The most up-to-date biography is John A. Farrell, *Richard Nixon: The Life* (New York: Doubleday, 2017). See 65–66 for Nixon's views on God and Wilson. Stephen Ambrose's *Nixon: The Triumph of a Politician, 1962–72* (New York: Simon & Schuster, 1989) provides an engaging appraisal of Nixon's comeback and first term. The best account of Nixon's White House years is Melvin Small's *The Presidency of Richard Nixon* (Lawrence: University of Kansas, 1999).

29. Richard M. Nixon, "Asia after Viet Nam," *Foreign Affairs*, October 1, 1967.

30. The best biography is Niall Ferguson, *Kissinger 1923–1968: The Idealist* (New York: Penguin Press, 2015). Walter Isaacson's *Kissinger: A Biography* (New York: Simon & Schuster, 1992) is lively and balanced. Marvin and Bernard Kalb's *Kissinger* (New York: Little, Brown & Co., 1974) gives a colorful, if adulatory, appraisal. For a less-flattering take on Kissinger's foreign policy, see Jussi Hanhimäki, *The Flawed Architect: Henry Kissinger and American Foreign Policy* (New York: Oxford Press, 2004). For the underpinnings of Kissinger's worldview, see Jeremi Suri, *Henry Kissinger and the American Century* (Cambridge, MA: Belknap Press, 2007). Kissinger's relationship with Nixon is covered in engrossing detail in Robert Dallek, *Nixon and Kissinger: Partners in Power* (New York: Harper Collins, 2007). The indispensable account of Nixon-Kissinger foreign policy is William Bundy, *A Tangled Web: The Making of Foreign Policy in the Nixon Presidency* (New York: Farrar, Straus and Giroux, 1998).

31. Kissinger was the first to make regular use of the title "national security advisor" as a shortened form of "special assistant for national security affairs."

32. Isaacson, 111.

33. The key source is Peter W. Dickson, *Kissinger and the Meaning of History* (Cambridge: Cambridge University Press, 1978); here, 4.

34. The philosophical dilemma at the heart of Kissinger's worldview is outlined in Dickson, chapter 2.

35. For a sense of the prevailing attitude toward diplomacy in the post–World War II era, see Hans J. Morgenthau, "Diplomacy," *Yale Law Journal* 55, no. 5 (August, 1946).

36. Kissinger, *World Restored*, 1–2.

37. Quoted in Ferguson, 316–317.

38. Henry A. Kissinger, "Central Issues of American Foreign Policy," in *Agenda for the Nation: Papers on Domestic and Foreign Policy Issues*, ed Kermit Gordon (Washington, DC: Brookings Institution, 1968), 585–614.

39. Isaacson, 136.

40. See Kissinger's critique of bureaucracy in "Domestic Structure and Foreign Policy," *Daedalus* 95, no. 2 (Spring 1966): 503–529; and Ferguson, 728–729.

41. For an overview of the NSC's creation and evolution, see David Rothkopf, *Running the World: The Inside Story of the National Security Council and the Architects of American Power* (New York: Public Affairs, 2006).

42. The Department of Defense became known as such in 1949.

43. See the memoranda dated December 27, 1968, January 7, 1969, and January 20, 1969, in *FRUS*, 1969–1976, Vol. II, 1–14 and 31–33.

44. For more on Kissinger's restructuring of the NSC, see Isaacson, 153ff.; Dallek, 84ff.; and Rothkopf, chapter 6.

45. Isaacson, 152.

46. See Bundy, 53; and Isaacson, 195–202.

47. Arne Westad argues that Nixon's instincts were hawkish but that he used diplomacy to buy time for the United States to get stronger. See Odd Arne Westad, *The Cold War: A World History* (New York: Basic Books, 2017), 398–389.

48. Kennedy, *Rise and Fall*, 384; and Tim Kane, "Global U.S. Troop Deployment, 1950–2005," Heritage Foundation, May 24, 2006.

49. Herring, *Colony to Superpower*, 752–754.

50. Colin S. Gray and Jeffrey G. Barlow, "Inexcusable Restraint: The Decline of American Military Power in the 1970s," *International Security* 10, no. 2 (Fall 1985): 51–52; and Henry A. Kissinger, *The White House Years* (Boston: Little, Brown & Co., 1979), 221.

51. Stephen Sestanovich, *Maximalist: America in the World from Truman to Obama* (New York: Vintage Books, 2014), 168.

52. Gray and Barlowe, 50.

53. The best account is Margaret MacMillan, *Nixon in China: The Week That Changed the World* (New York: Penguin, 2006).

54. There's some debate about how much Nixon had really thought through the Chinese opening before coming to office. See Michael J. Green, *By More than Providence: Grand Strategy and American Power in the Asia Pacific since 1783* (New York: Columbia University Press, 2017), 346–347.

55. John Pomfret, *The Beautiful Country and the Middle Kingdom* (New York: Henry Holt & Co., 2016), 440ff.

56. Pomfret, 429–430.

57. *FRUS*, 1964–1968, vol. XXX, doc. 302 and 303. Recent scholarship shows that Johnson remained much more open to the idea of engagement with China than was previously thought. See Victor S. Kaufman, *Confronting Communism: U.S. and British Policies toward China* (Columbia: University of Missouri Press, 2001) 182.

58. Raymond Garthoff argues that Nixon would have pursued the opening to China anyhow, but the situation in Vietnam gave the policy shift greater urgency. See Garthoff's *Détente and Confrontation: American-Soviet Relations from Nixon to Reagan* (Washington, DC: Brookings Institution, 1985), 249–250.

59. Kissinger, *Diplomacy*, 719–720 and 723.

60. Isaacson, 125–126.

61. See, for example, Kissinger's dismissive attitude toward triangulation in the minutes of the Senior Review Group meeting dated May 15, 1969, *FRUS*, 1969–1972, vol. XVII, doc. 13. See also Chris Tudda, *A Cold War Turning Point: Nion and China, 1969–1972* (Baton Rouge: Louisiana State University Press, 2012), chapter 2.

62. See "National Security Study Memorandum 14," February 5, 1969, *FRUS*, 1969–1972, volume XVII, doc. 4.

63. These debates are covered in Tudda, 10–11. For the CIA response to Nixon's tasking, see "Summary of the CIA Response to NSSM 14," undated, *FRUS*, 1969–1972, vol. XVII, doc. 12.

64. "Minutes of the Senior Review Group Meeting," May 15, 1969, *FRUS*, 1969–1972, vol. XVII, doc. 13.

65. Garthoff, 200–201. See also Richard Wich, *Sino-Soviet Crisis Politics: A Study of Political Change and Communication* (Cambridge, MA: Harvard University Press, 1980).

66. For a recent analysis of Brezhnev's strategy toward China and the United States, see Sergey Radchenko, *To Run the World* (Cambridge: Cambridge University Press, 2024).

67. Michael S. Gerson et al., "The Sino-Soviet Border Conflict: Deterrence, Escalation, and the Threat of Nuclear War in 1969," *Center for Naval Analysis*, November 2010. For the ceasefire, see Tudda, 34–35.

68. The key source is Anthony Saich, *From Rebel to Ruler* (Cambridge, MA: Harvard University Press, 2021).

69. Stéphane Courtois et al., *Black Book of Communism: Crimes, Terror, Repression* (Cambridge, MA: Harvard University Press, 1999), 4.

70. See the account by Mao's doctor in Li Zhisui, *The Private Chairman Mao* (New York: Random House, 1994), 358ff.

71. MacMillan, 141.

72. Altogether Chen Yi wrote or contributed to four strategy papers in this period. See the chronology in Chen Jian, *Zhou Enlai: A Life* (Cambridge, MA: Belknap Press, 2024), 617–622. The texts of all but the first can be found in Jian and Wilson, docs. 9, 11, and 12.

73. Westad, 366–367.

74. Tudda, 60.

75. Richard Nixon, *RN: The Memoirs of Richard Nixon* (New York: Grosset & Dunlap, 1978), 552; and Dallek, 340.

76. Kissinger, *White House Years*, 735.

77. Edward Luttwak, *The Rise of China vs. the Logic of Strategy* (Cambridge, MA: Belknap Press, 2012), 24ff.

78. Kissinger, *White House Years*, 743–7.

79. Percy Zucheng Fang, *Zhou Enlai: A Profile* (Beijing: Foreign Languages Press, 1986), 12; and Chen, *Zhou Enlai*, 13ff.

80. MacMillan, 44.

81. Fang, 100.

82. Chen, *Zhou Enlai*, 636.

83. Kissinger, *White House Years*, 752.

84. Kissinger, *White House Years*, 753.

85. Chen, *Zhou Enlai*, 635–636.

86. "NSSM 106—China Policy," February 16, 1971, *FRUS*, 1969–1972, vol. XVII, doc. 105.

87. Green, 349; and Tudda, 69ff.

88. MacMillan, 257.

89. Tudda (67) dates the start of triangulation to April 1971, just after the arrival of Zhou's invitation.

90. Kissinger, *White House Years*, 735. Over the summer, one of Kissinger's assistants, Winston Lord, wrote a series of memos that prioritized Chinese help on Vietnam alongside pressuring the Soviets and reducing Chinese support for insurgencies. See Tudda, 124; and Yafeng Xia, *Negotiating with the Enemy: U.S.-China Talks during the Cold War, 1949–1972* (Bloomington: Indiana University Press 2006), 164.

91. Kissinger, *White House Years*, 736.

92. Tudda, 60.

93. Chen, *Zhou Enlai*, 632; and Xia, 164–165.

94. MacMillan, 240 and 248. See also Nancy Bernkopf Tucker, *Strait Talk: United States-Taiwan Relations and the Crisis with China* (Cambridge, MA: Harvard University Press, 2008), chapter 2.

95. Xia, 164.

96. Tucker, 42 and 90.

97. Chen, *Zhou Enlai*, 635. Herring (*Colony to Superpower*, 778) notes that it was after Kissinger made concessions on Taiwan that Zhou said, "Good, these talks may now proceed."

98. Tudda, 101; and Kissinger, *White House Years*, 833–841.

99. Anatoly Dobrynin, *In Confidence: Moscow's Ambassador to America's Six Cold War Presidents, 1962–1986* (New York: Random House, 1995), 193 and 227. See also Svetlana Savranskaya and William Taubman, "Soviet Foreign Policy, 1962–1975," in *The Cambridge History of the Cold War*, ed. Melvyn P. Leffler and Odd Arne Westad (Cambridge: Cambridge University Press, 2010), 134–157.

100. For Nixon's defense of secrecy in diplomacy, see Nixon, *RN*, 550.

101. "Cablegram to Canberra," July 15, 1971, *Documents on Australian Foreign Policy* (hereafter *DAFP*), vol. 22, doc. 209.

102. See MacMillan, chapter 18 and Michael Schaller, "The Nixon 'Shocks' and U.S.-Japan Strategic Relations, 1969–74," National Security Archive, George Washington University, Working Paper No. 2, 1996, https://nsarchive2.gwu.edu/japan/schaller.htm.

103. Schaller, "The Nixon 'Shocks.'"

104. "Cablegram to Washington," July 18, 1971, *DAFP*, vol. 22, doc. 213.

105. Tucker, 45; Tudda, 102–103; and "Cablegram to Canberra," July 16, 1971, *DAFP*, vol. 22, doc. 211.

106. See, for example, Kissinger's memcon describing a heated interaction with leading conservative William F. Buckley Jr., in "Memorandum of Conversation with Conservative Opinion Leaders," August 12, 1971, National Security Archive, doc. 9, https://nsarchive2.gwu.edu/NSAEBB/NSAEBB193/.

107. Tudda, 108.

108. Nixon's approach was to support Communist China gaining a seat in the Security Council while fighting to prevent Taiwan's eviction from the General Assembly and endeavoring to make sure none of this interfered with rapprochement. See Tucker, 47–52; and MacMillan, 211–212.

109. Tabulated from Chen, *Zhou Enlai*, 638.

110. Green, 351.

111. Nixon, *RN*, 563.

112. Tudda, 184. Mao may have been bored by Nixon. See "Memcon of Nixon and Mao, February 21, 1972," in William Burr, ed., *The Kissinger Transcripts* (New York: New Press, 1998), 59ff.

113. Nixon, *RN*, 568–589; and Tudda, 186–187.

114. Tudda, 187.

115. Tudda, 188.

116. Tucker, 57.

117. Kissinger, *White House Years*, 1075; and Isaacson, 404.

118. MacMillan, 300.

119. Kissinger, *White House Years*, 1069 and 1086. While Kissinger seems to mock Nixon for getting "carried away" in his toast, recently released documents show that Kissinger later made statements to Zhou that were similar to those in Nixon's speech. See "Memorandum of Conversation with Zhou Enlai," June 20, 1972, National Security Archive, doc. 10, https://nsarchive2.gwu.edu/NSAEBB/NSAEBB193/.

120. For the public reception, see Tudda, 203; and MacMillan, 311. In his memoirs (*White House Years*, 1091–1092), Kissinger focused only on negative reactions, but as Dallek (369) points out, the press was mostly positive. For Reagan's reaction, see Kissinger, *White House Years*, 1093.

121. Tucker, 64.

122. Several historians have noted the blunders that Kissinger made in negotiating the SALT and ABM agreements, many of which stemmed from his exclusion of U.S. experts from the process. See, for example, Garthoff, 171; and Isaacson, 428–433. Most scholars believe that SALT did little to curb the arms race and may have even intensified it. See Robert Jervis, "The Many Faces of SALT," *Journal of Cold War Studies* 24, no. 4 (Fall 2022): 198–214; Marc Trachtenberg, "The United States and Strategic Arms Limitation during the Nixon-Kissinger Period: Building a Stable International System?," *Journal of Cold War Studies* 24 no. 4 (Fall 2022): 157–197; and Steven E. Miller, "Article Review 163: Miller on Trachtenberg and Jervis on SALT," *H-Diplo*, September 27, 2023.

123. Tom W. Smith, "The Polls: American Attitudes toward the Soviet Union and Communism," *Public Opinion Quarterly* 47, no. 2 (Summer 1983): 277–292.

124. Garthoff, 260.

125. Kissinger's premature announcement put Nixon in a bind because the process was far from complete and Nixon didn't want to create the impression that he was trying to force an outcome to coincide with the election. See Ambrose, 643ff.; and Nixon, *RN*, 706–707.

126. Herring, *Colony to Superpower*, 782.

127. Herring, *Colony to Superpower*, 783.

128. Dallek, 433.

129. The former include, significantly, Kissinger's role in brokering agreements between Israel and Egypt and Israel and Syria following the Yom Kippur War of 1973, which aren't covered in this book. See Martin Indyk, *Master of the Game: Henry Kissinger and the Art of Middle East* (New York: Knopf, 2021).

130. In a crowded field, see: Seymour M. Hersh, *The Price of Power: Kissinger in the Nixon White House* (New York: Summit Books, 1983); Christopher Hitchens, *The Trial of Henry Kissinger* (New York: Verso, 2001); and Dylan Matthews, "What Henry Kissinger Wrought," *Vox*, November 30, 2023; Norman Podhoretz, "Kissinger Reconsidered," *Commentary*, June 1982; and Patrick J. Buchanan, *Nixon's White House Wars: The Battles That Made and Broke a President and Divided America Forever* (New York: Crown Forum, 2017).

131. Green, 348.

132. Kissinger, *On China*, 275, and *Diplomacy*, 728.

133. Kissinger often said he preferred Bismarck's methods to Metternich's, but he spilt much more ink on the latter. It's reasonable to speculate that in his long years after government service, Kissinger came to see Metternich's cosmopolitanism as more palatable for modern audiences than Bismarck's Realpolitik.

134. See, for example, Kissinger, *White House Years*, 716, 840, 1046, 1086, 1217, 1245, and 1476.

135. Critics counter that Kissinger's focus on big-power relations fueled instability in the periphery. See Hanhimäki, xviii.

136. For more on the neglected concept of *recueillement* in geopolitics, see Jakub Grygiel, "Stand Up or Sit Down," *The American Interest*, March 7, 2014.

137. See, for example, Kissinger, *Diplomacy*, 728, and *World Order*, 222 and 225.

138. Garthoff, 240; and Kissinger, *On China*, 274. For more on the Chinese perspective of Sino-U.S. rapprochement, see Gong Li, "China's High-level Decision Making and the Thaw of Sino-American Relations," in *Re-Examining the Cold War: U.S.-China Diplomacy, 1954–1973*, ed. Robert S. Ross and Changbin Jiang (Cambridge, MA: Harvard University Press, 2001).

139. On one occasion, Zhou bluntly told Kissinger that America was trying to build a rigid order in the style of Metternich while China was using revolution to undermine that very order. See MacMillan, 208.

140. See Kissinger, *White House Years*, 522 and 752.

141. Chen, *Zhou Enlai*, 635.

142. Yafeng, 164.

143. Quoted in Green, 337.

144. Japan, South Korea, and the Philippines increased defense spending; Australia did not. For a positive appraisal of the Nixon Doctrine, see Green, 337ff.; and Andrew Kepinevich et al., eds., "Strategy in Austerity," Center for Strategic and Budgetary Assessments, 2012, 22ff. For a critical analysis, see Jussi Hanhimäki, "An Elusive Grand Design," in *Nixon in the World: American Foreign Relations, 1969–1977*, ed. Fredrik Logevall and Andrew Preston (New York: Oxford University Press, 2008), 38–39.

145. Kane, "Global U.S. Troop Deployments."

146. Stephen E. Miller, Article Review 163, *H-Diplo*, Robert Jervis International Security Studies Forum, September 27, 2023. For more on this line of reasoning, see John D. Maurer, "The Forgotten Side of Arms Control: Enhancing US Competitive Advantage, Offsetting Adversary Strengths," *War on the Rocks*, June 27, 2018.

147. Recent scholarship suggests that contrary to U.S. perceptions, Brezhnev was operating from a position of weakness. See Sergey Radchenko, "Strategies of Détente and

Competition: Brezhnev and Moscow's Cold War," in *The New Makers of Modern Strategy: From the Ancient World to the Digital Age*, ed. Hans Brands (Princeton, NJ: Princeton University Press, 2023), 817–840.

148. Bundy, 525.

149. Farrell, 464.

150. William A. Hunt, *Melvin Laird: The Foundation of the Post-Vietnam Military* (Washington, DC: Government Printing Office, 2015), 78–79.

151. Hal Brands, The *Twilight Struggle* (New Haven, CT: Yale University Press, 2022), 118.

152. Kiron K. Skinner et al., *Reagan in His Own Hand* (New York: Simon & Schuster, 2001), 25. See also Simon Miles, *Engaging the Evil Empire: Washington, Moscow, and the Beginning of the End of the Cold War* (Ithaca, NY: Cornell University Press, 2020), 4–6.

153. See Green, 399; Robert A. Manning, "Reagan's Chance Hit," *Foreign Policy*, Spring 1984, 87ff.; and Donald Stoker, *Purpose and Power: U.S. Grand Strategy from the Revolutionary Era to the Present* (Cambridge: Cambridge University Press, 2024), 518.

154. William Inboden, *The Peacemaker: Ronald Reagan, the Cold War, and the World on the Brink* (London: Penguin Random House, 2022), 281.

155. See, for example, John J. Mearsheimer, "The Inevitable Rivalry: America, China, and the Tragedy of Great-Power Politics," *Foreign Affairs*, November/December 2021.

156. Mead, 39.

157. Isaacson, 766.

158. Kissinger, *World Order*, 327.

Chapter Nine: The Necessity of Diplomacy

1. Maybe that's why the popular board game Diplomacy, despite its name, is actually a war game. Thus when we read that artificial intelligence (AI) can beat humans at this game, we're really being told that it can optimize alliance choices and offensive vectors for conquering territory, and not, as its boosters imply, that it is actually superior in negotiating skills. For AI's performance in the game, see Meta Fundamental AI Research Diplomacy Team (FAIR) et al., "Human-Level Play in the Game of Diplomacy by Combining Language Models with Strategic Reasoning," *Science* 378 (2022): 1067–1074.

2. The key source is Stephen M. Walt, *The Origins of Alliances* (Ithaca, NY: Cornell University Press, 1987).

3. The classic articulation of this argument is John G. Ikenberry, *After Victory: Institutions, Strategic Restraint, and the Rebuilding of Order after Major Wars* (Princeton, NJ: Princeton University Press, 2001).

4. See for example Bartoletti, 3ff.

5. Quoted in John Lewis Gaddis, *Strategies of Containment: A Critical Appraisal of American National Security Policy during the Cold War* (Oxford: Oxford University Press, 2005), 3.

6. For an elaboration of this tension, see Kennedy, *Rise and Fall*, 539–540.

7. See W. K. Marriot et. al., eds., *The Essential Writings of Machiavelli* (Premium Classic Books, 2020), 222–224; and Langer, 175.

8. All but Chamberlain were political liberals, and even Chamberlain followed the liberal trend of treating diplomacy as an extension of domestic politics that leaders use to remove the sources of conflict rather than applying constraints to an opponent.

9. Steinberg, 465–470.

10. See Victor Davis Hanson's chilling account of annihilation as an understudied phenomenon in history in *The End of Everything: How Wars Descend into Annihilation* (New York: Basic Books, 2024).

11. For more on the potential uses and limitations of AI in the field of diplomacy, see Andrew Moore, "How AI Could Revolutionize Diplomacy," *Foreign Policy*, March 21, 2023; Henry A. Kissinger, Eric Schmidt, and Daniel Huttenlocher, *The Age of AI: And Our Human Future* (New York: Little, Brown & Co., 2021); and Matthew Hutson, "How Artificial Intelligence Could Negotiate Better Deals for Humans," *Science*, September 11, 2017.

BIBLIOGRAPHY

Primary Sources

Albèri, Eugenio. *Le relazioni degli ambasciatori Veneti al Senato durante il secolo decimosesto.* Vol. 4. Firenze: Società Editrice Florentina, 1860.

Arneth, Alfred von. *Geschichte Maria Theresas.* Wien: W. Braumüller, 1870.

Avenel, M., ed. *Lettres, instructions diplomatiques et papiers d'état du Cardinal de Richelieu.* 8 vols. Paris: Imprimerie Nationale, 1853.

Beer, Adolf. *Archiv für österreichische Geschichte, Denkschriften des Fürsten Wenzel Kaunitz-Rittberg.* Wien: Karl Gerold's Sohn, 1872.

——, ed. *Aufzeichungen des Grafen William Bentinck über Maria Theresia.* Wien: C. Gerold's Sohn, 1871.

Bismarck, Otto von. *Gedanken und Erinnerungen von Otto Fürst von Bismarck.* 3 vols. Stuttgart: Cotta, 1922.

Boyce, D. George, ed. *The Crisis of British Power: The Imperial and Naval Papers of the Second Earl of Selborne, 1895–1910.* London: Historians' Press, 1990.

British Documents on the Origins of the War, 1898–1914. 11 Vols. London: Her Majesty's Stationery Office, 1924–1938.

Butler, A. J., trans. *Bismarck, The Memoirs.* Vol. 2. New York: Howard Fertig, 1966.

Champollion-Figeac, Aimé Louis. *Captivité du roi François Ier.* Paris: Imprimerie Royale, 1847.

Charrière, Ernest. *Négociations de la France dans le Levant: 1515–1547.* 4 vols. Paris: Imprimerie Royale, 1848.

Collection des ordonnances des rois de France: catalogue des actes de François Ier. 9 vols. Paris: Imprimerie Royale, 1907.

Correspondenz des Kaisers Karl V. 3 vols. Leipzig: F. A. Brockhaus, 1844.

Die Grosse Politik der Europäischen Kabinette, 1871–1914. Vols. III, IV, V, VI. Berlin: Deutsche Verlagsgesellschaft für Politik und Geschichte, 1922–1927.

Dilks, David. *The Diaries of Sir Alexander Cadogan, 1938–1945.* New York: G. P. Putnam's Sons, 1972.

Documents on Australian Foreign Policy. Vol. 22. 2, 2002. https://www.dfat.gov.au/about-us/publications/historical-documents/volume-22/Pages/default.

Documents on British Foreign Policy, 1919–1939. First series, vols. XVIII, XXVI, XXVII; second series, vols. XXI, XXIII, XIX; third series, vol. II. London: Her Majesty's Stationery Office, 1947–1986.

Dumont, Jean. *Corps universel diplomatique du droit des gens.* Vol. 1. Amsterdam: chez P. Brunel, R. et G. Wetstein, les Janssons Waesberge, l'Honore et Chatelain, 1726.

Essays by the Late Marquess of Salisbury. New York: Dutton, 1905.

Fink, Arthur S. *The Papers of Woodrow Wilson.* Vol. 40. Princeton, NJ: Princeton University Press, 1966.

Foreign Relations of the United States, 1952–1954; 1964–1968; 1969–1972; 1969–1976. Washington, DC: U.S. Government Printing Office, 1984-2006.

Given, John. *The Fragmentary History of Priscus: Attila, the Huns and the Roman Empire, AD 430–476.* Merchantville, NJ: Evolution Publishing, 2014.

Grillon, Pierre, ed. *Les papiers de Richelieu: section politique intérieure, correspondance et papiers d'état.* Vol. 1. Paris: A. Pedone, 1975.

Hill, Henry Bertram. *The Political Testament of Cardinal Richelieu.* Madison: University of Wisconsin Press, 1961.

Hughes, Daniel J. *Moltke on the Art of War: Selected Writings.* Novato, CA: Presidio Press, 1993.

Humphrey, David C., ed. *Foreign Relations of the United States, 1969–1976.* Vol. 2. Washington, DC: U.S. Government Printing Office, 2006.

Jacqueton, Gilbert. *La politique extérieure de Louise de Savoie: relations diplomatiques de la France et de l'Angleterre pendant la captivité de François Ier.* Paris: É. Bouillon, 1892.

Khevenhüller-Metsch, Rudolf Graf, and Hans Schlitter. *Aus der Zeit Maria Theresias. Tagebuch des Fürsten Johann Josef Khevenhüller-Metsch, 1742–1776.* Vol. 3. Wien: Adolf Holzhousen, 1910.

Kohl, Horst. *Die Politischen Reden des Fürsten Bismarck.* 14 vols. Stuttgart: Cotta, 1894.

Lucy, Henry W., ed. *Speeches of the Marquis of Salisbury.* London: Routledge, 1885.

Malalas, John. *The Chronicle of John Malalas.* Translated by Elizabeth Jeffreys, Michael Jeffreys, and Rodger Scott. Leiden: Brill, 2017.

Meisner, Otto Heinrich. *Denkwurdigkeiten des General-Feldmarschalls Alfred Grafen von Waldersee.* Vol. 1. Stuttgart: Deutsche Verlags-Anstalt, 1922.

Metternich, Clemens. *Aus Metternichs Nachgelassenen Papieren.* Edited by Alfons von Klinkowström. Vienna: Wilhelm Braumüller, 1880.

———. *Memoirs of Prince Metternich.* Edited by Prince Richard Metternich. London: Forgotten Books, 2012.

Moltke, Graf, and Ferdinand von Schmerfeld. *Die deutschen Aufmarschplane, 1870–1890.* Berlin: E. S. Mittler & Sohn, 1929.

National Security Archive Electronic Briefing Book No. 193. National Security Archive, George Washington University, 2006.

Oncken, Wilhelm. *Österreich und Preussen im Brefreiungskriege.* Vol. 1. Berlin: G. Grote, 1876.

Petitot, M., ed. *Mémoires du cardinal de Richelieu, sur le règne de Louis XIII.* 10 vols. Paris: Foucault, 1823.

Predelli, Riccardo. *I libri commemoriali della republica di Venezia: regesti.* Vol. 5. Cambridge: Cambridge University Press, 2012.

Pribram, Alfred Franzis. *The Secret Treaties of Austria-Hungary 1879–1914.* Vol. 4. Cambridge, MA: Harvard University Press, 1920.

Prokopios. *The Secret History: With Related Texts.* Edited by Anthony Kaldellis. Indianapolis, IN: Hackett, 2010.

Romanin, Samuele. *Storia documentata di Venezia.* Second edition. Vol. 3. Venice: Giusto Fuga, 1913.

Roper, A., A. Bosvile, and T. Leigh, eds. *Letters of the Cardinal Duke de Richelieu: Great Minister of State to Lewis [sic] XIII of France Faithfully Translated from the Original by T. B.* London, 1698.

Schlitter, Hans, ed. *Correspondance Secrète entre le Comte A. W. Kauitz-Rietberg et le Baron Ignaz de Koch.* Paris: E. Plon, Nourrit, 1899.

Schneider, Karl. *Aus Österreichs Vergangenheit, Nr. 11, Aus dem Briefwechsel Maria Theresias mit Joseph II.* Wien: Schulwissenschaftlicher Verlag, 1917.

Schwertfeger, Bernhard. *Die Diplomatischen Akten des Auswärtigen Amtes, 1871–1914.* 5 vols. Berlin: Deutsche Verlagsgesellschaft für Politik und Geschichte, 1927.

Self, Robert, ed. *The Neville Chamberlain Diary Letters.* Vol. 4. Aldershot, UK: Ashgate, 2000.

Sonnino, Paul. *The Political Testament of Cardinal Richelieu.* Lanham, MD: Rowman & Littlefield, 2020.

Thiriet, Freddy. *Régestes de délibérations du sénat de Venise concernant la Romanie.* Vol. 3. Paris: Mouton & Co., 1961.

Walker, Mack. *Metternich's Europe: Selected Documents.* London: Macmillan, 1968.

Secondary Sources

Acheson, Dean. *Power and Diplomacy.* Cambridge, MA: Harvard University Press, 1958.

———. *Present at the Creation.* New York: Norton, 1969.

Adams, Lestyn. *Brothers across the Ocean: British Foreign Policy and the Origins of the Anglo-American "Special Relationship" 1900–1905.* London: I. B. Tauris, 2005.

Adamthwaite, Anthony. "War Origins Again." *Journal of Modern History* 56, no. 1 (March 1984): 100–115.

Aksan, Virginia, and Daniel Goffman, eds. *The Early Modern Ottomans: Remapping the Empire*. Cambridge: Cambridge University Press, 2007.

Albrecht-Carrié, René. *A Diplomatic History of Europe Since the Congress of Vienna*. New York: Harper & Brothers, 1958.

Allison, Graham T. *Destined for War: Can America and China Escape Thucydides's Trap?* New York: Mariner Books, 2018.

———. *Essence of Decision: Explaining the Cuban Missile Crisis*. Boston: Little, Brown & Co., 1971.

Ambrose, Stephen. *Nixon: The Triumph of a Politician, 1962–72*. New York: Simon & Schuster, 1989.

Angelov, Alexander Borislavov. "Conversion and Empire: Byzantine Missionaries, Foreign Rulers, and Christian Narratives (ca. 300–900)." PhD dissertation, University of Michigan Library, 2011.

Avakov, Alexander V. *Two Thousand Years of Economic Statistics: Population, GDP at PPP, and GDP Per Capita*. Vol. 1. New York: Algora Publishing, 2017.

Babinger, Franz. *Mehmed the Conqueror and His Time*. Edited by William C. Hickman. Translated by Ralph Manheim. Princeton, NJ: Princeton University Press, 1978.

Baer, Marc David. *The Ottomans: Khans, Caesars, and Caliphs*. New York: Basic Books, 2021.

Baker, A. D., III. "Battlefleets and Diplomacy: Naval Disarmament between the Two World Wars." *Warship International* 26, no. 3 (1989): 217–255.

Barbaro, Nicolò. *Giornale Dell'assedio Di Costantinopoli, 1453*. Vienna: Libreria Tendler & Co., 1856.

Barkey, Karen. *Empire of Difference: The Ottomans in Comparative Perspective*. Cambridge: Cambridge University Press, 2008.

Barnett, Correlli. *The Collapse of British Power*. New York: Morrow, 1972.

Bartoletti, Andrea. *Escaping the Deadly Embrace: How Encirclement Causes Major War*. Ithaca, NY: Cornell University Press, 2022.

Bassett, Richard. *For God and Kaiser: The Imperial Austrian Army, 1619–1918*. New Haven, CT: Yale University Press, 2015.

Beale, Howard K. *Theodore Roosevelt and the Rise of America to World Power*. Baltimore: Johns Hopkins University Press, 1984.

Beales, Derek. *Joseph II: In the Shadow of Maria Theresa, 1741–1780*, Vol. 1. Cambridge: Cambridge University Press, 1987.

Becirovic, Muamer. *Clemens Wenzel von Metternich oder das Gleichgewicht der Mächte*. Hamburg: Osburg Verlag, 2024.

Beck, Robert J. "Munich's Lessons Reconsidered." *International Security* 14, no. 2 (Fall 1989): 161–191.

Beisner, Robert L. *Dean Acheson: A Life in the Cold War* (New York: Oxford Academic, 2023).

Bellaigue, Christopher de. *The Lion House: The Coming of a King*. New York: Farrar, Straus and Giroux, 2022.

Belloc, Hilaire. *Richelieu: A Study*. Philadelphia: J. B. Lippincott Co., 1929.

Berridge, G. R. *Diplomacy: Theory and Practice*. Sixth edition. London: Palgrave Macmillan, 2022.

Berridge, G. R., Maurice Keens-Soper, and T. G. Otte. *Diplomatic Theory from Machiavelli to Kissinger*. Basingstoke, UK: Palgrave, 2001.

Bersch, Julia, and Graciela Kaminsky. "Financial Globalization in the 19th Century: Germany as a Financial Center." George Washington University Working Paper, September 2008.

Best, Anthony, and Hugh Cortazzi, eds. *British Foreign Secretaries and Japan, 1850–1990: Aspects of the Evolution of British Foreign Policy*. Amsterdam: Amsterdam University Press, 2018.

Bew, John. *Castlereagh: A Life*. Oxford: Oxford University Press, 2012.

Bew, John, and Andrew Ehrhardt. "The Last Conservative Statesman." *The American Interest*, April 10, 2017.

Black, Jeremy. *A History of Diplomacy*. London: Reaktion Books, 2010.

Blanchard, Jean-Vincent. *Éminence: Cardinal Richelieu and the Rise of France*. New York: Walker & Co., 2011.

Blanning, Tim. *Frederick the Great: King of Prussia*. New York: Random House, 2016.

———. *The Pursuit of Glory: Five Revolutions That Made Modern Europe,1648–1815*. New York: Penguin Books, 2007.

Blockley, R. C. *East Roman Foreign Policy*. Leeds, UK: Francis Cairns, 1992.

———. "Subsidies and Diplomacy. Rome and Persia in Late Antiquity." *Phoenix* 39, no. 1 (Spring 1985): 62–74.

Bolger, Brian Patrick. "The Age of Diplomacy Is Over," *The National Interest*, December 4, 2023.

Bonney, Richard. *Society and Government in France under Richelieu and Mazarin, 1624–61*. Houndmills, UK: Macmillan, 1988.

———. *The Thirty Years' War 1618–1648*. Oxford: Osprey, 2002.

Bourne, Kenneth. *Britain and the Balance of Power in North America, 1815–1908*. Berkeley: University of California Press, 1967.

———. *The Foreign Policy of Victorian England, 1830–1902*. Oxford: Clarendon Press, 1970.

Bourrilly, Victor-Louis. *Guillaume du Bellay*. Paris: Société Nouveille de Librairie et D'Édition, 1905.

Bouverie, Tim. *Appeasement: Chamberlain, Hitler, and the Road to War*. New York: Tim Duggan Books, 2019.

Bowie, Robert R., and Richard H. Immerman. *Waging Peace: How Eisenhower Shaped an Enduring Cold War Strategy*. New York: Oxford University Press, 1998.

Boyce, R, and J. A. Maiolo, eds. *The Origins of World War Two: The Debate Continues*. New York: Palgrave Macmillan, 2003.

Brands, Hal, ed. *The New Makers of Modern Strategy: From the Ancient World to the Digital Age*. Princeton, NJ: Princeton University Press, 2023.

———. "The Triumph and Tragedy of Diplomatic History." *Texas National Security Review* 1, no. 1 (December 2017).

———. *The Twilight Struggle*. New Haven, CT: Yale University Press, 2022.

Braubach, Max. *Versailles und Wien von Ludwig XIV bis Kaunitz: die Vorstadien der diplomatischen Revolution im 18. Jahrhundert*. Bonn: L. Röhrscheid, 1952.

Bridge, F. R. *The Habsburg Monarchy among the Great Powers, 1815–1918*. Oxford: Berg Publishers, 1990.

Broadberry, Stephen, and Kevin H. O'Rourke, eds. *The Cambridge Economic History of Modern Europe*, Vol. 2: *1870 to the Present*. Cambridge: Cambridge University Press, 2010.

Brodie, Bernard, ed. *The Absolute Weapon: Atomic Power and World Order*. New York: Harcourt, 1946.

Broomhall, Susan, ed. *Women and Power at the French Court, 1483–1563*. Amsterdam: Amsterdam University Press, 2018.

Browning, Reed. *The War of the Austrian Succession*. New York: St. Martin's Press, 1995.

Brummett, Palmira. *Ottoman Seapower and Levantine Diplomacy in the Age of Discovery* Albany: State University of New York Press, 1994.

Buchanan, Patrick J. *Nixon's White House Wars: The Battles That Made and Broke a President and Divided America Forever*. New York: Crown Forum, 2017.

Bull, Hedley. *The Control of the Arms Race*. New York: Frederick A. Praeger, 1961.

Bundy, William. *A Tangled Web: The Making of Foreign Policy in the Nixon Presidency*. New York: Farrar, Straus and Giroux, 1998.

Burckhardt, Carl J. *Richelieu and His Age*. Translated by Bernard Hoy. 3 vols. New York: Harcourt, Brace & World, 1970.

———. *Richelieu and His Age: Assertion of Power and Cold War*. New York: Harcourt, Brace & World, 1970.

Burckhardt, Jacob. *The Civilization of the Renaissance in Italy*. London: George Allen & Unwin, 1921.

Burns, Alexander S., ed. *The Changing Face of Old Regime Warfare: Essays in Honour of Christopher Duffy*. Warwick, UK: Helion & Co., 2022.

Burns, William J. *The Back Channel: A Memoir of American Diplomacy and the Case for Its Renewal*. New York: Random House, 2020.

Burr, William, ed. *The Kissinger Transcripts*. New York: New Press, 1998.

Campanella, Tommaso. *A Discourse Touching the Spanish Monarchy*. London: Philemon Stephens, 1654.

Cassis, Youseff. *Capitals of Capital: A History of International Financial Centres, 1790–2005*. Cambridge: Cambridge University Press, 2006.

"Cato." *Guilty Men*. London: Victor Gollancz, 1940.

Cecil, Lamar. *The German Diplomatic Service, 1871–1914*. Princeton, NJ: Princeton University Press, 1976.

Center, Seth, and Emma Bates, eds. *After Disruption: Historical Perspectives on the Future of International Order*. Washington, DC: Center for Strategic and International Studies, 2020.

Chambers, D. S. *The Imperial Age of Venice 1380–1580*. London: Thames & Hudson, 1970.

Charmley, John. *Chamberlain and the Lost Peace*. Chicago: Ivan R. Dee, 1990.

——. *Splendid Isolation? Britain and the Balance of Power 1874–1914*. London: Hodder & Stoughton, 1999.

Chen, Jian, and David L. Wilson. "'All under the Heaven Is Great Chaos': Beijing, the Sino-Soviet Border Clashes and the Turn towards Sino-American Rapprochement, 1968–9." *Cold War International History Project Bulletin* 11, no. 157–175 (Winter 1998): 161.

Chojnacki, Stanley. "Social Identity in Renaissance Venice: The Second Serrata." *Renaissance Studies* 8, no. 4 (December 1994): 341–358.

Chrastil, Rachel. *Bismarck's War: The Franco-Prussian War and the Making of Modern Europe*. New York: Basic Books, 2023.

Church, William F. *Richelieu and Reason of State*. Princeton, NJ: Princeton University Press, 1972.

Churchill, Winston S. *The Second World War*, Vol. 1: *The Gathering Storm*. Boston: Houghton Mifflin, 1948.

Clark, Christopher. *Iron Kingdom: The Rise and Downfall of Prussia 1600–1947*. Cambridge, MA: Belknap Press, 2006.

——. *The Sleepwalkers: How Europe Went to War in 1914*. New York: Harper, 2014.

Clodfelter, Michael. *Warfare and Armed Conflicts: A Statistical Encyclopedia of Casualty and Other Figures, 1494–2007*. Jefferson, NC: McFarland & Co., 2008.

Cohen, Anver. "Joseph Chamberlain, Lord Lansdowne and British Foreign Policy 1901–1903: From Collaboration to Confrontation." *Australian Journal of Politics and History* 43, no. 2 (April 1997): 122–134.

Cohen, Eliot A. *Conquered into Liberty: Two Centuries of Battles along the Great Warpath That Made the American Way of War*. New York: Free Press, 2011.

Colby, Elbridge A., *The Strategy of Denial: American Defense in an Age of Great Power Competition*. New Haven, CT: Yale University Press, 2021.

Cooper, Andrew F., Jorge Heine, and Ramesh Thakur, eds. *The Oxford Handbook of Modern Diplomacy*. Oxford: Oxford University Press, 2013.

Corbett, Julian. *Some Principles of Maritime Strategy*. London: Longmans Green & Co., 1918.

Courtois, Stéphane, et al. *Black Book of Communism: Crimes, Terror, Repression*. Cambridge, MA: Harvard University Press, 1999.

Craig, Gordon A. *The Politics of the Prussian Army 1640–1945*. London: Oxford University Press, 1955.

Craig, Gordon A., and Felix Gilbert, eds. *The Diplomats 1919–1939*. Princeton, NJ: Princeton University Press, 1981.

Crankshaw, Edward. *Bismarck*. New York: Viking Press, 1981.

Crocker, Chester A., Fen Osler Hampson, and Pamela Aall, eds. *Diplomacy and the Future of World Order*. Washington, DC: Georgetown University Press, 2021.

Crowley, Roger. *City of Fortune: How Venice Ruled the Seas*. New York: Random House, 2013.

Croxton, Derek. "The Peace of Westphalia of 1648 and the Origins of Sovereignty." *International History Review* 21, no. 3 (September 1999): 569–591.

Dade, Eva Kathrin. *Madame de Pompadour: Die Mätresse und die Diplomatie.* Köln: Böhlau Verlag, 2010.

Daggett, Stephen. "Costs of Major U.S. Wars." Congressional Research Service, June 29, 2010.

Dallek, Robert. *Nixon and Kissinger: Partners in Power.* New York: Harper Collins, 2007.

Darwin, John. *The Empire Project: The Rise and Fall of the British World-System 1830–1970.* Cambridge: Cambridge University Press, 2009.

De Vivo, Filippo. "How to Read Venetian *Relazioni.*" *Renaissance and Reformation* 34, no. 1–2 (Winter-Spring 2011): 25–59.

De Wicquefort, M. *L'histoire des Provinces-Unies, confirmée & eclaircie par des preuves authentiques.* Vol. 3. The Hague: T. Johnson, 1719.

Decker, Michael J. *The Sasanian Empire at War: Persia, Rome, and the Rise of Islam.* Yardley, UK: Westholme, 2022.

Dehio, Ludwig. *The Precarious Balance: Four Centuries of the European Power Struggle.* New York: Random House, 1959.

Dickson, P.G.M. *Finance and Government under Maria Theresia: 1740–1780.* Oxford: Clarendon Press, 1987.

Dickson, Peter W. *Kissinger and the Meaning of History.* Cambridge: Cambridge University Press, 1978.

Dobrynin, Anatoly. *In Confidence: Moscow's Ambassador to America's Six Cold War Presidents, 1962–1986.* New York: Random House, 1995.

Dockrill, M. L., and Zara S. Steiner. "The Foreign Office at the Paris Peace Conference in 1919." *International History Review* 2, no. 1 (January 1980): 55–86.

Doelger, Franz. *Byzanz und die Europaeische Staatenwelt.* Ettal, Germany: Buch-Kunstverlag, 1953.

Downing, Brian M. *The Military Revolution and Political Change: Origins of Democracy and Autocracy in Early Modern Europe.* Princeton, NJ: Princeton University Press, 1992.

Drummond, Diane. "Sustained British Investment in Overseas Railways, 1830–1914." In *Across the Borders: Financing the World's Railways in the Nineteenth and Twentieth Centuries.* Aldershot, UK: Ashgate, 2008.

Duffy, Christopher. *The Army of Maria Theresa: The Armed Forces of Imperial Austria, 1740–1780.* New York: Hippocrene Books, 1977.

———. *The Military Experience in the Age of Reason.* New York: Atheneum, 1988.

Dursteler, Eric R. "The Bailo in Constantinople: Crisis and Career in Venice's Early Modern Diplomatic Corps." *Mediterranean Historical Review* 16, no. 2 (2001): 1–30.

Dwyer, Philip G., ed. *The Rise of Prussia 1700–1830.* London: Routledge, 2000.

Eizenstat, Stuart. *The Art of Diplomacy: How American Negotiators Reached Historic Agreements That Changed the World.* Lanham, MD: Rowman & Littlefield, 2024.

Elliott, J. H. *Richelieu and Olivares.* Cambridge: Cambridge University Press, 1984.

Fagniez, G. "La mission du père Joseph a Ratisbonne 1630 (Suite et Fin)." *Revue historique* 28, no. 1 (1885): 33–88.

Fairgrieve, James. *Geography and World Power.* London: University of London Press, 1927.

Fang, Percy Zucheng. *Zhou Enlai: A Profile.* Beijing: Foreign Language Press, 1986.

Farr, Jason. "Point: The Westphalia Legacy and the Modern Nation State." *International Social Science Review* 80, no. 3/4 (2005): 156–159.

Farrell, John A. *Richard Nixon: The Life.* New Haven, CT: Doubleday, 2017.

Feiling, Keith. *The Life of Neville Chamberlain.* Hamden, UK: Archon, 1970.

Ferguson, Niall. *Empire: The Rise and Demise of the British World Order and the Lessons for Global Power.* New York: Basic Books, 2002.

———. *Kissinger 1923-1968: The Idealist.* New York: Penguin Books, 2015.

———. *The Pity of War.* New York: Basic Books, 1999.

Ferguson, Wallace K., ed., et al. "Changing Attitudes Towards the State." In *Facets of the Renaissance.* New York: Harper & Row, 1963.

Fettweis, Christopher J. *The Pursuit of Dominance: 2000 Years of Superpower Grand Strategy.* Oxford, UK: Oxford University Press, 2023.

Figliuolo, Bruno. *Il diplomatico e il trattatista: Ermolao Barbaro ambasciatore della serenissima e il de officio legati.* Vol. 2. Naples: Guida, 1999.

Fishlow, Albert. "Lessons from the Past: Capital Markets during the 19th Century and the Interwar Period." *International Organization* 39, no. 3 (1985): 383–439.

Förster, Stig. "Der Deutsche Generalstab und die Illusion des Kurzen Krieges, 1871–1914: Metakritik Eines Mythos." In *Militärgeschichtliche Mitteilungen.* Vol. 54. Freiburg: Oldenbourg, 1995.

Fox, Edward Whiting. *History in Geographic Perspective: The Other France.* New York: W. W. Norton & Co., 1971.

Francke, Kuno, ed. *The German Classics of the Nineteenth and Twentieth Centuries.* Vol. 10. Project Gutenberg eBook, 2004.

Freedman, Lawrence. "Alliance and the British Way in Warfare." *Review of International Studies* 21, no. 2 (April, 1995): 145–158.

———. *Strategy: A History.* New York: Oxford University Press, 2013.

Freeman, John F. "Louise of Savoy: A Case of Maternal Opportunism." *Sixteenth Century Journal* 3, no. 2 (October 1972): 77–98.

Freeman, Philip, and David Kennedy, eds. "Diplomacy and War in the Relations between Byzantium and the Sassanids in the Fifth Century AD." In *The Defense of the Roman and Byzantine East: Proceedings of a Colloquium Held at the University of Sheffield.* Oxford: British Institute of Archaeology at Ankara, 1986.

French, David. *Deterrence, Coercion, and Appeasement: British Grand Strategy, 1919–1940.* Oxford: Oxford University Press, 2022.

Frieda, Leonie. *Francis I: The Maker of Modern France.* New York: Harper Collins, 2018.

Friedberg, Aaron. *The Weary Titan: Britain and the Experience of Relative Decline, 1985–1905.* Princeton, NJ: Princeton University Press, 2011.

Fubini, Riccardo. "L'ambasciatore Nel XV Secolo: Due Trattati E Una Biografia (Bernard De Rosier, Ermolao Barbaro, Vespasiano Da Bisticci)." *Mélanges de l'ecole française de Rome. moyen âge* 108, no. 2 (1996): 645–665.

Fukuyama, Francis. *The End of History and the Last Man.* New York: Free Press, 1992.

Fuller, Joseph Vincent. *Bismarck's Diplomacy at Its Zenith.* Cambridge, MA: Harvard University Press, 1967.

Furnia, Arthur H. *The Diplomacy of Appeasement: Anglo-French Relations and the Prelude to World War II, 1931–1938.* Washington, DC: University Press, 1960.

Gaddis, John Lewis. *The Cold War: A New History.* New York: Penguin Books, 2005.

———. *Strategies of Containment: A Critical Appraisal of American National Security Policy during the Cold War.* Oxford: Oxford University Press, 2005.

———. "What Is 'Grand Strategy'? American Grand Strategy after War." Unpublished manuscript. Triangle Institute for Security Studies and Duke University Program on American Grand Strategy, 2009.

Garthoff, Raymond. *Détente and Confrontation: American-Soviet Relations from Nixon to Reagan.* Washington, DC: Brookings Institution, 1985.

Gerson, Michael S., et al. "The Sino-Soviet Border Conflict Deterrence, Escalation, and the Threat of Nuclear War in 1969." Center for Naval Analysis, November 2010.

Gibbon, Edward. *The Decline and Fall of the Roman Empire.* Vol. 3. Alfred A. Knopf, 1993.

Gibbs, N. H. *Grand Strategy.* Vol. 1. London: Her Majesty's Stationery Office, 1976.

Gilbert, Felix. *To the Farewell Address: Ideas of Early American Foreign Policy.* Princeton, NJ: Princeton University Press, 1961.

Gilbert, Martin. *The Appeasers.* Boston: Houghton Mifflin, 1963.

Gilmour, David. *Curzon: Imperial Statesman 1859–1925.* New York: Farrar, Straus and Giroux, 2006.

Gilpin, Robert. *War and Change in World Politics.* Cambridge: Cambridge University Press, 1981.

Gluzman, Renard. *Venetian Shipping from the Days of Glory to Decline, 1453–1571.* Leiden: Brill, 2021.

Goerlitz, Walter. *History of the German General Staff 1657-194*. London: Westview, 1985.

Gooch, G. P., and J.H.B. Masterman. *A Century of British Foreign Policy*. London: Council for the Study of International Relations, 1917.

Gordon, C. D. *The Age of Attila: Fifth Century Byzantium and the Barbarians*. Ann Arbor: University of Michigan Press, 2013.

———. "Subsidies in Roman Imperial Defense." *Phoenix* 3, no. 2 (1949): 60–69.

Gordon, Kermit, ed. *Agenda for the Nation: Papers on Domestic and Foreign Policy Issues*. Washington, DC: Brookings Institution, 1968.

Gould, Eliga H. *Among the Powers of the Earth: The American Revolution and the Making of a New World Empire*. Cambridge, MA: Harvard University Press, 2014.

Gray, Colin S., and Jeffery G. Barlow. "Inexcusable Restraint: The Decline of American Military Power in the 1970s." *International Security* 10, no. 2 (Fall 1985): 27–69.

Greatrex, G., and Jonathan Bardill. "Antiochus the 'Praepositus': A Persian Eunuch at the Court of Theodosius II." *Dumbarton Oaks Papers* 50 (1996): 171–197.

Green, Michael J. *By More than Providence: Grand Strategy and American Power in the Asia Pacific since 1783*. New York: Columbia University Press, 2017.

Greene, Sally. "Peace in Whose Time? Neville Chamberlain's Other Mistake." *Anglican and Episcopal History* 64, no. 2 (June 1995): 138–147.

Grenville, J.A.S. "Lansdowne's Abortive Project of 12 March 1901 for a Secret Agreement with Germany." *Bulletin of the Institute of Historical Research* 27, no. 76 (November 1954): 201–213.

Grenville, John A. S. *Lord Salisbury and Foreign Policy*. London: Athlone Press, 1964.

Gross, Leo. "The Peace of Westphalia, 1648–1948." *American Journal of International Law* 42, no. 1 (January 1948): 20–41.

Grygiel, Jakub. *Great Powers and Geopolitical Change*. Baltimore: Johns Hopkins University Press, 2006.

———. *Return of the Barbarians: Confronting Non-State Actors from Ancient Rome to the Present*. Cambridge: Cambridge University Press, 2018.

———. "Stand Up or Sit Down." *The American Interest*, March 7, 2014.

Guérard, Albert. *France: A Modern History*. Ann Arbor: University of Michigan Press, 1969.

Guicciardini, Francesco. *The History of Italy*. London: Z. Stuart, 1763.

Hale, J. R., ed. *Renaissance Venice*. London: Faber and & Faber, 1974.

Hamerow, Theodore S., ed. "A Historic Necessity." In *Otto von Bismarck: A Historical Assessment*. Boston: D. C. Heath and Co., 1962.

Hamilton, Keith. *Bertie of Thame: Edwardian Ambassador*. Woodbridge, UK: Boydell Press, 1990.

Hamilton, Keith, and Richard Langhorne. *The Practice of Diplomacy: Its Evolution, Theory and Administration*. London: Routledge, 2011.

Hanhimäki, Jussi. *The Flawed Architect: Henry Kissinger and American Foreign Policy*. New York: Oxford University Press, 2004.

Hanson, Victor Davis. *The End of Everything: How Wars Descend into Annihilation*. New York: Basic Books, 2024.

Hart, B. H. Liddell. *The British Way of War*. London: Faber & Faber, 1932.

———. *The Defense of Britain*. London: Faber & Faber, 1939.

———. *Europe in Arms*. London: Faber & Faber, 1937.

Hayes, Bascom Barry. *Bismarck and Mitteleuropa*. London: Associated University Presses, 1994.

Hazard, Harry W., and Norman P. Zacour, eds. *A History of the Crusades: The Impact of the Crusades on Europe*. Vol. 6. Madison: University of Wisconsin Press, 1989.

Herring, George C. *America's Longest War: The United States and Vietnam, 1950-1975*. New York: Wiley, 1979.

———. *From Colony to Superpower: U.S. Foreign Relations since 1776*. New York: Oxford University Press, 2008.

———. *Years of Peril and Ambition, U.S. Foreign Relations, 1776-1921*. New York: Oxford University Press, 2017.

Hersh, Seymour M. *The Price of Power: Kissinger in the Nixon White House*. New York: Summit Books, 1983.

Hexter, J. H. *The Vision of Politics on the Eve of the Reformation: More, Machiavelli and Seysse*. New York: Basic Books, 1973.

Hill, David Jayne. *A History of Diplomacy in the International Development of Europe: The Struggle for Universal Empire*. Vol. 1. New York: Longmans, Green & Co., 1905.

Hinsley, F. H. *Power and the Pursuit of Peace*. Cambridge: Cambridge University Press, 1963.

Hitchens, Christopher. *The Trial of Henry Kissinger*. New York: Verso, 2001.

Höbelt, Lothar. "The Impact of the Rákóczi Rebellion on Habsburg Strategy: Incentives and Opportunity Costs." *War in History* 13, no. 1 (2006): 2–15.

Hochedlinger, Michael. *Austria's Wars of Emergence*. New York: Routledge, 2013.

Holborn, Hajo. "Bismarck's Realpolitik." *Journal of the History of Ideas* 21, no. 1 (March 1960): 84–98.

———. *A History of Modern Germany 1840–1945*. Princeton, NJ: Princeton University Press, 1982.

Hollingsworth, Mary. *Catherine de' Medici: The Life and Times of the Serpent Queen*. New York: Pegasus Books, 2024.

Holt, P. M., Ann K. S. Lambton, and Bernard Lewis, eds. *The Cambridge History of Islam: The Central Islamic Lands from Pre-Islamic Times to the First World War*. Vol. 1A. Cambridge: Cambridge University Press, 2008.

Hopkins, Keith, and M. K. Hopkins. "Eunuchs in Politics in the Later Roman Empire." *Proceedings of the Cambridge Philological Society* 189, no. 9 (1963): 62–80.

Howard, Christopher. "The Policy of Isolation." *Historical Journal* 10, no. 1 (1967): 77–88.

Howard, Michael. *The Continental Commitment and the British Way in Warfare: A Reappraisal*. London: Maurice Temple Smith, 1972.

Hoyer, Katja. *Blood and Iron: The Rise and Fall of the German Empire 1871–1918*. Cheltenham, UK: History Press, 2022.

Hunt, William A. *Melvin Laird: The Foundation of the Post-Vietnam Military*. Washington, DC: U.S. Government Printing Office, 2015.

Husband, William B. "Soviet Perceptions of U.S. 'Positions-of-Strength' Diplomacy in the 1970s." *World Politics* 31, no. 4 (July 1970): 495–517.

Hutson, Matthew. "How Artificial Intelligence Could Negotiate Better Deals for Humans." *Science*. September 11, 2017.

Ikenberry, John G. *After Victory: Institutions, Strategic Restraint, and the Rebuilding of Order after Major Wars*. Princeton, NJ: Princeton University Press, 2001.

Iluk, J. "The Export of Gold from the Roman Empire to Barbarian Countries from the 4th to the 6th Centuries." *Münstersche Beitraege zur Antiken Handelsgeschichte* 4, no. 1 (1985): 79–103.

Inalcik, Halil. *The Ottoman Empire: The Classical Age, 1300–1600*. London: Weidenfeld & Nicolson, 1973.

Inboden, William. *Peacemaker: Ronald Reagan, the Cold War, and the World on the Brink*. London: Penguin Random House, 2022.

Indyk, Martin. *Master of the Game: Henry Kissinger and the Art of Middle East*. New York: Knopf, 2021.

Ingrao, Charles W. *The Habsburg Monarchy, 1618–1815*. Second edition. New York: Cambridge University Press, 2000.

———. "Paul W. Schroeder's Balance of Power: Stability or Anarchy?" *International History Review* 16, no. 4 (November 1994): 681–700.

Isaacson, Walter. *Kissinger: A Biography*. New York: Simon & Schuster, 1992.

Isom-Verhaaren, Christine. *Allies with the Infidel: The Ottoman and French Alliance in the Sixteenth Century*. London: I. B. Tauris, 2011.

Jansen, Sharon L. *The Monstrous Regiment of Women: Female Rulers in Early Modern Europe*. New York: Palgrave Macmillan, 2002.

Jensen, De Lamar. "French Diplomacy and the Wars of Religion." *Sixteenth Century Journal* 5, no. 2 (25–43): October 1974.

———. "The Ottoman Turks in Sixteenth Century French Diplomacy." *Sixteenth Century Journal* 16, no. 4 (Winter 1985): 451–470.

Jervis, Robert. "Cooperation under the Security Dilemma." *World Politics* 30, no. 2 (January 1978): 167–214.

———. "The Many Faces of SALT." *Journal of Cold War Studies* 24, no. 4 (Fall 2022): 198–214.

———. *The Meaning of the Nuclear Revolution: Statecraft and the Prospect of Armageddon.* Ithaca, NY: Cornell University Press, 1990.

Jervis, Robert, Jack S. Levy, and David Wetzel, eds. *Systems, Stability, and Statecraft: Essays on the International History of Modern Europe* (New York: Palgrave Macmillan, 2004).

Jian, Chen. *Zhou Enlai: A Life.* Cambridge, MA: Belknap Press, 2024.

Jones, Archer. *The Art of War in the Western World.* Oxford: Oxford University Press, 1987.

Jones, W. R. "The Image of the Barbarian in Medieval Europe." *Comparative Studies in Society and History* 13, no. 4 (October 1971): 376–407.

Kagan, Donald. *The Outbreak of the Peloponnesian War.* Ithaca, NY: Cornell University Press, 1969.

Kagan, Robert. *Dangerous Nation.* London: Atlantic, 2006.

Kalb, Marvin, and Bernard Kalb. *Kissinger.* New York: Little, Brown & Co., 1974.

Kaldellis, Anthony. *The New Roman Empire: A History of Byzantium.* Oxford: Oxford University Press, 2023.

Kane, Tim. "Global U.S. Troop Deployment, 1950–2005." Heritage Foundation, May 24, 2006.

Kann, Robert A. "Metternich: A Reappraisal of His Impact on International Relations." *Journal of Modern History* 32, no. 4 (1960): 333–339.

Kaplan, Herbert H. *Russia and the Outbreak of the Seven Years' War.* Berkeley: University of California Press, 1968.

Kaplan, Lawrence S. *Colonies into Nations: American Diplomacy, 1763–1801.* New York: Macmillan, 1974.

Kaplan, Robert. *The Revenge of Geography: What the Map Tells Us about Coming Conflicts and the Battle against Fate.* New York: Random House, 2013.

Kaufman, Victor S. *Confronting Communism: U.S. and British Policies toward China.* Columbia: University of Missouri Press, 2001.

Keens-Soper, Maurice, and Karl W. Schweizer, eds. *François de Callières: The Art of Diplomacy.* New York: Leicester University Press, 1983.

Kennan, George F. *The Decline of Bismarck's European Order: Franco-Russian Relations, 1875–1890.* Princeton, NJ: Princeton University Press, 1979.

———. *Memoirs 1925–1950.* Boston: Little, Brown & Co., 1967.

———. "The Sources of Soviet Conduct." *Foreign Affairs,* July 1, 1947.

Kennedy, A. L. *Old Diplomacy and New, 1876–1922: From Salisbury to Lloyd-George.* London: Murray, 1922.

Kennedy, John F. "On Diplomacy in the Nuclear Age." *International Journal* 29, no. 1 (Winter 1973/1974): 67–70.

Kennedy, Paul. *The Realities behind Diplomacy: Background Influences on British External Policy, 1865–1980.* London: Allen & Unwin, 1981.

———. *The Rise of the Anglo-German Antagonism 1860–1914.* London: Allen & Unwin, 1980.

———. *The Rise and Fall of British Naval Mastery.* London: Macmillan, 1983.

———. *The Rise and Fall of the Great Powers.* London: Fontana, 1989.

———. *Strategy and Diplomacy 1870–1945.* London: Fontana, 1983.

———. "A Time to Appease." *The National Interest,* August 2010.

———. "The Tradition of Appeasement in British Foreign Policy 1865–1939." *British Journal of International Studies* 2, no. 3 (October 1976): 195–215.

Kennedy, Paul, and William Hitchcock, eds. "The Great Powers in the New International System, 1919–1923." In *From War to Peace.* New Haven, CT: Yale University Press, 2000.

Keohane, Nannerl O. *Philosophy and the State in France: The Renaissance to the Enlightenment.* Princeton, NJ: Princeton University Press, 1980.

Kepinevich, Andrew, et al. "Strategy in Austerity." Center for Strategic and Budgetary Assessments, 2012.

Kerry, Simon. *Lansdowne: The Last Great Whig.* London: Unicorn, 2017.

Kessel, Eberhard. *Moltke.* Stuttgart: Koehler Verlag, 1957.

Keynes, John Maynard. *The Economic Consequences of the Peace.* New York: Harcourt, Brace & Howe, 1920.

King, Margaret L. *The Death of the Child Valerio Marcello*. Chicago: University of Chicago Press, 1994.

Kissinger, Henry. *Diplomacy*. London: Simon & Schuster, 1994.

———. "Domestic Structure and Foreign Policy." *Daedalus* 95, no. 2 (Spring 1966): 503–529.

———. "Force and Diplomacy in the Nuclear Age." *Foreign Affairs*, April 1, 1956.

———. *On China*. New York: Penguin Books, 2012.

———. *The White House Years*. Boston: Little, Brown & Co., 1979.

———. *World Order*. London: Penguin Books, 2014.

———. *A World Restored: Metternich, Castlereagh and the Problems of Peace, 1812–22*. Boston: Houghton Mifflin, 1973.

Kissinger, Henry A., Eric Schmidt, and Daniel Huttenlocher. *The Age of AI: And Our Human Future*. New York: Little, Brown & Co., 2021.

Klingenstein, Grete. *Der Aufstieg des Hauses Kaunitz: Studien zur Herkunft und Bildung des Staatskanzlers Wenzel Anton*. Göttingen, Germany: Vandenhoeck & Ruprecht, 1975.

Knecht, R. J. *Francis I*. Cambridge: Cambridge University Press, 1982.

———. *Renaissance Warrior and Patron: The Reign of Francis*. Cambridge: Cambridge University Press, 1994.

———. *Richelieu*. New York: Longman, 1991.

———. *Rise and Fall of Renaissance France 1483–1610*. Oxford: Blackwell, 2001.

Kotkin, Stephen. "Five Futures of Russia." *Foreign Affairs*, April 18, 2024.

Kralev, Nicholas. *Diplomatic Tradecraft*. London: Cambridge University Press, 2024.

Krasner, Stephen. "Compromising Westphalia." *International Security* 20, no. 3 (Winter 1996): 115–151.

Kroenig, Matthew. *The Return of Great Power Rivalry: Democracy versus Autocracy from the Ancient World to the U.S. and China*. Oxford: Oxford University Press, 2020.

Kruger, Peter, and Paul Schroeder, eds. *The Transformation of European Politics, 1763–1848: Episode or Model in Modern History?* Munster, Germany: Lit Verlag, 2002.

Kundnani, Hans. *The Paradox of German Power*. Oxford: Oxford University Press, 2015.

Kupchan, Charles A. *How Enemies Become Friends: The Sources of Stable Peace*. Princeton, NJ: Princeton University Press, 2012.

Lambert, Andrew. *Seapower States*. New Haven, CT: Yale University Press, 2018.

Lane, Frederic C. *Venice: A Maritime Republic*. Baltimore: Johns Hopkins University Press, 1973.

Langer, William. *European Alliances and Alignments 1871–1890*. New York: Vintage Books, 1964.

Langhorne, Richard. "Current Developments in Diplomacy: Who Are the Diplomats Now?" *Diplomacy & Statecraft* 8, no. 2 (July 1997): 1–15.

Lattimore, Owen. *Inner Asian Frontiers of China*. Boston: Beacon Press, 1962.

Lauber, Emil. *Metternichs Kampf um die europaische Mitte: Struktur seiner Politik von 1809 bis 1815*. Vienna: A. Luser, 1939.

Lauren, Paul Gordon, Gordon A. Craig, and Alexander L. George. *Force and Statecraft: Diplomatic Challenges of Our Time*. Oxford: Oxford University Press, 2021.

Law, John E. "The Venetian Mainland State in the Fifteenth Century." *Transactions of the Royal Historical Society* 2 (1992): 153–174.

LeDonne, John P. *The Grand Strategy of the Russian Empire, 1650–1831*. Oxford: Oxford University Press, 2003.

Leffler, Melvyn P., and Odd Arne Westad, eds. *The Cambridge History of the Cold War*. Cambridge: Cambridge University Press, 2010.

Lentin, Antony. "Several Types of Ambiguity: Lloyd George at the Paris Peace Conference." *Diplomacy & Statecraft* 6, no. 1 (1995): 223–251.

Levy, James P. *Appeasement and Rearmament: Britain, 1936–1939*. Lanham, MD: Rowman & Littlefield, 2006.

Lewis, Bernard. *Istanbul and the Civilization of the Ottoman Empire*. Norman: University of Oklahoma Press, 1963.

Lieu, S.N.C., and G. Greatrex. *The Roman Eastern Frontier and the Persian Wars II, AD 363–630: A Narrative Sourcebook*. London: Routledge, 2002.

Lippmann, Walter. *U.S. Foreign Policy: Shield of the Republic*. New York: Little, Brown and Company, 1943.

Liska, George. *Nations in Alliance: The Limits of Interdependence*. Baltimore: Johns Hopkins University Press, 1967.

Lobell, Steven E. "Britain's Paradox: Cooperation or Punishment prior to World War I." *Review of International Studies* 27, no. 2 (April 2001): 169–186.

Logevall, Fredrik, and Kenneth Osgood. "The Ghost of Munich: America's Appeasement Complex." *World Affairs* 173, no. 2 (July/August 2010).

Logevall, Fredrik, and Andrew Preston, eds. *Nixon in the World: American Foreign Relations, 1969–1977*. New York: Oxford University Press, 2008.

Lord, Winston. *Kissinger on Kissinger: Reflections on Diplomacy, Grand Strategy, and Leadership*. New York: All Points Books, 2019.

Lucy, Henry W., ed. *Essays by the Late Marquess of Salisbury*. New York: Dutton, 1905.

Luttwak, Edward. *The Grand Strategy of the Byzantine Empire*. Cambridge, MA: Belknap Press, 2009.

———. *The Grand Strategy of the Roman Empire from the First Century A.D. to the Third*. Baltimore: Johns Hopkins University Press, 1976.

———. *The Rise of China vs. the Logic of Strategy*. Cambridge, MA: Belknap Press, 2012.

———. *Strategy: The Logic of War and Peace*. Cambridge, MA: Harvard University Press, 2002.

Lynn, John A. "Recalculating French Army Growth during the Grand Siècle, 1610–1715." *French Historical Studies* 18, no. 4 (Autumn 1994): 881–906.

MacFarquar, Frederick. "Mission to Mao." *New York Review of Books*, June 28, 2007.

Machiavelli, Niccolò. *An Account of the Affairs of France*. Hastings, UK: Delphi, 2017.

Mackinder, H. J. "The Geographical Pivot of History." *Geographical Journal* 23 (1904): 421–437.

MacMillan, Margaret. *Nixon in China: The Week That Changed the World*. New York: Penguin Books, 2006.

———. *Paris 1919*. New York: Random House, 2001.

———. *The War That Ended Peace: The Road to 1914*. New York: Random House, 2014.

Maddison, Angus. *The World Economy: A Millennial Perspective*. OECD Development Centre Studies, 2001.

Maenchen-Helfen, Otto J. *The World of the Huns: Studies in Their History and Culture*. Berkeley: University of California Press, 1973.

Magocsi, Paul Robert. *Historical Atlas of East Central Europe*. Seattle: University of Washington Press, 1993.

Mahan, Alfred Thayer. *The Influence of Sea Power upon History, 1660–1783*. Boston: Little, Brown & Co., 1890.

Mahnken, Thomas, Joseph Maiolo, and David Stevenson, eds. *Arms Races in International Politics: From the Nineteenth to the Twenty-First Century*. Oxford: Oxford University Press, 2016.

Mallett, M. E., and J. R. Hale. *The Military Organization of a Renaissance State: Venice c. 1400–1617*. Cambridge: Cambridge University Press, 1984.

Manning, Robert A. "Reagan's Chance Hit." *Foreign Policy*, Spring 1984.

Marks, Sally. "The Myths of Reparations." *Central European History* 11, no. 3 (1978): 231–255.

Marriott, J.A.R. *Anglo-Russian Relations 1686–1943*. Second edition. London: Metheun & Co., 1944.

Marriot, W. K. et. al., eds. *The Essential Writings of Machiavelli*. Premium Classic Books, 2020.

Massie, Robert K. *Dreadnought: Britain, Germany and the Coming of the Great War*. New York: Ballantine Books, 1992.

Matthews, Dylan. "What Henry Kissinger Wrought." *Vox*, November 30, 2023.

Mattingly, Garrett. "The First Resident Embassies: Mediaeval Italian Origins of Modern Diplomacy." *Speculum* 12, no. 4 (October 1937): 423–439.

———. *Renaissance Diplomacy*. New York: Russell & Russell, 1970.

Maurer, John D. "The Forgotten Side of Arms Control: Enhancing U.S. Competitive Advantage, Offsetting Adversary Strengths." *War on the Rocks*, June 27, 2018.

Maurseth, P. "Balance-of-Power Thinking from the Renaissance to the French Revolution." *Journal of Peace Research* 1, no. 2 (1964): 120–136.

May, Ernest R., ed. *American Cold War Strategy: Interpreting NSC 68*. Boston: St. Martin's Press, 1993.

———. *"Lessons" of the Past: The Use and Misuse of History in American Foreign Policy*. New York: Oxford University Press, 1973.

Mayer, Dorothy Moulton. *The Great Regent*. New York: Funk & Wagnalls, 1966.

McGill, William J. "The Roots of Policy: Kaunitz in Vienna and Versailles." *Journal of Modern History* 43, no. 2 (June 1971): 228–244.

McMeekin, Sean. *Stalin's War: A New History of World War II*. New York: Basic Books, 2021.

McNeill, William H. *Venice: The Hinge of Europe, 1081–1797*. Chicago: Chicago University Press, 1974.

McShea, Bronwen. *La Duchesse: The Life of Marie de Vignerot*. New York: Pegasus Books, 2023.

Mead, Walter Russell. *Special Providence: American Foreign Policy and How It Changed the World*. New York: Routledge, 2002.

Mearsheimer, John J. "The Inevitable Rivalry: America, China, and the Tragedy of Great-Power Politics." *Foreign Affairs*, November/December 2021.

———. *The Tragedy of Great Power Politics*. New York: W. W. Norton & Co., 2014.

Meinecke, Friedrich. *Machiavellism: The Doctrine of Raison d'État and Its Place in Modern History*. New Haven, CT: Yale University Press, 1962.

Melvin-Koushki, Matthew. "The Delicate Art of Aggression: Uzun Hasan's 'Fathnama' to Qaytbay of 1469." *Iranian Studies* 44, no. 2 (March 2011): 193–214.

Miles, Simon. *Engaging the Evil Empire: Washington, Moscow, and the Beginning of the End of the Cold War*. Ithaca, NY: Cornell University Press, 2020.

Millar, Fergus. "Government and Diplomacy in the Roman Empire during the First Three Centuries." *International History Review* 10, no. 3 (August 1988): 345–377.

———. *A Greek Roman Empire: Power and Belief under Theodosius II 408–450*. Berkeley: University of California Press, 2006.

Miller, Aaron David. "The End of Diplomacy?" *Foreign Policy*, February 3, 2010.

Miller, Steven E. "Article Review 163: Miller on Trachtenberg and Jervis on SALT." *H-Diplo* (blog), September 27, 2023.

Millward, Robert. "Geopolitics versus Market Structure Interventions in Europe's Infrastructure Industries, c. 1830–1939." *Business History* 53, no. 5 (August 2011): 673–687.

Milne, David. *Worldmaking: The Art and Science of American Diplomacy*. New York: Farrar, Straus and Giroux, 2015.

Mirski, Sean A. *We May Dominate the World: Ambition, Anxiety and the Rise of the American Colossus*. New York, NY: Public Affairs, 2023.

Mitchell, A. Wess. "Conservatives and Geopolitical Change." *National Review*, April 2, 2020.

———. *Grand Strategy of the Habsburg Empire*. Princeton, NJ: Princeton University Press, 2018.

Modelski, George, and William R. Thompson. *Seapower in Global Politics, 1494–1993*. London: Macmillan, 1988.

Monger, George. *The End of Isolation: British Foreign Policy, 1900–1907*. London: Thomas Nelson & Sons, 1963.

Moore, Andrew. "How AI Could Revolutionize Diplomacy." *Foreign Policy*. March 21, 2023.

Morgan, Kenneth. *Lloyd George*. London: Weidenfeld & Nicolson, 1974.

Morgenthau, Hans J. "Diplomacy." *Yale Law Journal* 55, no. 5 (August 1946): 1067–1081.

———. *Politics among Nations*. New York: Alfred A. Knopf, 1960.

Morris, Edmund. *Theodore Rex*. New York: Modern Library, 2002.

Mueller, Reinhold C. *The Venetian Money Market: Banks, Panics, and the Public Debt, 1200–1500*. Baltimore: Johns Hopkins University Press, 2019.

Murray, Williamson, and Richard Hart Sinnreich, eds. *The Shaping of Grand Strategy: Policy, Diplomacy, and War*. Cambridge: Cambridge University Press, 2011.

———. *Successful Strategies: Triumphing in War and Peace from Antiquity to the Present*. Cambridge: Cambridge University Press, 2014.

Nakhimovsky, Isaac. *The Holy Alliance: Liberalism and the Politics of Federation.* Princeton, NJ: Princeton University Press, 2024.

Narizny, Kevin. "Both Guns and Butter, or Neither: Class Interests in the Political Economy of Rearmament." *American Political Science Review* 97, no. 2 (May 2003): 203–220.

Neustadt, Richard E., and Ernest R. May. *Thinking in Time: The Uses of History for Decision-Makers.* New York: Free Press, 1986.

Nicolson, Harold. *The Congress of Vienna: A Study in Allied Unity.* New York: Harcourt, Brace & Co., 1946.

———. *Diplomacy.* New York: Galaxy Books, 1964.

———. *The Evolution of Diplomacy.* New York: Collier Books, 1966.

———. *Peacemaking 1919.* New York: Grosset & Dunlap, 1965.

———. *Portrait of a Diplomatist.* New York: Harcourt, Brace & Co., 1930.

Nish, Ian. *The Anglo-Japanese Alliance: The Diplomacy of Two Island Empires, 1894–1907.* London: Athlone Press, 1966.

Nixon, Richard M. "Asia after Viet Nam." *Foreign Affairs,* October 1, 1967.

———. *RN: The Memoirs of Richard Nixon.* New York: Grosset & Dunlap, 1978.

Norwich, John Julius. *Byzantium: The Early Centuries.* New York: Viking Press, 1989.

———. *Four Princes: Henry VIII, Francis I, Charles V, Suleiman the Magnificent and the Obsessions That Forged Modern Europe.* New York: Grove Press, 2016.

———. *A History of Venice.* New York: Vintage Books, 1989.

Nye, Joseph S. "Public Diplomacy in a Changing World." *Annals of the American Academy of Political and Social Science* 616 (March 2008): 94–109.

Obolensky, Dimitri. *Byzantium and the Slavs.* Crestwood, NY: St. Vladimir's Seminary Press, 1994.

O'Connell, C. P. *Richelieu.* Cleveland: World Publishing Co., 1968.

Osgood, Robert E. *Alliances and American Foreign Policy.* Baltimore: Johns Hopkins University Press, 1968.

Osiander, Andres. "Sovereignty, International Relations, and the Westphalian Myth." *International Organization* 55, no. 2 (Spring 2001): 251–287.

———. *The States System of Europe, 1640–1990: Peacemaking and the Conditions of International Stability.* Oxford: Oxford University Press, 1994.

Ostrogorsky, Georg. "The Byzantine Emperor and the Hierarchical World Order." *Slavonic and East European Review* 35, no. 84 (December 1956): 1–14.

———. *Geschichte des byzantinischen Staates.* München: Verlag C. H. Beck, 1975.

O'Toole, Patricia. *The Moralist: Woodrow Wilson and the World He Made.* New York: Simon & Schuster, 2019.

Otte, T. G. *The Foreign Office Mind: The Making of British Foreign Policy, 1865–1914.* Cambridge: Cambridge University Press, 2011.

———. "A Question of Leadership: Lord Salisbury, the Unionist Cabinet and Foreign Policy Making, 1895–1900." *Contemporary British History* 14, no. 4 (Winter 2000): 1–26.

Padover, Saul K. "Prince Kaunitz' Résumé of His Eastern Policy, 1763–71." *Journal of Modern History* 5, no. 3 (September, 1933): 352–365.

Pagès, G. *The Thirty Years War 1618–1648.* New York: Harper & Row, 1970.

Palmer, Alan. *Metternich: Councillor of Europe.* London: Phoenix Giant, 1997.

Papasotiriou, Charalampos. "The Role of Diplomacy in Byzantine Grand Strategy." Discussion paper. Centre for the Study of Diplomacy, University of Leicester, 1996.

Paret, Peter, and Michael Howard. *Carl von Clausewitz: On War.* Princeton, NJ: Princeton University Press, 1984.

Parker, David. *La Rochelle and the French Monarchy: Conflict and Order in Seventeenth-Century France.* London: Royal Historical Society, 1980.

Parker, Geoffrey. *Emperor: A New Life of Charles V.* New Haven, CT: Yale University Press, 2019.

———. *The Grand Strategy of Philip II.* London: Redwood, 2000.

———. "The 'Military Revolution,' 1560–1660—a Myth?" *Journal of Modern History* 48, no. 2 (June 1976): 196–214.

———. *The Military Revolution: Military Innovation and the Rise of the West, 1500–1800.* Cambridge: Cambridge University Press, 1988.

———. *The Thirty Years' War.* New York: Barnes & Noble Books, 1997.

Parrott, David. *The Business of War: Military Enterprise and Military Revolution in Early Modern Europe.* Cambridge: Cambridge University Press, 2012.

———. "French Military Organization in the 1630s: The Failure of Richelieu's Ministry." *Seventeenth-Century French Studies* 9, no. 1 (1987): 151–167.

———. "The Mantuan Succession, 1627–31: A Sovereignty Dispute in Early Modern Europe." *English Historical Review* 112, no. 445 (February 1997): 20–65.

———. *Richelieu's Army: War, Government and Society in France, 1624–1642.* Cambridge: Cambridge University Press, 2004.

Peden, G. C. *Arms, Economics and British Strategy: From Dreadnoughts to Hydrogen Bombs.* Cambridge: Cambridge University Press, 2007.

Penson, Lillian M. "The New Course in British Foreign Policy, 1892–1902." *Transactions of the Royal Historical Society* 25 (1943): 131.

Pflanze, Otto. *Bismarck and the Development of Germany.* 3 vols. Princeton, NJ: Princeton University Press, 1990.

Phillips, Adrian. *Fighting Churchill, Appeasing Hitler, Neville Chamberlain, Sir Horace Wilson, and Britain's Plight of Appeasement: 1937–1939.* New York: Pegasus Books, 2019.

Podhoretz, Norman. "Kissinger Reconsidered." *Commentary,* June 1982.

Pomfret, John. *The Beautiful Country and the Middle Kingdom.* New York: Henry Holt & Co., 2016.

Queller, Donald E. *The Office of Ambassador in the Middle Ages.* Princeton, NJ: Princeton Legacy Library, 1967.

Radchenko, Sergey. *To Run the World.* Cambridge: Cambridge University Press, 2024.

Rady, Martyn. *The Habsburgs: To Rule the World.* New York: Basic Books, 2020.

Rahe, Paul Anthony. *The Grand Strategy of Classical Sparta: The Persian Challenge.* New Haven, CT: Yale University Press, 2015.

Rehman, Iskander. "Raison d'État: Richelieu's Grand Strategy during the Thirty Years War." *Texas National Security Review* 2, no. 3 (June 2019).

Reid, Walter. *Neville Chamberlain: The Passionate Radical.* Edinburgh: Birlinn, 2021.

Riordan, Shaun. *The New Diplomacy.* Cambridge: Polity, 2003.

Ripsman, Norrin M., and Jack S. Levy. "Wishful Thinking or Buying Time? The Logic of British Appeasement in the 1930s." *International Security* 33, no. 2 (Fall 2008): 148–181.

Roberts, Andrew. *The Holy Fox: The Life of Lord Halifax.* London: Head of Zeus, 2019.

———. "Salisbury: The Empire Builder Who Never Was." *History Today,* October 1999.

———. *Salisbury: Victorian Titan.* London: Weidenfeld & Nicolson,1999.

———. *Seapower States.* New Haven, CT: Yale University Press, 2018.

Roberts, Michael. *Essays in Swedish History.* Minneapolis: University of Minnesota Press, 1967.

———. *Gustavus Adolphus: A History of Sweden 1611–1632.* 2 vols. London: Lowe & Brydone, 1965.

———. *Sweden as a Great Power 1611–1697, Government, Society, Foreign Policy.* New York: St. Martin's Press, 1968.

Roberts, Sir Ivor, ed. *Satow's Diplomatic Practice.* Seventh edition. Oxford: Oxford University Press, n.d.

Röhl, John C. G. *The Kaiser and His Court: Wilhelm II and the Government of Germany.* Cambridge: Cambridge University Press, 1994.

Roider Karl A., Jr. *Austria's Eastern Question 1700–1790.* Princeton, NJ: Princeton University Press, 1982.

———. "Grete Klingenstein, der Aufstieg des Houses Kaunitz." *Austrian History Yearbook* 14 (1978): 320–321.

Romano, Dennis. *The Likeness of Venice: A Life of Doge Francesco Foscari 1373–1457*. New Haven, CT: Yale University Press, 2007.

———. *Venice: The Remarkable History of the Lagoon City*. Oxford: Oxford University Press, 2023.

Rose, Norman. *Harold Nicolson*. London: Pimlico, 2006.

Ross, Robert S., and Changbin Jiang, eds. *Re-Examining the Cold War: U.S.-China Diplomacy, 1954–1973*. Cambridge, MA: Harvard University Press, 2001.

Rothenberg, Gunther. "The Austrian Army in the Age of Metternich." *Journal of Modern History* 40, no. 2 (June 1968): 156–165.

Rothenberg, Gunther E., Belá K. Király, and Peter F. Sugar, eds. *War and Society in East Central Europe*. New York: Brooklyn College Press, 1982.

Rothkopf, David. *Running the World: The Inside Story of the National Security Council and the Architects of American Power*. New York: Public Affairs, 2006.

Ruskin, John. *The Stones of Venice: The Foundations*. Vol. 1. New York: John Wiley & Sons, 1880.

Saich, Anthony, *From Rebel to Ruler*. Cambridge, MA: Harvard University Press, 2021.

Satow, Ernest Sir. *A Guide to Diplomatic Practice*. Vol. 1. Second edition. London: Longmans, Green & Co., 1922.

Savelle, Max. *The Origins of American Diplomacy: The International History of Angloamerica, 1492–1763*. New York: Macmillan, 1967.

Sbrik, Heinrich von. *Metternich: Der Staatsmann und der Mensch*. 3 vols. München: F. Bruckmann, 1925.

Schadlow, Nadia. "The Forgotten Element of Strategy." *The Atlantic*, June 22, 2023.

Schake, Kori. *Safe Passage: The Transition from British to American Hegemony*. Cambridge, MA: Harvard University Press, 2017.

Schaller, Michael. "The Nixon 'Shocks' And U.S.-Japan Strategic Relations, 1969–74." National Security Archive, George Washington University, 1996.

Schelling, Thomas C. *Arms and Influence*. New Haven, CT: Yale University Press, 1966.

Schilling, Lothar. *Kaunitz und das Renversement des Alliances: Studien zur Ausenpolitischen Konzeption Wenzel Antons von Kaunitz, historische Forschungen*. Vol. 50. Berlin: Duncker & Humbolt, 1993.

Schmidt, Eric. "Innovation Power: Why Technology Will Define the Future of Geopolitics." *Foreign Affairs*, March/April 2023.

Schnakenbourg, Eric, and Frédéric Dessberg, eds. "Les tentatives de mediations françaises dans les conflits suédo-polonais du XVII siècle: une diplomatie de la périphérie?" In *La France face aux crises et aux conflits des périphéries européennes et atlantiques du XVIIe au XXe siècle*. Rennes: Presses Universitaires de Rennes, 2016.

Schöllgen, Gregor, ed. *Escape Into War? The Foreign Policy of Imperial Germany*. Oxford: Berg, 1990.

Schroeder, Paul. *Metternich's Diplomacy at Its Zenith 1820–1823*. Austin: University of Texas Press, 2021.

———. *Systems, Stability and Statecraft: Essays on the International History of Modern Europe*. David Wetzel, Robert Jervis, and Jack S. Levy, eds. New York: Palgrave Macmillan, 2004.

———. *The Transformation of European Politics 1763–1848*. New York: Clarendon Press, 1994.

Scott, H. M. *The Emergence of the Eastern Powers*. Cambridge: Cambridge University Press, 2001.

Seabury, Paul, ed. *Balance of Power*. San Francisco: Chandler, 1965.

Self, Robert. *Neville Chamberlain: A Biography*. London: Routledge, 2006.

Sestanovich, Stephen. *Maximalist: America in the World from Truman to Obama*. New York: Vintage Books, 2014.

Setton, Kenneth M. *The Papacy and the Levant, 1204–1571: The Fifteenth Century*. Vol. 2. Philadelphia: American Philosophical Society, 1978.

Seward, Desmond. *Metternich: The First European*. New York: Viking Press, 1991.

———. *Prince of the Renaissance: The Life of François I*. London: Sphere Books, 1974.

Seyssel, Claude de. *The Monarchy of France*. Edited by Donald R. Kelley. Translated by J. H. Hexter. New Haven, CT: Yale University Press, 1981.

Shay, Robert Paul. *British Rearmament in the Thirties: Politics and Profits*. Princeton, NJ: Princeton University Press, 1977.

Shepherd, Jonathan, and Simon Franklin, eds. *Byzantine Diplomacy: Papers from the Twenty-Fourth Spring Symposium of Byzantine Studies, Cambridge, Society for the Promotion of Byzant, March 1990*. Aldershot, UK: Variorium Reprints, 1992.

Showalter, Denis. *The Wars of Frederick the Great*. New York: Longman, 1996.

———. *The Wars of German Unification*. Second edition. London: Bloomsbury, 2015.

Siemann, Wolfram. *Metternich: Strategist and Visionary*. Cambridge, MA: Harvard University Press, 2019.

Simms, Brendan. *Britain's Europe: A Thousand Years of Conflict and Cooperation*. London: Allen Lane, 2016.

———. *Europe: The Struggle for Supremacy, from 1453 to the Present*. New York: Basic Books, 2013.

———. "Strategies of Geopolitical Revolution: Hitler and Stalin." In *The New Makers of Modern Strategy: From the Ancient World to the Digital Age*. Princeton, NJ: Princeton University Press, 2023.

Simonova, Gabriela. "Byzantine Diplomacy and the Huns." *Macedonian Historical Review* 2, no. 2 (2011): 67–86.

Siracusa, Joseph M. *Diplomatic History: A Very Short Introduction*. Oxford: Oxford University Press, 2021.

Skinner, Kiron K. *Reagan in His Own Hand*. New York: Simon & Schuster, 2001.

Small, Melvin. *The Presidency of Richard Nixon*. Lawrence: University of Kansas, 1999.

Smith, J. Russell. "The World Entrepôt." *Journal of Political Economy* 18, no. 9 (November 1910): 697–713.

Smith, Tom W. "The Polls: American Attitudes toward the Soviet Union and Communism." *Public Opinion Quarterly* 47, no. 2 (Summer 1983): 277–292.

Sofka, James R. "Metternich's Theory of European Order: A Political Agenda for "Perpetual Peace". *Review of Politics* 60, no. 1 (Winter 1998): 115–149.

Sprout, Harold, and Margaret Sprout. *Toward a New Order of Sea Power: American Naval Policy and the World Scene, 1918-1922*. Princeton, NJ: Princeton University Press, 1943.

Steele, E. D. *Lord Salisbury: A Political Biography*. London: UCL Press, 1999.

Steil, Benn. *The Battle of Bretton Woods: John Maynard Keynes, Harry Dexter White, and the Making of a New World Order*. Princeton, NJ: Princeton University Press, 2014.

Steinberg, Jonathan. *Bismarck: A Life*. Oxford: Oxford University Press, 2011.

Steiner, Barry. *Bernard Brodie and the Foundations of American Nuclear Strategy*. Lawrence: University of Kansas Press, 1991.

Steiner, Zara S. *The Foreign Office and Foreign Policy, 1898-1914*. London: Cambridge University Press, 1969.

———. *The Triumph of the Dark: European International History, 1933-1939*. Oxford: Oxford University Press, 2011.

Stieb, Joseph. "History Has No Lessons for You: A Warning for Policymakers." *War on the Rocks*, February 6, 2024.

Stoker, Donald. *Purpose and Power: U.S. Grand Strategy from the Revolutionary Era to the Present*. Cambridge: Cambridge University Press, 2024.

Stoler, Mark A. "War and Diplomacy: Or, Clausewitz for Diplomatic Historians." *Diplomatic History* 29, no. 1 (January 2005): 1–26.

Stollberg-Rilinger, Barbara. *The Holy Roman Empire: A Short History*. Princeton, NJ: Princeton University Press, 2018.

———. *Maria Theresa: The Habsburg Empress in Her Time*. Princeton, NJ: Princeton University Press, 2021.

Stone, James. *The War Scare of 1875: Bismarck and Europe in the Mid-1870s*. Stuttgart: Franz Steiner Verlag, 2011.

Strassler, Robert B., ed. *The Landmark Thucydides*. New York: Simon & Schuster, 1996.

Strausz-Hupé, Robert, William R. Kintner, and Stefan T. Possony. *A Forward Strategy for America*. New York: Harper & Brothers, 1961.

Strayer, Joseph R. *On the Medieval Origins of the Modern State*. Princeton, NJ: Princeton University Press, 1970.

Sturdy, David J. *Richelieu and Mazarin: A Study in Statesmanship*. New York: Palgrave Macmillan, 2005.

Suri, Jeremi. *Henry Kissinger and the American Century*. Cambridge, MA: Belknap Press, 2007.

Szabo, Franz. *Kaunitz and Enlightened Absolutism 1753–1780*. Cambridge: Cambridge University Press, 1994.

———. "Prince Kaunitz and the Balance of Power." *International History Review* 1, no. 3 (1979): 399–408.

———. *The Seven Years War in Europe: 1756–1763*. London: Routledge, 2007.

Taylor, A.J.P. *Bismarck: The Man and Statesman*. London: H. Hamilton, 1985.

———. *Origins of the Second World War*. New York: Atheneum, 1983.

———. *The Struggle for Mastery in Europe 1848–1918*. Oxford: Oxford University Press, 1988.

Temperley, H.W.V. *A History of the Peace Conference of Paris*. 6 vols. London: H. Frowde, 1920–1924.

Thayer, William Roscoe. *A Short History of Venice*. Boston: Houghton, Mifflin & Co., 1908.

Thompson, E. A. *The Huns*. Oxford: Blackwell, 1996.

Thompson, William R., ed. *Great Power Rivalries*. Columbia: University of South Carolina Press, 1999.

Toft, Monica Duffy. "The Dangerous Rise of Kinetic Diplomacy." *War on the Rocks*, May 14, 2023.

Toft, Monica Duffy, and Sidita Kushi. *Dying by the Sword: The Militarization of U.S. Foreign Policy*. New York: Oxford Academic, 2023.

Tougher, Shaun. *The Eunuch in Byzantine History and Society*. London: Routledge, 2008.

Trachtenberg, Marc. "Reparation at the Paris Peace Conference." *Journal of Modern History* 51, no. 1 (March 1979): 24–55.

———. "The United States and Strategic Arms Limitation during the Nixon-Kissinger Period: Building a Stable International System?" *Journal of Cold War Studies* 24, no. 4 (Fall 2022): 157–197.

Treadgold, Warren. *A History of the Byzantine State and Society*. Stanford, CA: Stanford University Press, 1997.

Treisman, Daniel. "Rational Appeasement." *International Organization* 58, no. 2 (Spring 2004): 345–373.

Trevor-Roper, Hugh. *Europe's Physician: The Various Life of Sir Theodore de Mayerne*. New Haven, CT: Yale University Press, 2006.

Trubowitz, Peter, and Peter Harris. "When States Appease: British Appeasement in the 1930s." *Review of International Studies* 41, no. 2 (April 2015): 289–311.

Tucker, Nancy Bernkopf. *Strait Talk: United States-Taiwan Relations and the Crisis with China*. Cambridge, MA: Harvard University Press, 2008.

Tudda, Chris. *A Cold War Turning Point: Nixon and China, 1969–1972*. Baton Rouge: Louisiana State University Press, 2012.

Urbach, Karina. "Between Saviour and Villain: 100 Years of Bismarck Biographies." *Historical Journal* 41, no. 4 (December 1998): 1141–1160.

Urbach, Karina, and Brendan Simms, eds. *Die Rückkehr der "Grossen Männer": Staatsmänner im Krieg. Ein deutsche-britischer Vergleich*. Berlin: De Gruyter, 2010.

Vagts, Alfred. "The Balance of Power: Growth of an Idea," *World Politics* 1, no. 1 (October 1948): 82–101.

Walt, Stephen M. *The Origins of Alliances*. Ithaca, NY: Cornell University Press, 1987.

Ward, Sir A. W., Sir. G. W. Prothero, and Sir Stanley Leathes, eds. *The Cambridge Modern History: The Restoration*. Vol. 10. Cambridge: Cambridge University Press, 1934.

Warman, Roberta M. "The Erosion of Foreign Office Influence in the Making of Foreign Policy, 1916–1918." *Historical Journal* 15, no. 1(1972): 133–159.

Wawro, Geoffrey. *The Austro-Prussian War: Austria's War with Prussia and Italy in 1866*. Cambridge: Cambridge University Press, 1996.

Weil, Patrick. *Madman in the White House: Sigmund Freud, Ambassador Bullitt, and the Lost Psychobiography of Woodrow Wilson.* Cambridge, MA: Harvard University Press, 2023.

Wertheim, Stephen. *Tomorrow, the World: The Birth of U.S. Global Supremacy.* Cambridge, MA: Belknap Press, 2020.

Westad, Odd Arne. *The Cold War: A World History.* New York: Basic Books, 2017.

Wetzel, David, Robert Jervis, and Jack S. Levy, eds. *Systems, Stability and Statecraft: Essays on the International History of Modern Europe.* New York: Palgrave Macmillan, 2004.

Whittow, Mark. *The Making of Byzantium.* Berkeley: University of California Press, 1996.

Whyte, A. F. *The Practice of Diplomacy.* London: Constable & Co., 1919.

Wich, Richard. *Sino-Soviet Crisis Politics: A Study of Political Change and Communication.* Cambridge, MA: Harvard University Press, 1980.

Wight, Martin. *Power Politics.* New York: Continuum, 2004.

Williams, Beryl J. "The Strategic Background to the Anglo-Russian Entente of August 1907." *Historical Journal* 9, no. 3 (1966): 360–373.

Wilson, James Graham. *America's Cold Warrior.* Ithaca, NY: Cornell University Press, 2024.

Wilson, K., ed. *British Foreign Secretaries and Foreign Policy: From Crimean War to First World War.* London: n.p., 1987.

Wilson, Keith M. *The Policy of the Entente.* Cambridge: Cambridge University Press, 2009.

Wilson, Peter H. *Heart of Europe: A History of the Holy Roman Empire.* Cambridge, MA: Belknap Press, 2016.

———. *Iron and Blood: A Military History of the German-Speaking Peoples since 1500.* Cambridge, MA: Belknap Press, 2023.

———. *The Thirty Years War: Europe's Tragedy.* Cambridge, MA: Belknap Press, 2011.

Wittek, Paul. *Rise of the Ottoman Empire.* London: Royal Asiatic Society, 1938.

Xia, Yafeng. *Negotiating with the Enemy: U.S.-China Talks during the Cold War, 1949–1972.* Bloomington: Indiana University Press, 2006.

Yorke, Claire, and Alastair Masser, eds. *New Perspectives in Diplomacy.* London: I. B. Tauris, 2021.

Zamoyski, Adam. *Rites of Peace: The Fall of Napoleon and the Congress of Vienna.* London: Harper Perennial, 2008.

Zarate, Robert, and Henry Sokolski, eds. *Nuclear Heuristics: Selected Writings of Albert and Roberta Wohlstetter.* Washington, DC: Strategic Studies Institute, 2009.

Zhisui, Li. *The Private Chairman Mao.* New York: Random House, 1994.

Zoellick, Robert B. *America in the World: A History of U.S. Diplomacy and Foreign Policy.* New York, NY. Grand Central Publishing, 2021.

Zosimus. *New History.* Translated by Ronald T. Ridley. Leiden and Boston: Brill, 2017.

Zuber, Terence. *German War Planning 1891–1914: Sources and Interpretations.* Martlesham, UK: Boydell Press, 2004.

A NOTE ON THE TYPE

THIS BOOK has been composed in Miller, a Scotch Roman typeface designed by Matthew Carter and first released by Font Bureau in 1997. It resembles Monticello, the typeface developed for The Papers of Thomas Jefferson in the 1940s by C. H. Griffith and P. J. Conkwright and reinterpreted in digital form by Carter in 2003.

Pleasant Jefferson ("P. J.") Conkwright (1905–1986) was Typographer at Princeton University Press from 1939 to 1970. He was an acclaimed book designer and AIGA Medalist.

The ornament used throughout this book was designed by Pierre Simon Fournier (1712–1768) and was a favorite of Conkwright's, used in his design of the *Princeton University Library Chronicle*.

GPSR Authorized Representative: Easy Access System Europe - Mustamäe tee
50, 10621 Tallinn, Estonia, gpsr.requests@easproject.com